WHAT MUSIC IS

HERBERT WEINSTOCK is well known in the world of music. Among the many books he has written on music are *Men of Music, The World of Opera* (both in collaboration with Wallace Brockway), *Tchaikovsky, Handel, Chopin: The Man and His Music, Music as an Art,* and *Donizetti.* Mr. Weinstock regularly reviews recordings for the *Saturday Review* and has been a frequent contributor to the *Encyclopedia Americana* and the *Americana Annual.*

WHAT MUSIC IS

Herbert Weinstock

A new revised and expanded edition of an earlier book
by the same author, *Music as an Art*.

Dolphin Books
Doubleday & Company, Inc., Garden City, New York

The music quoted on pages 323 and 324 is from TROIS MOUVEMENTS DE PÉTROUCHKA, by Igor Stravinsky. Copyright 1922 by Édition Russe de Musique for all countries. Copyright assigned 1947 to Boosey and Hawkes, Inc., New York. Used by permission.

The music quoted on pages 328–29 is from LE SACRE DU PRINTEMPS, by Igor Stravinsky. Copyright 1921 by Édition Russe de Musique for all countries. Printed by Arrangement with Boosey and Hawkes, Inc., New York. Used by permission.

The music quoted on page 346 is from WIND QUINTET, Opus 26, by Arnold Schönberg. Copyright 1925 by Universal Edition, A. G., Vienna; renewed 1952 by Gertrud Schönberg; by permission of Gertrud Schönberg.

What Music Is was originally published in hardcover by Doubleday & Company, Inc., in 1966.

Dolphin Books edition: 1968

Musical Autography by Ben Weber

ACKNOWLEDGMENTS

For me to express my sincere thanks to everyone who was helpful to me in writing the present book (or my earlier book entitled *Music as an Art,* published by Harcourt, Brace and Company in 1953, from which much of its contents has been adapted and simplified) would be impossible. Ben Meiselman read—or listened while I read—many sections of the manuscript; he never failed to make happy suggestions in the direction of simplification and greater clarity. Sam Morgenstern willingly and helpfully answered many questions regarding theory and technique. Three Doubleday editors—Mr. Tom McCormack, Miss Vicki Garriques, and Miss Denise Rathbun—worked on early versions of the text far beyond the mere call of duty. To all these people, and to many whom it is impossible to name here, I am genuinely grateful.

Herbert Weinstock

CONTENTS

SOME AIMS AND DEFINITIONS –
AND AN APOLOGY

What Music Is was not meant to be—and is not—a history of
music or an inclusive survey of the composers whose works
now constitute even its most familiar literature. The
ruling aim of this book is to be helpful by sticking very
close to the tones out of which music is made. The book
tries to show how they are arranged by composers and performed by instrumentalists, singers, and conductors, how
they can be apprehended, understood, and enjoyed most
easily by listeners without technical musical training. That
is a very large order, one that this (or any other) book can
fill only in part. Nonetheless, it is a worthy aim. The role
that a book on the understanding and appreciation of music
as an art and a science can play best for its readers is that
of preparing them to listen, to listen better, to *hear* with
more awareness and information what music is, what happens in it. No book can listen for them, and it is precisely
in individual listening removed as far as possible from mere
hearing (or, worse, the overhearing that modern conditions
increasingly make inescapable) that music achieves the most
rewarding and valuable of its functions. It performs several
other actual and imputed functions, some of them in the
realm of therapeutics, but those are no interest of this book,
which is concerned with music exclusively as one of the
fine arts.

Valuable time almost always can be saved if the people
discussing anything will make clear exactly what each of
them is talking or writing about. Every exposition of ideas
can benefit from definition of the principal terms being
used. Here, at the beginning, then, let us define the subject
matter of this book, what will be under discussion throughout it.

For "music," the key word itself, I have meant to keep in mind the inclusive and suggestive first clause of the definition in *Webster's New International Dictionary*, Second Edition: "The science or art of pleasing, expressive, or intelligible combination of tones . . ." That is what the word "music" refers to in the title of this book and in the following pages.

This is—the fact must be faced—a book about music appreciation. Now, the term "music appreciation" has acquired a bad name among musicians, historians of music, and musicologists, and for very good reasons. Of the reprehensible artifices, stratagems, and duplicities in which what often is called "the music-appreciation racket" has indulged, the most apparently persuasive has at the same time been the most dangerous and harmful. It has been a way of dodging all the real issues by pretending that music is largely a substitute means for communicating specific ideas, emotions, even pictures. I have vowed to avoid any sort of attempted translation of music into nonmusical terms, of extramusical terms into music. I do not believe, that is, that the opening section of Beethoven's C-sharp-minor sonata, Opus 27, No. 2, is about moonlight on water. I am much closer to believing that it is "about" melodies and the key of C-sharp minor and triplets and ties and dotted notes and gradations of soft and loud, that it deals musically with musical materials. I am, of course, aware from personal experience and from accounts of the experiences of others that by suggestion, association, and acts of memory and projection music can and does evoke in listeners' minds many ideas, emotions, pictures, and even stories with plots. But I regard such subjective reactions as by-products of listening to music rather than as constituents of music itself.

Webster defines "appreciation" as "Act of appreciation; appraisal; estimation; full recognition of worth; recognition through the senses, esp. with delicacy of perception." Comprehensive enough, that series of approximately synonymous phrases and words will serve to establish my understanding of what the "appreciation" in "music appreciation" must mean in the hands of any writer wanting to be of assistance to his readers and not to deceive them.

This book, to sum up, is meant to be a preliminary guide or companion for those who are attracted by or interested in the "science or art of pleasing, expressive, or* intelligible combination of tones." The publisher and I hope that the book will help its readers to appraise existing and perhaps future products of that science and art, to estimate them, to recognize their worth (or, in some notable instances, lack of worth) fully, to listen with newly acquired "delicacy of perception."

I present the constructive materials of music in a loosely evolving chronological order, with plenty of dates. But I am very far from believing or intending to suggest that the music of, say, the seventeenth century had "progressed" beyond that of the sixteenth or that of the second half of the twentieth century beyond that of its first half. An art does not "progress": it merely changes, and each work of art is a unique happening, not just one step along a road rising constantly into a better world. I have used a continuous narrative historical framework only because it affords the easiest, least repetitious way to discuss the means by which composers have organized their musical materials in the hope of making them available to listeners.

To attempt any relationship with music beyond that of bathing pleasantly and inertly in sounds, it is absolutely essential to be able to read at least a single, unaccompanied line of notes and other musical signals and know what they mean. For that reason, I have provided a "Foreword for Those Who Do Not Know How to Read Music." With a modicum of effort on the reader's part, the Foreword will enable him to approach a simple musical quotation in the state of mind in which, because he knows how to read English, he approached the present sentence. The Foreword should, of course, be skipped over by any reader already acquainted with at least the simplest forms of musical notation.

Inevitably—I would say rightly—this book is both personal and "prejudiced." Being human, I naturally hope that many

* I feel strongly that this "or" should have been "and." I do not, that is, understand how a science or art can please or express anything if its constituent parts are not intelligible.

readers will come to share my own convictions, judgments, and biases. What I consider to be far more important, however, is that each reader should acquire from this book, and from other books and experiences that he will encounter later, the background information and guides to attentive and informed listening which will enable him to shape his own convictions, judgments, and biases. To suppose, as some people do suppose, that too much knowledge or awareness will impair musical pleasure is to deny that music is either an art or a science, thus reducing it to a source of purely physical response. If music were that and nothing more, it would not have become the magnificent accomplishment of the human mind and spirit which Western civilization in particular* long has recognized it to be.

Herbert Weinstock

* This book makes no attempt to deal with the music of the Orient or of other non-European or non-Europe-derived cultures, most of which is built upon assumptions alien to the Western mentality. It refers exclusively to European music, which gradually has come to have almost world-wide distribution and vitality.

FOREWORD

For Those Who Do Not Know How to Read Music

(Double-starred words and terms will be found defined in the Glossary of Musical Terms, beginning on page 365.)

Musical notes[1] and their relative positions on, above, and below the five horizontal lines making up a staff** indicate:

1. comparative and absolute *duration* of tones;
2. comparative and absolute *pitch* of tones.

Roughly speaking, the passage of time in music is indicated by the *horizontal* placement of notes (time passes as one reads music from left to right), whereas differences in pitch are indicated by *vertical* placement. A composer's other indications to the performer or reader are transmitted by other symbols and by conventional words. Such symbols and words are of great importance to performance and to any thorough understanding of a composer's wishes. But they are not immediately germane to our purposes here, and therefore are not discussed.

Duration

The *comparative duration* of tones is a different quality from speed (tempo). It has to do with the comparative lengths of time indicated by the different note-values at whatever speed. As their names indicate, a whole-note repre-

[1] In common practice, the words "tone" and "note" are used as though synonymous. I have tried, however, to use "tone" to indicate a heard sound, "note" to indicate the printed symbol.

sents twice as much duration as a half-note whether the music is to be performed swiftly or slowly, just as a distance of one mile is twice as long as that of half a mile whether traversed at six miles per hour or six hundred.

The longest integer of comparative musical duration in modern use is a *whole-note*, represented as a hollow oval: 𝅝. Half the duration of a whole-note is occupied by a *half-note*, represented as a hollow oval with a stem rising or descending from it: 𝅗𝅥 , 𝅗𝅥 . Half of a half-note is a *quarter-note*, a solid circle or oval with a stem: 𝅘𝅥 , 𝅘𝅥 . Similarly, half of a quarter-note is an *eighth-note*, a solid circle or oval with a stem and one flag: 𝅘𝅥𝅮, 𝅘𝅥𝅮 ; half of an eighth-note is a *sixteenth-note*, a solid circle or oval with a stem and two flags: 𝅘𝅥𝅯, 𝅘𝅥𝅯 ; half of a sixteenth-note is a *thirty-second-note*, a solid circle or oval with a stem and three flags: 𝅘𝅥𝅰, 𝅘𝅥𝅰 ; and half of a thirty-second-note is a *sixty-fourth-note*, a solid circle or oval with a stem and four flags: 𝅘𝅥𝅱, 𝅘𝅥𝅱 .[2]

This is simple mathematics, any whole being divisible into two halves, four quarters or fourths, eight eighths, etc. Beginning with the hollow whole-note, musical notation di-

[2] This is standard American terminology. The English use another terminology, which sometimes appears in books published in the United States. That terminology, with its American equivalents, is: *semibreve*—whole-note; *minim*—half-note; *crotchet*—quarter-note; *quaver*—eighth-note; *semiquaver*—sixteenth-note; *demisemiquaver*—thirty-second-note; *hemidemisemiquaver*—sixty-fourth-note. For anyone curious as to why a *whole*-note should be called a *semi*breve, it should be explained that in older notation a note with the duration value of two whole-notes existed and was called a *breve*; it was represented by two vertical lines connected by two heavier horizontal lines (▯) or by a hollow oval squeezed in between two vertical lines (◖|).

vides duration value in half by adding a stem; then it goes on with the series of halvings, first by filling in the hollow, then by adding a flag, then another flag, etc., producing this progression:

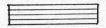

Composers sometimes increase the duration value of a note *by half* by placing a dot immediately *after* it (dots *under* or *over* notes do not relate to duration). Thus, ○• indicates a whole-note *plus* half of its duration value, or a "one-and-a-half-note." Similarly, ♩• indicates quarter-note plus value of an eighth-note, or a three-eighths-note. Again, simple mathematics. In the comparatively rare instances in which a note is followed by *two* dots, the second dot adds half the duration value of the first dot. Thus, ♩•• indicates half-note plus quarter-note plus eighth-note, or seven-eighths-note. Any dot after a note or another dot adds half of the duration value of the symbol immediately preceding it.

The meter, or pattern of basic beats or felt pulsation, in most Western music can be ticked off in groups of 1-2, 1-2; 1-2-3, 1-2-3; or 1-2-3-4, 1-2-3-4. The duration of one of these metric groups is called a *measure* because it measures out the comparative duration of such a group of beats. A measure is indicated in printed music by being enclosed between vertical lines called bar-lines. A single measure on a staff looks like this:

All but exceptional pieces of printed music are made up of a succession of such measures:

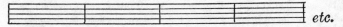
etc.

If the number of constantly repeated basic beats per measure is two or four, the musical passage is said to be in *duple* (that is, double) *time*. If the number of basic beats is three or six, the music is said to be in triple time.[3]

In the preponderance of musical compositions, the composer has decided that at a given place he wants each of the basic beats in his measures to be a quarter-note, eighth-note, or sixteenth-note (though basic beats of whole-notes and of notes shorter than sixteenths occasionally will be encountered). Suppose that he has decided to write music in three-beat measures, each beat to occupy the comparative duration of a quarter-note. We then say that the music is in "three-quarter" time. Similarly, if he decides upon four-beat measures, with each beat occupying the comparative duration of an eighth-note, the music is said to be in "four-eighth" time (or, idiomatically, "four-eight" time).

So that anyone reading music need not travel some distance into it before becoming aware of what "time" it is in, composers place at the beginning of each composition or section of a composition a *time-signature* stating the number and comparative duration of the basic beats in the succeeding measures. If a composer writes $\frac{3}{8}$ at the opening of a composition or section, he thereby tells us that each succeeding measure *until a different time-signature appears* will be in three-eighth time—that each measure will have three basic beats, each beat with the comparative duration of an eighth-note. If the time signature is $\frac{4}{4}$, we are being told that each measure will be in four-quarter ("four-four") time—that is, each measure will have four basic beats, each

[3] Subtleties not requiring exposition here arise when the number of basic beats per measure is a multiple of both two and three—as six or twelve. In such situations, other criteria often determine whether the time is duple or triple. Also, measures in which the repetitive basic pulse is neither duple nor triple—when it is five or seven—are sensed by most Western (as differentiated from Russian and Oriental) listeners as "compound." That is, the modern Western ear feels five beats as two-plus-three or three-plus-two, etc., the entire modern Western musical experience having predisposed us to hear all repeated groups of beats in twos, threes, fours, and sometimes sixes.

beat with the comparative duration of a quarter-note.[4] And so forth.

Let us look at the first nine measures of Beethoven's Piano Sonata Opus** 79 to decide what they tell us about the mathematics of note-values:

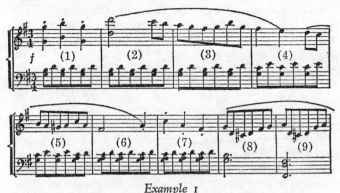

Example 1

Disregarding the first two symbols on both staffs because they refer to pitch rather than to duration, we arrive at the symbol $\frac{3}{4}$, meaning that this music is in three-quarter time: it is to have three basic beats to each measure, each beat with the mathematical value of a quarter-note.

In the first measure, the three successive quarter-note octaves** are easy to see and to count. On the lower staff, however, the total measure duration of three quarters is filled out by six eighth-notes.[5]

[4] Four-four time often is referred to as "common time" and usually is indicated by the C, thus:

When this letter C is vertically bisected by a line, ₵, the indication is that the time will be *"alla breve,"* meaning $\frac{2}{2}$, a measure of two basic beats, each of them being a half-note.

[5] Both the octaves on the upper staff and the thirds** on the lower staff represent tones to be sounded together. And exactly because they are sounded together, we speak of each of them as "a" quarter-note and "an" eighth-note. Even a chord** of five or six notes

It is extremely helpful to notice that the mathematical relationships among the notes on the two staffs are kept clear to the eye by the horizontal locations of the notes themselves. Two successive eighth-notes on the bottom staff, that is, will be allotted exactly the same amount of horizontal space as one quarter-note on the upper staff. This visual indication of the relative durations of notes on separate staffs (or on the same staff) is maintained unchangingly in printed music, so that it always is possible to see at a glance what tones are to be played simultaneously or kept sounding together.

In measure 2 of Example 1, the upper staff fills out its quota of three quarters by means of one half-note and two eighth-notes, whereas the bottom staff continues with six eighth-notes per measure. In measure 4, however, the upper staff makes three quarters of duration out of one quarter, another quarter, and two eighths. Note especially the bottom staff in measures 8 and 9: here the three quarters' duration consists in each case of a half-note followed by a dot —that is, a half plus a quarter, or the required three quarters.

Now let us examine the final two measures of the same Beethoven sonata:

Example 2

The time-signature effective for this movement** is $\frac{2}{4}$ (not shown). The bottom staff of measure 1 has eight sixteenth-notes, mathematically equal to the required two quarters. But what about the upper staff of measure 1 and both staffs of measure 2?

The upper staff of measure 1 appears to contain only two

sounded simultaneously would thus be referred to as "a" whole-note, sixty-fourth-note, or whatever, when counting out a measure.

xxiv

eighth-notes, measure 2 to have only one eighth-note in each staff. Neither situation would fill out the indicated measure duration of two quarters.

Here Beethoven wanted silences between tones. Therefore, he used symbols, called *rests*, to measure out the silence in durations that could be added to those of the tones themselves and give a total duration of two quarters. Such rests come in durations to match the lengths of all notes, from whole-notes to sixty-fourth notes. Exactly like notes, they also can be dotted and double-dotted. They look like this:

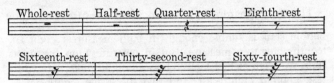

(Note that the visual difference between a whole-rest and a half-rest is that the former appears *below* a staff line, the latter *above* a staff line.)

WITHIN A COMPLETE MEASURE, THE CUMULATED DURATION VALUE OF NOTES AND RESTS ALWAYS EQUALS THE DURATION VALUE INDICATED BY THE TIME-SIGNATURE. (At the beginnings and ends of compositions and sections of compositions, incomplete measures often occur.)

Now let us return to Example 2. In the upper staff of measure 1, we find: an eighth-note, an eighth-rest, another eighth-note, and another eighth-rest—a total of four eighths, which mathematically equals the $\frac{2}{4}$ of the time-signature. In measure 2: an eighth-note, an eighth-rest, and a quarter-rest—two eighths and one quarter, again exactly equal to the $\frac{2}{4}$ of the time-signature. (Notice again how the horizontal location of both notes and rests tells us at a glance what sounds or silences are occurring simultaneously or enduring together.)

But supposing that a composer desires three notes on the upper staff to occupy the duration of four notes on the lower one? Our system of notation supplies half-notes, quarter-notes, etc., but not third-notes, fifth-notes, sixth-notes, etc. How this lack has been filled can be shown in two measures from the same Beethoven sonata:

Example 3

The time-signature in effect in these measures is $\frac{2}{4}$. The bottom staff is simple enough in both measures: eight sixteenth-notes to a measure. But in measure 1 on the upper staff, we seem at first look to find an eighth-note, an eighth-rest, another eighth-rest, and two successive eighth-notes—a total duration of five eighth, one eighth more than we can accommodate. But notice the small figure 3 under the semifinal eighth-note. It means that the *written* duration of three eighth-notes (here actually an eighth-rest and two eighth-notes) is to be compressed evenly into the actual *sounding* duration of two eighth-notes (four sixteenth-notes). The correct count of the indicated durations in measure 1, upper staff, therefore is: eighth-note, eighth-rest, and eighth-rest-plus-two-eighth-notes, the three last units marked (by the 3) to occupy the actual duration value of two eighths. The *actual* value remains correct because the group of three eighth values (an eighth-rest and two eighth-notes) will occupy the duration of only two eighths. So, by adding one eighth, one eighth, and the equivalent of two eighths, we arrive at four eighths, equal to the necessary two quarters.

The notation on the upper staff of measure 2 in Example 3 is merely that of the second half of measure 1 repeated twice—that is, two times the equivalent of two eighths, or the desired two quarters.[6]

[6] This "three-against-four," as it is called, may be difficult to play or sing (try tapping out three even beats with your right hand while tapping out four even beats with your left hand). But it is not difficult to understand mathematically. In the length of time required to

Here is a comparatively complex measure from Beethoven's Piano Sonata Opus 81a, nicknamed *"Les Adieux"*:

Example 4

The time-signature in effect in this measure is $\frac{2}{4}$. What must be looked at thoughtfully here is that the stems of some of the notes go up, whereas the stems of others go down. In both staffs, the line of notes with rising stems represents a single strand of musical material, that of those with descending stems another such strand.

IN SUCH CASES, THE CUMULATED DURATION VALUE OF ALL THE NOTES IN A MEASURE WHICH HAVE STEMS GOING IN THE SAME DIRECTION ON A SINGLE STAFF WILL EQUAL THAT INDICATED BY THE TIME SIGNATURE, here $\frac{2}{4}$.

Is that true of the notes in Example 4? Take those with ascending stems on the upper staff: a quarter-note, two sets of three sixteenth-notes (each set marked by a 3) as equivalent to two sixteenths—that is, a quarter plus four sixteenths, the desired two quarters. Now the notes with descending stems on the upper staff: an eighth-note, an eighth-note, a sixteenth-note, a sixteenth-rest, an eighth-rest—one eighth

---

play four sixteenth-notes on the bottom staff, three notes must be played on the upper. Each of the upper staff's "eighths," then, has been given the arbitrary duration value of one third of four sixteenths, or one twelfth. As the upper staff measure contains six of these, we have six twelfths, equal to the required two quarters. (In effect, that is, the upper staff in this measure is in triple time, the lower staff in duple time.) There is logic here. Similar interrelationships, likewise indicated by small numerals located like the 3s in Example 3 (though sometimes above rather than below the notes), justify four-against-five, five-against-six, etc.

plus one eighth plus one sixteenth plus one sixteenth plus one eighth, equal to two quarters.

The bottom staff in Example 4 is easy to count out: rising stems—a quarter-note, an eighth-note, an eighth-rest, equal to two quarters; descending stems—four eighth-notes, equal to two quarters. (As explained in Footnote 5, the fact that two or more notes of the same value appear on a single stem does not in any way alter the duration value.)

It should be reiterated here that tempo—the over-all speed at which music is played or sung—affects the *actual* duration of tones and silences, but has no influence on the mathematical relationships among notes, their *comparative* durations.

That is all that we must know about symbols of comparative duration in order to be able to read the basic facts of duration in simple forms of musical notation.[7] "Ornamental" notes, such as those provided for by trills, grace-notes, turns, and mordents, though essential to the actual performance of any music, do not effect what is here referred to as the basic facts of duration; they are mentioned and discussed in the body of the text itself.

Pitch

Sound is the end result of vibrations set up in the air or other vibrating medium and beating against our eardrums.

[7] Something must be said about the horizontal curved lines that appear in musical notation. In Example 1, such a line, beginning above the first note of measure 2 and extending to the second note of measure 4, indicates phrasing, and is called a *slur* or *phrase-mark*. That is, the section of the music beneath or above such a line is regarded by the composer or editor as either a complete musical idea or a self-contained sector of a musical idea. Such a slur is a suggestion to the performer as to what we loosely call "interpretation," and has no direct effect on either duration or pitch. In Example 4, however, the curved line at the beginning of each staff connects two notes of identical pitch. These are not slurs, but *ties*. Their purpose is to indicate that the note is not to be struck a second time, but is to be held down for the duration value of the notes so tied together. The note with the rising stem at the beginning of both staffs is to be struck and held: in the upper clef for the duration value of a quarter-note plus a sixteenth-note; in the lower staff for the duration value of a quarter-note plus an eighth-note.

We call a sound "high" if the vibrations are rapid, "low" if they are slow. The frequency of vibrations determines pitch. Whereas the elapsing of musical time is represented *horizontally* on a page of printed music (reading from left to right), relative pitches vary *vertically* on musical staffs—"higher" notes higher up on the lines and spaces of a staff, "lower" notes lower down (and, similarly, a staff representing higher tones placed above a staff representing lower tones).

Some musical instruments—and for our purposes notably the piano—are of fixed pitch: the performer does not control the pitches of the individual tones, which are established by the construction of the instrument and/or by a tuner. But with the human voice and on instruments not of fixed pitch—such as the violin—the performer must establish the pitch of each tone as he produces it. In the present discussion, all references are to music for the piano, that instrument being the most commonly available and being written for in one of the simplest manners.

Piano music generally is written on, above, and below two staffs. The upper, or higher, staff usually is indicated by the "clef**-sign" that appears in Example 1, upper staff, as the first symbol. This is called the G clef or treble clef:

The lower staff ("lower" also in pitch) usually is indicated by the clef-sign that appears as the first symbol in the lower staff of Example 1. This is called the F clef or bass clef: 𝄢.[8] Other clef-signs are used for some other purposes and instruments, but they need not enter our discussion here.

Each line and each space on, above, or below a staff rep-

[8] Notes above and below staffs using either the treble or the bass clef may be represented in diverse ways. The composer may draw in extra staff lines above or below the regular staff and then place notes either on such lines or in the spaces between them. Or he may write *8va* above or below certain notes to indicate that they are to be played an octave above or below the notes actually written (*16va* similarly raises or lowers notes by two whole octaves).

resents a specific key on the piano. Each of the keys—and their corresponding notes and tones—is represented by a letter of the alphabet. Only the letters from A to G are used, and the series of letters starts over again in each octave (the interval covered by eight diatonic tones, as C-D-E-F-G-A-B-C).

Here is a plan of the middle of a piano keyboard containing all the keys corresponding to the tones within two octaves:

The white key immediately to the left of the group of two black keys is called C wherever it appears on the keyboard; the C appearing in the middle of the keyboard is called middle C. Middle C is represented in usual piano notation by an extra line added either just below the treble clef or just above the bass clef. Rising or descending from that extra line between the two clefs, each succeeding line and each succeeding space on, above, or below the staff indicates the adjacent key on the keyboard. The space *above* the extra line representing middle C therefore represents the next white key to the right: D. The line above that space (actually the bottom line of the treble clef) represents the next white key to the right: E—and so forth. Similarly, the space *below* the extra line for middle C represents the next white key to the left: B; the line below that space (the top line of the bass clef) represents A—and so on:

In a majority of instances, the lines and spaces of the treble clef represent keys above middle C which are played by the pianist's right hand; those of the bass clef represent keys below middle C which are played by the left hand.

In Western music, an octave is most commonly covered in seven diatonic** steps and therefore consists of eight tones—as, for example, C-D-E-F-G-A-B-C. The distance (difference in pitch) between one piano key and the key immediately adjacent to it on either side is called a half-tone, and the distance between one piano key and a key separated from it by one other key is therefore called a whole-tone. We therefore say that the octave scale C-D-E-F-G-A-B-C is made up of a whole-tone (C-D, one key intervening), another whole-tone (D-E), a half-tone (E-F, no key intervening), a whole tone (F-G), another whole-tone (G-A), another whole-tone (A-B), and a final half-tone (B-C). This is a common "major scale"—called C major because it begins and ends on C. A comparable scale, with the identical whole-tone and half-tone intervals, may begin on any tone as long as the same formula of progression is maintained (reading upward) as 1. whole-tone, 2. whole-tone, 3. half-tone, 4. whole-tone, 5. whole-tone, 6. whole-tone, 7. half-tone. The commonest "minor" scale may also begin on any tone, but has a distinct formula of progression upward: 1. whole-tone, 2. half-tone, 3. whole-tone, 4. whole-tone, 5. half-tone, 6. tone-and-a-half, 7. half-tone (an example is A-B-C-D-E-F-G sharp [the black key between G and A] -A). Beginning and ending on A, this scale is referred to as that of A minor.

THE DISTANCE FROM ANY KEY ON THE PIANO TO ANY ADJACENT KEY IS A HALF-TONE. THE DISTANCE FROM ANY KEY TO A KEY SEPARATED FROM IT BY ONE OTHER KEY IS A WHOLE-TONE. BY EXTENSION, THE DISTANCE FROM ANY KEY TO A KEY SEPARATED FROM IT BY TWO OTHER KEYS IS A TONE-AND-A-HALF, THAT FROM ANY KEY TO ANOTHER SEPARATED FROM IT BY THREE OTHER KEYS IS TWO WHOLE-TONES, ETC. THE EIGHT TONES ENCLOSING A DIATONIC PIANO OCTAVE ARE COVERED BY A SCALE IN SEVEN STEPS (major: 1, 1, ½, 1, 1, 1, ½; "harmonic" minor, such as the A-minor scale cited above: 1, ½, 1, 1, ½, 1½, ½). Any "diatonic" scale, whether major or minor, thus covers an octave, a total "width" of six whole-tones.

But how does our traditional notation represent tones not inherent in the C-major scale (the one beginning and ending on C and being played—uniquely among major scales —all on the white piano keys)? By the addition of symbols called sharps, flats, naturals, double-sharps, and double-flats, which look like this: sharp ♯, flat ♭, natural ♮, double-sharp ✕, double-flat ♭♭.

A *sharp* has the effect of raising the note a half-tone. A *flat* similarly lowers the note a half-tone. A *natural* temporarily cancels the effect of a preceding sharp or flat. A *double-sharp* raises the note a whole-tone; a *double-flat* similarly lowers the note a whole-tone. Keys represented by either sharps or flats may be either white keys or black keys (thus, for example, the key represented as C♯ is the black key between C and D, but the key represented by C♭—that is, the key one half-tone below C—is the white key that under other circumstances is called B). The important fact to remember is that a sharp indicates that the note to be played is one adjacent key higher than that of the line or space on which the note is written, that a flat similarly indicates that the note to be played is one adjacent key lower than that of the line or space on which the note is written. This is *always* the case, and the obvious fact that C♯ and D♭ represent the same key, note, and tone on a piano is irrelevant to this part of our discussion.

These symbols appear in several ways and several different locations. Look at Example 1. You will see that after the symbols indicating the treble clef and bass clef at the beginning of the first measure, a sharp appears on the upper treble line representing F and on the fourth bass line, likewise representing F. When sharps or flats appear in this location they are called the key signature. The key signature in Example 1 means that EVERY F THAT FOLLOWS THEREFORE WILL BE PLAYED AS F♯ (F♯ being the key immediately above F) UNTIL (a) this section of the composition ends, (b) a new key-signature is substituted, or (c) a natural sign, ♮, before an F in either treble clef or bass clef indicates that the effect of the "signature F♯" is canceled for the duration of that measure or a sharp is placed before a succeeding F within that measure.

Now look at Example 3, bass clef, first measure. The signature F♯ still is in effect here. For that reason, the sixth sixteenth-note ordinarily would be an F♯. But Beethoven wanted an F here, and he therefore canceled the effect of the signature F♯ temporarily by placing a natural sign before the note. The power of this natural sign really ends at the bar-line to its right—but notice that in the next measure a sharp is placed before the same note—to remind the performer that the signature F♯ still rules despite the natural inserted in the preceding measure.

A KEY-SIGNATURE SHARP OR FLAT APPLIES TO EVERY NOTE FOLLOWING IT UNTIL ITS EFFECT IS CANCELED TEMPORARILY (FOR THE DURATION OF A MEASURE IN WHICH ANOTHER SYMBOL IS APPLIED TO THE SAME NOTE) OR PERMANENTLY (BY THE APPEARANCE OF A NEW KEY-SIGNATURE). Notice, also, that, for example, an F♯ in the key-signature effects all Fs on the keyboard, not merely the F represented by the line or space on which it is placed in the key-signature.

Now let us look at the comparatively complex measure from Beethoven's Piano Sonata Opus 81a appearing in Example 4. Here the ruling key-signature contains three flats —effecting the tones B, E, and A. Also, because the music for both the right hand and the left lies relatively high up on the keyboard, Beethoven has notated both the right-hand part and the left-hand part on the treble clef, thus avoiding the use of many lines added above the bass clef. (At the end of this very measure, however, the insertion on the lower staff of the bass-clef sign indicates that the succeeding measures in that staff are notated in the bass clef.)

Taking the upper staff first, let us look at the notes that have rising stems. The first quarter-note is a B♭, the key-signature containing a B♭ requiring that all Bs be flatted. The first and second notes of the following triplet of sixteenth-notes also are B♭ for the same reason; the third sixteenth-note is a C. The first note of the second triplet of sixteenth-notes would be an A♭ (as required by the key-signature), but is preceded by a natural sign, and therefore is an A. The next note is another B♭. Then, wanting an A♭, but having raised the preceding A♭ to A by the use of the natural sign, Beethoven now re-establishes the effect of the key-signature by writing a flat sign before the A.

Now, still on the upper staff, let us examine the notes with descending stems. The first eighth-note is a D. The second is an E♭, as required by the key-signature. The third note, a sixteenth-note, has a "reminder" natural before it because it is an F—and in the preceding measure Beethoven had raised F to F♯ by inserting an "accidental" sharp before an F. The natural sign now restores it to a natural F.

Now, looking at the lower staff (which, here, be it remembered, is also notated in the treble clef), the notes with rising stems are a B♭, as required by the key-signature, and a second B♭. Of the pairs of notes with descending stems, the first pair consists of an F (with a natural sign before it because of an accidental F♯ in the preceding measure) and an A♭ (with a flat before it because of an accidental A♮ in the preceding measure). The second pair is an E♭, as required by the key-signature, and a G. The third pair is a D and an F, the fourth pair a B♭, as required by the key-signature, and a D.

If we keep in mind that (1) a sharp raises any note a half-tone, whereas a flat lowers it the same distance; (2) a double-sharp (𝄪) raises a note a whole-tone, whereas a double-flat (♭♭) lowers it the same distance; (3) a key-signature flat or sharp remains in effect until canceled—either temporarily by the insertion of another symbol within a measure or permanently by the insertion of a new key-signature—we shall be able to decipher simple piano notation with regard to the position and pitch of notes.

Here are two examples each of major and harmonic[9]

[9] One of the greatest difficulties in discussion of music is its complex nomenclature. Only those interested in the history of music and the history of its usages should bother about the *reasons* for that nomenclature. But here it must be pointed out that the distance from, say, C to D, in addition to being called a whole-tone is also called a "major second," whereas the distance from, say, C to C♯ is called both a half-tone and a "minor second." Similarly the distance from C to E is called both two whole-tones and a major third, whereas that

minor scales, one of each with a key-signature in sharps, one of each with a key-signature in flats:

from C to E♭ is called both a tone-and-a-half and a minor third. And the fundamental difference between a major *scale* and a minor *scale* is that the major contains a *major* (that is, wider) third between its first three tones (as C to E), whereas a *minor* scale contains a *minor* (that is, narrower) third between its first three tones (as C to E♭). Ordinarily, minor scales come in two varieties, called "melodic" minor and "harmonic" minor. The "harmonic" minor scale is the one exemplified in the text by A-B-C-D-E-F-G♯-A; it contains exactly the same tones whether it is played upward or downward: that is, the descending form of the A-B-C-D-E-F-G♯-A harmonic minor scale is the same notes reversed: A-G♯-F-E-D-C-B-A. But the corresponding *melodic* minor scale not only is built up on a differing system of intervals (1, ½, 1, 1, 1, 1, ½), but also changes when played downward (when it reads 1, 1, ½, 1, 1, ½, 1)—as, for example, A-B-C-D-E-F♯-G♯-A ascending, but A-G-F-E-D-C-B-A descending. The *Harvard Dictionary of Music* well explains the difference between the ascending and descending melodic minor scales: "The aesthetic justification for this lies in the fact that, without the flatted seventh and sixth [in our example, that is, the alteration of G♯ to G, F♯ to F], the descending minor scale would sound like a major scale until its sixth tone [C in our example] is reached. Since the minor scale just described is evolved from melodic considerations (upward and downward movement), it is called 'melodic minor scale.'" Like major scales, either harmonic or melodic minor scales may be begun on any note whatever—as long as the properly spaced-out intervals occur at the proper locations within them.

CHAPTER I

The Emergence of Music

Nobody is likely ever to know how music began. Primeval men may have begun it by repeating and arranging howls and shouts with which they found themselves accompanying walking, working, or dancing. Perhaps, in some confused preliminary manner, other primeval men began to arrange successions of tones in attempts to imitate sounds in nature: wind, running water, animal cries, falling trees, thunder. The tones may have been produced in their own throats or by striking either hollowed tree trunks or stretched animal hides. Many other possibilities exist. But no purported description of the beginning of music, however solemn and apparently well documented, contains much more than unsupported speculation. One of the guesses that seem likeliest is that music as an art was born at the moment when a man first recognized the power of organized sounds to assist him in appeasing and beseeching the Unknown, in whipping up his spirits to make war on his fellows, or in helping him to capture and possess a female.

What is certain is that the surviving music of Western civilization tended, until recently, to divide into two large categories, each with its own purposes and practices. These have been sacred or ecclesiastical music and secular, popular, or vulgar music. The first category has included the music that men and women have employed while adoring, invoking, and placating powerful forces outside themselves. In the second category has been the music expressing their attitudes toward themselves and each other, their dreams and powerful wishes, and the tangible universe.

Gregorian Chant

From early in the seventh century, the dominating sacred music in Western (Roman Catholic) Christendom consisted of the collection of melodies known as Gregorian chant because the contents of the collection had been made official by the Church during the pontificate of St. Gregory, pope from 590 to 604. Rome's leading position as the seat of the papacy enabled Gregorian chant to supersede other, similar groups of sacred melodies.

The melodies of Gregorian chant, intended to be sung in connection with sections of the liturgy, are plainsong. Plainsong consists of a single vocal tone followed at a relatively indeterminate interval of time either by the same tone or by another tone separated from it by a predetermined interval of pitch, and then by another tone and another. It never is a combination of several independent melodies sung simultaneously (the later form of music known as polyphony) or a succession of interrelated groups of tones sounded together (the "harmonic" texture of most music later than the heyday of polyphony).

The chant melodies, that is, are alien to our modern Western conception of music. Further, they were intended for chanting without instrumental accompaniment, though from early times the organ and perhaps other instruments often supported them by duplicating the sung tones. In the modern sense of the word "accompaniment," such duplication of melodic tones does not constitute accompaniment. Each of the chant melodies is a strand of single tones in which only the pitch relationships among the tones sung are fixed definitely. The duration of the tones is not fixed, or originally was not fixed, but became fixed by tradition. It originally varied with the length or brevity of the vowels in the text syllables. The volume and timbre (or tonal color) of plainsong in unadulterated form were not predetermined: they were accidental functions of the voice or voices of the priest or chanting choir, traditionally male.

Psychologically, we of today are poorly equipped to hear Gregorian chant or other unaccompanied single-tone melodies because we instinctively and silently—and most often unconsciously—supply each heard tone with unsounded tones to support or accompany it. Some of these unsounded tones almost certainly occurred to the minds even of the earliest listeners, as they are inherent in the physical structure of musical sound itself. But we unquestionably hear them much more definitely. Our brains, that is, hear any melody as if it were moving forward on the support of changing chords or even as integers of such chords. In much of the most familiar music, in fact, the tones of the most prominent melody are simply the highest tones of such a succession of chords.

Since early in the Renaissance, music has been thought of as at once horizontal and vertical: as made up of one or more melodies flowing through time (the medium in which music exists, just as space is the medium of the plastic arts) or moving from left to right on a page *and* as a sequence of chords each sounded all at once and read up and down on a page. This way of thinking about and hearing music is so deeply native to us as to make it difficult, if not altogether impossible, for us to hear the sinuous Gregorian melodies as they must have sounded to chanters and listeners at the time of their codification and for some centuries thereafter.

We almost inevitably find plainsong "peculiar." In musical terms, this "peculiarity" results from the absence of mathematically measured-out repetitive rhythm and of chordal sequences, accompaniment, and the resulting harmony. It results also from the order of the pitch intervals by which plainsong proceeds and from the frequent occurrence in it of several tones to a single text syllable. Plainsong has varying rhythms of its own, of course, music devoid of rhythm being inconceivable. But the rhythms of plainsong resemble those of prose, whereas the basic repetitive rhythms of most later music (at least until well into the twentieth century) resemble those of poetry written in recurring patterns of accent. Whether classical or ultramodern piece, sonata or symphony, opera or musical comedy, ragtime or bossa nova, almost all the Western music with which we are

3

familiar has a repetitive rhythmic pattern absent from plain-song.

Besides the exoticism that strikes us when we hear an un-accompanied melody moving through time in proselike rhythms without chordal or harmonic support, plainsong bears the additional strangeness of all music that lies out-side our now traditional system of keys and scales. "Key" is essentially the construction of music on the framework of a scale covering an octave in seven steps, each of the scale tones existing for the time being in an established or cus-tomary relation to one chief tone, called the principal or tonic (that is, tone-ic). This concept, known as "tonality," became sovereign in European music after 1500 and began to deliquesce only after 1875. The well-defined scales used in this arbitrary system are of two chief varieties, either of which—"major" and "minor"—may be begun on any tone.

The only important difference between one major or minor scale and another major or minor scale is in its loca-tion in pitch. The interior arrangement of pitch intervals between the successive tones in, for example, the B-major scale is identical with that in the F-major scale, and the same identity of arrangement exists among the minor scales.

The Ecclesiastical Modes

Gregorian chant, however, long preceded our major-minor system. It used another system of scales known as ec-clesiastical modes, almost certainly Oriental and Greek in origin (but it must be noted that the extremely theoretical so-called "Greek modes," which lie outside the scope of this book, are something altogether different). The most impor-tant fact about these "ecclesiastical modes" is that the dis-tinguishing differences among them lie in the varying arrangements of the successive pitch intervals within them. One ecclesiastical mode differs from another, that is, not as one of our major scales differs from another major scale, one of our minor scales from another minor scale—in having an identical arrangement of pitch intervals in a different sector of the tonal gamut—but as any one of our major scales differs from any of our minor scales—in having a different succession of pitch intervals in whatever sector of the tonal gamut.

Notes and Notation

The evolving notation in which Gregorian chant came to be written down differed from our modern notation, not only in appearance, but also in significance and scope. With something approaching exactness, modern notation can indicate details of pitch, duration, accent, volume, speed, and several other qualities. But the neumes—as the signs in plainsong notation were called—indicated much less; also, they were not always intended to mean what they said. At a very early date, musicians felt an imperative need to make use of the tones between those regarded as constituting one or another of the ecclesiastical modes. Such tones foreign to the scale came to be known as "accidentals," and we may in a preliminary way think of them usefully (though only temporarily) as roughly equivalent to the black notes of a piano keyboard if sounded in relation to the major scale produced by beginning with a C and sounding all the white notes up to and including the next higher C.

Driven by this imperative need, musicians tacitly agreed that at certain melodic junctures, accidentals were to be sung instead of the tones apparently asked for by the neumes. The cause of this willful self-deception was that the preceding curve of a melody might seem to the musician's ear (which enacts all the musical "laws" that get obeyed) to require a semitone interval where the mode being employed did not allow for one. That cause, in fact, was the dawning desire for some of the harmonic events that we of today feel to be implicit in any melody whatever. From our point of view, the neumes can be scarcely more than a mnemonic device. No modern person not already familiar with a Gregorian plainsong melody could sing it properly merely by reading it as notated on a parchment before him. The neumes, in fact, served mostly to recall to a singer the profile and general progress of a melody that already was more or less familiar to him.

The jealously guarded though largely theoretical purity of the liturgical music of the Church, already sullied by the custom of interpolating accidental tones, was marred even more, probably after 700, by a custom that appears to have migrated from Byzantium. This was the interpolation of new melodic passages into existing Gregorian melodies. The cause again was the creative urges of musicians. These theoretically extraneous additions, which came to be called "tropes," soon were being included and accepted in the chanting of most varieties of liturgical song. And before very long, tropes began to flower within tropes. One variety known as a "sequence" gradually attracted additional text words to itself. These sequences became so elaborate that they threatened the comprehensibility of the sacred texts, and in the mid-sixteenth century, the Council of Trent therefore ordered nearly all of them deleted. The best-known of those upon which no ban was placed are the *Dies irae,* sung on the Friday of Passion Week, and the *Stabat mater,* sung on the third Sunday in September. The *Dies irae* melody remains familiar outside the Church because it has been adapted by such relatively modern composers as Franz Liszt, Hector Berlioz, and Serge Rachmaninoff for compositional purposes of their own.

From early in the Middle Ages on, then, an unrestrainable urge to tamper with the isolated purity of plainsong has been evident. That tendency, closely related to the physical make-up of musical sound itself, remained suspect from an ecclesiastical point of view. But for some seven centuries it produced the chief art music of the Western world.

Beginning in early times, the groups chanting plainsong in churches contained both men and boys. The difference in pitch between the preadolescent male voice and that of a mature man inevitably resulted in the same melody's being sung simultaneously at two different pitches—the men, let us say, sang a D while the boys sang the D one octave higher. At other periods in various parts of Europe, the pitch distance between the two sorts of voices theoretically singing the same melody was less than a full octave. Sometimes that distance was of three tones, five tones, or six. But

—and it is essential to believe this, however unlikely it now may seem to us—the performing singers did not think of the result of the singing of two simultaneous different tones as being a *combination* of two different tones. They felt that they all were singing one melody, the same melody, and the practice of singing plainsong in constantly parallel octaves, fifths, or other pitch intervals therefore did not dilute significantly the conception of music as made up of one single-tone melody without accompaniment. The simultaneous combinations of tones that nevertheless occurred remained not so much unimportant as unnoticed. As we listen to men and boys chanting a melody in constantly parallel intervals, the resulting combinations of tones often sound purposeless, if not ugly. And so they probably would have sounded to singers in earlier times if their ears and brains had been accustomed to thinking of music as we think of it, as at once vertical and horizontal, melodic and harmonic.

Early Polyphony

What seems to have happened next, however, changed that conception of what music was. This was the simultaneous singing of two or more *different* single-tone melodies: polyphony. The mere evolution of polyphony naturally hastened the existing tendency to drift farther and farther from the strait theoretical purity of Gregorian chant. Creative experimentation with temptations hidden in the very structure of musical sound itself had led to the attractive notion of singing two or more different melodies simultaneously. In the churches, one melody now was thought of as fundamental. This *"cantus firmus,"* or fixed song, usually was from the Gregorian collection. To it the singers added one or more other melodies adapted from secular music or composed for the purpose.

The resulting powerfully expressive new musical texture created serious problems for both composers and singers. The evolving solutions of those very problems produced a large part of the music and the musical history of the Western Church up to roughly 1600.

Measured Music and Counterpoint

If one melody is to be fitted into simultaneous singing with another melody, both melodies somehow must be measured out in recognizable divisions of duration which can be matched one to the other. A singer in polyphony, that is, no longer could depend for the durations of his tones—as a man singing a single melody could—upon his own individual interpretations of the length-emphasis suggested by the vowels in the words he was singing. New notation therefore became essential, and music came to be marked off into regular and recurring divisions of time. The name *musica mensurata*—measured music—survives in our use of the word "measure" for the space between two vertical lines in printed music. By about the mid-1100s, six so-called "rhythmic modes" had evolved. These made it possible to fit together as of equal measured duration musical units that were thought of as corresponding to various sorts of poetic feet: trochees, iambs, dactyls, anapaests, spondees, and occasionally tribrachs, words known to everyone who ever has analyzed poetic meter.

Full polyphony was not "invented" and did not emerge suddenly and fully developed. Evolving slowly from performances in which two simultaneous voices remained separated by an unchanging interval in pitch (that is, truly were singing the same melody at a constant pitch interval from one another), polyphony first began to deviate from this unchanging parallel at the openings and closes of melodic phrases or units. The two voices began to end frequently "in unison"—on the identical tone. When the interval between the two singing voices no longer was an octave, but (preponderantly) a fifth or a fourth, both voices began to be duplicated at a pitch distance of an octave, so that four "voices" actually were singing, two of them duplications of the other two at octave intervals.

When strictly parallel movement between the fundamental melody—often called the "tenor"—and the added melody—"duplum"—began to be avoided as monotonous, the relative movement often became oblique. That is, one voice

8

remained relatively stationary in pitch while the other moved closer to it or farther from it, thus producing constant fluctuations in the width of the pitch intervals between the two. Or contrary motion might intervene: the voices both might move toward or away from one another. In some surviving examples of eleventh-century polyphony, in fact, two voices at first widely separated in pitch actually cross one another, thus exchanging relative pitch positions.

Another important development was singing in which literal counterpoint (*punctum contra punctum*, the singing of a tone in one voice against a tone in the other voice or voices) was dropped in favor of singing two, three, or even four successive tones in one voice against a single tone in the other. During the twelfth century, the duplum in fact often flowered into groups of tones, each group being sung against a single tone in the basic plainsong tenor. In works by the twelfth-century musician Perotinus, two more melodies (triplum and quadruplum) became attached to the tenor and duplum, thus producing genuine four-voice ("four-part") polyphony. As a result of these increasing complexities, rhythm for a time became more and more strict, being limited to versions of what we now call three-beat or triple time.

During the musical era later dubbed the *ars antiqua*—the decades leading up to 1300—music inched very far away from the unencumbered single-tone melodies of Gregorian chant. The secularization and increased expressive scope of the art were evolving with self-compounding speed. In one sense, of course, duplum, triplum, and quadruplum melodies sung against all (or, in some surviving examples, sometimes only sections) of a Gregorian melody already were secular even though they retained sacred texts. They were not, that is to say, in themselves from the Gregorian collection. But in many surviving examples of *ars antiqua* polyphony, the tendency toward secularization had gone much farther: none of the melodies was Gregorian. Even the basic melody or tenor, by then usually referred to as the *cantus firmus* or *canto fermo*, was itself either adapted from secular music or freshly composed.

The most fruitful polyphonic form developed toward the close of the *ars antiqua* was the motet, which appears to have come into existence when one or more of the added polyphonic voices sang distinct text words of its own. The added texts were likely to include commentary on the immediately preceding text words of the *cantus firmus*. But by the end of the 1200s, additionally, motets were being arranged and sung in which the *cantus firmus* might be a Gregorian melody and retain its liturgical text, whereas added voices sang profane—and not seldom obscene—texts. These motets, largely French, were of truly bewildering complexity: each of the two or three or four melodies not only might have its own text, but also might be cast in a repetitive rhythmic pattern ("rhythmic mode") different from the rhythmic patterns of its companions.

It is not now, and never was, possible to understand even most of the text when so complex a motet is sung. By the time when the so-called *ars nova* era set in—about 1300—polyphonic music in some instances had become an extremely self-conscious, complicated, and all but autonomous technique. Not only had it absorbed secularity; it also had begun to confess the probability that it would in itself become entirely secular.

Early Secular Music

Before glancing briefly at the music of the *ars nova*, however, we should note a few large facts about the wholly secular music that undoubtedly existed outside the Church even early in the Middle Ages.

The reason for our almost complete unfamiliarity with very early Western secular music is clear. The learning that had led to the more or less effective notation of music was that of monks and other churchmen. Those scholars and scribes had no reason to wish to preserve the songs and dance tunes of highroad, market place, and pleasure resort, the haunts of the laity. But the certainty that such popular music existed is attested to both by common sense and by the findings of literary and social historians. Historians of music, on the other hand, too often have overlooked or implicitly denied its existence. The result of this tacit falsification has been a treatment of Church music and its practices as though they had existed and evolved until just before the dawn of the Renaissance in a vacuum penetrated (from about 1100 on) only by the musics of the troubadours, minnesingers, and trouvères. The result of that treatment has been musical history crowded with palpable nonsense.

All the music of the modern Western world has inherited practices from (among numerous other sources) both the music of the medieval Church and the secular music of the Middle Ages, including varieties of what has come to be called folk music and the perhaps more individually controlled music of minstrels, goliards, and jongleurs. (Incidentally, the vague notion that "folk music" is or could be the result of spontaneous generation by a tribe or other group of people is untenable. Every musical cell must originally have been the creation of a single individual, however much the intervention of other individuals or even of a group may have altered it later.)

The Troubadours

The earliest important body of non-Church music of which sizable remnants survive intact naturally is that of the first secular musicians sufficiently educated to have been able to note it down. These were the troubadours, aristocratic and often princely poet-musicians who flourished in Provence and Catalonia from about 1100 on. The geographical situation of Provence and Catalonia, as well as many details in the surviving troubadour works, suggests borrowings from Spain and, via Spain, from North Africa. The love poetry so assiduously cultivated at the court of the Carolingian rulers between 750 and 950 and the cult of ecstatic adoration of the Virgin also probably supplied the troubadours with creatively accepted hints.

The art of the troubadours was gallant, intricate, and flowery. The fact that some pictorial representations of their singing show performers holding musical instruments was thought until recently to prove that their poem-songs had something like modern instrumental accompaniment. But later students have become almost certain that the troubadours used instruments only to duplicate the sung melodies strictly or with trifling divergences—or for brief purely instrumental preludes, interludes, and postludes, probably extemporized on the spot. No proof survives that the music of the troubadours was anything but monophonic—that is, single-voiced. But it had begun to disregard the ecclesiastical modes, tending toward basic scales much nearer to the major scale as we know it.

The musico-poetic achievements and techniques of the troubadours seem to have spread out gradually through Spain proper, Portugal, Italy, England, Northern France, and the states of Germany. In all regions, they unquestionably absorbed or were absorbed into already existing forms of secular song and probably dance. The most immediately fruitful descendants of the troubadour art were those in Germany and Northern France, where it helped to germinate, respectively, the art of the minnesingers and that of the trouvères.

The Minnesingers

The flowering, in the minnesingers (from the German *Minnesänger*, love singers), of the only known considerable German music of the Middle Ages dated from about 1156, when Friedrich I ("Barbarossa"), Holy Roman Emperor, married Beatrix, heiress of Upper Burgundy. With this princess, French influences impregnated the German court. The names of the Provençal troubadours are known only to specialists, but those of three of the minnesingers—Tannhäuser, Walther von der Vogelweide, and Wolfram von Eschenbach—are widely remembered because seven centuries later Richard Wagner wove into a popular opera supposed incidents from their lives and from an actual song-contest that was held during the thirteenth century. Most surviving minnesinger melodies stick closer to the ecclesiastical modes than do those of most known troubadour songs.

The Trouvères

The trouvères of Northern France flourished in the middle of the twelfth century, notably with Blondel de Nesles and Quesnes de Béthune, both aristocrats. They included Thibault IV, King of Navarre, and died out with Adam de la Halle, a commoner, in 1287. About eight hundred of their poem-songs survive complete. Their texts now often are classified in groups by subject, but their musical forms became so important that in fact text patterns began to be adapted to them. For that reason, certain of these trouvère patterns sometimes are looked upon as the first truly independent musical forms.

Monophony: Sacred and Secular

Both as to classifications and as to interpretation of the exact manner of performance, the surviving works of the troubadours, minnesingers, trouvères, their counterparts elsewhere, and their immediate successors (including the fifteenth-century German Meistersinger, or mastersingers, from whom Richard Wagner later drew subject matter for another opera) still set scholars to quibbling. What is important for the musical amateur to remember is that the music of all these groups almost certainly was monophonic. Like Gregorian chant, it consisted entirely of single-tone melodies sung without either harmony or accompaniment as we now conceive them. In this respect at least, all wholly secular music before the Renaissance was as distant from our own ruling musical conceptions as was plainsong. Pre-Renaissance secular music, in fact, was much closer to Gregorian chant than to any post-Renaissance music. But it was on the verge of internal changes as important to the evolution of music as an art as the elaboration of perspective was to the developments in painting after Cimabue and Giotto.

Although it is self-evident that sacred music and secular music could not have existed for centuries side by side in completely non-intercommunicating compartments, music as the fine art we think it to be almost certainly did not begin to come into existence until they had started to interact constantly and profoundly.

By the end of the twelfth century, polyphony was firmly entrenched in all Church music except Gregorian chant itself. It had produced musical creations of enduring strength. Within polyphony, however, music was beginning rapidly to abandon the purely horizontal view—of however many distinct melodies flowing forward with whatever resulting simultaneous pitch intervals—for a mixture of that horizontal view and a vertical view. That mixture prefigured the close relationship between many later harmonic practices and the physical nature of musical sound itself. Not very much later, as much careful attention would be paid by musicians to chords and to a logic of chordal succession as to the forward motion of separate or simultaneous strands of melody. Thus chords and what they implied and evoked and suggested were shortly being studied and employed for their own power in clarifying musical logic and supporting musical construction. Instrumental music (which already had a long, though still mostly unknown, history) would come into its own. Along with such independent purely instrumental music—ancillary to it—would emerge the astonishingly fecund conception of melody proceeding forward on a support of chordal, nonpolyphonic accompaniment. For these and other reasons, the two centuries that began about the year 1301 can be looked upon sensibly as the first era of a new musical world or system. They produced the earliest surviving music with which ordinary nonscholarly music-loving listeners can feel any large measure of sympathetic identification.

CHAPTER II

Musical Periods as Historic Tools

When discussing music—as when discussing any other art or, for that matter, general history—the definition of periods is not much more than a convenience for easy identification and reference. If such arbitrary periods are understood as units in a series of separate happenings, their use becomes dangerously misleading. Forms, usages, influences, and manners flow along, mostly without sudden interruption, intermingling, dying away, coming to birth or to rebirth. The date 1301, for example, is a significant signpost along the path of musical evolution. But the new varieties of music which ripened immediately following that turn into the fourteenth century were not sudden unprepared-for blossomings in the garden of a single composer or group of composers. They happened to appear at a given time, but their long roots were deep in the past and their plants had been germinating for decades and centuries, unnoticed perhaps in gardens of other plants in other stages of growth, ripening, flowering, and decay.

Ars Nova

From one point of view (likely to be ours), the fourteenth century may conveniently be looked at as a period during which the fifteenth was gestating. But it also was the period during which the twelfth and thirteenth centuries were dying away, and we shall make a crippling error if we do not linger long enough with the fourteenth century to realize that it produced astonishing and admirable blossoms of its own. During its first decades, writers on the practice and theory of music began to indicate their awareness of musical change by referring to the music of their predecessors as the *ars antiqua*. Philippe de Vitry (1291–1361), a bishop of Meaux, near Paris, was probably the first theorist-poet-musician to call the music of his own period the *ars nova*. Viewed from a temporal distance of more than six centuries, the most noticeable changes from the "old art" to the "new art" can supply us with one key to the condition of Western music in the age of Dante and Giotto.

Despite the encroachments of all variety of secular and semisecular usages, the music of the *ars antiqua* had remained predominately Gothic, sacred, and ecclesiastical. But the gay courtly music of the troubadours and trouvères had begun to mix with it, altering its patterns and rhythms and nourishing its urge to greater freedom. This secularizing tendency—allied as it was with a movement toward bringing musical practices into closer consonance with the physical structure of musical sound itself—helped to produce the *ars nova*, which, much more than the *ars antiqua*, was a music of laymen and a music driving toward artistic autonomy.

Developing with special richness of achievement in France and Italy, but having related developments in England and elsewhere, this music of the early fourteenth century was (in so far as judgments based entirely on surviving music can be correct) most expressive as created by Guillaume de Machaut, a French poet-composer who lived from about 1300 to 1377, and by such Italians as Jacopo da Bologna, Giovanni da Cascia, and the somewhat later Francesco Landino (or Landini). The differences between the French manifestations of the *ars nova* and the Italian were significant. South of the Alps, neither the *ars antiqua* nor the trouvères had flourished. Unlike their French contemporaries, fourteenth-century Italian musicians were not in the position of following and having to digest such well-defined achievements in style and technique. They developed more independently, and therefore differently.

Regional and national differences aside, typical music of the *ars nova* differed from typical music of the *ars antiqua* most noticeably in that it increasingly employed measures in duple time (in company with the previously more frequent triple-time measures); in that it succumbed to the increasingly urgent desire to conceive music both horizontally and vertically; in that it extended the function of the full triad** (C-E-G, F-A-C, and so forth), which later became the radiating heart of harmonic activity; and in that it was even more free than its immediate predecessor in admitting what it considered to be dissonances** on all but the first beats of measures and those which closed melodic phrases or other musical units.

Machaut

Guillaume de Machaut, like most of the troubadours, minnesingers, trouvères, and even Meistersinger, was as much a poet as he was a composer. Chaucer, about forty years his junior, was acquainted with his poetry, from which he quoted, if not with his music. In his person, Machaut brought together for a remarkable late harvest the traditions of the trouvères and the manners of the Gothic ecclesiastical musicians of the *ars antiqua*. He was in holy orders, and he composed the earliest polyphonic setting of the Mass known to be the work of a single individual (the only earlier Mass that may have been composed by one musician now is generally thought to have been the work of several men). He also composed numerous secular songs. He handled his musical materials with ease and with a still unmistakable originality, bringing his vast musical erudition to serve a fresh conception of music as an increasingly autonomous art.

Many of Machaut's surviving compositions are not polyphonic, but so many of them consist of one vocal melody and one, two, or three simultaneous melodies for instruments that he may be thought of as one of the earliest musicians to write melodies designed to be sung to instrumental accompaniment—a novelty still often assigned to the early-seventeenth-century pioneers of opera. Deviating far from his trouvère models, Machaut composed rondeaux that to some extent resemble later art songs for a single voice accompanied by two or three instruments. The "accompaniments" do not serve the later purpose of chordal support to be found in most modern song-accompaniments: they still are predominantly polyphonic.

Isorhythms and Imitation

In his motets, Machaut strove toward all-over patterns of rhythmic unity by making use of isorhythms, that system of codifying a few set patterns of alternating time values in which the number of times a pattern was repeated within a composition or section depended upon the desired or necessary length of the musical unit. Isorhythms may be regarded as a kind of variation in which a rhythm is applied to differing successions of melodic tones. Machaut also used a constructive principle that has remained one major form of musical syntax ever since: imitation (which, needless to say, he did not "invent"). Imitation is what takes place in polyphonic texture when a melody or melodic fragment that just has been sung or played is repeated in the same pitch or a different pitch by one or more other voices or instruments while the first voice or instrument proceeds to other materials. This is the ruling procedure of many musical forms, including canon, catch, fugue, and round.

The round, perhaps the simplest form of imitation, is familiar to anyone who ever has taken part in singing "Oh how lovely is the evening," "Scotland's burning," or "Frère Jacques." One voice initiates the melody. When it has advanced a predetermined distance, the second voice enters with the beginning of the same melody. Then third and at times fourth voices enter with similar predetermined delays.

The principle of the round is imitative, rhythmic, and repetitive. As soon as the first voice has completed the entire melody, it may start all over again, and thus the several voices may continue to go "round and round" until—after a certain number of repetitions—each voice, beginning with the first, stops singing as it reaches the end of the melody. In a round, the imitating voices sing either in the same pitch as the first voice or at an interval of one octave from it. In a strict canon, the imitating voices may repeat the melody at the interval of a fourth, a fifth, or some other pitch distance from the initiating voice. In the canon, too, the imitating voices do not always wait for the completion of a melodic phrase by the preceding voice (as they do in the round), but may enter at a variety of different points.

"My end is my beginning"

Machaut made extremely adept use of canon in his motets, while in some of his rondeaux he foreshadowed the almost incredibly complicated "puzzle-canons" of a later period. The rondeau originally had been a dance-song of fresh simplicity, but in Machaut's hands it often became an intellectual game requiring the concentrated attention demanded by the effort to solve a difficult puzzle. The most renowned of his compositions of this sort is called *"Ma fin est mon commencement"* (My end is my beginning), a statement that is factual. In modern notation, as quoted by Gustave Reese in *Music in the Middle Ages* (W. W. Norton & Company, Inc.), the piece looks like this:

("Ma fin est mon commencement"—Machaut)

Example 5

This astonishing composition is for one singing voice and two instruments. The melody of the vocal part (upper line of notes on the bottom staff) also is used for the instrumental part that here appears on the top staff, *but as reversed note by note,* proceeding backward throughout. The other instrumental part (bottom melody on bottom staff) has a different melody. This reaches a conclusion halfway through the piece, at the double bar line. Thereafter it too proceeds backward until reaching its own first note.

"Ma fin est mon commencement" displays another characteristic of the *ars nova* which continues to be an important element of musical construction: syncopation, the temporary displacement of regular, expected accents. In the third and fourth measures of this rondeau, upper staff, one variety of syncopation is produced by the absence of notes on the first, most important beats. This shifts the expected first-beat accent subtly to the second half of that beat, almost with the effect of talk interrupted by a sudden intake of breath. In the eighth measure, upper melody on bottom staff, another variety of syncopation is produced by the holding-over *through the important first beat* of a tone first sounded on the weaker fourth beat of the preceding measure. Machaut used syncopation in motets organized with the repetitive isorhythms, thus producing then unexampled rhythmic elaboration and interest. With respect to this special sort of rhythmic complexity, some of his compositions scarcely were matched before the twentieth century.

When composing polyphonically, Machaut often made no use of existing melodies, but created all of his materials. In his view, the art of musical creation rapidly was becoming the conscious activity we think it today: the preparation of an entirely original whole, rather than, as in some early practices, the embedding of one or more borrowed elements in newly devised original material. Later composers, of course, at times have reverted to that earlier practice: Tchaikovsky wove his *Mozartiana* suite around melodies used by Mozart; Edvard Grieg composed for performance at a second piano original pieces intended to be played while Mozart sonatas were being played at the first piano; Igor Stravinsky built his ballet score *Le Baiser de la fée* on hints borrowed from pieces by Tchaikovsky. Sets of variations** on borrowed themes are numerous.

Consonance and Intervals

Machaut and some other musicians of his time occasionally treated all the voices or parts in a composition with nearly equal emphasis. Looked at vertically, such many-voiced compositions appear to the modern eye to pay strict attention to consonance** at certain important points and to disregard it at others. As in some earlier and many later pieces, the voices are likely to begin in perfect consonance—that is, are likely to be separated as they start by an octave, a fifth, or a fourth. They are likely to return to one of these perfect consonances for points of repose or finality, such as the ends or melodies or of melodic phrases. Between any two of these consonant points, however, the intervals very often not only are dissonances, but also dissonances in sequences that would have been inconceivable to most eighteenth- and nineteenth-century musicians. Although the intervals separating simultaneously sounding tones were becoming more and more the objects of composers' fascinated attention, what remained of prime interest was melodic profile. Strictly forward melodic movement of however many individual but simultaneous voices was still more central than vertical, chordal structure or any logic of chordal succession.

Musicians as gifted as Machaut and Landino created expressive and in themselves satisfying musical structures by using the newly evolved freedoms of the *ars nova* as additional to older procedures. In composing his Mass for four voices, Machaut stayed as faithful to the older ways of ecclesiastical polyphony as was possible for a man living fully in a later era. But when composing other pieces, he evinced his interest in producing, by whatever means would render it expressive and pleasing, music that would support and display the verbal texts he had selected or written.

Landino wandered farther still from earlier practices, allowing his versions of ballata, caccia, madrigal,[1] and other forms to be shaped in part by the sensuous, lush turns of melody native to his homeland which to this day are spoken of as "Italian." These pieces almost certainly were not intended for performance by voices alone. Stringed instruments, mostly of varieties now obsolete, both plucked and bowed, the small portable organ called *organetto,* recorders (end-blown flutes), and possibly other wind instruments may have been intended to play with the voices or, in some instances, even to replace them.

In Landino's surviving compositions, especially as they must have sounded when he himself was one of the performing group (he was an accomplished performer on organ, lute, flute, and other instruments, including at least one of his own invention), music was slipping altogether from its belated Gothic period. The art was shedding its hieratic medieval rigidity, its purposeful and often powerfully evocative narrowness. To replace those qualities, it was preparing to take on some of the graciousness, the curving, soft, almost fleshly allure of the Renaissance. Landino, the last great exponent of the *ars nova,* died in 1397. By that year, Donatello and Fra Angelico had been born and the wonderful English musician John Dunstable was a grown man.

From the mid-seventh century on, the ways of musicians in the British Isles were much like those of their Continental colleagues. The chief differences to be discerned in English and Irish music of that period clearly resulted from differences in their folk music and from the tendency, apparently more advanced in the islands than in France and other Continental regions, to use the local or national language in addition to, or instead of, Latin. A number of

[1] The madrigal of the *ars nova* period was not the sort of vocal piece indicated by the same word during the sixteenth century and later. It referred to a much more strictly applied poetico-musical pattern of which the later madrigal was a very freely interpreted imitation.

special musical practices inevitably developed, but these remain refinements that now are of interest only to scholars. Also, although Britain and Ireland were somewhat isolated geographically, communication between them and Continental centers of culture was constant. Influences flowed in both directions across the English Channel and the North Sea.

"Sumer is icumen in"

Because fewer documents on the early history of music survive in Britain and Ireland than in several Continental countries, less is known of insular than of Continental practices and developments. But the earliest-known preserved example of written-out polyphony is a musical illustration in *Musica Enchiriadis,* a theoretical treatise written out in England or Ireland in the ninth century. And by the early decades of the fourteenth century (possibly, though improbably, before the middle of the thirteenth), there had been written out in England one of the most enduringly famous of musical compositions, "Sumer is icumen in," known as the "Reading rota"—that is, the round discovered at Reading Abbey.

Unless this astonishingly elaborate and expressive composition is to be regarded as the result of an isolated upthrust of individual genius of an unparalleled sort, it inescapably suggests that the techniques of polyphonic composition were more advanced in England than elsewhere by the date of its noting-down. "Sumer is icumen in" frequently is sung today because of the lively beauty of its melodies, whose springtime freshness has remained unaffected by six or seven centuries of time and change. As an early example of imitation, it is all but incredible: it actually consists of two simultaneously sung rounds, the upper one for four voices, the lower one for two.

"Sumer is icumen in" is of enormous interest technically. The voices of the upper, four-part round enter successively at distances of four measures. The lower, two-part round continues, so that when the fourth upper-round voice comes in, six voices actually are singing together, which they continue to do for at least thirty-four measures. They may have been meant to do so for more than thirty-four measures, for though the piece appears to end when the first voice has completed the melody once, no intrinsic reason suggests itself why it could not continue until the final voice also had completed the melody (the other voices, meanwhile, having fallen silent one by one). Also, the piece appears to be in what we know as the major mode: each staff of the manuscript has a B♭ set down at its beginning, this being in our modern notation the indication or "key signature" for F major (or for D minor, clearly not intended here).

Further interest inheres in "Sumer is icumen in" because it makes use of a ground bass, or *basso ostinato,* another compositional method still in use. This indicates a melody or melodic fragment used as the lowest part of a composition, where it is repeated over and over, usually below varying melodic and other occurrences in the other parts or voices. In this piece, the two lowest voices actually constitute a double ground bass that in itself is a round. Then, too, the "Reading rota" not only is secular, but is in a local (Wessex) dialect. In modern English, its opening words mean: "Summer is coming in. The cuckoos sing loudly." True, it also has a Latin text, written under the lines of the upper round and beginning *"Perspice Christicola."* But the Latin words do not fit the melody nearly so smoothly as the words in Wessex dialect: they possibly may have been added so that the music could be sung in Reading Abbey, where the famous manuscript, now in the British Museum, was discovered.

"Sumer is icumen in" contains no notable dissonances. If sung from a replica of the manuscript, it ends upon a chord containing the three tones of the full tonic triad of F major (F, A, and C). It is extremely smooth in both harmony and texture. Above all other qualities, it presents the euphonious sweetness that was to be singled out a century later by Continental musicians as being peculiarly English. This stylistic element, so remote from the stiff, dissonant angularity of much earlier polyphony, was to help fertilize the great Burgundian-Flemish schools of polyphonic composition, schools initiated by men who either had studied with John Dunstable (1370?–1453) or were his indirect artistic heirs.

Dunstable

The surviving compositions of Dunstable chiefly differ from the French works of his era in their much more marked tendency toward later evolutions of vertical and harmonic thinking. When they employ three voices, the resulting three-note chords are preponderantly consonant; they move forward through time with something directly ancestral to the harmonic motion that—as codified and then legislated—was to govern much musical architecture of the seventeenth and eighteenth centuries and most of the nineteenth century as well. John Dunstable was what scarcely a composer before him could be called: a great inventor of persuasive melodies. His compositions also evidence careful consideration for sonority in itself, for the full, pleasing *sound* of the music. This either was something new or something that Dunstable had acquired from now unknown British musicians and himself had developed startlingly. The suggestion often has been advanced that Dunstable's suave and charming manner represented the preservation and development of a native English liking for euphony which somehow had escaped the powerful, pointed influence of Gothic Continental polyphony. Yet Dunstable's taste for melismata** approaching the purely decorative *fioriture*** of later Italian music appears to indicate that he was acquainted with very similar melodic decorations in the music of the late Italian *ars nova*.

Although nothing certain is known of Dunstable's life and career, it is generally believed that he died in 1453 (the very year of the surrender of Constantinople to the Ottoman Turks which was to have so important a role in producing the Renaissance). It also is believed that he was very old at the time of his death and that for a time he had served as master of a musical establishment kept in Paris by a brother of Henry V. Almost as much as his native genius, his presence on the Continent in the early decades of the

26

fifteenth century, particularly at a musical center as important as Paris, would help to explain both his great fame and the otherwise odd fact that most of his surviving compositions have been discovered outside England. It also would help to explain the clear evidence of contemporary Continental procedures in his music and his own profound, enduring influence on his Continental contemporaries and immediate successors. He seems to have appeared at the close of a long period of vital development in British music, to have combined British procedures with certain Continental customs to the advantage of both creative streams, and to have left the resulting fusion to Continental composers rather than to his compatriots, who soon were to be put into long eclipse by Burgundian and Flemish master musicians.

The compositions of Dunstable and of such a composer-contemporary of his as Lionel (or Leonel) Power do not, of course, bespeak anything like a fully developed harmonic system. But many of their pieces do show a strong feeling for chords and for a logical interrelationship among chords, the very elements that later would determine the formulation and practice of such a system. Abandoning exclusive consideration of melodic strands as such, composers long since had begun to insist on the potential musical significance of the intervals between simultaneously sounded tones.

The Ear's Wisdom

Although, as remarked earlier, in earlier polyphony consonant combinations of tones had been expected at the openings and closes of melodic units and sometimes at other important musical junctures, there had been no prevailing sensation that a certain sort of dissonance ought to be "resolved"—that is, succeeded by a specific, defined consonance having the almost therapeutic effect of "healing" the dissonance. This strong feeling for an inherent logic of chordal succession is the most important operative tenet of the harmonic system of most eighteenth- and nineteenth-century music. It did not exist in Dunstable's mind or era.

But it was to be derived in part from unchanging mathematical relationships discoverable in the physical make-up of musical sound itself, and long before its codification by schoolmen, composers were responding to instinctive understanding of some of its components.

One expression of that instinctive understanding was the procedure called *faux-bourdon* or *faulxbordon*—false bass—one variety of which, known as English discant, was natural to Dunstable and his British coevals. The reasoning behind *faux-bourdon* was complicated and not devoid of mystification. Its effect in practice was a series of parallel sixth-chords such as F-D followed by E-C, F-D, G-E, etc. Between the outlying voices, the third voice moved along parallel to the lower voice, removed from it by a third. The resulting three-note chords were F-A-D, E-G-C, F-A-D, G-B-E, etc. And the acceptance of these resulting thirds (F-A, E-G, G-B, etc.) as "consonant" or pleasant intervals marked *faux-bourdon* as an important thrust toward the harmony of later days. Furthermore (and here the mystification enters in), if we transpose the top voice—which the complex theory behind *faux-bourdon* ruled to be the "real bass"—down an octave, we produce a series of full triads (D-F-A, C-E-G, D-F-A, E-G-B, etc.), which is how practitioners of *faux-bourdon* actually *heard* the three-note chords. And the full triad was to be the armature on which the modern system of harmony was to be modeled. English discant, arrived at or explained by a different but equally complicated sort of theoretical reasoning, resulted in chords much like those in *faux-bourdon*, and therefore was just as likely to urge music toward the elaboration of harmony.

Both *faux-bourdon* and English discant as made use of by Dunstable imply a heightened feeling for the independence and interrelationships of chords. Similarly, the constant admission, if not in writing music, then in performing it, of accidentals underlined this increased tendency to think harmonically, though it was in itself primarily a melodic procedure. The importance of accidentals in inching all music in the direction of harmonic thought was particularly great when an accidental was used to raise by a semitone the seventh tone of a scale. The result of such a raising of the seventh tone was the introduction of a semitone rather than a whole tone between the seventh and eighth tones of the scale. The presence of a semitone there is invariable in our modern diatonic scales, both major and minor. These musical methods responded to demands by the listening brain, which instinctively understood more about the physical make-up of musical sound than earlier compositional procedures had demonstrated.

The awakening of this sort of consciousness produced a long step from earlier polyphony toward what now is thought of as the classical system of harmony. It defined the available store of forward-tending, almost harmonic devices available to European composers during the first decades of the fifteenth century. Music remained preponderantly vocal, as it had been in the period of the *ars antiqua,* but in that of the *ars nova* instruments were increasing their importance both as used in accompaniment to singing and as played alone for their own varieties of expressiveness. Music for the organ and other instruments, notably plucked and bowed strings, stood on the verge of idiomatic as well as physical independence of the human voice. Compositions already were being performed widely by instruments alone. In actual performance of supposedly vocal polyphonic pieces, some or all of the "voices" often were played rather than sung. In the continuing ebb and surge of these intermingling usages and means, Europe during the succeeding century was to enter upon one of its greatest periods of musical creation.

CHAPTER III

A Slow-swinging Pendulum

The history of Western music, looked at in cross section, may be viewed as a series of swings between experimentation and summation, alternations of longer and shorter periods of expansion of technical means, and of consolidation of the uses of those means.

The Burgundian School

"Burgundian School" is a name given to a group of composers who lived during an interregnum between the musical manners of the *ars nova* and the heyday of the Netherlandish masters. In another view, "Burgundian School" may be merely a plausible label for two great musical creators who fit poorly elsewhere: Gilles Binchois (1400?–67) and Guillaume Dufay (1400?–74). Their works present the most successful combination of the best of the *ars nova* and the sweetening flavor represented by Dunstable. The result of that combination was music of the most sensuous tenderness.

Cambrai and Dijon were centers of a musical style that yearned away from the complex, extraordinarily learned music of the *ars nova* toward a more direct, more seemingly personal mode of expression. The turn was occasioned in part by a strong preference for orderliness and consolidation, for tradition over experiment. The *ars nova* had been rich in novelty; its motion had been centrifugal or forward. The Burgundians cared remarkably little for novelty in that sense; their movement was centripetal and inward. Their achievements in creating persuasive and beautiful music were large, but except for their gradual production of a few harmonic devices, they look, from a historical point of view, almost reactionary. As the culmination of one entire view and practice of musical developments, their music could have been succeeded only by gradually devitalized repetition and aping, by stagnation, or by another era of experiment (they were, that is, composers in the artistic position occupied in the eighteenth century by Johann Sebastian Bach and Handel, in the nineteenth by Johannes Brahms).

Binchois and Dufay

Binchois and Dufay carried forward the establishment of the full triad as the deepest foundation of a logic of chordal progression. Their feeling for the relative importance of the tones constituting a scale came closer than that of their immediate predecessors to what was to be considered normal from late in the seventeenth century until very recently. Besides ceding a prominent role to the full triad, the Burgundians developed a strong feeling about the melodic-harmonic use of the seventh tone of a scale.

A harmonic pattern that moves to a sensation of temporary or permanent finality is called a cadence, and the last chord of a closing cadence must have the key-tone (the first tone of the scale being employed) as its chief constituent. Melodically, this tonic is most often approached from the tone immediately below it, the seventh tone of the scale in use—what is called most often the "leading tone." In approaching this final tonic, the Burgundians often employed what looks to us like two leading tones: first the seventh tone of the scale, then the sixth, and only then the tonic. Thus, if the tonic was C, the melodic notes at the end of a Burgundian composition often were B, A, C, whereas A, B, C would be a much more common later way of ordering the same tones at the same location in a composition. Landino had made some use of this double leading tone, producing what sometimes is called the "Landino cadence," but with Binchois and Dufay it became customary and lent their final cadences, for modern ears at least, a curious sort of indecision or instability.

The newly acquired importance of the full triad (which came to be regarded as an interval of a third superimposed on another third—as, for example, E-G superimposed on C-E to produce C-E-G) underlined the basic importance of the third. The triad was interpreted by Binchois, Dufay, and their Burgundian confreres by the principles of *fauxbourdon*. When looked at vertically, their music therefore often contains extended series of such chords as C-E-A and G-B-E, which contain both thirds (C-E, G-B) and sixths (C-A, G-E). This produces a chordal series very unlike the octave-fifth angularity of earlier days. A mixture, musically speaking, of Gothic and later manners, it tends toward the curving, softer-textured idioms of the Renaissance. Melodically it accompanied the advance into a new day.

Sacred and Secular
in Burgundian Music

The composers of the Burgundian School displayed a lively new interest in writing music for the changing sections (Proper of the Mass) of the liturgical text, finding in it reasons for the creation of new musical materials. In their settings of the Ordinary, or unchanging sections, of the Mass they often reached toward an over-all musical unification by employing one basic theme or melody throughout but in varying guises. Dufay, for example, was one of the earliest composers to adapt the secular song "*L'Homme armé*" to this purpose, thus helping to establish a vogue for that song which endured into the seventeenth century. In structural intention, these thematically unified Masses resemble the symphonies of César Franck and other composers of the nineteenth century in which all or part of a single thematic melody is heard in each movement "cyclically."

The Burgundians placed the motet halfway between sacred and secular practices. The usual motet no longer was multitextual or multilingual. No longer was it usually built upon a *cantus firmus*. Becoming the celebratory music performed as a grand tribute to a victory, coronation, royal wedding, or other large public occasion, it had begun to employ the same text in all its voices and to make use of no pre-existing *cantus firmus* at all or to use fragments of one in what may still have been thought of as the lowest voice but in actuality was the highest.

Dufay was a composer of sacred music who also wrote some music that was secular. But Gilles Binchois's three-part secular songs occupy so eminent a position among his works as to make him appear more a secular composer than a sacred one. These *chansons* are almost exactly songs in the modern sense: the musical clothing of a poetic text. Binchois's *chansons* are softer, less harsh and rugged, less overtly male music than almost any earlier music had been on the Continent. Burgundian music in general most often seems to require such descriptive adjectives as plaintive, sensuous, mellow, feminine, and sentimental. This is particularly true of the music of Binchois, for Dufay strikes us as much the more vigorous of the two leaders.

In both their sacred and their secular works, the Burgundians inevitably admitted close acquaintance with the technical innovations of Machaut and his contemporaries. They became particularly adept at building forms out of imitation, especially canonic imitation. Within these forms, however, they remained content to perform superbly musical actions that their predecessors had performed well. No artistic discontent, no restless or challenging search for new methods is exhaled by their music. But their sheer dexterity still can astonish us, not only as true virtuosity always astonishes, but also as expressivity.

In one example of close-meshed Burgundian imitation, an *Agnus Dei* from Dufay's *"L'Homme armé"* Mass, the quoted melody employed as the *cantus firmus* is sung backward and then reversed to be sung forward in diminution (that is, in notes half as long in duration as those previously used). In the four-voice web of the *Agnus Dei*, it could be recognized thus only by a highly trained, sensitive, and constantly, fiercely attentive listener. But to recognize it at all, even if only through the eyes, is to add something to our understanding of one way in which Dufay made music. For the musical value is only incidentally dependent on this learned device: the musical point is that this reversed melodic line has been fitted into a relationship with other melodic lines in such a way as to produce excellent music. Both the scholarly cleverness *and* the musical value increase when, nineteen measures from the close of the *Agnus Dei,* that same melodic line appears moving in shortened tones.

Uses of the Learned Device

When Dufay's *Agnus Dei* is being sung, it is so difficult to pick out the *cantus firmus* from among the other voices that it fairly may be said that its very presence (not to mention that it is one musical phrase of the song "*L'Homme armé*" sung forward after being sung backward) is for the composer's satisfaction and the admiration of our eyes. But what it is worth while repeating is that as music the *Agnus Dei* is for the ear and for the glory of God.

Many surviving Dufay and Binchois scores do not make clear to us whether a given melodic line was intended for the human voice or for an instrument. We know, nonetheless, that the Burgundians surely made wide use of instruments. By their epoch, indeed, instruments had arrogated to themselves such importance that we must know at least a little about them in order to be able to imagine, however approximately and imperfectly, the true character of Burgundian music as it originally was performed.

Early Instruments

The end-blown flute known as the recorder occupied a primary position in the instrumental parts and a few wholly instrumental compositions of Dufay and Binchois, as did several sizes and varieties of organ. Of other wind instruments, perhaps the most widely used were the shawm and the trombone.

The shawm, ancestral to the modern oboe, English horn,[1]

[1] The modern instrument called "English horn" actually (like the bassoon) is a larger oboe. In modern usage, a horn is a brass instru-

bassoon, and contrabassoon, was a wind instrument in which the sound-producing element was a pair of flexible reeds so placed within a wooden tube that the pressure of the player's breath caused them to vibrate against one another. It was made in several sizes, from one with about the pitch-range of the present oboe to one not too far removed from that of the modern contrabassoon.

The fifteenth-century trombone differed but little from the one used today in orchestras and bands. Evolved partly from a medieval instrument called a sacbut (or sackbut), the trombone really is a deep-voiced trumpet. When the mechanisms of most other wind instruments were still insufficiently developed to permit the players to produce all the tones desirable in musical performance, the trombone already had been equipped with the slide mechanism that enables the player to produce all the semitones within the instrument's range. The trombone therefore could all but match the human voice in flexibility, and was not restricted, as many other wind instruments still were, to use in fanfares and military signaling.

Of stringed instruments, the Burgundian composers particularly favored the viols. These incarnations of such medieval bowed instruments as the rebec, vielle, and lyra entered their heyday about 1500 and were superseded by the violins before 1650. They differed from the modern family of violins chiefly in that their back customarily was flat rather than gently rounded; in that their upper body sloped away from their neck on either side rather than springing straight out from it; in that they had six strings instead of the violins' four; in that they had horizontal frets like those of a guitar rather than a smooth neck; in that their bridge, and therefore the alignment of their strings, was almost flat instead of being rounded (an arrangement that facilitated the bowing of more than two strings at a time); in that even in their smallest sizes they were held downward be-

---

ment lacking the vibrating reeds characteristic of the oboes and usually having a conical bore—that is, an air column whose circumference increases away from the mouthpiece. "English horn," as the designation of a large oboe, therefore, is only a well-established misnomer.

tween the player's knees or on them rather than being placed (as the later violins and violas are) in a semihorizontal position against the player's neck and shoulder; and that the stick of their bow was curved outward rather than made straight or nearly straight. The chief difference in sound—resulting from the differences in construction—between almost any viol and almost any member of the violin family of comparable size is that the viols, though possessing suave, delicate tonal color, lacked brilliance and easily were covered by the sounds of other instruments. Violin, viola, cello (really violoncello), and contrabass (or double-bass),[2] the leading violins, are incomparably more brilliant and audible than their viol predecessors.

The Music of Chivalry

With these and some other instruments, Binchois, Dufay, and other, lesser Burgundians delighted to employ the uppermost register of the male singing voice. They cherished the crying, depersonalized color of vocal tone produced in the throats of boys and very high tenors, and even the "artificial" tone known as falsetto. Because falsetto is produced high in the throat, it affects many modern listeners as unpleasantly nasal, but when it is used sensitively it has, even in small volume, a color distinct from any other, and therefore highly useful to a composer, particularly to a composer not otherwise equipped with a very wide choice of timbres.

The Burgundians composed motets and Masses reflecting the chivalric, medieval-into-Renaissance elegance of a ducal aristocracy. Their secular music was apt entertainment for the courtiers of Philip the Good and Charles the Bold. Either their application of their wide musical erudition was not so self-conscious as that of the later *ars nova* masters had been or to us it simply does not seem so elaborate because it almost constantly was placed at the disposi-

---

[2] The doublebass or contrabass or "bass fiddle" or "bull fiddle" sometimes is classified as a viol. Indeed, its proper full name probably is double-bass viol. In fact, it is half a viol and half a violin, its descent from true viols being most noticeable in its sloping shoulders.

tion of an aristocratic mode of expression. The still-charming music of Binchois and Dufay brings us an echo of the elegant way of life that was to disappear (as was independent Burgundy itself) before the end of the fifteenth century. It is the way of life made familiar to our eyes by the paintings of Hubert and Jan van Eyck.

Okeghem

Jean de Okeghem (1430?–95?), perhaps a pupil of Binchois or Dufay, high musical servant to Charles VII and Louis XI, was an all but exact contemporary of Jean Fouquet and François Villon. He asserts a reasonable claim to a high position among all teachers of musical theory and practice. He was to attract one pupil—Josquin des Prés—who would outglow all preceding musicians in personal expressiveness and in the sort of pervasive musicality of which Mozart has become the best-known exemplar. Scholars regard Okeghem as one founder of a school of Netherlandish composers who inherited a very rich legacy from the Burgundians and then, by adding to it, rapidly expanded the technical resources of the art of music.

If, in one sense, a comparison of Josquin des Prés to Mozart is useful, so in another may be that of Okeghem to the great modern methodologist and composer Arnold Schoenberg. For Okeghem was an intellectual, fascinated by the mathematical possibilities in musical relationships, wonderful at designing musical puzzles that latter-day theorists have delighted to solve. But he was no more a desiccated academic than Schoenberg, for he wrote music that some of his contemporaries judged to be marvelously expressive and beautiful. But it was his destiny, created in large part by his own musical nature, to be outshone by Josquin his pupil and to go down in musical history as an innovator and setter of new patterns. "With Okeghem, in fact," Cecil Gray wrote in *The History of Music*, "the art of polyphony goes to school and is set to perform tasks, frequently dull and thankless in themselves, but constituting the discipline and exercise which are a necessary preliminary to any fruitful development."

Okeghem composed numerous Masses, about twenty of which survive. He also left behind motets, *chansons,* and canons—including puzzle canons noted down in cryptograms that allow of several different solutions. One of his Masses is headed *Cujusvi toni*—In Whatever Mode. It purposely lacks clef-signs, the result being that, having chosen a mode in which to perform it, the singers also had to supply clefs in such a way that pleasant interrelationships could be maintained among the individual voices. Also, of course, they had to insert accidentals.

"Paper" Music

Notorious among Okeghem's displays of technical legerdemain is a canon called *Deo gratias.* This is essentially "paper music," more to be admired by the astonished eyes than heard by the unconvinced ear. But it is an indicative example of the learning and virtuosity of technique at which fifteenth-century musical creation had arrived. The words *"Deo gratias"* are repeated and repeated throughout the canon, which calls for thirty-six singers, nine each of altos, sopranos, tenors, and basses. The altos start the complex proceedings, entering one by one for nine successive measures, each of them beginning the melody anew, but not always at the same pitch. When all nine of the altos finally are singing together, the sopranos enter similarly, one by one, measure after measure, until eighteen voices are singing eighteen fragments of the same melody at once. When the tenors begin to add their voices, however, the altos fall silent; when the basses begin to enter, the sopranos desist. The thirty-six voices never sing all together, but even eighteen voices singing sections of a single melody make, structurally speaking, a musical mesh of very considerable complexity. The trouble with the *Deo gratias* canon as interesting or convincing music is that Okeghem, needing to avoid fierce outbursts of undesired dissonance, had to select or design his melody with a degree of care that finally resulted in a parched monotony.

This sort of game among experts is a world distant from Gregorian chant or its first simple adaptations intended to exalt the glory of God. Josquin des Prés was to play it successfully for even higher intellectual stakes in *Qui habitat in adjutorio*, a canon to full text. In it, six each of sopranos, altos, tenors, and basses finally succeeded in singing simultaneously twenty-four sections of a single melody.

When, in 1501, Ottaviano dei Petrucci, expanding the young process of printing music from movable metal type, issued the first important musical book ever thus printed, he included no pieces by Jean de Okeghem. But of Okeghem's more winning and musically more gracious contemporary, Jacob Obrecht, he put two secular compositions into this *Harmonice musices odhecaton A*. Later on, eight of Obrecht's Masses, as well as many of his motets and *chansons*, were printed.

Obrecht and the Polyphonic Chanson

The polyphonic *chanson*, though likely to be cast, at least in part, in one of the patterns that had descended from the troubadours and trouvères, was inclining toward a new simplicity. It also was signaling a tendency to new patterns, often used but once and then discarded, which were related to the shape and significance of their texts. Okeghem and, particularly, Obrecht put into secular *chansons* some of their most winning musical ideas. Although these *chansons* probably were conceived either as entirely vocal pieces or as largely vocal pieces with instrumental support, evidence suggests that the possibility of wholly instrumental performances was not ruled out. At times the melodic line of each voice was played by a single instrument.

Like many of his Netherlandish and other northern European coevals, Obrecht helped to spread the new virtuosity to Italy by living and working there. He served both Ercole d'Este—the patron of Ariosto—and Lorenzo de' Medici ("the Magnificent"). He attracted no musical protégé so famous as Josquin des Prés (whose music often seems to show more influence by Obrecht than by Okeghem), but at one time numbered among his pupils the great scholar Desiderius Erasmus. Most of his works are settings of Latin texts, but his French *chansons* uncover a lively secular temperament. One of them has the timeless subject *Tant que notre argent durera* ("As long as our money lasts"). On the basis of one setting, for use during Holy Week, of the Passion of Christ—including the Seven Last Words—Obrecht long was cited as having composed a forerunner of Johann Sebastian Bach's great Matthew and John Passions. But this large polyphonic structure (in which no attempt is made at the Bachian dramatic differentiation of roles) no longer is believed by scholars to be Obrecht's work.

The Music of the Netherlanders

The Netherlandish School[3] was partly a reaction against the increasing secularization heralded by Dunstable, Machaut, Dufay, and Binchois. If assessed quantitatively, its products were more sacred in emphasis. It concentrated on the Mass and the sacred motet. Using scriptural texts, the Netherlanders habitually composed motets for four, five, six, and more voices. Whereas Okeghem's surviving motets indicate a preference for a *cantus firmus* in long-held tones, with the other voices uncoiling melismatically, Obrecht and his followers developed the more specifically harmonic manner of conceiving the voices as to be heard together vertically, in chords. This concept, known as the "familiar" style, resulted in a texture allowing the Latin syllables of the text to be understood easily. All the singers pronounce the same syllables simultaneously, to tones held for equal durations. In both manners, the most talented and accomplished of the Netherlanders created music of enduring beauty, helping to express with certainty the religious attitudes of the epoch in which such men as Botticelli, Leonardo da Vinci, and Albrecht Dürer were painting and Christopher Columbus was sailing west in search of Cathay.

The Mass quoting all or fragments of a secular melody continued to attract the creative attention of the Nether-

---

[3] "Late Burgundian School" and "Middle Flemish School" are names occasionally applied to various groupings of the northern-born composers of this era. But Netherlandish seems more accurately inclusive when the group embraces Belgians, Hollanders, and belated Burgundians.

landers. The long-popular *"L'Homme armé"* still challenged the ingenuity of composers in these *"cantus firmus* Masses," so called because the adapted melody was used in the tenor as a true *cantus firmus*. Both Okeghem and Obrecht employed other secular melodies that were known popularly as accompanying amorous or narrative texts in the local language. Both men also composed what appear to be wholly original Masses in which no previously existing melodies are embedded.

Evolution of Instrumental Music

So complex and absorbing of inventiveness had the available techniques of vocal polyphony become, so adept were choristers in the great churches of the Netherlands, France, and Italy, that independent instrumental music advanced little in those regions during this period. Music for instruments was both composed and performed there, but its comparatively feeble development (except, perhaps, as the alternate method of performing primarily vocal music) proves that it did not enlist the full energies of the most accomplished composers of the time, who continued to be more attracted to the possibilities inherent in combinations of language and vocal sound.

No purely instrumental music fully comparable in scope to the best vocal compositions of Okeghem, Obrecht, and Josquin made its appearance before the seventeenth-century days of the surpassing northern organists. Instruments went on changing and differentiating themselves, notably early or ancestral forms of the harpsichord (strings plucked by plectra activated from a keyboard), the clavichord (strings vibrated by wedges fastened to the back of lever-like keys extended from a keyboard, the wedges also serving to "divide" the strings into varying lengths, and thus to determine their sounding pitch as the player's fingers do on violin strings), and various sorts and conditions of flutes, horns, recorders, and viols.

Josquin des Prés

This was the musical universe in which Josquin des Prés (1445?-1521) reached his resplendent maturity, the most honored and glittering individual in the history of music to his day. Not primarily an experimenter or innovator, Josquin (in this resembling Johann Sebastian Bach) most fully exploited the technical resources at hand, putting them masterfully at the service of an intensely poetic sensibility and a copious imagination. His Masses and motets are not significantly different in techniques from those of his immediate predecessors and his contemporaries. They simply were achieved better, more expressively, whether judged obliquely as appropriate settings of text or abstractly as music. Ronsard, the leading French poet of the time, placed Josquin at the head of "excelling workers in the art [of music]," while Henricus Glareanus gave him in music the rank held in poetry by Vergil. His works were published widely while he lived, and were performed all over Europe. Martin Luther, a musically learned man, said: "Musicians do with notes what they can. Josquin does with them what he wishes."

Josquin was worldly and sophisticated. His music gleams with wit and is alive with humor. He could play musical paper-games with the cleverest of his contemporaries. But he was more interested in sound, its effective manipulation and its beauties. Sometimes he was dissatisfied with one of his new compositions when he heard it sung; then he would alter its notes to make it *sound* better. For sheer glory of sounding voices, his six-part masterpieces may never have been exceeded. He contributed comparatively little to the morphology of musical technique, much to music as expressive creation. Except for his influence upon his pupils and imitators, he changed music's direction but little—much less, for example, than Okeghem. But the repertoire of vocal polyphony would be more impoverished by the deletion of his surviving works than by the loss of Okeghem's.

Josquin blazed like a sun. In that brilliance, the lesser lights of his most talented and craftsmanlike contemporaries

43

now seem to have paled. To forget those others or to leave their music unperformed would be a mistake. But in any study of musical *means,* of music's parts of speech, Josquin himself must accept a small place, the others none. Their names retain an undoubted flowery charm—Loyset Compère, Pierre de la Rue, Jean Mouton, Antoine Brumel, the Huguenots Claude Goudimel and Claude le Jeune—or a fine strength, as with Heinrich Isaak. But the practices of the art of music were not modified materially by what they composed.

The Sixteenth-Century Madrigal

In the middle years of the sixteenth century, the evolution of the polyphonic *chanson* in France was paralleled in Italy by that of the later type of madrigal. This was at first and for some decades chiefly the work of Flemings living in Italy and of Italians. Not by any measurement a strict musical form, the sixteenth-century madrigal was a vocal composition for three, four, and later five unaccompanied singers. Its texts dealt with nature, love, and death. The manners of madrigal performance suggest those of later chamber music, for the singers most often sat at a table with their scores before them. The entire atmosphere was intentionally intimate.

Madrigals composed in the 1530s by such Flemish musicians as Jacob Arcadelt (1514?–70?) and Philippe Verdelot, such native Italians as Girolamo Carlo and Costanzo Festa (?–1545) consisted of a leading melodic line accompanied by other voices. They were, that is, preponderantly homophonic in texture. Thereafter, these madrigals tended to become much more polyphonic. The finest examples of the Venetian Flemings such as Adrian Willaert (1480?–1562), Cipriano de (or van) Rore (1516–65), and Philippe de Monte (1521?–1603) are made of five voices substantially equal in interest. In their hands, in fact, the madrigal was becoming the secular counterpart of the sacred motet.

The later sixteenth-century madrigal evolved into a highly integrated poetico-musical means for expressing intense personal emotions. The high Renaissance by then was at hand, and many of these flowery madrigals show some defining characteristics of what later men came to call Romantic music. Such men as Willaert, Rore, and the later Carlo Gesualdo (1560?–1613) searched eagerly for more expressiveness. This search led them to previously unheard-of frequent melodic use of semitone intervals not native to the scales they employed—that is, toward chromaticism. The combination of several simultaneous chromatic melodies inevitably produced chromatic chordal progressions and an examination of the logic of such progressions. This chromaticism still lends the madrigals of Willaert, Rore, Gesualdo, and some others their peculiar, intense, plaintive quality.

In Italy, the madrigal constantly became more complex. At last it not only was cast in so idiosyncratic a style as that of Carlo Gesualdo, but also evoked the virtuoso singer and established programmatic and coloristic effects. Scarcely an important Italian musician of the second half of the sixteenth century and the first years of the seventeenth but wrote into madrigals some of the most personal and characteristic of his music. Also, the madrigal spread to England (where it optionally came to be called ayre, canzonet, sonet, or just song), to Spain, and to the states of Germany. Of these offshoots, by far the most productive was the English, of which the first surpassing master was the greatest composer Britain yet had produced: William Byrd (1543–1623), a somewhat older contemporary of Shakespeare.

CHAPTER IV

Further Evolution of Polyphony

The techniques of composition inherited, developed, and changed by the Burgundian, German, and Netherlandish composers were spread across Western Europe by their practitioners as they labored in the chapels of kings, princes, dukes, cardinals, and popes. As the ill-defined period now referred to as the Renaissance began, the Netherlands proper witnessed a decline in the supremacy of local music while Netherlandish inheritors, altering their teachers' practices in personal, local, and national ways, unconsciously began to prepare another of music's great periods of accomplishment. This time, the light was to blaze chiefly in Italy, Spain, and England. Vocal polyphony was to achieve its freest and, at the same time, formally most successful manifestation in the period after Josquin des Prés chiefly in the music of four men. Only one of them was a Fleming by birth, and by career even he was as international as Igor Stravinsky. The other three were an Italian, a Spaniard, and an Englishman.

Orlando di Lasso, Palestrina, Victoria, Byrd

The Fleming Roland de Laittre (whose name commonly is Latinized as Orlandus Lassus or Italianized as Orlando di Lasso), Palestrina, and Victoria often are erroneously exalted above both Josquin and William Byrd. Although they perhaps were superior in certain respects, such superiority was at most a matter of shading. What matters here is what each of these composers did to alter the techniques and means of music and how each used the language of music—both as he encountered it and as he changed it in the process of adapting it to his own changing purposes. We shall find that the men who brought a musical period to its close were Palestrina, Orlando di Lasso, and Victoria, not Josquin and Byrd. We shall find Byrd clearly foreshadowing the musical future by being almost equally attracted by—and adept at—vocal and instrumental composition. Never again since Orlando di Lasso and Palestrina died in 1594 and Victoria in 1613 have the most accomplished composers worked primarily in vocal polyphony.

Music at a Frontier

The year of Victoria's death marked one of the most clearly visible boundaries in the history of music. On the far side of it, music had meant singing; on this side, in most of the civilized Western world, it would mean music for voices and music for instruments in varying proportions. For centuries on that far side, music had meant polyphony; on this side, music would come to mean, in varying proportions, polyphony (or its parallel, instrumental counterpoint) and chordal harmony and accompanied melody. Before reaching that boundary, music had meant largely sacred music, with composed secular music comparatively unimpressive in quantity; on passing that boundary, music began to mean secular and sacred music in varying proportions, with the secular predominating more and more. Before 1613 was reached, however, the musical era that first topped the heights in Josquin's maturity was to produce in unaccompanied vocal polyphony some of the most magnificent of all musical creations.

Developments Toward Harmony

Melody, which was basic to music from any discoverable beginnings of the art and is basic to it today, meanwhile was being forced increasingly to share its leading role with harmony. A brief backward glance will remind us that the earliest forms of polyphony contained germs of what we have come to call harmony, most notably the germs that always have lurked in the physical make-up of musical sound itself. In many of the earliest known examples of polyphony, a *duplum* exactly paralleled the *tenor,* thus (if looked at vertically) producing simultaneous combinations of tones which were almost, but not quite, in the modern sense, chords. (The word "chord" now is customarily reserved for combinations of three or more simultaneously sounded or clearly implied tones.) Usually at intervals of a fifth or a fourth, but additionally in octaves and thirds, this type of parallel *órganum* was not, in any recently agreed-upon meaning of the word, harmony. But it made that harmony inevitable if music was not mortally to limit itself but was instead to go on evolving new means. How closely the gradual acceptance of different intervals as consonant was related to the physical nature of musical sound becomes clear when we examine the nature of an ordinary musical tone.

Overtones

Except in very special instances that mostly can be produced only in laboratories, a musical tone is not a single "pure" tone, but is a composite. It consists, that is, of the main tone, called a fundamental, and a number of other, less easily audible tones, called overtones, harmonics, or upper partials. We do not ordinarily "hear" these overtones as separate from the fundamental. But the presence or absence of certain of them and the degree of audibility in which certain of them occur are the elements that make up the distinctive tone color—called timbre—of the instrument or human voice producing the tone. Supposing that the tone sounded is a C, the first ten overtones produced will be:

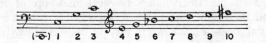

For any tone other than C, the overtones produced will be in the same intervallic relations to it as those in the example are to C.

The cause of overtones is the unchanging fact that any vibrating body vibrates simultaneously throughout itself and throughout one half, one third, one fourth, and so forth, of itself. It therefore sends into the air, to be picked up by our eardrums, not only the fundamental (loudest) sound produced by vibrating throughout itself, but also the overtones produced by vibration of its mathematically determinable sections. These overtone vibrations most usually have an amplitude (loudness) of only between one fifth and one fiftieth of that of the fundamental tone.

Anyone who wants to "hear" overtones in order to prove to himself that they exist can do so with a piano. Depress silently any key, preferably at or below the middle of the keyboard, then forcefully strike the key one octave above it, releasing it immediately. What you will hear sounding is not the tone represented by the lower key still being held down, but that of the key just struck and released—the key that here represents the first overtone of the tone represented by the silently depressed key, the string for which now is producing not its own tone, but its first overtone. Go one step farther, to the second overtone. Depress silently, for example, a C. Then strike forcefully and immediately release the G next above it. What you will hear sounding is the G, the second overtone of C.

What should be noticed particularly here is that the first overtone is removed from the fundamental by an octave, the second from the first by a fifth, the third from the second by a fourth, and the fourth from the third by a third—and that this is almost exactly the historical sequence in which the octave, fifth, fourth, and third were accepted as consonant or pleasant, and therefore as widely useful in composition. This historical acceptance, that is to say, was rooted in the unchanging physical make-up of musical sound itself. And the physical, inescapable presence in all musical tones of overtones in varying degrees of partial audibility was probably the major reason why harmony in the modern understanding of the term inevitably developed as a technique of musical construction.

Phases of Organum

By the end of the tenth century, the wholly parallel phase of organum had begun to cede place to a freer type, in which the duplum—often by then the higher of two voices or parts—moved in oblique and contrary motion and broke into several successive tones to each tone in the tenor. This still was not harmony, for the forward, horizontal movement of distinct melodies remained the ruling factor in the minds of composers and performers. Although some combinations of simultaneous tones, some intervals (notably octaves, fifths, and fourths) were felt to be more pleasant, more permissible, than others, no well-defined structural concept had emerged dealing with the manner in which one interval best might succeed another. Here we come upon the essential difference of meaning between "chord" (two or, most strictly, three or more different tones sounded together) and "harmony" (the arranged, orderly succession of chords and of relationships among them).

During the first half of the twelfth century, free organum split into variants of itself. One of these variants was different only in rhythm: instead of moving by the free meters of earlier organum, which had been determined by the lengths of the syllables in Latin texts, it was regulated by the rhythmic modes. In other variants, a triplum and quadruplum were added to the tenor and duplum, thus producing a texture that resembles, but is not, three- and four-part harmony. It is not harmony because it still is seen as a succession of incidentally related chords, each of which occurs only because constituent tones of several melodies happen to occur simultaneously thus at given points. Melismata (originally groups of several tones sung to a single syllable) had become elaborate: the principal voice often was slowed down so that the other voice or voices could sing whole groups of tones to each of its tones. Music, that is, was yearning toward harmony, making use of many of its future materials without truly becoming harmonic. Any examination of music of the period banishes all doubt that its composers increasingly were aware of vertical, chordal structure. But a succession of chords is not in itself harmony unless the relations among the chords have had an important effect upon the selection of tones used. The status of organum during the twelfth century can best be described as protoharmonic.

Consonance and Dissonance

Feelings about consonance and dissonance meanwhile developed and changed, as they always have. Consonance is not much more than the name given to the pleasant or restful effect that certain intervals and successions of intervals produce upon listeners; dissonance is its opposite, the relatively unpleasant, dissatisfied, and therefore unrestful effect that certain other combinations of tones evoke. Such feelings always are in large part subjective: they constantly shift, not only from century to century, but also individually, as experienced by a single listener at different stages in his musical sophistication. These subjective feelings, however, also represent the responses of the ear and the mind to aspects of the constitution of sound itself. Some eras, some ears, some minds, are more tolerant than others; some find *this* pleasant and *that* unpleasant, whereas others find both either pleasant or unpleasant or merely reverse the *this* and the *that*. This agitated and endlessly discussed subject is a physico-psychological mixture as little explicable by present-day knowledge as is the basic difference between a cheap tune and a noble melody.

The earliest surviving examples of órganum prove that singers and listeners of its time found both the fifth and the fourth to be pleasant intervals. Further, as the voices remained parallel for most of the duration of a composition, we can be certain that the ears and minds of singers and listeners were not jarred unduly by sequences of fifths and fourths. By the early nineteenth century, on the contrary, though both the fourth and the fifth still were held to be consonances, a sequence or series of parallel fifths was considered by theoreticians and academic teachers (who had their reasons) to be a compositional sin. The octave certainly has been a consonance always: it is not possible to conceive of an octave, in itself, as dissonant. But, again, scholastic harmony later would find *in that very fact* sufficient reasons for considering a series of parallel octaves compositionally sinful.

During the eleventh and twelfth centuries such previously ostracized chordal intervals as the sixth and the third began to assert their usefulness. But they still were considered, if not somewhat dissonant, at least less consonant—that is, restless and relatively unpleasant—and therefore were avoided at the openings and closings of compositions, as indeed they were until the twentieth century. Further, intervals that even today are regarded by many musicians as dissonances, such as sevenths and seconds, occurred only where they could be followed at once by a recognized consonance, which was felt, so to speak, to be able to erase their unpleasantness. This is a straight harmonic concept: that the presence of one interval or chord can make desirable (or, in reverse, be retroactively excused by) the presence of another interval or chord. Even though such dissonant-consonant sequences occurred because the forward movement of simultaneous melodies produced them incidentally, the fact that they had become numerous shows that the harmonic sense had begun to be one of the architectural means of composition.

Sometimes a composer felt that he could heighten interest in the shape or profile of a melody by "decorating" one of its tones—that is, by preceding a tone with a briefly sounded nearby tone, usually the tone just above or just below it. Known as an "appoggiatura" (from the Italian verb *appoggiare*, meaning "to rest on"), this incidental tone often formed, with a tone heard simultaneously in another voice or part, a dissonant interval. Because the appoggiatura was heard very briefly, however, it produced only a very fleeting dissonance. Or a dissonance might occur between the sounding of two consonances because of the composer's feeling for the way his separate melodies must move onward. When harmonic practices came to be codified, this sort of nonharmonic tone was denominated a "passing" tone because it occurred in passage from one consonant or basic interval to another and because any dissonance of which it was an integer was thus quickly succeeded by a healing consonance.

The Ear's Awareness

The listening musical mind constantly was enlarging its awareness and its hospitality. An interval that one century felt as dissonant might be heard so often by the next century as to be accepted with no sensation of restlessness or unpleasantness. The later century then would come to regard that interval as consonant. Theorists, listeners, composers, and performers constantly have become more tolerant, until in our own time many people have said that, though consonance and dissonance temporarily have had reality, they are unimportant absolutely and should be disregarded in favor of other, more important musical considerations. Not all ears and minds travel at the same speed or to the same regions, and the complaint of many music-lovers that too much twentieth-century music is "discordant" really means that more recent composers have felt formerly dissonant junctions and sequences of tones to be both pleasant in themselves and worthy of prominence—"consonant" in every sense but that implied by abstruse theoretical considerations. To their own satisfaction and that of a growing minority of listeners, they have reduced "consonant" and "dissonant" to the condition of purely historico-technical terms.

Those of us who have been formed largely on the music of the eighteenth and nineteenth and early twentieth centuries cannot help finding the masterpieces of the true golden age of vocal polyphony a little exotic in texture. They remain on the other side of what, until music's yesterday, was the farthest limit of our own age. Palestrina may sound modern if contrasted with Dunstable or Binchois, but he sounds ancient, somehow loose and texturally indecisive (despite the surpassing loveliness of many of his melodies) if we listen to him with mental ears that have been conquered by Bach, Handel, Haydn, Mozart, and Beethoven.

54

Of Palestrina, Orlando di Lasso, Victoria, Byrd, and their contemporaries and less mighty successors what, for us, is true of Gregorian chant still is true: if we want to try to hear their music almost as they heard themselves, we must make every effort to listen to it as melody upon melody moving forward in time. This is not true of all of Byrd's music, some of which—as we shortly shall see—had stopped being polyphony. But in general the best music of the sixteenth century, despite its protoharmonic features, still was intentionally pure melody before it was anything else.

Palestrina

With the Italian Giovanni Pierluigi da Palestrina (1525?–94), the Flemish Orlando di Lasso (1530?–94), the Spanish Tomás Luis de Victoria (1535?–1613), and the English William Byrd (1543–1623), unaccompanied vocal polyphony reached its Himalayas, points so high in artistic accomplishment that to rise beyond them quite simply became impossible. Of the three great Continental polyphonists, only Victoria may strike today's average ear as notably original, and that semblance of originality probably results in large part from our unfamiliarity with his Spanish predecessors. For these great musicians added astonishingly little to the materials, to the historic evolution, of musical means. They were summations of the past. In their music they brought to final ripening the developments with which this book thus far has been concerned. They did not, in any positive or weighty sense, point toward the future or hint at what their most important successors would do to and for the art of music. In their air of temporary finality they belong, not with pathfinders like Okeghem, Haydn, Beethoven, Wagner, Schoenberg, and Stravinsky, but with the monumental composers who have satisfied themselves and their listeners by doing superbly what others already had done, men like Josquin des Prés, Johann Sebastian Bach, and Johannes Brahms.

Palestrina, who was invited by Pope Gregory XIII to edit the body of Gregorian chant in the gradual and the antiphonary—a task that he did not live to complete—was endowed with unsleeping good taste. Devoting himself largely to Church music—nearly one hundred of his Masses survive, for example—he composed nothing excessive, almost nothing that was not superbly devotional, extremely little that was not right and just in whole and in detail. His worldly positions gave the most highly trained chapel singers into his hands more often than not, and for the greater glory of God he strained their capabilities to the limit, but never beyond it.

As the late Dr. Curt Sachs pointed out, these singers, and most notably those in the Papal Chapel, "were famous for their skill in dissolving the plain notation on their music sheets in fluent graces and coloraturas." We must not, that is, suppose that actual performances of Palestrina's music—or of that of his contemporaries—were confined to the notes set down by the composer. Such a supposition would be roughly equivalent to the widespread false notion that the Greek temples of which the bleached gray or buff-colored ruins survive showed those colors when new—whereas in fact they originally were painted in what might strike us as rather gaudy colors. When the music of Palestrina was new, the Renaissance was in blossom and the day still was far distant (Dr. Sachs set it as late as 1800) when performers would be expected to sound only the notes on the score before them. It is difficult to agree, however, with "purists" who bewail the fact that (to quote Sachs again) "the solemn, stately voice parts of Roman polyphony were never heard in the sober form that the scores suggest." It is senseless, that is, to apply a Protestant prejudice in favor of simplicity to Roman Catholic music of the Renaissance. The real point, however, is that the greatest examples of Roman polyphony were conceived so magnificently that no amount of expert decoration could mask effectively their structural strength and beauty.

Palestrina's music must often seem to us as impersonal, as nonsubjective as Gregorian chant itself, for he had the genius to transmute his passion, his large emotional energy into the terms of the sacred music of his era—polyphonic and modal, but with occasional clauses and sentences all but fully harmonic. He composed some secular music, including madrigals honoring the glories of Italian women, but his major effort went into the weaving of musical fabrics strong enough to resist time. With good reason, then, he is regarded as one of the greatest of all composers.

Orlando di Lasso

A man of altogether different nature was Orlando di Lasso. A minor diplomat, a friend and confidant of the politically powerful, he somehow found time to become one of the most productive composers of all time. His known compositions run to nearly two thousand. In one sense, he alone in his era points toward the future: he often is dramatic to the edge of theatricality, and thus seems to prefigure the imminent emergence of opera. But he is more clearly the summation and climax of the musical traditions of northern Europe. Beside Orlando's brawling vigor, Palestrina well may sound a little pallid at first; beside the almost incredible abundance of Orlando's motets, madrigals, villanelle, psalms, French *chansons,* German lieder, and music in other forms, Palestrina's scope may at first appear a little small. But Orlando, for all his suave mastery, never approached Palestrina's unflawed purity of style, the element that finally gives the Italian's music the strength that inheres in any perfectly proportioned structure. Only in his Masses and his powerful Seven Penitential Psalms did Orlando equal the fervor and formal perfections of his outstanding contemporary.

Victoria

Victoria, a Spaniard, was the first mystic to be a great musician. Alone of the sixteenth-century masters, he wrote no secular music whatever: he looked upon his compositions as manifestations of mystical religious devotion. To modern listeners with ears and minds that respond sympathetically to Victoria's Masses, motets, and great *Officium defunctorum* (Requiem), his music swirls with a heady, curious mixture of the sacred and the not-quite-sublimated fleshly, glows with almost neurasthenic intensity. In the melodic ways by which Victoria sometimes seems to hint at the African and gypsy turns that have lent more recent Spanish music its peculiar color, we can locate one of the causes of his unquestionable difference from his contemporaries, a quality not always easy to distinguish from eccentricity. Certainly, religious passion seldom has been suggested by music of such direct intensity. Appropriate and suggestive critically is the fact that Victoria was a contemporary both of El Greco and of those God-driven Spanish mystics Teresa of Ávila and Ignatius Loyola.

To these peaks music had been led by the innate necessity to do something to plainsong and other simple melodic lines. For centuries, composers had been celebrating the Christian God and helping their fellow men to worship Him through the beauty of many voices lifted together. Instrumental music had seemed less effective in carrying out their purpose, and most composers had given it only very incidental attention. But while Palestrina, Orlando, and Victoria were living and dying, there occurred in Italy, Spain, the Netherlands, France, and the Germanies, and across the Channel in Britain, a number of feeble beginnings of developments that shortly would leave abandoned in the past many of the techniques that they had employed.

William Byrd

The first master composer to divide his creative efforts appreciably, in quality if not in quantity, between unaccompanied, sacred vocal polyphony and secular instrumental pieces was, in fact, a slightly younger contemporary of the great completers. He was England's foremost composer after John Dunstable, William Byrd.

The learned Belgian musicologist François-Joseph Fétis once wrote that "Byrd was the Palestrina and the Orlando di Lasso of England." That judgment in itself would indicate that if Byrd had composed nothing but his three Masses (one each for three, four, and five voices), he still would lay claim to an exalted position in the history of music. His contributions to the earliest known book of Latin motets to be published in England (*Cantiones quae ab argumento sacrae vocantur*, 1575) also are marvels of expressive contrapuntal composition for as many as eight voices. Although that book was in part the work of Thomas Tallis (1505?–85), possibly Byrd's teacher and certainly for a time his colleague in the Chapel Royal, Byrd later published collections of sacred songs that were entirely his own. Among these latter, the two groups of *Gradualia* (1605, 1607) are wonderful combinings of self-sufficiently expressive music and the apt, incisive setting of Latin texts.

Byrd also composed music for use in the Church of England. Here, naturally encountering few set patterns on which to mold his materials, he was forced to evolve musical forms from the hints and trials that he could find around him. He succeeded so brilliantly that English liturgical music kept for a long time (perhaps too long a time) the patterns that he evolved. From his teeming musical imagination and untiring hand poured psalms, anthems, preces, sacred songs, and whole sacred services. Of these last, the so-called Great Service is a masterwork as impressive as his Catholic Mass in five voices.

This protean Englishman was deeply and permanently marked by the manners of the Italian madrigal. That influence is very apparent in his sacred music, whether Latin or English—in frequent imitations of nonmusical sounds, in a dramatic boldness almost as striking as Orlando di Lasso's. The English madrigal was to enjoy a variegated flowering, and William Byrd's contributions to it added both to the strength of its colors and to the sweetness of its perfume. If compared with the firmest and most vivid of Byrd's madrigals, in fact, even the piercingly tender pieces of such other Englishmen as Thomas Morley (1557–1603?), Thomas Weelkes (?–1623), John Wilbye (1574–1638), and Orlando Gibbons (1583–1625) seem to lack some final vitality.

Byrd's vocal compositions more than suffice to establish him as a sovereign musical creator. But what more clearly helped to shape the nature of the musical future was his understanding and sure-handed writing for instruments. To his songs for solo voice, for example, he composed accompaniments for four viols, accompaniments that remain astonishing, considering their date, for their true instrumentality of style. In texture they are almost string quartets, far more original in conception than the lute accompaniments to the ever-charming songs of John Dowland (1563–1626). Byrd went farther still, composing fantaisies for groups of three, four, five, and six instruments (even one for seven instruments) which well may be the oldest composed string music entirely independent of vocal style. Although he was adept at writing for the various sizes of viols, he also helped to formulate the futures of the later-developed violin, viola, and violoncello, using them together in chamber music of a charm comparable to that of the string trios and quartets of Joseph Haydn.

Variation and Dance

The music that had been composed earlier than that of Byrd and his younger contemporary, John Bull (1562–1628), for early forms of the clavichord and harpsichord largely had been polyphonic vocal music directly transcribed—or at least music conceived as a parallel to vocal polyphony. But Byrd, writing probably for the primitive harpsichord known as the virginal, or "pair of virginals,"[1] found ideas and time to delineate a style and a texture based directly upon the capabilities of its keyboard. Here he deserted polyphony for homophony, the musical texture in which melody is supported on accompanying tones or chords. He created the keyboard variation, a form that remains viable today, having undergone constant extension and change and having evoked enduring music from, among many, Johann Sebastian Bach, Handel, Haydn, Mozart, Beethoven, and Brahms. Some of Byrd's virginal pieces, to be sure, are adaptations of previously existing vocal music,

[1] The derivation of the name virginal for a harpsichord is uncertain. It may have become attached to the instrument because it was considered particularly appropriate for playing by young girls, or it may have reflected the Latin word for the rod or jack that was animated by the virginal's keys: *virga*. The idea that it honored Elizabeth, "the Virgin Queen," is disproved by the occurrence of the word before her reign. Equally uncertain is the very confusing phrase "pair of virginals" as referring to a single instrument.

but even they have been translated wholly into terms idiomatic to the keyboard. He employed dance forms (*"pavana,"* *"galiardo"*) on the keyboard too, prefiguring the dance-form suites of Bach and Handel. Although Byrd was a great religious and vocal composer, his historical influence was most germinative in the direction of the increasing secularization and instrumentalization of music. In his own person he bridged the golden era of religious vocal polyphony and the first important era of music that dispensed with the human voice.

CHAPTER V

The Organ

The organ traditionally descends from the syrinx, or pipes of Pan, a small row of mouth-blown pipes bound together side by side in a flat triangular shape. But it first attained something of its modern character at Alexandria, in Egypt, about the middle of the third century B.C. Its history is as complex as its structure. Its construction is based on the principle that air released under pressure through a series of pipes of varying sizes will produce tones of varying pitch and timbre.** In modern organs, the release of air is controlled from one or more keyboards, by foot-operated pedals, and by hand-operated pistons. Various mechanisms have been developed to make possible the sounding of two and more pipes at once by the operation of one controlling unit. Handily the most complex of all musical instruments, as well as in many instances the largest, the organ occurs in unnumbered variations of size, make-up, and flexibility.

Increasingly until about 1300, the organ in Western Europe supported or doubled the single melodic line of plainsong or the *vox principalis* or tenor in such early polyphony as órganum. Technical limitations and both the audibility and the multiplicity of its jangling overtones long kept the organ from use in purely instrumental polyphony: on the organs of earlier periods, the performance of any complicated polyphony evokes an unsortable blur of undesired tonal interrelationships. During the thirteenth and fourteenth centuries, however, in part as a result of improvements in the designing of the instruments, a variety of the vocal sequence-trope began to be composed for the organ alone.

The Organ and Polyphony

Known as the *estampie,* this polyphonic organ form varied in pattern. Most commonly, it consisted of from four to seven melodic sections, each played twice in succession. These sections, called *puncti* (points), each had two different endings or closes, one for the first statement, the other for the second. The evolution of the *estampie* from secular vocal music is suggested clearly by this verselike pattern. In all probability, the *estampie* first developed as accompaniment to dancing.

While the organ constantly became more complicated and more flexible, English, Italian, and German organists and composers were working out methods of noting down music to be played on it. Tablatures, as these notations were called, also were used increasingly for noting down the music of such other instruments as virginals, flutes, lutes, guitars, and viols. They differed from the notation for vocal music chiefly in that they substituted alphabetic letters, numbers, or conventional symbols for notes. Also, when used for keyboard instruments, the tablatures were intended to be read as successions of vertical groups rather than as distinct lines of horizontal melody.

During the fourteenth century, *estampies* and instrumental motets were set down in organ tablature: the instrument had begun to be used for the solo performance of complex music. The German organists employed tablatures widely during the fifteenth century, and later wrote out in them, not only such transplanted Italian vocal forms as the *ricercar* and *canzona,* but also free preludes, examples of a quasi-improvisational form wholly native to the keyboard. In the free preludes preserved in tablatures dating from about 1450 on, German organists composed brief pieces that were not consistently either monophonic or polyphonic. Their alternations of chords with passages in single notes was to become standard practice of the first half of the eighteenth century, when Handel and Bach flourished. These fifteenth-century organists also built into increasingly massive instrumental compositions the Protestant hymn melodies called chorales, evolving such instrumental forms as the chorale prelude and chorale fantasia.

Organists:
German, Spanish, Italian, Netherlandish

The first salient name in German organ composition is that of Conrad Paumann (1410?–73). Although born blind, Paumann became a performer of extraordinary proficiency on, among other instruments, organ, lute, and flute. He was honored by emperors, princes, and dukes, and was decorated by the pope. A relative handful of Paumann's organ compositions survives, and among them most appear to be simple two-voice exercises for the training of other organists. Another blind organist, Arnolt Schlick the elder (1460?–1517?), composed instrumental arrangements of chorales which already are almost chorale preludes.

A very remarkable, though still little known, school of organ composition flourished in sixteenth-century Spain. Its towering figure was Antonio de Cabezón (1510–66), still another blind organist, the organ always having been par excellence the instrument of the blind. Cabezón resembled William Byrd in his strong feeling for the idiomatic nature of keyboard composition, as also in his development of variation techniques. Serving both Charles V and Philip II as organist and harpsichordist, Cabezón evolved a courtly instrumental art of great originality. In Italy, meanwhile, another important school of organists evolved. Its most prominent members were the Venetian Gabrielis, Andrea the uncle (1510?–86) and Giovanni the nephew (1557–1612), and the most renowned organ virtuoso of his time, Girolamo Frescobaldi (1583–1643), a composer of large talent. In France, too, Jean Titelouze (1563–1633) initiated a national school of organ-playing and composition for the organ.

Sweelinck

But the surpassing period of organ music was inaugurated by a Netherlander who, when very young, may have studied in Italy with Andrea Gabrieli: Jan Pieterszoon Sweelinck (1562–1621). It was partly through Sweelinck's friendship with John Bull and their exchange of compositions and musical compliments that the discoveries of the English keyboard composers influenced the highly fertile school of North German organists which was to culminate in Johann Sebastian Bach; Bull himself was an accomplished organist and composer for the organ. Sweelinck, a musician of genius, gave increased importance to the pedals, thus helping to enlarge the organ's resources for both composer and performer. From the *ricercari* and fantasias composed by his predecessors and contemporaries, Sweelinck evolved real fugues for organ, thus setting a pattern as important as that of the free prelude.

Fugue

Fugue is the most richly organized form of imitation. In fugue, a short melody or melodic fragment is stated first by one voice or part and then taken up, in imitation, by other voices or parts, usually three or four in number (though other numbers occur). The voices or parts enter in quick succession; the melody or fragments of melody must appear in all of them. Other melodic materials often are added to employ voices or parts when they are not occupied with pronouncing the chief melody; in this, fugue diverges from strict canon or round, in which no material other than the theme itself is used. As developed and altered by both major and minor composers, fugue became malleable enough to emerge as one of the most fruitful and widely used of musical devices as long as counterpoint ruled. Its usefulness inevitably diminished in the first era of homophony, but resurged when counterpoint and harmony began to be mixed skillfully. To our own day, even in the hands of the most extreme experimenters, fugue has continued to delight composers by its unremitting challenge to ingenuity, listeners by its expressive and climactic potentialities.

Sweelinck also borrowed the variation principle and made superior creative use of purely instrumental figurations, thus in general prefiguring the organ and harpsichord compositions of Bach. Although he was also an accomplished creator of secular and sacred vocal music, in which he combined a learned use of imitation with a forward-tending sense of rhythm, Sweelinck now is best known as a composer for organ. His pupils and emulators formed a real constellation. One of them, Samuel Scheidt (1587–1654), reacted in irritation against the "coloristic" tablatures being issued all around him—coloristic here meaning a manner of composition in which musically meaningless *colorature* were appended to almost every important note. In the third volume of his history-making *Tabulatura nova* (1624), Scheidt disclosed sacred organ music of sober, powerful expressiveness. Making extensive use of fugal forms, Scheidt also prepared the way for the Northern Baroque, the so-called "Gothic" style, which expanded the length of organ compositions, including the toccata, another instrumental form of enduring usefulness.

Sonata, Cantata, Toccata

The exact musical meanings of terms alter with time, but it is instructive to notice the differences originally implied by the words *sonata* (in which instruments were sounded), *cantata* (in which voices sang), and *toccata* (in which sounds were touched into vibration through a keyboard). Andrea Gabrieli had composed toccatas in which, as in free preludes, chords and single-note passages alternated. In the toccatas of the Gothic style, there were also contrapuntal passages in *fugato*—that is, fuguelike matter imbedded in music not strictly fugal. The toccata, that is, was becoming an extended keyboard composition in which composers felt increasingly free to lodge the most varied musical thoughts.

Organists:
North, Middle, and South German

In large outline, the genealogy that led from Scheidt to Johann Sebastian Bach was double, consisting of both a North German line and a Middle German line. The Gothic style was chiefly the province of the Northerners, outstanding among whom were Johann Adam Reinken (1623–1722), Dietrich Buxtehude (1637–1707), and Vincent Lübeck (1654–1740). The Middle German line began with Heinrich Bach (1615–92), grandfather of Johann Sebastian, and included Johann Pachelbel (1635–1706), Johann Kuhnau (1660–1722), and several members of the prolific Bach family. These men tended to content themselves with organ compositions shorter and simpler than those elaborated by their northern colleagues.

A little to one side of this double genealogy stood the school of South German organists. Predominantly Roman Catholic (in contrast to the mostly Protestant lines from Scheidt to Bach and Handel), the South Germans absorbed Italian and French manners and naturally proceeded without the Protestant chorales so basic to the music of the other Germans. The earliest important South German organ composer was Johann Jacob Froberger (1616–67). A pupil of the magnificent Frescobaldi, Froberger favored the toccata, several varieties of *canzona*-with-variations, and the capriccio, which he interpreted as still another sort of variation-*canzona*. He was intimate with the keyboard compositions of his contemporaries in France, and he imported many of their novel practices into German organ music. In his harpsichord compositions, indeed, he followed the French way of combining short, dancelike movements, developing the keyboard suite, a varied and important form later cultivated by both Handel and Bach. Froberger's influence on other South Germans shows most strongly in the fact that his successors nearly always preferred Italian and French practices to those of other regions of the Germanies.

The Modes and Chordal Logic

Both Netherlandish and German organists also wrote vocal music, sacred and secular, and pieces for rapidly evolving forms of clavichord and harpsichord. In whatever medium and in whatever pattern they cast their musical thoughts, they were unknowingly hastening the end of polyphony's sovereignty. All of them felt free to introduce homophonic passages into polyphonic textures. Most of them showed disregard of, even unfamiliarity with, modal usages. Coming into view in the faded leaves of their published music is the major-minor division of classic harmony.

More important even than the willing acceptance and employment of an increased variety of chords was the increasingly strong underlying assumption that some chords naturally "resolve" into others, evoke a desire for certain other chords to follow them. Some chords are relatively static, seem not to bespeak onward movement. Others ask for fulfillment, appear to require other combinations of tones for the release of the psychological tension, however small, which they themselves set up. The profound assumption that there is a natural logic of chord progression is, as already has been pointed out, a theorem of harmony as understood in the eighteenth and nineteenth centuries.

Once the medieval modal system had all but been left entirely to the past, once the sensation of chordal logic had diluted the belief that music was either a single unaccompanied melody or a fabric of discrete melodies moving forward in time together, then the classic system of harmony had become almost inevitable. But antimodernists who speak as though that classical system of harmony had been established (or legislated) forever, who claim that artistic sanity requires its present dominance too, forget that it achieved its perfections slowly, in response to *changing* demands of the listening ear. When the listening ear no longer demands change in response to outward and inward logic and stimuli, the only predictable destiny for the art of music is stultification.

Further evidence of the drift toward classic harmony marks the music of the sixteenth and seventeenth centuries, whether among the several schools of German organists or among their Italian, French, and English coevals. It is the waxing prominence of the first (tonic), fifth (dominant), and fourth (subdominant) degrees of any given diatonic scale. This incipient hierarchy among the scale-tones was closely responsible for the increasing desire and ability to move, in the midst of a composition or section, from one tonality (key) to another, though this "modulation" still was achieved with difficulty and under limited conditions.

Music, though still in part thought of as consisting of forward-moving autonomous vocal lines or instrumental parts, was falling under semicodified vertical regulations. The very profiles of composed melodies began to be functions of the composer's wish to employ chords in logical succession and—at important junctures of grammatical and syntactical force—to base them on certain tones of the diatonic scale being used. Also, nonpolyphonic music was being written with the influence of certain scale-degrees and specific chordal progressions dominant in the composers' minds. What it is reasonable to call harmonic considerations had started to displace purely polyphonic or contrapuntal concepts. Music already had moved light-years away from plainsong: it was scarcely recognizable as the art that had consisted of melody and nothing else only a few centuries earlier.

What here is referred to as classic harmony developed gradually during many centuries. That evolution was a slow definition by small adoptions and codifications rather than the abrupt product of one man, one group of men, or even one school or century. In a wide, loose, but nonetheless real sense, that slow formulation began at the mythical moment when the first elementary polyphony thrust out of monophony and the physical constitution of musical sound. In a useful sense it may be said that the keystone of its central edifice, the major and minor scales and keys, had been installed by 1722, when Johann Sebastian Bach completed the twenty-four preludes and fugues—one of each in every major and minor key—which make up Part I of *The Well-Tempered Clavier*.

But classic harmony consists of more than just that central edifice. For its complete definition it had to await the heyday of Haydn, Mozart, and all but the latest Beethoven. During the entire seventeenth century, it was coming more and more to hold sway over musical creation, but without being spoken of or even foreseen as quite what at last it became. (At the exact mythical moment when classic harmony was complete and supreme, of course, it began to become something else. The parlor game of nominating that moment has been played often and has produced widely separated answers. One composition often named as the *locus classicus* of pure classic harmony's special euphony is Mozart's Symphony No. 39, in E♭ major.) During the seventeenth century, that is, harmony still was coexisting on something like even terms with the last blooming of pure polyphony. And pure polyphony is, except as an occasional device, by definition inimical to classic harmony. In one sense, in fact, the two textures cannot coexist.

Listening to Polyphony and Homophony

Many so-called polyphonic or contrapuntal compositions written in the eighteenth, nineteenth, and twentieth centuries are not in reality polyphonic or contrapuntal. Their true texture is homophony: they consist of a dominating or principal melody or of principal melodies supported on pseudo-contrapuntal accompaniment consisting of present or implied chords. The essential difference between monophony and polyphony is simple to state and easy to understand: it is the difference between a single melody and two or more simultaneous but independent melodies. But the essential difference between polyphony and homophony is more complex because it is to be located largely in intention and understanding. Homophony is easy to detect in simple compositions, where it can be seen as a single melody accompanied by chords that are not accidental results of the superimposition of two or more additional melodies upon one another. When, however, homophony becomes complex to the degree at which almost every tone of the leading melody is one constituent of a chord, we often encounter a musical fabric that has most of the visual signs of polyphony.

That sort of apparently polyphonic or contrapuntal music often must be listened to with detailed attention if we are to be able to determine what its primary texture really is— and therefore whether the performer is performing it, and we ourselves hearing it, properly. If the composer's intention was homophonic, then the separate "melodies" that, by ingenuity, often can be detached from the forward-moving chords by the process of reading one interior tone from one chord, one from the next, and so on, are incidental. If this is the case, insistence on polyphonic performance or listening will falsify the composer's intention and devaluate his music. If, however, two or more independent melodies assert themselves together, the composition or passage is polyphonic even though the accidentally formed chords can be interpreted by strict rules of academic harmony. Such compositions or passages must be performed ("interpreted") with some emphasis on the separate melodies, and must be listened to with some similar emphasis. For to perform or listen to them with the diminished attention to interior details usually desirable with homophony is to mistake the significance of their discourse.

We have seen polyphony unintentionally weakened by increased recognition of the powers, duties, and interests of chords; by the wasting-away of the medieval or Church modes; by the gradual assertion of modern diatonic scales; and by the seductions of melody with accompaniment. A further telling blow against polyphony as music's ruling texture was struck consciously as the sixteenth century turned into the seventeenth. It came from an unexpected and relatively weak quarter. For a time, nevertheless, it was decisive. It altered both the fabric and the history of music and even exerted some social influence on the areas in which it flourished. Its results persist today. The scene was Florence, the immediate occasion the self-conscious birth of opera as an artistic form.

CHAPTER VI

Opera

For more than a millennium now, musicians and theorists of music have been arguing about the philosophy, nature, techniques, and ethics of the music of ancient Greece. The small amount of reliable evidence which survives—most of it literary and sculptural—remains pathetically inadequate. As a result, most of the disputes have produced little more than spun-out theorizing, alternately of the most fascinating sort and the most boring. During the years just before 1600, a group of largely amateur musicians in courtly Florence decided that they knew precisely how music had acted as a partner in the production of Greek drama. In demonstrating the mistaken precision of their knowledge, they produced by far the most vital and long-lived offspring of this unending argument. This attempt to re-create the conditions under which they supposed Greek plays to have been supported upon music was what led the men who met in the palace of Giovanni Bardi, Count of Vernio, to evolve the opera.

The honor of being the first true opera usually is conceded to *Dafne* (1597), by Jacopo Peri (1561?–1633?). Its music unhappily has been lost. Its immediate successors were a *Euridice* by Peri and one by Giulio Caccini (1558–1615?), and they survive. Both are musically thin, pallid, and rigid. Their importance in the evolution of musical style (in contradistinction to their obvious importance in the history of opera) lay in their being all but entirely homophonic. Homophony was a central support of the structure of beliefs about Greek music which had been erected by Count

73

Bardi's courtiers. What prevented these earliest operas from becoming vital musico-dramatic wholes was not their almost complete avoidance of polyphony, but the fact that their composers were hobbled by the self-conscious novelty of their musical procedures and by a decisive lack of talent for expressiveness.

Peri, Caccini, and their friends—including Vincenzo Galilei (1533?–91), father of the great astronomer Galileo Galilei—were certain that Greek tragic actors had recited syllables on tones of prescribed, varying pitch and that they had been accompanied in a simple manner by instruments. Consequently, they laid out musical lines dictated by the spoken rhythm of the Italian words in their chosen texts, with accents falling as they would fall in normal or slightly heightened speech. They referred to this musical prosody as the *"stile recitativo,"* or reciting style, and thus bequeathed to the terminology of opera the word recitative, which later came to be applied to something rather different. Their meager semimelodies were supported on chords sounded by a small scattering of instruments (notably lutes and forms of harpsichord) whose business it was to pronounce this *basso continuo* (thorough bass**) as long as the singing voices went on pronouncing the verbal text. Only at the end of dramatically important scenes did they vary this monotonous half-song, half-speech by introducing choruses and songs in regular musical meters or by attempts at autonomous melody. Their choruses and songs were intended to accompany small pantomimes or ballets—so early had opera begun to learn its manners. Otherwise, however, the poverty-stricken, purportedly Greek "drama with music" went helplessly on.

Texture in the First Operas

The following excerpt from Giulio Caccini's *Euridice* displays (in modern notation) the bare bones of this earliest of operatic textures. The notes here printed in the bass clef are no more than shorthand indications to the instrumentalists of the chords desired. In some cases, it will be seen, this bass is "figured"—that is, has small superior numbers or accidentals meant to indicate the chord to be built on that particular note. The excerpt is taken from the opening of a prologue sung by Tragedy:

After the indicated *ritornello***—the only purely instrumental passages were brief sections of this nature—six additional verses were sung, apparently without the slightest variation in the music. Yet much of the future of musical style can be foreseen in this impoverished excerpt: here, in full clarity, are to be seen at work the assumptions that (1)

melody rests upon an accompanying bass and (2) a logic of chordal succession exists, to be recognized and obeyed.

Polyphony played a very small role in these Florentine operas, and even then usually in the simplest note-against-note manner. In the hands of any but a master composer, in fact, polyphony and theatrical action mix very poorly. The dramatic poet's ideal musical texture customarily remains accompanied melody. Even earlier than the experimental operas of Peri and Caccini had been some curious, often musically attractive madrigal comedies, composed by, among others, Orazio Vecchi (1550–1603) and Alessandro Striggio (1535?–87). These had been polyphonic settings, in chains of madrigals, of quasi-dramatic poems related to the *commedia dell'arte*. Earlier still had been the liturgical musical plays of the Middle Ages and the "mysteries" of the very early Renaissance. But modern scholarship reasonably refuses these forerunners positions as the "first" operas.

The Bardi Camerata

No single person or group of persons could have invented the sonata or the concerto. But members of the Bardi *camerata* (that is, men who met in a room) deserve the honor now accorded them, for they did very consciously foresee opera. Italian dramatic poetry happened in their era to have evolved exactly the sort of drama which then could best be set to music. This was the pastoral eclogue. The poets were Torquato Tasso, Giovanni Battista Guarini, and Ottavio Rinuccini. Their verse dramas—intact, excerpted, revised, adapted, and imitated—became the sources of opera librettos** in numbers now beyond all possibility of computation. Rinuccini wrote the texts of both of the first two operas, *Dafne* and *Euridice*. Such texts as Tasso's *Aminta* and *Rinaldo* and Guarini's *Il Pastor fido* were set to music over and over. Whole generations of librettists mined the rich veins of Tasso's *Gerusalemme liberata*, having discovered that they could isolate from its pseudo-epic structure the dramatic episodes that they craved and could employ for operatic purposes.

No more than Columbus did the composers influenced by

the Bardi *camerata* realize, at least at first, that what they had discovered was not a new route to a known world, but a new world. The Greek performance of tragic drama was the Cathay that they sought; they almost certainly died believing that they had reached it. Their operas as such, however, were musically sickly. But for the accident of their also being intensely fertile, their kind would have died out with them, unsung and forgotten. Peri and Caccini, however, had been granted the gift of serendipity: they inadvertently had hit upon a multiple musico-dramatic form that their musical successors and betters would raise not infrequently to greatness. For their secure place in operatic history, they are indebted in part to the happiest of chances.

Monteverdi and Orfeo

Early in 1567, moreover, a composer of genius had been born in Cremona. Claudio Monteverdi (1567–1643) snatched up the Florentine novelty and used it to prove himself a musical dramatist of a power seldom surpassed. Monteverdi lived to be nearly seventy-seven, and in the course of accomplishing much else, he refashioned the Peri-Caccini pseudo-Greek play-with-music into a genre endowed with seemingly eternal vitality. His *Orfeo* (1607), with a libretto by Alessandro Striggio the younger (son of the composer mentioned above), is the earliest opera that still repays staged performance.

Orfeo has proved to be so symptomatic of opera's subsequent history that Monteverdi, who did not "invent" the form, rightly is considered its preceptor. His score begins with a "toccata" played by an instrumental ensemble. Although this consists, as Professor Donald Jay Grout pointed out in *A Short History of Opera*, of nothing more than "a dressed-up version of the customary opening fanfare," it led directly to the operatic overture and prelude. The five acts of *Orfeo* contain twenty-five more purely instrumental pieces. Monteverdi desired a full-bodied accompaniment, much richer in color, harmony, and even contrapuntal development than the Florentine founding fathers had allowed. Peri, who had sung the role of Orpheus when his own *Eu-*

ridice had been performed at the Pitti Palace in Florence on October 6, 1600, had been content on that occasion to have his opera equipped with only four instruments: in the printed preface to his opera, he referred to them as *gravicembalo, chitarrone, lira grande,* and *liuto grosso.*[1] Monteverdi's *Orfeo* asks for at least forty instruments, including violins, viols, harpsichords, harps, lutes, small organs, trombones, and trumpets. Although this opera contains no single passage in which most of these instruments are sounded together, and though more use is made of them in the frequent purely instrumental passages than as accompaniment to the singing, this was rich, intoxicating fare if contrasted with Peri's exceedingly thin instrumentation.

Far from consisting of a string of recitatives lightened by occasional strophic songs or choruses, Monteverdi's *Orfeo* is a musical whole planned as elaborately and unified almost as thoroughly as a fine symphony or concerto. Each of its five acts has a well-defined scheme both of color and of layout which helps toward this pervading unity. Fragments of the same instrumental music appear several times and in various of the acts, again contributing strongly to a sense of unification. The musical texture is astonishingly responsive to the atmosphere and situations of Striggio's poem as it sensitively shifts its texture and coloration with the emotions and fortunes of the characters. Here, very early in opera's career, the drive toward music at once implicated and characteristic rather than merely decorative or self-sufficient is realized. Monteverdi did not, out of theory, disdain any musical device available to him: he used all the applicable resources of his era and his learning (which was vast) as means toward the creation of a full-bodied musico-dramatic entity.

In Act III of *Orfeo* occurs *"Possente spirto,"* Orpheus' moving supplication of the underworld spirits. It is the most renowned of the excerpts from Monteverdi's operas except for *"Lasciatemi morire,"* which is all that has survived of his

---

[1] *Gravicembalo* refers to a form of harpsichord; *chitarrone* to a long-bodied bass lute; *lira grande* to a collateral relative of the violin, but larger, with numerous strings so placed as to make chord-playing relatively easy; *liuto grosso* to a short-bodied bass lute.

second opera, *Arianna*. "*Possente spirto*" is an elaborately organized unit consisting of a melody presented and then followed by four strophic sections, each of which might be described as an ornamented variation on it. Each section has been given its own sympathetic accompaniment, such as two violins, two cornetts,** two harps, and two violins with one *basso da brazzo*, this last a form of violoncello. At times the instruments support or reinforce the voice; at others they compete with Orpheus in a manner that later developed into often standardized contests between soprano and flute. Listened to as expressive music apart from its theatrical context, "*Possente spirto*" is no less impressive than that more familiar aria of Plutonic supplication of a later day, "*Divinités du Styx,*" from Gluck's *Alceste*. Nonetheless, it loses much by being listened to out of context: it is primarily a climax in the evocation of Orpheus' tragedy, not merely beautiful dramatic music, but also forceful theater.

Few modern listeners could sit comfortably through a complete performance of Peri's *Euridice*. In recent years, however, many have found Monteverdi's *Orfeo* a substantial and deeply moving theatrical and musical experience. Few facts better illustrate the chasm between intention and genius than that these two early operas (as well as Caccini's *Euridice*), composed within a single decade and both setting the same Greek legend dealing with the power of music, are so widely disparate in artistic accomplishment and values.

Nuove Musiche

In 1602, Caccini had published a collection of vocal pieces in the monodic texture of his operatic recitative and with thorough-bass accompaniment. This publication, called *Nuove musiche* (New Music), became not only a manifesto of the antipolyphonic movement, but also the source of the name now generally given to it. The "new music" found its purest expression in the works of inferior composers because basically it demanded that music serve poetry faithfully and without asserting its own autonomy. This was in part a reasonable rebellion against the over-elaborated polyphonic manners of motets and madrigals in which musical complexities had begun to render all but impossible any understanding of the sung words. The "new music" was a sibling of opera. It assisted the development of the great baroque musical forms of cantata and oratorio. And it erected a barrier between the Netherlandish traditions of vocal polyphony and the music of the seventeenth century and after.

But this same "new music," if strictly interpreted and evolved, would have reduced a once-great art to slavery. Monteverdi combined its procedures with those of polyphony, adding several variants of his own devising. He was one of the composers who put music first and thereby saved the art from such a future of servitude, keeping it free in the cause of expressiveness instead. In his dramatic cantata *Il Combattimento di Tancredi e Clorinda* (1624), with text derived from Tasso's *Gerusalemme liberata,* he announced what he called the *"stile concitato"* (literally "excited style") for the rendering of rage and agitation. This amounted to the free use of string tremolo,** the rapid repetition of one tone by means of short, rapid bowings. In this important forerunner of the myriads of not-quite-operas satisfied with cantata state, he also indicated the striking together of swords by the use of string *pizzicato,* a plucking of strings by the player's fingers.

Although the musical forces required for performance of *Il Combattimento* are fewer than those required for *Orfeo,* its musical expressiveness is achieved much more clearly for its own sake, a sign of the gradual reassertion of the power of music even when used to illustrate a text. And in Monteverdi's last opera, *L'Incoronazione di Poppea* (1642), written when he was nearly seventy-five, further prime developments become obvious. The exact instrumentation of this opera cannot now be determined because the only surviving copy of the manuscript does not specify it. What is clear, however, is that this is primarily an opera to be sung. Every available ounce of Monteverdi's creative energy was concentrated here on compacting an effective, unified musicodramatic whole. The balance among text, music, and theatrical viability which he achieved here was as distant from the text-overbalanced experiments of the Florentine *camerata* as from the music-overbalanced operas of some later days, in which composers sank their librettos in favor of virtuosic singing or their own overweening assertiveness.

L'Incoronazione di Poppea

The history of opera can be represented by a graph, with a line oscillating between these extremes of domination. All the so-called "reforms" of opera have been reactions against one or another of these excesses. The ideal itself has been certain since Monteverdi's time (which does not mean that a great enough composer cannot create a great opera at or near either extreme): it is the assumption, as in *L'Incoronazione di Poppea*, of the music and the text into a new, living unit. This assumption would be so complete in the ideal opera that no tag ends of music, text, or mere theatricality would extend beyond the areas occupied by the newly created unit.

Opera had begun with mythological subjects. Although similar subjects were to be composed always, *L'Incoronazione*, making use of a pseudo-historic episode from Roman history, initiated the more human opera with a masterwork. In it, the personalities of Nero, Poppea, and the other chief protagonists—including Valletto, a page boy destined to reappear in many guises in later operas—are created by music with the sort of psychological verisimilitude which was to attain a splendid fullness in Mozart's *Le Nozze di Figaro* and *Don Giovanni*.

Despite—or perhaps because of—its development of opera, cantata, and oratorio, the seventeenth century, whatever its proliferation of magnificent musical creations, now necessarily appears somewhat overshadowed by the towering musical centuries on either side of it. Happening, as it did happen, after the most glorious achievements of pure vocal polyphony and before the powerful grace of the high baroque and classic-rococo Viennese periods, it reveals an understandable tentativeness, the uncertainties of an experimental age. To understand its most important accomplishments in changing and expanding the materials available

81

to composers, we best had look at this variegated century region by region. In experimental vitality, in tentativeness, and in regional specializations, it much resembles the first fifty years of the twentieth century.

Persistence of Polyphony

Throughout the extremely complex history of music in Italy between roughly 1575 and 1700 run the threads of several contests whose outcomes proved to be of first importance to the entire vocabulary of music as an art. First was the challenge to the weakening government of polyphony by the alliance of monody and homophony. Then came the attempts to balance the architectural roles of instruments with the role of the human voice. Additional turmoil was supplied by an unremitting determination to develop formally satisfying relations between melody and accompaniment. Underlying and suffusing this alternately revolutionary and reactionary activity—with most musicians oscillating between or mixing the two—was an irregular march toward the unsuspected terrain of classic harmony.

In the northern countries, the flowering of polyphonic organ music and the consequent evolution of such noble instrumental forms of polyphony as the organ chorale and the fugue may be interpreted as a final effort by the polyphonic organism to adjust itself to a new environment created by nonvocal and harmonic music. The best pieces by Sweelinck and Buxtehude proffer melodies of fine emotional range, themes wholly distinct in profile and procedure from those of earlier epochs. Often they tempt us to listen to them as melody with accompaniment. But melody with accompaniment was not their chief structural principle, and to yield to that temptation is to disregard and miss their true character. They remained many-voiced structures, webs that denied any pre-eminence to a single line of melody.

In Italy, on the contrary, though contrapuntal usages did not disappear, but went on producing extraordinary, vital music, accompanied melody more and more claimed a first position among expressive means. Here, from the point of view of musical architecture, lay the chief significance of the melodically poor Florentine operas. Here too resided the chief historical meaning of many Italian developments of instrumental and vocal-instrumental music, of the emergence of purely instrumental melodies in many varieties of sonata and concerto, as well as of such vocal genres as *aria* and *arioso*. *Basso continuo* supplied one method of freeing melody from its cloak of many voices, of displaying its naked form. The *continuo* did not become lost in the harmonic fabric of eighteenth-century music until it had influenced for all time all music consisting entirely or in part of accompanied melody.

Let us examine the relative and shifting emphases that these usages, manners, styles, and forms adopted and suggested. Such an examination is of first importance because an awareness of a composer's intentions is essential both to listening to his music and to judging the aptness with which it is being performed. To listen to polyphonically intended music, it is absolutely necessary not to concentrate attention on a single thread of melody; to listen polyphonically to music designed as accompanied melody is about equivalent to expecting to experience tragic emotions while watching a farce.

Sonata

When looking at the historic and evolving meanings attached to the word sonata, we must first cleanse our minds of all the additions to its meaning which have been made since the time of Joseph Haydn. This word did not originally bear the chief significance that we now automatically attach to it: it did not, that is, describe a musical composition for one or more instruments which was divided into three or four separate sections, each of them likely to be constructed according to some more or less established pattern.

As explained earlier, the word sonata originally indicated no more than a composition "sounded"—in contrast to one that was sung (cantata) or one that was touched (toccata) on a keyboard. From the mid-sixteenth century to about the mid-seventeenth, sonata was a generic label attached to many sorts of pieces intended primarily for instruments other than organ, clavichord, and harpsichord. During that hundred years, many sonatas were composed which bear no relationship whatever to the specific patterns of composing to which the label soon was transferred.

At the same time, early forms of the musical patterns to which the word sonata later was to be applied were known originally under other names. Musicologists commonly find one of the earliest of these in certain Franco-Flemish *chansons* of the early sixteenth century composed by such men as Claude de Sermisy (1490?–1562) and Clément Jannequin (sixteenth century). Jannequin—a composer still noted for his remarkably naturalistic imitations of the noises of barnyard, hunt, and battlefield—frequently built four-voice *chansons* on a tripartite (ternary) ABA pattern: that is, two statements of the same musical section separated by a contrasting middle section (B) in another mood and another tempo.

These northern *chansons* became extremely popular in Italy. The fact that their texts were likely to be in either French or Flemish, added to a current Italian tendency to transfer vocal compositions to instruments, led local composers to arrange them for solo instruments or instrumental groups. Andrea Gabrieli, the great Venetian, published in 1571 his *Canzoni alla francese per l'organo* (French Chansons for the Organ). Not content with thus giving new raiment to the works of outlanders, Italian musicians began also to compose pieces of this genre directly for instruments, calling them usually *canzoni da sonare* (*chansons* to be sounded). These were written both for keyboard instruments and for small groups of nonkeyboard instruments; some of the earliest among them apparently were intended for performance either way ad libitum. They were couched in variants of ternary form—ABA, ABB, occasionally even AAB—and in expanded patterns such as AABC. Gradually, however, a real difference was established between *canzoni* for keyboard instruments and those for ensembles (which often included one or more keyboard instruments). Keyboard *canzoni* tended to lose the overtly sectional pattern. Becoming more compact and retaining their predominantly polyphonic texture, they contributed to the emergence of the keyboard fugue. In Germany, in fact, pieces that in Italy probably would have carried the generic name *canzona* often were headed *Fuge*.

Canzoni composed for small instrumental ensembles gradually drifted toward the pattern we now call sonata. Of many varieties and patterns as evolved by composers of the late sixteenth century and early seventeenth, they attained their most (in our sense) sonata-like shape in the hands of Girolamo Frescobaldi. His *canzoni* freely mingle homophonic passages with contrapuntal passages making large use of imitation. In them, a change from polyphonic to homophonic usually indicates an alteration in tempo, greater swiftness of performance being desired for polyphonic sections than for homophonic. Frescobaldi's *canzoni* published between 1623 and 1634 definitely were sonata-like, especially in their contrasts between contiguous sections. In them, and in the *canzoni* of Frescobaldi's contemporaries and immediate successors, the *canzona* began to contract toward the ABA pattern of perfect ternary form. After the middle of the seventeenth century, this sort of *canzona* increasingly was called sonata, the older word being reserved more and more for fugal compositions or for single fugal movements in otherwise preponderantly homophonic sonatas in several movements.

Giovanni Legrenzi (1626-90) and other Venetians produced, during the late seventeenth century and early eighteenth, *sonate* related ever more closely to the classic Viennese sonata. Instead of being one-movement pieces laid out in continuous, contrasted sections, these were highly organized compositions in several movements. One pattern employed was AbCdA—A being a rapid movement fugal in texture, C a homophonic movement in triple time, b and d contrasting slower sections. Giuseppe Torelli (1658-1708) worked out a variant of this pattern: four movements arranged as slow, fast, slow, fast. Known as *sonata da chiesa* (church sonata, in complex, uncertain contrast to the so-called *sonata da camera*, or chamber sonata),[2] this proved to

[2] Primarily a development from the less organically unified suite of separate pieces, the *sonata da camera* tended toward the classic sonata only as it also tended to merge with the *sonata da chiesa*.

85

be an extremely fertile pattern. It was favored by the great Italian violinist Arcangelo Corelli (1653–1713) and many other composers of the time. Later Italians were likely to compose *sonate* in three, five, six, and even more movements: they returned only occasionally to the four movements of Legrenzi's *sonate*. It was left to German composers, notably Johann Sebastian Bach and Handel, and to the great French violinist Jean-Marie Leclair (1697–1764) to carry the four-movement ABCD *sonata da chiesa* pattern to the threshold of the classic Viennese period. (Further discussion of the sonata and its changing terminology will be found on pages 142–53.)

Concerto

Like the English word concert, the Italian *concerto* has been derived from the Latin verb *concertare*, meaning to contend or to debate, with an implication that the contention is co-operative and for shared results, that one is debating with one's peer in a friendly fashion. The term was first used in music to distinguish accompanied vocal music from *a cappella* singing (singing "for the chapel"—that is, unaccompanied choral singing). It was used by many Italian composers after 1575, notably by Giovanni Gabrieli, who in 1587 published a book of pieces by his uncle, Andrea Gabrieli, and himself, calling it *Canti concerti a 6, 7, 8, 10, e 16 voci* (Concerted Songs for 6, 7, 8, 10, and 16 Voices). The term became attached to both polyphonic and monodic vocal music supported either by organ or by small ensembles of instruments. It persisted in this sense for about a century, Johann Sebastian Bach having labeled certain of his cantatas *Concerten*.

Only when forms of the word *concerto* began to be applied to instrumental music did it begin to indicate pieces that, however uncertainly, we should likely recognize as concertos. With music for instrumental groups, *concerto* at first literally indicated contention or debate. Within the ensemble, one division of instruments would alternate with another, "struggling" or "debating" for the privilege of contributing most strikingly to a satisfactory whole. Many such compositions were labeled *concerti* in Italy; but many that might have been labeled so were called *canzoni, sonate,* and even *sinfonie,* having been looked at for other characteristics. (As late as 1873, a French composer—Édouard Lalo—gave the name *Symphonie espagnole* to a large composition for violin and orchestra which has most of the determining marks of a concerto for solo instrument; Vincent d'Indy reasonably might have called his *Symphonie sur un chant montagnard français,* 1887, a concerto for piano and orchestra.)

Under whatever label it appeared, the musical principle of concerted playing became a major aspect of musical architecture. Italian composers of the early seventeenth century often called it the *"stile moderno,"* as when, in the 1620s, Dario Castello issued groups of *canzoni* for keyboard, winds, and strings, as *Sonate concertate in stile moderno.* Throughout the 1600s, numerous Italians composed these concerted pieces, mostly single movements divided into sections by alternation of the instruments or groups of instruments. In the last quarter of the century, however, compositions in the concerted texture—increasingly called concertos by then—tended to fragment into several movements and to be preponderantly homophonic, consisting very largely of chordally accompanied melody. The word *concerto,* nevertheless, went on capaciously housing several distinct sorts of music. Of these, the concerto for a soloist and (or against) an ensemble did not emerge fully developed until the eighteenth century. Two other late-seventeenth-century sorts of concerto require mention here.

The so-called *concerto-sinfonia* failed to survive except as it devolved upon and expanded into other forms. Its basic principle was alternation of sections in differing styles though all performed on the same instruments. In it, for example, a solemn passage in which all the instruments sounded together would be followed by a passage in which a few of them exerted all their technical brilliance while the rest provided a somewhat recessive background. The *concerto-sinfonia* required virtuosity of instrumental technique, particularly from the players of those instruments which could be made to stand out from the general concourse. In part it produced, and was produced by, the first virtuoso violinists; it evolved almost directly into the *concerto grosso*.

Concerto Grosso

A *concerto grosso* is a composition for instrumental ensemble in which a small number of a group of instruments plays in contrast against all of the other instruments in full grouping. The smaller group is called the *concertino* or *principale*, the whole ensemble the *tutti*, *ripieni*, or simply (and confusingly) *concerto*. Early composers in this genre were Corelli and the half-mythical Alessandro Stradella (1645?–82). Their *sinfonie* or *concerti* still hung backward toward the fragmentary structures of the *canzoni*, often being built out of many brief, highly contrasted movements. By the beginning of the eighteenth century, the distinction between a *concerto grosso* and a *concerto* for solo instrument and orchestra was becoming sharp. By then, the *concertino* in a *concerto grosso* commonly consisted of two violins with cello and harpsichord thorough bass, the *ripieni* of a string orchestra and harpsichord—to which still later practice at times added both woodwinds and brasses. Corelli himself, having composed earlier in some of the ancestral patterns, lived to write—in his so-called "Opus 6," of which the eighth piece is the familiar *Christmas Concerto*—superbly assured masterpieces that differ from the final developments of the *concerto grosso* only in that they usually have five and more movements.

Another Italian violin virtuoso, Francesco Geminiani (1687–1762) consistently confined the *concerto grosso* to the four-movement pattern of the *sonata da chiesa*. Still another violinist, Antonio Vivaldi (1675?–1741), favoring an ABA sequence of movements—fast, slow, fast—established a pattern that was followed by Johann Sebastian Bach in four of the best-known of all *concerti grossi*—his six so-called "Brandenburg" Concertos. Imitating Vivaldi, who was a very talented if slightly repetitive composer, Bach also adapted the Italian's brilliant style, whereas Handel, in his scarcely less remarkable *concerti grossi* continued to prefer the five or more movements and less advanced manner of his friend Arcangelo Corelli.

During the late eighteenth and nineteenth centuries, the *concerto grosso* was to drop from sight almost completely. But its texture was retained in movements of suites, symphonies, and solo concertos (especially double and triple concertos). The solo concerto, however, was to become a typical genre of the nineteenth century, which was strewn with hundreds of piano concertos and violin concertos, to name only two sorts. The twentieth century, however, has witnessed a return to the past in search of viable formal usages. So modern a composer as Igor Stravinsky has composed several *concerti grossi*. The genre has emerged, alive and vital, after its period underground.

Aria and Arioso

Aria is the Italian word for air, often with the secondary meaning of breath. Its application to song is easy to understand, as is the English use in a related connotation of the word air. The Italian word now is generally reserved for a lengthy accompanied solo song not in strophic form—that is, not repeating the same music to differing textual divisions, but being one continuous unfolding of music, especially as in a solo song in an opera. It has not borne this significance always.

Aria as a musical term is said to have appeared in print for the first time in the *Arie di canzon francese* published in 1579 by Marc'Antonio Ingegneri (1550?–92), a teacher of Monteverdi. Ingegneri used the word to differentiate certain textless but polyphonic songs among his madrigals. In the *Nuove musiche*, Caccini placed the word above examples of monody which were brief and built on strophic principles. During the seventeenth century, the aria underwent a bewildering series of incarnations and metamorphoses. Willi Apel pointed out, in the *Harvard Dictionary of Music*, that *"aria"* was used during the seventeenth and eighteenth centuries by German composers to indicate songs that became direct ancestors of the strophic German Lieder of the eighteenth and nineteenth centuries. Thus, one variety of early aria descended to a rich national musical form often somewhat foolishly cited as inimical to its other important descendant, the full-fledged opera aria.

During the first half of the seventeenth century, what composers called an aria often was in reality that compromise between true song and recitative which later usage termed *arioso*. Like the instrumental *concerto grosso* and sonata, the aria also borrowed and altered patterns from the *canzona*, organizations employing rapidly contrasted brief sections. Still other arias were constructed of a chief melody soaring above an accompanying bass made of a brief semi-melody repeated over and over: a *basso ostinato*.

Aria da Capo

The first variety of aria to be preferred above all others was in the ternary ABA pattern that pervades musical form in many ways. This was the *aria da capo* ("aria from the head," in the sense of beginning), in which, after a contrasting middle section, the first section is repeated. In later *arie da capo*, the relationship between the A and B sections often was that between a major key and the minor key having the same key-signature, called the relative minor. Sometimes A and B were sternly in contrast; more often, the difference between them was less dramatic.

The *aria da capo* captivated composers and singers and, through them, listeners. Monteverdi had hinted at it in both his first opera and his last. Other Italian composers cultivated it with constancy. Alessandro Scarlatti (1659–1725), not bothered by the unlikelihood that a real person would express thoughts or show emotions in ternary form (he knew the difference between life and art), filled his many operas with characters singing *arie da capo*. Every *prima donna* (literally, first lady) and leading *castrato* (castrated male soprano or alto) tried to triumph by using *arie da capo* as platforms on which to perform astonishing vocal gymnastic feats. Operas tended, in fact, to become chains of *arie da capo*, often of surpassing beauty in themselves, but at last inevitably becoming detrimental to the dramatic component.

This excessive emphasis helped to bring on one of the several "reforms" of opera.

Composers and librettists, determined to reduce the arrogance of singers and to restore the central role of the libretto, tried to revert toward an improved variant of the Florentine operatic style. First they attacked the *aria da capo* for its lack of verisimilitude. Then, more sensibly, they insisted that any aria, whatever its pattern, must be fitted more appropriately into an operatic fabric. The renowned eighteenth-century "reformer of opera" Christoph Willibald von Gluck (1714–87) reacted against the aria—of which his own earlier operas had been full—in favor of a sort of Lied. Richard Wagner (1813–83), another reformer, wanted to banish the aria from music drama altogether; this was one central effort in his attempt to make an opera an uninterrupted dramatic whole. The *Pelléas et Mélisande* of Claude Debussy (1862–1918) contains nothing that can be called an aria.

Yet that form of extended song has produced, not only some of the most attractive and—at times—dramatic operatic music, but also many of the apparently nonoperatic wonders that dot the oratorios, cantatas, and passions of Handel and Johann Sebastian Bach. It also has been composed for its own sake, apart from any larger framework, as in the concert arias of Mozart and Beethoven. To denounce it or refuse it careful attention because of the gymnastic excesses to which pandering composers and vacuous star singers sometimes have led it is both futile and foolish.

Continuo, Basso Continuo, Thorough Bass, Figured Bass

Continuo (an accompaniment in the form of a submelodic element repeated throughout a composition or section of a composition); *basso continuo* (a bass accompaniment so continuing); thorough bass (an English translation of *basso continuo,* "thorough" being here a form of "through"); and figured bass (an accompaniment of this nature notated in a sort of shorthand, with figures or musical symbols to indicate chords desired)—these terms represent important musical means evolved during the sixteenth and seventeenth centuries. Like the concepts of sonata, concerto, aria, opera, cantata, and oratorio, they were available to those eighteenth-century musicians who were to sum up the immediate past in a massif of final achievement and to those (Carl Philipp Emanuel Bach, Joseph Haydn, Mozart) who were to evolve the musical manners that we have come to call Viennese, rococo, classical, or some combination of those terms.

Continuo

In 1587, Alessandro Striggio had written out a part for the organist in a motet by using the merest suggestions of the supporting chords required. In slightly later similar parts, some single notes are topped by sharps or flats to suggest that either major or minor triads are desired. In the earliest surviving opera scores, the *Euridice*s of Caccini and Peri, a related *basso continuo* uses Arabic numerals to indicate the wished-for chordal support. This "figured bass" became—and for a long time remained—the usual way of notating thorough bass. Some form of *continuo,* figured or unfigured, became so integral a part of compositions that the high baroque period of music (roughly from the beginning of the seventeenth century to Handel's death in 1759) often is called the "thorough-bass period."

The musical significance of *continuo* lies in its being the foundation of a harmonically logical structure in which chordal succession creates an important element of the logic. In religious music, the *continuo* often was meant to be played by the organ, but in secular compositions, thorough-bass parts soon were intended for a harpsichord and—in an effort to give additional strength to the substructure—a cello, viola da gamba, and/or bassoon. The use of one or more melody-carrying instruments was essential as long as the bass retained some melodic character of its own. But in the eighteenth century, the bass began to lose that life and to tend toward chordal accompaniment as such. Then the harpsichord gradually took over the accompanying role without any other instrument. Also, the musician playing the accompanying harpsichord became, in effect, the leader of the ensemble, a position that he kept as late as the 1790s.

A modern performer faced with a keyboard *continuo*, whether figured or unfigured, must be ready either to improvise discreetly or to play some editor's arbitrary "realization" (writing-out) of what he is to play. When, for example, we listen to a Handel violin sonata, we must understand that of the notes being played by the harpsichord or piano, Handel actually indicated only the bass: the performer either is improvising the treble or playing a version of it provided by an editor. This means that there may be as many versions of the sonata as there are players—and that the "rightness" or "wrongness" of a given version is a function of the individual performer's or editor's education, understanding, and taste.

Although these and related practices grew out of improvisational ways of using instruments in polyphonic music, they asserted their full weight only when applied to monody. All were signally effective in helping to evolve musical means by which melodies could be supported harmonically.

Basso Ostinato

Basso ostinato, a device as old as polyphony itself and still often used, is of a different nature. *Ostinato* (obstinate, in the sense of persistent) is applied to a fragment of melody or quasi-melody which recurs quickly and often, on the pitch and in the voice part of its original appearance. It may occur in any voice, but because it proved peculiarly useful in the bass, the term *basso ostinato* has become familiar. (Turn back to the discussion of "Sumer is icumen in," pages 24–26, for a discussion of one of the earliest surviving examples of *basso ostinato*.) The equivalent term in English is ground bass or simply ground. Like imitation, it is a form of lengthening by repetition, of which variation also is the child. But *basso ostinato* involves a fresh view that proved to be of structural and esthetic value: that of continuous variation or new creation presented against a repeated, unchanging, customarily simple background. Grounds made up of nothing more than four successive tones repeated over and over often have supported music so elaborate that a listener may fail altogether to notice their presence.

"When I am laid in earth"

The most renowned of all passacaglias,** Johann Sebastian Bach's in C minor—but not every passacaglia—is built on a ground bass. So are two of Johannes Brahms's most satisfying finales, that of his *Variations on a Theme by Haydn* and the passacaglia finale of his Fourth Symphony. So is the magnificent lament of Dido in Henry Purcell's opera *Dido and Aeneas*, "When I am laid in earth." Purcell's use of *basso ostinato* is so intensely effective that it is worth noting here as one demonstration of the way by which an accomplished craftsman can wring emotional power from an apparently dry-as-dust device. Here is the ground that is stated seven times in "When I am laid in earth":

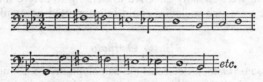

In its predominantly descending one-octave (G to G) motion, this semimelody evokes pathos. This is enhanced by the fact that the descent from G as far as D is made by semitones. Not musically very meaningful in itself, this six-measure ground, when Dido's vocal melody was added above it, proved flawless for Purcell's tragic purpose.

One all but complete presentation of the ground serves as an introduction to the aria: Dido begins to sing only with its closing note. Her melody, rhythmically much more varied than this ground, and of stronger musical interest because of its greater variety of up-and-down motion, meshes with it exquisitely. The stately progress of the falling ground is relentless. Yet Purcell did not interfere with the logical relation of text and vocal line even to avoid what—if looked at without regard for dramatic or pervasive musical effect —clearly are dissonances. Most of these are resolved quickly —are followed, that is, by assuaging consonances—so that in performance they scarcely project from the mostly consonant combinations. But they occur, and by occurring intensify the emotional atmosphere. In creating a vocal melody related sensitively to the profile of the ground bass, Purcell by no means confined himself. On the contrary, he used the device to compose one of his greatest arias.

Purcell, of course, could have composed a continuously unfolding bass accompaniment to his vocal melody, a more varied support than this constantly reiterated ground. But here he wanted exactly the grave, stately effect evoked by the ground (Dido is the Queen of Carthage) even when the listener, attending to the aria as a whole and as an important juncture in the opera, is not directly aware of its separate existence. Also, more than a mere probability exists that the melody actually resulted from the ground, that, having selected the ground itself, Purcell sketched in a vocal melody that would both mesh with it and symbolize the emotional distress expressed by the text. He was not performing a learned stunt; he was composing music out of a creative imagination freed of restriction by the very handling of this useful musical device.

Sonata, concerto, aria, arioso, *basso continuo, basso ostinato*—these and other methods, forms, and devices of performance were instrumentalities in the continuing emergence of homophony, monody, melody chordally accompanied along protoharmonic lines. They provided both present areas for composition and roads into the future. All of them reached a high development in Italy, though not there exclusively. They flourished through those seventeenth-century changes in musical syntax and grammar which a schooled musician of 1675 could consider natural, whereas his forerunner in 1575 would have thought them either devoid of meaning or full of a different meaning. All discussions of the rich musical life of seventeenth-century Italy necessarily are crowded with the terms evoked to designate them.

CHAPTER VII

The German States:
Heinrich Schütz

In the states of Germany during the seventeenth century, differences of musical background, local taste, individual talent, and religious observance continued to produce music with emphases and formal procedures very different from those burgeoning at the same time in Italy. Some of the remarkable northern developments of keyboard music already have been discussed: the appearance of free preludes, toccatas, fugues, variations, capriccios, and suites with shapes and textures distinct from those of vocal music. But the most intensely German musician of the seventeenth century was not primarily an organist or an instrumental composer. His salient contribution to musical change was a fusion of older northern polyphonic practices and some of the newer manners of the south. He has been called the "father of German music" because some of his compositions seem to have led directly to those of Johann Sebastian Bach. He was born exactly one century before Bach. He was Heinrich Schütz (1585–1672).

The Landgrave of Hesse-Cassel, Schütz's employer, took note of his musical talent and sent him to Italy in 1609 to study under Giovanni Gabrieli. That his studies were pursued at Venice under an organist of St. Mark's Cathedral was to have peculiarly direct results both on the style of Schütz's compositions and on their forms and patterns. St. Mark's is laid out in a Venetian adaptation of Byzantine church architecture: its ground plan is that of a Greek cross, so that its transept and nave divide each other into halves. Because its congregation therefore could not stand in relation to the choir as congregations stood in churches laid out in the form of the long crucifix or Latin cross, its choir was divided into two sections, one section being placed in each arm of the transept. By the time Schütz arrived to be Giovanni Gabrieli's student, St. Mark's was the home of a form of choral music making a virtue of this necessity. Gabrieli had prepared choral works for two groups of singers, works that took constructive advantage of this division of the choir and the possibilities of contrast and response thus afforded him. Nor had he been satisfied to manipulate only the two choral groups: some of his pieces were truly polychoric—that is, were conceived for three and four separate choirs.

Pure Splendors of Sound

Gabrieli's polychoric compositions roughly parallel paintings in which the resources of chiaroscuro have been summoned to heighten the emotional impact. His truly "concerted" choral groups compete for the honor of contributing most to the realization of his musico-religious intentions. He enjoyed the widest contrasts, those between very high and very low human voices, between single voices and one or more choirs, between soft (*piano*) and loud (*forte*), between the tone colors of voices and those of instruments, particularly the brasses. He was enamored of pure splendors of sound: his employment of the voice, whether solo or in masses, was in part instrumental. In his creative imagination, the human voice was becoming one instrument among many; perhaps, with the organ, the most important of them all, but no longer a ruler in isolated supremacy. Gabrieli joined glinting and shattering brass sounds to those of organs and voices, producing firmly controlled avalanches of sonority not matched in monumental quality until the oratorios of Handel.

Into the resulting musical climate, the twenty-four-year-old Heinrich Schütz moved as a pupil of the sixty-two-year-old Gabrieli. The year was 1609. In the Germany from which Schütz had come, the homophonic, monodic, not quite harmonic music budding all across Italy remained all but unknown. Schütz himself, returning to Cassel after Gabrieli's death in 1612, successfully imported that music into the north and mixed it with the north's own music. In 1619, while living at Dresden, Schütz published twenty-six settings of the Psalms. He had scored them for eight and more voices or solo parts, two, three, and four choirs, and a *basso continuo* for one or more organs, with additional accompaniment by lutes, strings, trumpets, and other instruments. Students find in these Psalms, besides the obvious external signs of Gabrieli's mastership, the indirect influence of the Florentine opera-makers' concept of vocal declamation. In them, also, Schütz has combined and alternated homophony, monody, and polyphony, using them all toward highly expressive ends.

A Passion by Schütz

Four years after publishing the Psalms settings, Schütz supplied the Electoral Chapel at Dresden with a setting, for use on Easter, of the story of Christ's Resurrection. For many years, it had been the custom in numerous German churches to sing the story of the Passion during Holy Week, that of the Resurrection on Easter Sunday. One of Schütz's predecessors at Dresden, the Italian Antonio Scandello (1517–80), had provided musical settings for both. Surviving copies and partial copies of these prove that they were unaccompanied choruses, recitative solos, duets, trios, and quartets. The individual characters in the stories were not, except for the Evangelist—whose part is a recitation for solo voice—assigned in theatrical manner to a single singer. Peter, for example, was represented by a trio of choristers, Christ by a quartet.

Schütz's setting of the Resurrection story is scored for singers accompanied by instruments. He has moved in the direction of theatrical verisimilitude, too, in that when the music for an individual protagonist is given to more than one melodic line (continuing a motet procedure), he has indicated that one of the parts may be omitted or played by an instrument. His Three Marys sing three separate vocal melodies; two angels are assigned a duet. That the eleven Disciples do not sing eleven polyphonically interwoven separate melodic strands, but perform a six-part chorus, indicates no diminution in dramatic realism, but only the fact that Schütz was more involved in musical truth than in the working-out of a technical prodigy. His Resurrection setting is a bold step away from pure vocal polyphony of strict liturgical cast and toward that balance of polyphony and homophony, of liturgy and theatrically realistic drama, which was to flower in all majesty in the cantatas and Passions of Johann Sebastian Bach and the oratorios of Handel.

Schütz's Resurrection oratorio dates from 1623. Two years after that, he published a collection of forty-one *Cantiones sacrae* (Sacred Songs) in which the Latin texts were scored for four voices with a *basso continuo* for organ. His formal usage here was a compromise between the motet (polyphony) and the concerto (polyphony-homophony). It also was an attempt to preserve some of the antique strength of the old ecclesiastical modes in the face of chordal motion that often suggests a harmony moving by semitones (chromatically).

Diatonic and Chromatic

Diatonic, it will be recalled, describes an octave-wide scale (for example, C-D-E-F-G-A-B-C) made up of seven steps, some of them whole tones, some semitones. The chromatic scale, on the other hand, covers an octave in twelve semitone steps (for example, C-C♯-D-D♯-E-F-F♯-G-G♯-A-A♯-B-C). Scales, whether diatonic or chromatic, usually have, for a composer, about the importance that vocabulary has for a poet. What really matters, musically speaking, is what the composer builds from combinations of tones selected from or related to the scales. Using mostly the tones native to a diatonic scale in a given passage, a composer writes a diatonic passage containing diatonic intervals making up diatonic chords involved in activities of diatonic harmony. Conversely, if he freely *and structurally* introduces tones not native to the prevailing diatonic scale, he writes a chromatic passage containing chromatic intervals making up chromatically moving chords involved in chromatic harmony.

Composers habitually introduce chromatic intervals into diatonic chords without obliterating the predominant diatonicism. Similarly, chromatically constructed chords may be introduced into diatonic harmony without destroying its predominant diatonicism. The question of whether a given passage, chord, or harmony is diatonic or chromatic frequently allows several differing answers. It generally is decided on the basis of the prevailing wind. A mostly chromatic example is called chromatic with diatonic aspects; in reverse, a mostly diatonic example is diatonic with chromatic aspects. A composition without at least tinges of both became all but inconceivable early in the evolution of harmonic music.

Oriental music long has been richly chromatic. But Western music remained all but exclusively diatonic until the middle of the sixteenth century. As remarked earlier, the first European composers to make free structural use of chromaticism were Flemings living in Italy: such men as Adrian Willaert and Cipriano de Rore. Many Italians composing during the second half of the sixteenth century made experimental uses of chromaticism. Notable among them was one of the most spectacular and talented eccentrics in musical history, Carlo Gesualdo, Prince of Venosa. Inhabiting a brilliantly lighted cul-de-sac of his own, Gesualdo so sensitized his musical responses to nuances in his madrigal texts that his harmonic practices fled entirely beyond what his contemporaries considered reason. He composed chromatic melodies and then wove them together with disregard for diatonic probity. Historical development happened to leave his fiercely expressive madrigals to one side of the main road: his contemporaries and their immediate followers remained much more conservatively diatonic. Three centuries and more later, the composers who might have found Gesualdo's example useful had all but forgotten his existence. The twentieth century has rediscovered him.

Sweelinck, almost exactly Gesualdo's contemporary, but

quite uninfluenced either by him or by the slightly less idiosyncratic Luca Marenzio (1553–99), let himself stray into chromaticism chiefly when composing fugues. He enjoyed the problems and solutions presented by a chromatically developing principal subject for fugal treatment; even more, his followers and some of his German coevals introduced such chromatic semimelodies as answers or countersubjects in fugues that remained mostly diatonic. But Schütz, in his *Cantiones sacrae* of 1625, seems, in one sense, to have gone back behind Sweelinck; he appears to be returning to the supposedly moribund ecclesiastical modes, finding there a basic substance onto which he could graft the newer, more directly expressive chromaticism inherent in concerted music of the melody-with-accompaniment sort evolved in Venice, and particularly by Giovanni Gabrieli.

Early Opera in Germany

Still acting as the persuasive ambassador, Schütz in 1627 composed (or arranged and composed) the first German opera. Rinuccini's text of the first opera, *Dafne* (1597), had been translated into German in the expectation that Peri's music for it could be sung to the translation when the opera was staged at Torgau in 1627 for a royal wedding. Peri's music, however, married to the Italian syllables, would not fit the different German words. So Schütz apparently composed a new score to the translated text. That score, like Peri's original one, has been lost.

In 1629, Schütz returned to Italy in his forty-fifth year, going to a Venice musically much altered since he first had visited it seventeen years before. The vogue of the solo voice, carrying a melody to intense dramatic effects, had increased notably. Harmonic textures were more highly seasoned with dissonances employed expressively. Instruments rapidly were supplanting the earlier accompaniments by massed voices. While in Venice, Schütz published the first of his three collections of *Symphoniae sacrae*. Some of these twenty settings in Latin of biblical texts, though called "symphonies," a term used loosely at the time, are in reality cantatas or small oratorios.

Opera, originating almost exactly at 1600, constituted the first new formal achievement in the monodic manner. Near the hour of its birth, that manner also found, in the cantata and its larger extension, the oratorio, nontheatrical forms of almost equal durability. The cantata had existed in embryo in collections issued by both Peri and Caccini before 1610, appearing there as a monodic substitute for the polyphonic madrigal of the preceding century. Tightly wrought pieces of sectional, often strophic, construction, some of these cantatas consisted of alternating passages for voices and for instruments, the voices pronouncing both recitative and almost-arias deserving the name of arioso. Related through ancestry and pattern to forms of the instrumental *canzona* which led to both the fugue and the sonata, this sort of cantata became a favorite with such Italian composers as Luigi Rossi[1] (1598–1653), Marc'Antonio Cesti (1623–69), and, above all, Giacomo Carissimi (1605–74).

Carissimi brought the third great formal genre of monodic music to its first maturity. The oratorio, descended somewhat indirectly from so-called "dialogue tropes" of the years between 925 and 1075, from the ensuing biblical plays with music, from the later "mysteries"—which also in part led to the serious drama of Western Europe—and from other semiliturgical musical plays, achieved its name and much of its enduring character in the middle 1500s. It was then that St. Philip Neri founded the Order of Oratorians, with headquarters in a Roman oratory (literally, a place for prayer). Parts of the services in the oratory were semitheatrical presentations intended for popular approval, adaptations in polyphonic vocal style of the earlier mysteries.

Many religious musico-dramatic works of the turn of the seventeenth century defy classification. The *Rappresentazione di anima e di corpo* of Emilio de' Cavalieri (1550?–

---

[1] Patronized by Cardinal Mazarin, Rossi spent some time in Paris. His *Orfeo*, translated into French as *Le Mariage d'Orphée et Eurydice*, was one of the earliest operas to cross the Alps from Italy; it was sung at Paris in March 1647.

1602) is alternately called the first oratorio and one of the earliest true operas. We no longer think of oratorio as employing such elaborate stage settings and costumes as were used in the first performance of this work by a friend of Peri and Caccini, but it was an oratorio in spirit. Carissimi, however, composed works that, even as presented at that time, would fall completely within our present understanding of the word oratorio. Many Masses and Passions can be distinguished from oratorios only in that their texts are liturgical. But even this distinction breaks down when confronted with oratorios that have scriptural and liturgical texts. It is helpful to consider some Masses and Passions —even such a work as Johann Sebastian Bach's *Magnificat* —as varieties of oratorio intended for use during religious services.

Carissimi performed his sacred music dramas without settings or costumes, but he articulated them with devotion and musical strength out of chorus, recitative, arioso, solos, groups of soloists, instrumental passages, monody, homophony, polyphony, concerted voices and instruments, and free use of the then most advanced harmonic idiom. Thus, he left models on which many future composers, Handel included, were to exercise their ingenuity and expose their genius.

Acquainted with the music of Monteverdi and Carissimi, aware from direct experience of the Italian cantata and oratorio, Schütz spent most of the rest of his long life in the Germanies. He went on pouring out compositions that combined the older strengths of northern polyphony with the sensuous dramatic allure of the younger southern monody, varying the proportions accurately in view of particular and momentary purposes. Of his later works, the most important were (1645) the *Seven Words of Christ on the Cross*; (1664) the *History of the Joyous and Merciful Birth of the Son of God and Mary*—an oratorio; and (1665–66) musical treatments of Christ's Passion as narrated by Matthew, Luke, and John. Brought down to us in imperfect preservation, these intensely sensitive last works, composed two decades before the births of Handel and Johann Sebastian Bach, are in no way stylistically inferior to Handel's

Messiah and Bach's *St. Matthew Passion,* from which they differ notably in dispensing entirely with instruments. They were first fruits of the consummation of the wholly remarkable marriage of Germanic and Italianate musical genius which has come to be called the German baroque.

Seventeenth-Century France: Lully

Seventeenth-century France, lying between the Italy of Corelli, Alessandro Scarlatti, and Carissimi and the Germanies of Schütz and the great northern organists, asserted its national character largely in its way of absorbing and remaking one or both foreign influences. French music became more Italian than German, but nonetheless remained French. In the compositions of one Gallicized Italian and one quintessential Frenchman, France contributed musical forms, musical atmospheres, and technical practices of the first importance, as well as music that, if listened to properly, remains entirely delightful. These men were Jean-Baptiste Lully (1632–87) and François Couperin (1668–1733), called *"le grand"* to distinguish him from the numerous other composers in his family. Lully's talents filled ballet and opera with fresh emphases, molded one enduring pattern of overture, and significantly developed the instrumental suite. Couperin was a major formulator of keyboard manners.

Lully's proficiency as a violinist, unexampled at the time in France, attracted the attention of Louis XIV. As the leader of the king's ensemble called *Les Petits Violons,* Lully wrote instrumental music rich in contrapuntal effects but tending to harmonic poverty. He gradually left behind the texture formed by assigning chief melodies to single instruments. He increasingly favored a more even distribution of notes among the instruments employed, finally reaching an over-all balance that can properly be called orchestral. In ballet, he carried on the already established French tradition of theatrical presentation of largely mythical and allegorical subjects by means of a group of dancers, a tradition that dated from the 1400s. By his time, both the costumes and scenery used in ballet had become very lavish;

the stage machinery often was much more impressive than either the music or the dancing. One of the best-known of the earlier ballets of which the music has survived, the *Ballet Comique de la royne*, was danced first in 1581.

In Lully's versatile hands, the music for ballets, beginning with the *Ballet de la nuit* (1653), consisted more and more of sharply defined brief dance forms. Enduring and often used among these were the minuet, *rigaudon, bourrée,* gavotte, and *passepied.* Grouped into suites (or, later, composed especially as parts of suites), these musical patterns proved central to the evolution of both orchestral music and keyboard music. In the history of ballet as such, Lully remains significant because he enlivened the previously monotonous stately movements with rapid steps and because he developed the importance of the star danseuse, complete with pirouettes and other twinkling attractions.

When Lully started to compose operas, his genius led him to become a key figure in the entire story of French art. With his setting of Philippe Quinault's *Les Fêtes de l'Amour et de Bacchus,* staged on November 15, 1672, the long, various pageant of French opera really was inaugurated. The two men were to produce twenty operas together. To subjects pseudo-historical or mythological, Lully matched music of understanding variety and suppleness. Not satisfied with the recitative manner of his operatic predecessors—the "dry" recitative or *recitativo secco,* that semisong, semideclamation accompanied only by harpsichord or a related instrument—he treated the connective tissue between arias or dances in such a manner as to raise it closer to full musical autonomy. To the recitative he gave, first of all, accompaniment more varied than most composers had given it, though Monteverdi had experimented with (and Schütz had made considerable use of) *recitativo stromentato* (instrumented) or *accompagnato* (accompanied). Lully, who had spoken Italian first, paid the most careful attention to French prosody, molding his accents and rhythms to the native shape of the language, often altering musical meter several times within a brief space. His arias and passages in arioso were written so as to be not only expressive but also concise, orderly, and neat in ways still thought of as musically French.

Because of Lully's strong sense of proportion, he lent grace to almost everything that he attempted. Equally admirable was his sense of timing, which taught him to introduce shifts from *recitativo stromentato* to arioso, from singing to dancing, from solo to duet or chorus, thus producing that variety which saved his operas from the monotony that without them might have blanketed musico-dramatic works in which the use of chordal harmony nearly always remained unadventurous and stiff.

The Opera Overture

When the earliest operas had had any instrumental introduction, it usually had been either an extended instrumental flourish, a sort of attention-gathering fanfare, or accompaniment to a staged scene called a prologue. This latter served the double purpose of pointing out the meaning and symbolic significance of the action to follow and of dedicating the performance and the work (usually in the most florid courtiers' language) to a king, prince, or noble patron. Soon, however, more extended purely instrumental overtures became customary, often before each of the several acts. Occurring in various patterns and under a multitude of designations, these gradually settled into two distinct forms. One, the "Italian" overture favored by Alessandro Scarlatti, typically consisted of three sections or movements: fast, slow, fast. Many Venetian composers of operas favored the "*canzona*-overture," formally allied to the *sonata da chiesa* and often labeled simply "sonata." This was likely to consist of a slow section in duple rhythm and a contrasting section in faster triple rhythm. This latter was the pattern that Lully enlarged into the "French" overture, the earliest known example of which led off (1658) his *ballet de cour* called *Alcidiane*.

As a pattern, the Lullyan overture most often began with a slow section intended to evoke grandeur. Often repeated, this typically was succeeded by a rapid section in which a brief melodic subject was dealt with semifugally. This two-part pattern evinced vitality and usefulness for a long time, toward the end of which it was elongated by addition of a very broad slow close, thus in effect becoming slow-fast-slow and exactly reversing the "Italian" fast-slow-fast pattern. The Lullyan overture did not have to bear any close relation to the opera that it preceded: it was therefore easily detached, easily written apart, for its own sake as autonomous music. As such, this "French" overture soon existed outside the opera house, having become a useful pattern for instrumental music, one that would yield precedence only, in the mid-eighteenth century, to the classic sonata and symphony.

Instrumental Suites

The seventeenth century established the custom of performing (or at least of publishing) groups of instrumental dance movements. Lully would seem to have reached this practice independently in part, so that his conception of the suite was individual with him. Skeleton performances of some of his ballets and operas were given by entirely instrumental forces, the music played being the overture and a selection of the dances. But neither Lully nor other composers of his era in France took advantage of the resulting suite pattern as inviting composition for its own sake. But German composers, one of the earliest of them being Johann Sigismund Kusser (or Cousser, 1660–1727), took it over. With the suite itself sometimes called "ouverture," these constellations of brief dances, preceded by a "French" overture, were composed by Johann Sebastian Bach, his immediate forerunners, and his immediate successors. During the second half of the eighteenth century, however, this type of suite, like the "French" overture itself, gradually was abandoned as a form of composition. In later musical eras, the suite has tended to return to its original nature as a group of selections from a long work. Such are the suites from Edvard Grieg's incidental music for *Peer Gynt* and from Tchaikovsky's ballet *The Nutcracker*. Occasionally, a composer will write a suite of independent music. Examples are Darius Milhaud's *Suite provençale* and *Suite française*.

Lully's life and creative mentality lay wholly within the boundaries of the baroque, which in music may be said to have begun in Italy about 1575 and to have closed on the death of Handel in London in 1759. But François Couperin lived, physically and intellectually, as long in the eighteenth century as in the seventeenth. For forty-eight years he was a contemporary of Bach, Handel, and Domenico Scarlatti. And though the actual dates of his life (1668–1733) fall within the baroque period, he himself announced a different musical age and style, the so-called rococo. (The word baroque is derived from a Portuguese noun meaning a pearl of irregular shape. Rococo, coming from the French word for rock, originally indicated types of artificial rockwork and pierced shellwork.)

In music, the baroque may be defined as an exuberant evolution of means capable of carrying drama, pathos, and passion, the rococo as a shifting within and away from the baroque—from expression to elegance, from the bodying-forth of majesty to its elaborate ornamentation, from large gestures to small gestures wrought in fine detail. The rococo was first of all a French offshoot of the baroque. It manifested itself in architecture, in interior decoration, in literature, music, and painting—in which last its first great practitioner was Watteau (1684–1721). The rococo laid claim to less territory than the baroque had yearned for; its children were content with scintillating achievements small in scale but perfect in proportion. The French rococo dallied with the frivolous and the erotic, for its hope was to make aristocratic life not only more sumptuous, but also more entertaining. Probably it is fair to say that whereas, in music at least, the baroque had expressed, examined, and tried to extend life, the rococo commented upon it, stylized and decorated it. To denigrate the baroque as overladen or stylistically corrupt, the rococo as trivial and passionless, is to fail in historic comprehension and to deny by implication the very central meaning of style.

Couperin became the first musical master of the rococo. Although a notable organist, he survives now chiefly through his four volumes of *pièces pour le clavecin* (that is, pieces for the harpsichord). In them, he crowned the school of French harpsichord composers which had been founded by Jacques Champion de Chambonnières (1602–72?). The several members of this line also had composed suites of pieces—suites not in the Lullyan sense of selections from longer works, but simply groups of brief pieces all in one key. These harpsichord suites neither developed a true pattern nor settled upon usual successions or varieties of dance forms for inclusion. Couperin, indeed, tended to drop true dance forms altogether, constituting his *ordres* (as he called his suites) from pieces wholly original as to pattern and form, sections with such flowery rococo titles as *Les Vergers fleuris, Soeur Monique,* and *Les Barricades mystérieuses.*

A universe distant from music intended to praise or placate God or to exalt His representative at Versailles, Couperin's *ordres* were meant to entertain by purely musical means people at once sophisticated enough and sufficiently concentrated to appreciate their fine points. This music often seems to lay claim to nothing more exalted than equality to jewelry or stucco scrollwork; yet it asserts music's self-sufficiency in a new way. Despite Couperin's descriptive titles and amusing mimicry of nonmusical sounds, his finest pieces remain pure music, unallied to religion, drama, or any other nonmusical activity. By this mild assertion of his art's independence, Couperin helped to make possible the great classic period that began with Luigi Boccherini (1743–1805) and Joseph Haydn (1732–1809).

One does not look for Gothic splendors at Le Petit Trianon—or accuse François Couperin *le grand* of heartlessness. His perfectly proportioned, delightful *ordres* are neither searching dramatic symbols nor profound emotional equivalents. Despite their titles, they are not "program music." Despite their touches of naturalistic imitation—of the clucking of hens, the clicking of heels—they are asked to provide more than they can or were intended to provide if they are listened to for more than their formal grace, their mellifluous progressions and lively figurations, their sweet, artificial aroma of courtly gallantry. Cecil Gray, in *The History of Music*, wrote that Couperin had been praised unduly by such modern French musicians as Debussy and Maurice Ravel, adding suggestively that his harpsichord pieces recall "china shepherdesses and similar antiques of the period." If nicely interpreted, that phrase suggests not only the exact nature of Couperin's musical originality, but also a sensible manner of approaching his charming *ordres*. It also makes certain that they must be played and heard, not on the modern piano, but on the harpsichord.

England: Henry Purcell

Charles II, returning to England from the court of Louis XIV, where he almost certainly became familiar with the music of Lully, carried to London the setting and the demand for a new musical style. England, not so devoid of good composers as many nineteenth-century historians made her appear, nonetheless had fallen upon musically evil days, poor in nurture and formal support for a maturing composer. The short career of Henry Purcell (1658?–95), for all the beauty it produced, unquestionably suffered in such artistic surroundings. And that was an English tragedy, for Purcell's failure to found a tradition that could be adapted by eighteenth-century Englishmen led to Italian and German musical supremacy in England. For two centuries after Purcell's death, no Englishman, in fact, would find around him or in his own person develop the musical sustenance essential to firmness of style. Only toward the end of the nineteenth century and in the twentieth has truly English music been composed which can survive in the company of Byrd, the finest of the madrigalists, John Blow, and Henry Purcell.

Purcell was remarkable both for his fresh spontaneity and for his Mozartean versatility. In *Dido and Aeneas* (1689), his only true opera (and that being given an amateur performance, no English public for opera yet being in existence), he managed, in the face of the poet laureate Nahum Tate's legendarily silly libretto, to create a formally unflawed small work taking advantage of the best practices of the Continental musicians of his time. To methods he held in common with such an Italian as Pietro Francesco Cavalli (1602–76), Purcell added an evocative sincerity and depth of feeling unique with him. (See pages 94–95 for discussion of Dido's Lament from this opera.)

To *Dido and Aeneas,* as well as to his not quite operatic music for several plays, Purcell also brought hints taken from such of his predecessors as had composed masques, those English counterparts of the French *ballets de cour:* the poet-composer Thomas Campion (1565–1620), Henry Lawes (1596–1662)—who composed the music for the most renowned of all masques, John Milton's *Comus*—Matthew Locke (1630?–77), and Christopher Gibbons (1615–76), a son of Orlando Gibbons. And Purcell's use of balletic interludes such as the "Triumphing Dance" and "Dance of Witches and Sailors" in *Dido and Aeneas* probably indicates familiarity with at least some scores by Lully.

In choral music, both religious and secular, Purcell likewise towered above his English contemporaries and matched the Continental creations of the period. He long served in several capacities in the Chapel Royal. His *Ode on St. Cecilia's Day* (1692, the finest of several such odes that he composed) and *Te Deum and Jubilate* (1694) wonderfully realize combinations of choral composition and full instrumental accompaniment in a truly orchestral style. The texture is Purcell's own mixture of polyphony and monody. In his purely instrumental music—sonatas (those of 1683 were so called for almost the first time in England) for two violins, violoncello or *viola da gamba,* and *continuo* (organ or harpsichord); fantazias (so spelled) for three, four, and five instruments; and harpsichord suites of short movements —he revealed his era's increasing mastery of manners not native to vocal music. In them, too, he half-consciously revealed the waxing discomfort that seventeenth-century composers of talent increasingly felt within the constricting limits of the few keys that the tuning and other limitations of their instruments forced them to accept within entire sections or movements. In each of his suites, Purcell confined himself to a single tonic key, each of the short sections to a simple binary form, in which each section was meant to be played twice in succession.

Binary and Ternary Form

Simple binary form, with the A section in the tonic key, the B section in the key based on the fifth tone (dominant) in the scale of that key, but moving back to the tonic for the ending, was certain to lose its popularity with composers when freer movement from one key to another (modulation) became possible and encouraged the emergence of larger, more complex forms (often binary too). To Purcell, simple ternary form was available easily only by repetition of an A section after a B, and he used even that almost exclusively in *arie da capo*. In the sense that the patterns and forms and techniques available to him failed to evoke and display to fullest advantage all the inclinations evidenced by his musical imagination, and as he himself remained an adapter and ameliorator of already existing forms, it probably is fair to say of him, as Harvey Grace wrote in *The International Cyclopedia of Music and Musicians,* that "he was a frustrated genius, born in a transition period, a century too soon (or perhaps too late: with his skill and invention what a figure he would have been among the Elizabethans!)."

Of most creative artists, this sort of speculative criticism, any criticism of what they are not rather than of what they are, is footless. But of Purcell it seems keenly relevant. *Dido and Aeneas,* the *Te Deum and Jubilate,* the *Ode on St. Cecilia's Day,* and some of the sonatas, fantazias, and suites were the last major creations of the transitional ("becoming") period that just preceded that of free modulation and expanded instrumental forms. But the general suggestion of Purcell's music as a whole is, if not quite of frustration, at least of an incomplete harvest. Certain musical tools and means that he needed but did not live long enough to obtain lay just ahead, beyond his reach, in Johann Sebastian Bach's *The Well-Tempered Clavier,* Handel's oratorios, and both the music and the theoretical and intellectual formulations of Jean-Philippe Rameau.

CHAPTER VIII

Tuning and Temperament

On an accurately tuned modern piano, any octave is an interval bounded by two tones of which one vibrates exactly twice as rapidly as the other. On that same piano, however (and on any present-day instrument of fixed pitch), any perfect fifth is an interval bounded by two tones of which one vibrates *very slightly less* than one and one-half times as rapidly as the other; any major third demonstrates a further narrowing of distance between its outside tones as compared with that of a natural or "overtone" third.

This discrepancy between pure intervals—those existing in unchanging mathematical relationships among the overtones or partials that sound (audibly or inaudibly) when a single musical tone is sounded (*see* pages 49–51)—and those created artificially on our instruments of fixed pitch is a time-honored compromise between nature and art. It was necessitated by the arbitrary, artistically motivated, "unnatural" division of our octave into twelve exactly equal semitones. This division was forced upon Western music by the gradual accretion of additional semitones to its fundamental alphabet, the semitones most often represented in our notation by sharps, flats, and sometimes naturals. The wider use of keys marked by several sharps or flats resulted in the possibility, almost the necessity, of shifting from one key to another within a composition or musical section. This modulation from one key to another was possible in rudimentary, limited ways in some systems of tuning employed before the general adoption of our present system, called equal temperament (temperament meaning tuning). But it became difficult or impossible in those systems when music began to be composed in keys using numerous accidentals. With the human voice and on instruments not of fixed pitch—of which violins and trombones are examples—unlimited modulation always has been theoretically possible.

Equal Temperament

Several systems of tuning were tried before equal temperament was formulated and accepted. Much of Western European music composed between 1500 and 1700, and an appreciable portion of that composed in the Germanies up to 1800 and in England and France up to 1850, was conceived for performance on instruments tuned (or, in the case of some instruments not of fixed pitch, played) in the "meantone" system, which used a fifth very slightly narrower than the pure perfect fifth. All such music is somewhat misrepresented as performed today on instruments tuned or played in equal temperament. But the theoretical disparity is far greater than any actually audible difference: the ear will make almost any small adjustment rapidly and to its own satisfaction. (Broadwood, a renowned English manufacturer of pianos, did not design its instruments for—or tune them in—equal temperament until 1846. In *The Oxford Companion to Music*, Percy A. Scholes pointed out that therefore a Broadwood piano built and tuned earlier than 1846 would have been unsuited to performance of either Beethoven or Chopin.)

To quote the *Harvard Dictionary of Music*, what was required for complex modulations and for keys marked by more than two sharps or flats was a system of tuning which would not be "perfect in the simple keys and intolerably wrong in the others," but would "spread the inevitable inaccuracy over all the tones and keys." That method, in use throughout the Western world since 1850, came to be called equal temperament because it solved the problem by arbitrarily dividing the octave into twelve equal semitones. The application of this "unnatural" mathematics has enabled us to use the tone next higher than any C as either C♯ or D♭; to use any C as B♯ when we wish; to use one tone as both G♯ and A♭, and so on.

The inevitable, necessary deviation from purity had been spread evenly over the octave and the keyboard. Except for the octaves, the intervals consequently produced on our instruments of fixed pitch usually do not coincide with the overtone intervals produced by each individual tone. Therefore, we constantly create a peculiarly mixed sort of misty dissonance not audible enough to upset any but the most phenomenally oversensitized ears. In fact, this misty dissonance, which is present constantly, has become an integral element in the sonorous material of music, and we might sense its absence with considerable discomfort now if we were suddenly to hear that instrumental chimera, a piano or other fixed-pitch instrument on which all the intervals were pure.

With equal temperament, composers have been able to be generous in their use of sharps and flats; they have been able to modulate with ease from one key to another. The price paid for this ability is the conventional falsification of every interval but the octave. As a completely, unthinkingly accepted convention, this distortion might be compared in some ways to that other convention by which perspective was achieved in painting.

Overgenerously, several individuals have been credited with the "invention" of equal temperament. One of them, Andreas Werckmeister (1645–1706), was an organist who studied and wrote extensively about all the thorny problems involved in tuning organs and keyboard stringed instruments. Werckmeister was working toward a system very like equal temperament, but he was not the first to do so—and he never succeeded in formulating it as it now is used. Another "inventor" of equal temperament was Johann Sebastian Bach (1685–1750), long assigned this honor because in 1722 he composed *Das wohltemperirte Clavier* (*The Well-Tempered*—that is, properly tuned—*Clavier*). This volume contained one prelude and one ensuing fugue in each of the twenty-four major and minor keys. That fact was taken to indicate an instrument tuned so as to be much closer to our equal temperament than to the meantone tuning then in general use. But no proof exists that Bach's own keyboard instruments were in equal temperament as we know it; he well may have expected an instrument to be retuned between pairs of pieces. To retune an eighteenth-century harpsichord was comparatively easy, and Bach's "well-tempering" can be produced by tuning major thirds a little wide, perfect fifths a little narrow within the given key; the result is a temperament somewhere between meantone and equal.

The Size of Semitones

Aristoxenus (fourth century B.C.), a pupil of Aristotle, wrote one of the earliest known theoretical treatises on music. He is said to have advocated a tuning system (in reality, it was a system of performance) with many elements of equal temperament. Certainly, Bartolomé Ramos de Pareja (1440?–1521?), an erudite Spanish musician, issued in Bologna in 1482 a book in which something close to equal temperament is described, being inherent in the circumstance that on the necks of guitarlike instruments the frets put there to indicate finger placement—showing, that is, where the player's left-hand fingers should be pressed down on the strings to divide them—were placed equal semitones apart. That inevitably resulted in a scale of equal semitones. During the sixteenth century, the need for something resembling equal temperament was sensed clearly. One proposed system would have split the octave into twelve semitones, of which two would have been slightly narrower than the other ten. Adrian Willaert asked for the acceptance of a system that would have been equal temperament if it had been adopted. Vincenzo Galilei, a member of the Bardi *camerata*, proposed the adoption of a semitone narrower than that of equal temperament by less than one twelve-hundredth of the width of an octave. Gioseffe Zarlino (1517–90), choirmaster of St. Mark's Cathedral at Venice, wrote passages about lute-fingering which are equivalent to asking that the lute be fingered like the *vihuela,* a viol-like ancestor of the guitar; that too would have amounted to equal temperament.

The drive toward equal semitones became still more urgent during the seventeenth century. Some of the English virginalists, including John Bull, composed music containing so much modulation that it calls for instruments tuned somewhere near equal temperament. Marin Mersenne (1588–1648), a French savant, delineated the equal-semitone theory in full. Johann Caspar von Kerll (1627–93), a leading German composer of the period just before Handel and Bach, composed one piece that modulates to or from every key. Johann Caspar Ferdinand Fischer (1665?–1738) published in 1702 a set of preludes and fugues for organ pedagogy in which nineteen of the twenty-four major and minor keys are represented. Handel's friend Johann Mattheson (1681–1764) issued in 1719 an *Exemplarische Organisten Probe* in which all twenty-four of them appear. Bach's *Well-Tempered Clavier* followed in 1722.[1] Others of his compositions, as well as many by Handel, imply by their harmonic texture that they were conceived by men who envisaged instruments tuned near equal temperament.

Harmony, Key, Tonality, Modulation

What had been making equal temperament desirable and, finally, inescapable was the increasing rapid trend toward classic harmony, the emergence of sharply defined sensations of key or tonality, and the consequent importance of modulation as one of the syntactical processes of music.

By the time of Handel and Bach and their contemporaries, music had become a very complex, greatly various, self-confident art. The formal patterns at the disposition of composers were numerous, supple, and satisfactory. Monody had set the melodic sense free in new regions; music had learned that monody and polyphony need not be mutually

---

[1] Only the first volume of twenty-four preludes and fugues was called *Das wohltemperirte Clavier* by Bach, though the second volume, adding twenty-four more preludes and fugues, follows the same scheme. The two volumes together often are referred to as "The Forty-Eight."

exclusive. The gradual approach to equal temperament was adding free modulation to the composer's means. The development of the pianoforte was about to supply it with its most useful single instrument after the organ and the violin. Its right to autonomy, its creators' free choice as to whether they would compose music to a text or music for its own sake, was unquestioned. All that was required for the blossoming of a musical era as fruitful as the most fertile periods of the past was composers emotionally and mentally equipped to seize upon and organize this wealth of means.

One Golden Age

Whether the means evoked the men or the men merely chanced to be able to employ the means, the most important period in musical history after that of the vocal polyphonists may be dated, in one way, by the births of Jean-Philippe Rameau in 1683, Johann Sebastian Bach and Handel in 1685, Christoph Willibald von Gluck in 1714, Joseph Haydn in 1732, Wolfgang Amadeus Mozart in 1756, and Ludwig van Beethoven in 1770—all within a span of eighty-seven years. The work of these master composers never should have been allowed (as it has) to cast into shadow the music of their predecessors and successors, or to make us undervalue that of their many less impressive, less technically important contemporaries. But it nonetheless is true that between Rameau's birth in 1683 and Beethoven's death in 1827 music summed up its past in rows of magnificent compositions and advanced confidently into three or four remarkable futures.

Genius may either be accepted without question or "explained" in terms of biographical, psychological, or other analysis. Recognizing genius as a term, albeit vague, for a mixture of qualities which cannot be described better at reasonable length, it is dealt with here only in examining the specific creative actions of indicative geniuses as they applied and enriched the vocabulary of music, as they asserted and proved its cohesiveness and probity as expressive creation. To explore the 1683–1827 period, it is essential to look inquiringly at harmony, at the continuing evolution of formal patterns, at the flowering of the oratorio, cantata, and Passion, and at development of the orchestra and the piano—as well as to examine the most significant of those periodic crises which have marked the history of opera. The first stages of all these inquiries have been made in the preceding pages. Now some relevant developments in harmony must be isolated.

Harmony

The word harmony is derived from a Greek word, *harmos*, which meant a fitting-together. In its barest musical sense, harmony means no more than the simultaneous sounding or fitting-together of two or more tones, a meaning that later usage has transferred to the word chord. Webster indicates this by first defining harmony as "musical consonance" and then suggesting that it refers to "pleasant" simultaneities, *i.e.*, combinations of tones whose simultaneity is widely accepted as proper or consonant. This application of the word remains useful in reference to much music of the seventeenth, eighteenth, and nineteenth centuries. From our point of vantage in history, however, its value diminishes rapidly with reference to music composed before 1600 and after roughly 1875.

Harmony in its widest and most useful application to music refers to the unfolding structure defined by the make-up, orderly progression, and interrelationships of chords. In this usage the word is distinguished, not only (as Webster states) from those other important terms, melody and rhythm, but also from polyphony. Harmony is the forward motion of vertical units (chords); polyphony is the forward motion of horizontal units (melodies). Music began as melody; chords at first were one thing that happened to melodies when two or more of them were sounded simultaneously and human ears began to take an interest in the implications and significances of the combinations of tones that, as a result, were sounded together. In that sense, harmony is what happens to both melodies and chords when chords succeed one another and our ears recognize relationships among them.

The briefest consideration of polyphony must convince us that all music except that consisting of one melody and nothing else—and even such music as we are likely to understand it now—is harmonic by the terms of our evolving definition. But it was not until the half century from 1550 to 1600, which led up to the emergence of opera and the assertion of *le nuove musiche,* that composers and listeners placed important emphasis upon harmonic relationships as constituent materials of the musical art. The pressure of this importance grew constantly, itself helping to hasten the adoption of equal temperament, to strengthen the sense of tonality or key, and finally to bring about the system here referred to as "classic harmony." During the first quarter of the eighteenth century, several theorists bent upon explaining actual musical occurrences and upon attempting to legislate both present and past proprieties insisted upon harmony as a foremost analytic and constructive principle. Especially and enduringly effective among them were Johann Joseph Fux (1660–1741) and Rameau.

In view of the fact that many musical practices of earlier eras are discussed in harmonic *terms,* the actual arrangement of harmonic *knowledge* has seemed to many to have occurred surprisingly late in music's history. But the data for that knowledge, the very logics with which it deals, were impossible and devoid of meaning before the realization of the classic system of keys and tonality. And that system was impossible under the musical philosophy of the ecclesiastical modes or any of their variations and extensions short of the twenty-four diatonic major and minor scales or keys. The system itself was evolved from the relations within and among those very scales and keys.

The Tonic

Of almost every musical work in existence except some of the most recent, it may be said that it exists logically in relationships between one principal tone (its tonic or tone-ic) and all of the other tones it employs. Gregorian chant recognized in each of its melodies the primacy of one tone. The domination of one tone, the existence of a tonic, that is, appears to be a first law of music. All music was tonal until some of it, in the twentieth century, became atonal. The constant presence in a composition or musical section of one tonic (or several successive tonics) is the basic premise of any system of tonal harmony.

Modulation

The concepts called tonality and modulation share a basic assumption: that chords have functions, bear esthetic-psychological relationships to one another, and tend to invite the subsequent sounding of certain other chords. Thus, if a composition mostly in C major arrives, after a time, back at the tonic triad of that key (C-E-G) in any position (C-E-G, E-G-C, or G-C-E), and whether that triad is sounded "close" or with its constituent tones spread out over more than one octave, the composer has arrived at a strategic point for modulating smoothly into one of several other keys. He may decide to regard C-E-G at this point as the subdominant triad of G major and to modulate temporarily into that key by so treating it. Or he may regard C-E-G as the triad on the seventh degree of the key of D minor and move temporarily into that key. In this and related procedures, the chord being thought of as belonging simultaneously to two different keys is called a pivot chord; it supplies the modulatory device most often used.

Another sort of modulation can be prepared for by some insistence upon one tone common to the key in hand and to a chord preselected to prove an entrance into a new key. After the tone has been given enough prominence, the composer may announce the new chord of which it also is a constituent. A third method of modulation, called enharmonic, may be simply (if somewhat inaccurately) described as that of considering what has been, let us say, G♯ as having become A♭—on an instrument tuned in equal temperament actually the same key and tone, but viewed in given contexts as having different functions and implications. After the eighteenth century, some composers began to feel it possible to move from one key to another without modulating—by simply ceasing to compose in one key and starting at once to compose in another. This action can be called "modulating" only by a distention of that word.

Modulation has supplied music with one of its psychologically most forceful methods of providing variety. It not only presents a way of showing melodies, chords, and comments upon them in different pitches, but also alters the functions and relative weights of individual tones. In the key of C major, for example, C is the tonic, and tends to be heard in chords at points of rest or finality; if the composer modulates to G major, however, C becomes the subdominant, and is heard in a new way, while G (formerly the dominant of C major) becomes the much more settled tonic. Modulation, that is to say, supplies perspective, shifting ambiguities, and felt resolutions unavailable to music remaining unchangingly in a single key.

Major-Minor

Similarly, the differences between major and minor, once they became sufficiently established, supplied composers with a tool without which most compositions of the centuries immediately before ours would have been inconceivable. Listeners and composers generally have agreed that major scales and major keys are brighter, "happier," than the more somber, more easily lugubrious minor scales and keys; but very many instances can be cited of "sad" music in major keys, of "gay" music in minor keys. For the real significance of the major-minor relationship is far subtler than a distinction between gaiety and sorrow: it supplies a further enrichment of perspective, of possibilities of modulation. To move from a major key to a minor one or vice versa usually is a more appreciable shifting of values than motion from one major key to another or one minor key to another. Further, it always is interestingly possible to modulate, say, from C major to C minor, two keys having the same tonic (C), dominant (G), and subdominant (F), but otherwise differing greatly in internal relationships.

A composer's selection of a major key or a minor key is relatively easy to understand. But why does a composer choose to couch a given composition or section in one major key rather than another, one minor key rather than another? Partly for the ease and naturalness with which, in the chosen key, his tones and chords can be played on the instrument or instruments he is using. In unaccompanied vocal music, his reason might be the pitches of the desired human voices: any major or minor key is higher or lower than any other major or minor key in over-all pitch. This consideration may play some part, too, in choosing keys for instrumental music.

In the meantone temperament—and, in fact, in any system of tuning other than equal temperament—some actual difference in the arrangement of intervals existed between one key and another. But in equal temperament, the arrangements of intervals between the scale tones of one major key and another (or one minor key and another) is completely identical. In composing in equal temperament, a choice of key is made partly for the reasons cited above and partly for subjective psychological reasons that defy analysis, though their intense reality in composers' minds cannot be denied. Some composers favor certain keys, appear to connect certain keys with certain moods or atmospheres. But except for questions of over-all pitch—which, by affecting the semiaudibility of overtones, also affect tone-color or timbre—and questions of performance ease and in relations to other keys, one major key is exactly like another major key, one minor identical to another. Except as influenced by the practical considerations mentioned, conscious or unconscious, a preference for one key above another is either subjective or mystical, and therefore properly speaking lies beyond or outside the possibility of logical explanation.

CHAPTER IX

Cantata

In the monodic innovations that evolved at the opening of the seventeenth century in Italy, opera and oratorio were paralleled by a smaller instrumental-vocal form, the cantata. The earliest known examples of cantata belong to the type later called *cantata da camera* (chamber cantata) to distinguish it from the *cantata da chiesa* (church cantata). As early as 1610, both Caccini and Peri, the very men who ushered opera into its career as a distinct form of stage music, had composed pieces lying somewhere between the aria and the cantata. These were extended vocal pieces in which a form of the variation principle was used: the same instrumental accompaniment was used for numerous stanzas or strophes, each of which had a different vocal melody. A form of the word "cantata" was applied to compositions of this nature for the first time in 1620, in the *Cantade et arie a voce sola* (Cantatas and Arias for Solo Voice) of Alessandro Grandi (?–1630?). The cantata, from its earliest days, bred elaborate examples in which sections of aria were contrasted with sections of recitative and arioso, even with purely instrumental *ritornelli*. By the days of Luigi Rossi, Marc'Antonio Cesti, and Giacomo Carissimi, the cantata had become a mixed genre tending toward standardization as a vocal-instrumental equivalent of the *canzona da sonare*.

This standardization of the cantata gave it the pattern aAbB, two sections of recitative (small letters) each introducing contrasted arias—again parallel to similar patterns in the purely instrumental *canzona*. This variety of cantata, in turn, helped to turn the *canzona* toward *sonata da camera* and *sonata da chiesa*. Alessandro Scarlatti composed between six hundred and seven hundred cantatas planned this way. Such immediate successors of Scarlatti as Leonardo Vinci, Niccolò Jommelli, and Leonardo Leo varied the pattern somewhat but employed the cantata predominantly for the secular purpose of expressing amorous and other emotions and passions through virtuoso singers.

Handel, who began to compose cantatas when visiting Italy as a young man, largely remained content to follow the Scarlattian manner. About eighty of Handel's Italian cantatas are known; nearly all of them are pastoral or amorous operas-in-miniature for one or two voices with instrumental accompaniment. Handel also wrote numerous vocal duets with *continuo* to Italian texts, and even two similar vocal trios. All of his cantatas and cantata-like pieces are highly decorative and conventional; they are full of notably Italianate melody. Perhaps the best-known of them are *Nel dolce dell'obblio*, *Fillide ed Aminta*, and *Apollo e Dafne*.

The Italianate cantata soon spread to Germany. There, because the influence of the evangelical church was pervasive, it was chiefly the *cantata da chiesa*. Heinrich Schütz made use of the pattern but did not adopt its name. The somewhat similar pieces of Dietrich Buxtehude further elaborated the form, giving important roles to both chorus and instrumental ensembles. The German cantatas of the seventeenth century usually were more solemn, more emotionally dramatic than the Italian. They show typical Teutonic emphasis on elaboration of texture, as against Italian insistence on song. In Germany, the use of the music or text, or both, of the chorales—those endlessly pliable German Protestant hymns—gave rise to the chorale cantata, much favored by Johann Sebastian Bach. The early chorale cantatas differed from the more Italianate cantatas of Buxtehude chiefly in that they made free use of chorale melodies and texts instead of being built wholly of freely composed melody on texts adapted from the Bible or written especially for musical setting.

Music and Pietism

Of the most signal importance to the entire future of music in Germany, especially because of its influence upon Bach, was the struggle between the Pietist followers of Philipp Jakob Spener (1635–1705) and August Hermann Francke (1663–1727) and the less narrowly religious, more worldly generality of evangelical Lutherans. The Pietists actively preached the necessity for expiating sin by repentance, the superiority of heartfelt devotion over intellectual conviction, and the desirability of experiencing as facts both regeneration and sanctification. They disapproved of the secularizing of music in the German churches, attacking it violently. They saw correctly that the old chorales were losing their centrality in the music of the churches and were being replaced by musical styles borrowed from secular sources, and from opera in particular. Special objects of their attacks included Johann Kuhnau and Handel's teacher, Friedrich Wilhelm Zachau (1663–1712), both of whom had composed numerous cantatas in the newer, more liberated manner.

In defense of the new church music arose Erdmann Neumeister (1671–1756), a pastor with literary talent. Deliberately challenging the Pietistic demand that cantata texts be simplified and confined largely to biblical quotation and chorale texts, Neumeister rearranged many of his own sermons in poetic form and published them for the use of composers. He developed a variety of text which quoted verbatim both from the German Bible and the chorales, but also included verse of his own, parts of it often so planned as to require setting in the form of *arie da capo*—surely "operatic" from the Pietist point of view. Numerous composers, among them Bach and the astonishingly prolific Georg Philipp Telemann (1681–1767), responded by setting Neumeister's texts and those of his disciples and imitators such as Picander (pseudonym of Christian Friedrich Henrici, 1700–64) and Salomo Franck (1659–1725). To set a text by Neumeister, Picander, or Franck above a choral *cantus firmus* was all but impossible; the result was a remarkable, sudden liberation of German composers' imaginations.

The Bach Cantatas

Some two hundred and thirty of Bach's cantatas survive, mostly religious, but a few of them secular. These vary greatly in style, manner, pattern, length, and vocal and instrumental forces employed. An average Bach cantata opens with a chorus, then alternates recitative and arias (sometimes duets) for up to three soloists, and ends with a freely harmonized chorale melody. The choruses in Bach's cantatas are largely fugal, but the monodic origins of cantata can be heard in the solos. The finest of Bach's cantatas are lyrico-dramatic masterpieces of constantly unfolding baroque luxuriousness; they contain some of the most sincerely expressive religious music ever conceived.

The Passion: Bach

The combined religious and musical influences that molded the German cantatas similarly molded German settings of the Passion of Christ, with text from Matthew, Mark, Luke, or John. Passions had been composed as early as the twelfth century, if not earlier. In Italy, they had been couched successively in the motet manner of the great era of vocal polyphony and in the monodic oratorio manner of the early seventeenth century. Finally, in Germany, they were composed homophonically, to texts in the vernacular. The baroque composers brought to their settings of versions of the Passion story all the resources of instrumentation, chorale, aria, and recitative. Thus the Passion approached very close to the oratorio. As already mentioned, Schütz composed Passions of extraordinary beauty. At the beginning of the eighteenth century, the use of verbatim biblical quotation in Passion texts began to decline, being alternated with specially written texts using dramatic or allegorical paraphrases of the great tragic story. Popular texts of this sort were written by Barthold Heinrich Brockes (1680–1747) and Picander. Brockes's *Der für die Sünden der Welt gemarterte und sterbende Jesus* (*Jesus Martyred and Dying for the Sins of the World*) was set by many composers, including Reinhard Keiser (1674–1739), Telemann, and Handel.

Bach's *St. Matthew Passion*, composed in 1729 to a Picander text, is wonderfully pathetic music that may be likened to a chain of cantatas. Each of its cantata-like sections culminates in a chorale. The voice of Christ is accompanied by a quartet of stringed instruments, giving it a luminous contrast to the other, more fully accompanied voices. Every sort of available dramatic, realistic, and imitative effect here is brought to bear in a series of choruses, recitatives, and arias, profoundly pious, but not Pietistic. Somewhat less satisfactory as a stylistic unity is Bach's only other surviving Passion,[1] the *St. John Passion* (1723), which contains an alto aria—"*Es ist vollbracht*"—which perhaps is superior in tragic utterance to any single section of the *St. Matthew Passion*.

The Mass

Coincident with the emergence of monody, though not certainly caused by it, was a decline in both the quantity and the general quality of musical settings of the Roman Catholic Mass. After the great sixteenth-century Orlando di Lasso and Palestrina, their first equal in both religious and musical grandeur was one of the most magnificent of all musical creations, Bach's Mass in B minor, over which he labored intermittently from 1733 to 1738. A composition of then unexampled proportions and esthetic loftiness, the Mass differs little from Bach's Passions in musical usages, widely from them in spirit. In effect it is a liturgical oratorio, the text being the Kyrie, Gloria, Credo, Sanctus, and Agnus Dei of the Ordinary of the Mass. It reflects Bach's inward piety as surely as the later Masses of Haydn and Mozart reflect more strictly musical attitudes. For grave

[1] Bach is believed to have composed five Passions, but three of them have been lost. A *St. Luke Passion* once believed to be his now is recognized as spurious.

and profoundly affective magnificence, the Mass in B minor was most nearly matched by the *Missa solemnis* that Beethoven composed as his Opus 123 (1819–23).

The Oratorio: Handel

The oratorio, meanwhile, still revealed its descent from the mysteries, those acted-out episodes from the Bible and the lives of the saints, and its relation to the secular theatrical entertainments of the 1500s and 1600s. Carissimi's important contributions to the evolution of this form already have been discussed. Like its smaller relative, the cantata, the oratorio rapidly increased the participation of the chorus. By the 1730s, when Handel tired of the London public's fluctuating reception of his Italian operas and turned his full attention to oratorio, it was ripe for his mastery. He looked upon the form as a musical giant capable of accepting his mightiest choral outbursts, a large ensemble of instruments, and the most baroque-operatic manner of singing. The chorus in a Handelian oratorio revives a basic feature of the Greek drama in a way that Caccini and Peri had neglected: its role very often is that of commentator upon the chief elements of the narrative text.

Setting English words, Handel in the most successful of his many oratorios expressed for the people of England their sense of imperial expansion. His rolling choruses, his celebrations of heroes (biblical mostly, but easily thought of as English), the sweet melodic streams of his love songs and arias of pathos—these guaranteed his oratorios an enduring popularity with large audiences, many of whose members were not seriously musical. It is scarcely too confining to say that the crowning masterpieces of the musical baroque were Bach's *St. Matthew Passion* and B-minor Mass and such of Handel's oratorios as *Israel in Egypt* and *Messiah*.

The Oratorio: C. P. E. Bach and Haydn

After Handel's masterworks, oratorio passed the zenith of its usefulness, partly because its sort of musical drama was replaced to a large extent by purely instrumental music in versions of the sonata manner that is itself a drama of musical ideas. The subsequent history of oratorio becomes a tally of occasional lonely accomplishments rising above surrounding flatlands. Carl Philipp Emanuel Bach composed several oratorios that contain individual numbers of considerable attraction and power, but in them we read that the baroque era—the very cause and home of the form—had ended somewhat before the birth of a new musical era of equal artistic fertility. The C. P. E. Bach oratorios—of which possibly the best is *Die Auferstehung und Himmelfahrt Jesu* (*The Resurrection and Ascension of Jesus*, 1787)—can only strike trained modern listeners as indecisive mixtures of the grand baroque manner of the composer's father and the style of Joseph Haydn.

In old age, Haydn presented the end of the eighteenth century with the greatest of its religious oratorios, *The Creation* (1797), and at the age of sixty-nine completed the greatest secular oratorio of the succeeding century, *The Seasons* (1801), the latter a setting of a German translation of James Thomson's *The Seasons*. Into the formation of these sure, artistically ripe works went Haydn's knowledge of Handel; much of what Haydn had learned during a lifetime of untiring composition; instrumental music in derived sonata manner; his enduring affection for the life of field, farm, and sky; hints from Mozart's handling of *Singspiel* and opera; and Haydn's own striking genius for absorbing these (and many more) influences without submerging his own stanch, forthright, winning personality. Of the baroque majesty that Handel had harnessed sixty years before, Haydn's masterpieces kept only what still was viable: they are classical works making full and relevant use of the classical orchestra and of the ripened procedures of classical harmony.

The Decline of Oratorio

After Haydn, the quality of newly composed oratorios again declined sharply. Mendelssohn's *St. Paul* (1836) and *Elijah* (1846), though once looked upon, particularly in England, as of Handelian quality, have lost much of their apparent strength. Their belated assumption of the exterior baroque manners of Handel and Bach has failed to stay well mated to Mendelssohn's own essentially romantic, lyric, undramatic idiom. In the second half of the nineteenth century, however, three quasi-oratorios were to demonstrate that a composer still might employ chorus, soloists, and orchestra to create quite un-Handelian works of power and beauty. Hector Berlioz (1803–69) composed *L'Enfance du Christ* (*The Infant Christ*) and *La Damnation de Faust*; Johannes Brahms (1833–97) wrote *Ein deutsches Requiem*. The first is a gravely simple, lyrical retelling of the events immediately following the birth of Jesus, the second a quasi-operatica "dramatic legend" that Berlioz at first called a "concert opera." The last is an extended funeral lament marked by Brahms's tremendous grasp of classical musical techniques and his intensely romantic musical character. Although entitled *A German Requiem*, this is not a Requiem Mass, for the text is Brahms's own selection of passages from the German Bible rather than the specific Roman Catholic liturgical text. For that reason, it is a religious oratorio rather than a Mass.

Such later composers as Igor Stravinsky, Paul Hindemith, Sir William Walton, and Arthur Honegger composed large works that may be classified as oratorios, oratorios-with-ballet, opera-oratorios, and other mixed genres. But neither sacred nor secular oratorio remained, in the twentieth century, so dominant a factor in musical creation as, for example, ballet became in its early decades. Far too often, the present-day musical audience's knowledge of oratorio is gained entirely from amateur or semiprofessional performances of that superb but difficult and uncharacteristic masterwork of 1741, Handel's *Messiah*. In truth the musical world of our day has lost many of the techniques of baroque oratorio performance, not least among them the *bel canto* that Handel expected from the singers of *Israel in Egypt*, *Messiah*, and *Jephtha* as much as from the demigods and amorous mythological heroes and heroines of his florid Italian operas. Under the conditions of the modern musical world, oratorio inevitably has become museum music in performance and a dead form in practice.

CHAPTER X

Choosing Instruments

Renaissance composers who had made autonomous use of instrumental ensembles usually had favored wind instruments; generally speaking, they had kept stringed instruments in subordinate positions. And though seventeenth-century composers increased the participation of the strings, the practice of writing out only the melody and the *basso continuo*, particularly where it implied the participation of instruments for which no notes were written down, proves that orchestration or instrumentation was not yet of prime importance to composers. The practice also leaves performers of later periods unable to determine exactly what instruments really were used. Some composers, to be sure, gave the most careful attention to the combining of instruments. Monteverdi did so, as noted in connection with his *Orfeo*. Preponderantly, however, it is difficult for a modern musician to determine why a seventeenth-century composer employed one instrument rather than another (or even rather than a human voice), so indeterminately was the "orchestration" of that era related to the unique, characteristic abilities, timbres, and other special qualities of the individual instruments used.

The seventeenth-century composers often increased the roles played by bowed stringed instruments, notably the various sizes of violins, which were much better adapted to ensemble use than were the recessive viols. They continued, also, to place wind and bowed stringed instruments together in varying proportions. But in the sense in which we now think of "the" orchestra—that nineteenth-century instrument —the seventeenth and early eighteenth centuries had no settled body of instruments and no customary distribution of functions among those used.

The makers of musical instruments continued to alter, improve, and find new uses for existing instruments and to evolve new ones both on their own initiative and at the promptings of composers and performers. Toward the close of the seventeenth century, an important addition to the unity and capacity of instrumental ensembles was made when the kettledrums (*timpani*) came to be considered a necessary component. The kettledrums proved to be of the greatest value for rhythmic accents, for laying down a background for the other instruments, and—as felt especially by Johann Sebastian Bach—for representing triumph and joyful demonstration. Bach, Handel, and their contemporaries, however, naturally continued to treat the human voice and the instruments as bearers of contrapuntally felt strands of melody. Except in specifically "pictorial" or onomatopoeic sections, they usually did not compose music whose character was determined importantly by the special capabilities of the grouped instruments. They certainly did not think in terms of a standardized orchestra, but continued to assign identical melodic lines to several instruments together: they wrote for flutes and oboes parts that as well could have been assigned to strings (and vice versa) and used the same distribution of instrumental parts throughout movements and even entire compositions.

The Baroque Ensemble

To pity Bach and Handel for not having enjoyed the advantage of—for not having had the wit to invent—the orchestra of Beethoven's maturity is foolish. Their instrumentation, determined by its value in performing contrapuntal music, did exactly what they demanded of it. To "reorchestrate" the music of the first half of the eighteenth century, to give it the "advantages" of the huge, pliable, greatly various body of instruments which the orchestra later became, is to denature and falsify it. Reinstrumentation of this sort is roughly equivalent to repainting one of the canvases of the pre-Giotto Italian religious masters to give it the "advantage" of later-day discoveries about perspective. Equally silly is trying to listen to, say, the "Brandenburg" Concertos or orchestral suites of Bach or the *concerti grossi* of Handel as if they were rudimentarily orchestrated nineteenth-century music. This music must be listened to as and for what it is, in the full realization that melodies not only are its essential trait, but also supply almost its sole reason for existence, however advanced may be its harmonic raiment, rhythmic insistence, and occasional splashes of characteristic instrumental coloring. Even when mistakenly played by the full complement of a modern symphony orchestra, it still remains remote in character from such a twentieth-century piece as Debussy's *La Mer,* in which the characteristic effects of finically selected instruments, both individually and in constantly shifting groups, are as essentially creative and integral a part of the music as its melody, rhythm, and harmony.

Rameau and Orchestration

In the instrumental ensemble music of Jean-Philippe Rameau—which was contemporary with that of Vivaldi, Bach, and Handel—the manners and conception of instrumentation began to change. Rameau was what neither of his great German confreres was: an intellectual, an inquirer, explorer, experimenter. He became a leader in the codification of eighteenth-century harmonic practices. He explored the inner natures of several instruments, most particularly the members of the flute and oboe families. For these instruments he composed truly orchestral parts that only they could perform, parts growing as much out of the instruments themselves and what they could be made to do as out of Rameau's wish to make a certain melodic or supporting line more or less audible. He began to inch toward the later concept of coloristic or characteristic orchestration. Suggestively, if inexactly, we might say that, whereas Bach, Vivaldi, and Handel were more interested in the music they composed than in the specific timbres through which its constituent tones reached listeners, Rameau's attitude often was exactly the opposite.

Bach's Instrumentation

Bach's six "Brandenburg" Concertos, now the most familiar of his purely instrumental ensemble music, demonstrate that his choice of instruments was made as much in the interests of contrapuntal clarity as for the emotional effects of timbres. Bach's own instrumentation, still of a *concerto grosso* nature, also shows that no settled group of orchestral instruments yet had been evolved. Here are the forces that he called for in the "Brandenburgs":

1st F major	2nd F major	3rd G major	4th G major	5th D major	6th Bb major
2 horns	oboe	strings	2 flutes	flute	2 violas
3 oboes	trumpet	cembalo	*à bec*	violin	da braccio
bassoon	flute	*continuo*	violin	strings	2 violas
violin	violin		strings	cembalo	da gamba
piccolo	strings		cembalo	*continuo*	cello
strings	cembalo		*continuo*	and solo	cembalo
cembalo	*continuo*				*continuo*
continuo					

(The violin *piccolo* was smaller than the regular violin: its penetrating tone derived from its being tuned one-third higher than the customary instrument. Flutes *à bec*, by which Bach indicated a variety of recorder, had an end mouthpiece, whereas the modern orchestral flute has no mouthpiece at all, being held in a transverse position and blown through a hole near one end: technically the player of a modern flute blows *across*, rather than *into*, the hole. The viola da braccio was a viol held against the shoulders, as opposed to the viola da gamba, which was held between (and at times on) the knees; most theorists regard the viola da braccio as an immediate ancestor of the second member of the modern violin family, the viola. The viola da gamba, held upon or between the knees, was a bass viol.)

The principal body of tone, then, in all six of the "Brandenburg" Concertos is supplied by bowed stringed instruments. The Sixth, lacking both violins and any body of strings, nonetheless calls for five bowed—and no wind—instruments. In all six, too, there is a cembalo *continuo*, i.e., a figured bass part for harpsichord used mostly to outline and support the harmonies. In the Fifth, this broadens out into a solo part, giving this piece something the nature of a concerto for soloist and small orchestra. Two of the "Brandenburgs"—the Third and Sixth—are for strings and harpsichord alone; two—the Fourth and Fifth—are for strings, woodwinds, and harpsichord; in only two—the First and Second—is brass added to strings, woodwind, and harpsichord: horns in the First, a trumpet in the Second. Although in modern performances the tendency is to substitute violin for violin *piccolo*, transverse flutes for the flutes *à bec*, members of the violin family for the viols, and a piano for the harpsichord—changes generally justified by reference to the increased size of modern auditoriums and to other altered circumstances of performance, but all robbing the listener of the effects Bach intended—the "Brandenburgs" can be heard (particularly on recordings) as they originally were conceived. In either the original texture or some more or less tasteful falsification, they remain far removed from what later musicians have thought of as "orchestral music."

The "Brandenburg" Concertos are as disparate in formal design as in instrumentation. The Third consists of only two movements, both of them rapid. The Second, Fourth, Fifth, and Sixth are each made up of three movements in the conventional Italian overture order: fast, slow, fast. The First, however, adds to three movements in that sequence a fourth movement compacted of dances: a minuet with trio,[1] a *polacca*, or Polish dance, and the minuet repeated with a different trio.

All but completely absent from the "Brandenburg" Concertos and other instrumental ensemble music of the first half of the eighteenth century is the principle of contrasting themes within a single movement, the principle destined to give life to the classical sonata, symphony, and string quar-

[1] "Trio" here refers to a contrasting middle section played between the first presentation and the repetition of the principal section of a movement. This use of the word emerged from the custom of Lully and others—including Bach in the movement here discussed—of composing these contrasting middle sections for only three instruments. (The trio here is for two oboes and bassoon, whereas the principal minuet, both as presented first and as repeated after the trio, is for the larger body of instruments.) Later composers tended to forget this origin of this use of "trio," and to employ the word to designate the middle section of any movement in ABA form.

tet. Instead, the individual movements are, rare exceptions aside, each either the expansion or prolongation of one musical idea or (as with the fourth movement of the First "Brandenburg") in effect a continuous suite of separate ideas. Within a movement, the baroque composers fractured one musical idea into its natural segments and simultaneously added them together again without any indications of divisions, thus making them free-flowing, continuous musical textures. The great kinetic power of baroque music resides in the apparently inexhaustible decorative details by means of which it is continued for long durations, repeating the same fundamental idea over and over, not so much seeing it constantly in new lights (variation) as constantly seeing it more and more nearly whole. At times the effect of listening to one movement by Bach or Handel or Vivaldi invites comparison to that of approaching closer and closer to a great baroque building, until its totality is discovered at last to consist of uncounted thousands of small carvings, cartouches, and scrollworks, each in the only right place and all contributing to the structural unity.

Not only were long sections of movements, and often entire movements themselves, of one unchanging instrumental-ensemble color in most baroque music; they also were largely of one unchanging volume. Dynamics, the constructive application of changing loudness and softness, still was mostly a question of the number of instruments being played. Such absolute essentials of modern orchestral music as prolonged gradual increases and decreases (*crescendos* and *decrescendos*) of volume, sudden increases and decreases, and sudden silences after a loud climax, though hinted at earlier, played no important role in baroque instrumental music. They began to be used in several widely separated centers of musical activity, Prague and Vienna included, toward the middle of the eighteenth century.

The Mannheim Orchestra

The most productive of these orchestral proving grounds was the famous orchestra of the Elector Palatine Karl Theodor at Mannheim. As conducted by Johann Stamitz (1717–

57) and by such of his successors as his sons Karl (1746–1801) and Anton (1754–1809) and by Christian Cannabich (1731–98), this was the first modern orchestra. An innovator sometimes called a fanatic, Johann Stamitz fused a more or less permanent body of instrumentalists into an ensemble of virtuoso quality which became renowned throughout Europe.

The Mannheim orchestra and the music composed especially for it by its conductors were increasingly, and at last essentially, noncontrapuntal in emphasis. Homophony was increasingly the favored texture, a group of violins being entrusted with most of the leading melodies while other instruments supplied harmonic chordal support. With the temporary decline of counterpoint as chief texture, such tectonic musical means as imitation (including fugue) temporarily went by the board. When the necessity of maintaining the clarity of separate but simultaneous melodic strands no longer was the primary concern, the speed of performance could be increased. True orchestral prestos** resulted, whereas no Bach, Vivaldi, or Handel movement for instrumental ensemble should be played faster than a well-considered allegro.** Also, the Mannheim orchestra could and did produce sudden, immediate, very loud (*fortissimo*) and very soft (*pianissimo*) passages; long, graduated crescendos and decrescendos; single loud chords (*sforzato* or *sforzando*) in the midst of softer passages; telling sudden silences of the entire ensemble, often next after a fortissimo climax; string *tremolo***; and very rapid broken** chords.

The compositions of the Mannheim conductors, like the works of many stylistic innovators, generally fail to satisfy as artistic wholes, whatever their eighteenth-century charm of manners. But the suppleness, the virtuosic precision, introduced into ensemble playing by the Stamitzes, Cannabich, and Ignaz Holzbauer (1711–83) affected the entire future of music. Without them or their equivalent, the orchestral compositions of Carl Philipp Emanuel Bach, Boccherini, Haydn, Mozart, and Beethoven, as well as the entire orchestral repertoire ever since, would have been impossible. When the Mannheim orchestra was at its zenith,

141

a customary, semicodified grouping of instrumental tones had been made as reliable and useful and varied an artistic medium as the organ.

The Mannheim orchestra, far from providing a good medium for the performance of baroque music, would have been as detrimental to its style as is a modern symphony orchestra in full battle array. It had developed in response to a slow shifting in the very nature of the music being composed. Men like Giovanni Battista Sammartini (1701–75) in Milan and Georg Christoph Wagenseil (1715–77) in Vienna, occurring in a stream of artistic evolution which had produced Stamitz, were creating the music for which the Mannheim orchestra and the orchestras elsewhere which soon imitated it were not only a proper performing medium, but also the only exact instruments in existence.

The Classical Sonata

At the heart of this new instrumental-ensemble music lay the first achievements of the classical sonata, perhaps the most complex, exception-ridden, fought-over subject in musical history. About the use of its terminology, in whatever language, experts quickly fall to quarreling; no two historians or musicologists exactly agree as to what a sonata is—or was—or how it came to be—or stopped being—just that. In broadest outline, and in the hope of avoiding the most tensely controversial points, the essential facts are these:

1. The classical sonata blossomed only when preponderantly homophonic texture was substituted for preponderantly contrapuntal texture. The gradual replacement of the latter by the former can be watched in the brilliant violin sonatas of Corelli and Vivaldi. A further enrichment of homophonic, dramatic ("operatic") treatment of themes (as opposed to continuous contrapuntal presentation of substantially unchanging melodies) can be seen in the works of Sammartini, Stamitz, and C. P. E. Bach. Dramatic contrast, homophony, intense emotional expressivity—these were the elements from which C. P. E. Bach constructed his

transitional art. They also are the central elements of the classical sonata.

2. The pattern of the Italian overture (fast, slow, fast) was emphasized by Alessandro Scarlatti; Vivaldi adopted it as the pattern of a large majority of his hundreds of concertos. Johann Sebastian Bach accepted it almost without question: he used it, with small variations, in organ sonatas, the Italian Concerto for solo harpsichord, and four of the six "Brandenburg" Concertos. Sonatas for harpsichord composed during the late 1700s also were generally cast in three movements. Italian harpsichord sonatas of this period also occur in only two movements. Domenico Scarlatti (1685–1757), son of the great Alessandro, long was supposed to have formed almost all of his sonatas in one movement, but research by Ralph Kirkpatrick showed that many of his so-called "*sonate*" were built in pairs that since have drifted apart, and therefore really were in two-movement form. With Johann Stamitz's invariable practice of composing symphonies and several-movement pieces for chamber ensembles in four movements (often fast, slow, minuet, fast), the symphony and the chamber piece (quartet, quintet, trio, and so forth) began to be more or less set as four-movement sonatas. The sonata for solo instrument and the concerto, however, tended to retain the three-movement pattern. Although exceptions are extremely numerous, the eighteenth century increasingly accepted the following meanings for these interrelated terms:

(a) *sonata*—a three-movement work for solo instrument, alone or accompanied by one or a few other instruments;

(b) *symphony*—a four-movement work for large instrumental ensemble;

(c) *concerto*—a three-movement work for large instrumental ensemble in which one or more solo instruments or a group of instruments plays a leading role;

(d) *trio, quartet, quintet, sextet,* and so forth—a four-movement work for three, four, five, or six (or more) players.

3. Certain formal patterns came to be associated with, and then to be required of, certain movements of sonatas, symphonies, concertos, and chamber pieces. Most of the movements in such compositions, in both the baroque period and the rococo period, were binary: Section A was presented and repeated, then Section B was presented and repeated, giving the two-division pattern AABB. An exception was the dance-form known as the minuet (originally, in French, *menuet,* derived from *menu,* meaning small, and referring to the dance's small steps). This characteristically had a trio,** the resulting pattern therefore being ABA. Gradually, however, the first movements of sonatas for any instrument or group of instruments began to develop an independent pattern of its own. Exceedingly difficult to isolate in pure state, this pattern is spoken of confusingly by two inappropriate designations: "sonata-form" and "first-movement form." "Sonata-form" is ambiguous because what it is meant to indicate is not the form of "a" sonata, but that of one movement of a sonata; "first-movement form" is equally misleading because the pattern also is used very often for other movements. In accepting the better of the two misnomers, it will be referred to here as first-movement form after a warning that nothing untoward has happened when a third or (as sometimes happened later on) fourth movement proves to be couched in it.

First-Movement Form

In broad terms again, first-movement form is a three-section pattern, the comparative lengths and importances of the three sections differing from composition to composition. The main melodic material is presented as an *exposition,* examined and commented upon in a *development,* and then repeated in variant state in a *recapitulation.* Sometimes a brief formal conclusion known as a *coda* (Italian for tail) is added as a peroration or summation at the end.

Sonata: Exposition

What is exposed, demonstrated, or set forth in this section of first-movement form is not often a single melody: it is more often several melodies or melodic ideas or constructive melodic fragments, referred to as themes. The exposition customarily ends with a conventional sign $\left(:\|\right)$, which indicates that the section is to be repeated. In many instances, in fact, the composer has supplied it with two different endings, one that smoothly leads back to its beginning, another that ends it with some sense of finality before the *development* begins—and at the same time supplies modulation to that next section.

The musical materials set forth in the exposition commonly are grouped into two systems, often misleadingly called "first theme" and "second theme," though each "theme" may be composed of several melodies or melodic fragments. Traditionally the first system is vigorous and dramatic, the second somewhat more pastoral or lyric. The first system almost invariably is composed in the tonic key of the movement (C major if the key signature of the movement indicates that key, Bb minor if the key signature of the movement indicates that key). The second system usually is in the key of the dominant if the movement as a whole is in a major key (it will be in G major, that is, if the movement is in C major, in F♯ major if the movement is in B major) or in the relative major key if the movement as a whole is in a minor key (C major if the movement is in A minor, Ab major if the movement is in F minor). In a very large number of classical first movements, the final melody or melodic fragment of the second system is strong and prominent; it is referred to as the "closing theme" because it culminates the exposition.

Sonata: Development

This is the dramatic center of first-movement form, that section of a movement in which the relationships among the ideas already set forth are examined and heightened. Just as classic harmony reached maturity in the sonata for one or more instruments, so the dramatic contest at the heart of the sonata matured in this section. An operatic broadness of thematic drama was considered permissible here, where the melodic hints and rhythmic and harmonic tensions of the materials are revealed, released, or set in movement. In many sonatas of the early classic period, the development section of the first movement uses no materials not presented first in the exposition; in later sonatas, composers felt free to introduce new materials in the development for contrast or in order to intensify dramatic effect.

In the development section of first-movement form, the composer may dissect some or all of his melodies or thematic fragments, presenting them in fragment so as to learn what can be evoked from them. He may modulate into and out of several keys, but usually will avoid those keys which he has used in the exposition. He may modulate with rainbow brilliance and swiftness. He may treat one of the thematic elements—and not necessarily the most imposing one—in imitation or combine it fugally with another element (for fugal passages had become common in predominantly homophonic music); he may present one or more of his ideas with the length of the notes doubled ("in augmentation") or halved ("in diminution"); he may turn one melody upside down ("inversion") or present it exactly backward ("cancrizans"—*i.e.*, like a crab). He may, that is, employ erudite scholastic devices from the polyphonic past, showing how one of his melodies or fragments can be simultaneously inverted, played backward, and made into a brief canon. The almost unlimited possibilities of manipulation are wasted, of course, if they do not make listeners feel that the materials they encountered for the first time in the exposition have become involved vitally in new activity.

Any composer with a gift for melody can produce relatively satisfying expositions, but to produce satisfying developments requires firm and searching intellectual command of the multifarious techniques of composition. However exquisite the materials exposed, for example, in many of Franz Schubert's sonata expositions, however much more melodiously compelling per se those expositions may be than corresponding places in Beethoven's sonatas, Schubert's neglect or lack of interest or inability to think with Beethoven's concentrated power often has resulted in developments that sound long, dull, loose-textured, or in other ways greatly inferior to Beethoven's. This does not necessarily mean that Schubert did not master the conception of first-movement form; what it certainly means is that the materials spontaneously occurring to Schubert (few traces of like spontaneity appear in Beethoven) often were not well suited to the classic compositional techniques.

Because the development is dramatic rather than expository, it naturally is not repeated entire, as the exposition usually is.

Sonata: Recapitulation

In a majority of classical examples of first-movement form, the recapitulation presents again all the thematic materials heard first in the exposition, though most often with changes in the connective tissue (sometimes referred to as "bridge passages," "intermediate groups," or "connecting groups"), and with the second melodic system of the exposition given in the tonic key rather than (as in the exposition itself) in the dominant key; it is esthetically essential to end a movement in the tonic if the sensation of enclosure or finality is to be provided. As a result, the recapitulation often is considerably shorter than the exposition.

Ways and Varieties of Sonata:
Symphony, Concerto, Chamber Piece

This, then—exposition, development, recapitulation—is the general ground plan of classical first-movement form, "sonata-form," or "sonata-allegro form," a pattern almost never encountered without variants dictated by genius or whim. The pattern has been used with moribund results by composers who lacked taste or did not evolve materials basically adapted to this sort of manipulation. It very often was the vehicle of the loftiest musical imaginings and compositional adventures of Haydn, Mozart, and Beethoven. It never was a formula for the creation of good music. Several other patterns found equally good uses. But first-movement form nonetheless was one of the most important means by which composers of the classical era contained, delineated, and balanced some of their finest music.

By no means all sonatas, symphonies, concertos, and sonata-based chamber pieces of the high classical period were given first movements in one or another variety of this pattern. Mozart's Sonata in A major, K. 331 (1778), for example, begins with a movement made up of a theme and six variations. Beethoven employed the theme-and-variation pattern for the opening movement of his Ab-major piano sonata, Opus 26, whereas in the so-called "Moonlight" Sonata, in C♯ minor, Opus 27, No. 2, he began with a movement evolved from an unchanging rhythmic figure. This latter certainly is not in first-movement form, for which reason, among other reasons, Beethoven carefully designated the sonata a *"sonata quasi una fantasia"* (sonata like a fantasia). Several other patterns were used. But it remains generally true that first-movement form was favored by Haydn, Mozart, Beethoven, and Schubert as the best pattern for opening movements, that during their era other first-movement patterns were deviations from the customary. They also employed first-movement form for slow second movements and for final movements. This pattern, that is, was at first—and long remained—the distinguishing formal mark of the sonata for one or more instruments.

Sonata: Second Movement

Second movements of classical sonatas nearly always were slow movements, in necessary contrast to the traditionally rapid opening movements in first-movement form. If a second movement, too, was not laid out in first-movement form, it was likely to be composed in some variety of binary or ternary form, though it too occasionally turned up as a theme and variations. At first glance, such a binary pattern as that of first-movement form—which might be represented as AABa, with A representing the exposition, presented twice; B the development; a the recapitulation, some variant of A—may look much like the ternary pattern of the *aria da capo*, ABA. In fact, some musicologists have said that first-movement form is ternary. The difference between the two forms lies primarily in the fact that in first-movement form the B is derived from the A, while in the ternary *aria da capo* form, the whole *raison d'être* of the B is its utter difference from the A. Like such simpler binary patterns as AB and AABB, however, the first-movement AABa pattern consists of two counterbalancing elements of approximately equal importance even though they often vary in length. In classical sonata usage, also, A-as-leading-to-B and B-as-first-presented bear a mirror relation to each other with respect to key. Section A, that is, most often starts in the tonic key of the movement and (as repeated) moves to the dominant or, if the ruling key is a minor, to the relative major; the B section then reverses this modulatory motion, returning to the tonic.

When true ternary form—ABA—is used in the classical sonata, Section A most often begins *and* ends in the tonic key of the movement; Section B usually is composed in the dominant key of that tonic, its relative major or minor, or its parallel key. (A "parallel" key has the same tonic tone as the key to which it is parallel, but is major if that key is minor, minor if that key is major; thus, the parallel key to C major is C minor, whereas the dominant of C major is G major and C major's relative minor is A minor.) Such ternary form likewise begins *and* ends the B section in the same key. While the A and B of binary form as used in first-movement form within the classical sonata usually have, harmonically speaking, a mirror relationship, forming a continuous whole with a peak of connecting modulation where they join, the ABA of ternary form must achieve unity in more subtle ways, being made up of self-enclosed sections, harmonically speaking.

Sonata: Third Movement

Whereas the second movement of a classical sonata may be cast in first-movement form, theme-and-variation form, or some variety of either binary or ternary pattern, the third movement (appearing in symphonies and chamber pieces, whereas the solo sonata and the concerto often omit this movement) nearly always is a minuet (early in the classical era) or a scherzo** (Beethoven and later). This is a special sort of ABA ternary form in which each of the sections will betray its origin in a dance form and will itself be in binary pattern. Because both the minuet and the scherzo are relatively rapid movements in triple time employing a ternary pattern, the difference between them is easy to define only in examples widely separated as to time of composition or as to the distinctive styles of composers. A typical early Haydn minuet is courtly and polished; a typical Beethoven scherzo is brusque, often humorously rough, and sometimes fantastic. But early Beethoven scherzos are very like Haydn or Mozart minuets in everything but some stigmata of the composer's most individual gesture and tone of voice.

We may well ask: what differentiates the ABA (AABa) of first-movement form from the ABA of the minuet-trio-minuet or scherzo-trio-scherzo? Some minuets or scherzos, in fact, could be analyzed as perfect examples of binary first-movement form except that they usually lack the essential internal key relationships and are ternary—and that they most often appear without any developmental activity in the B section.

Sonata: Final Movement

The fourth movement (or, in solo sonata and concerto, the third, final movement) most often is a very rapid movement in first-movement form, rondo-form,** or theme-and-variation form. Rondo-form evolved from the *rondeau,* a pattern favored by such French harpsichord composers as Chambonnières, Couperin *le grand,* and Rameau. In their view, the rondeau was a refrain pattern, *i.e.,* one in which a short thematic integer was repeated with contrasting materials between each two of its appearances. One such pattern might be represented as ABACADAEA. In many French harpsichord pieces, too, the key relationships among these sections were elaborated delicately. Section A, known as the refrain, always would be repeated in its original key, but Section B (these alternating sections often were referred to as *couplets*) would be in that same tonic key, whereas Section C would appear in the dominant, Section D in the relative major or minor, and Section E in the parallel key. In the rondo-form of classical sonatas, the couplets came to be limited to three, the form thus crystalizing as ABACADA or, rather, as ABACABA, as the third couplet very commonly repeated the first. In classical terminology, the A came to be known as the rondo; the couplets were referred to as diversions or episodes.

All sonata movements may be preceded by several sorts of introductions and followed by several sorts of codas. Either the introduction or the coda may take on large proportions, so large in some cases that they can be interpreted as sections of additional development. Even when this happens, however, the essential AABa form often is preserved intact and visible in movements partaking of first-movement form.

The over-all pattern of the classical sonata, then, though often written and spoken about as though it had been a straitjacket restraining originality and creativity, in actuality was an endlessly variable collection of possible ground-plan suggestions rather than a collection of accurate maps. Each movement could be any one of a number of things, each thing occurring in a wide variety of possible shapes. Yet a sonata—at least, a classical sonata—is unmistakably different from a fantasia or a set of variations or a rhapsodic composition in a single movement. At its heart lies the concept of a several-movement composition in the fast-slow-fast succession (solo sonata and concerto) or the fast-slow-minuet (scherzo)-fast order (symphony and chamber piece). Its dynamism was derived from drama and contrast, the contrast being of speed, of key, of melodic temper and disposition.

The classical sonata exploited the powerful, delicate principle of unity through diversity.

Sonatas for Ensembles: Symphony

What differentiates the form of a classical solo sonata from that of a symphony, the classical sonata for orchestra? Substantially they are alike, if pattern alone be considered, though the symphony very often begins with an introduction leading up to that point within the form at which the solo sonata usually begins. The important differences between the classical solo sonata and the classical symphony tended more and more to be of treatment and expansiveness, though both Beethoven and Schubert, later in their creative lives, composed solo sonatas that justly can be called symphonic in scope. In general, then, a classical symphony is an extended four-movement sonata for orchestra.

Sonata and Chamber Music

What about the difference between a classical solo sonata and a classical string trio, piano trio, string quartet, clarinet quintet, or string sextet? Substantially, all of them are alike in pattern, though in early classical chamber pieces for strings alone the patterns were manipulated so as to give the leading ("first") violin a stellar role and in such later works as posed a wind instrument or piano against strings, the same sort of manipulation was repeated. But in general a classical chamber piece in sonata form is quite simply an extended four-movement sonata for several instruments.

Sonata and Concerto

What differentiates the form of a classical solo sonata from that of a classical concerto for one or more solo instruments and orchestra? Like the early solo sonata, the concerto tends to have only three movements. (The enormous Brahms Concerto for piano and orchestra in Bb major, Opus 83, is uncharacteristically in four movements, but other factors as well make it doubtful that this is rightly to be called a classical concerto.) The scherzo never became as native to the concerto as to the symphony and chamber piece. While making almost invariable use of first-movement form in its opening movement, the concerto modified it. The exposition most often is played complete by the orchestra. Then it is repeated for orchestra and soloist, again in the tonic key, but leading to a second ending that modulates to the dominant. Midway in the recapitulation, but nearer its close than its beginning, the orchestra almost always pauses on a well-defined six-four chord[2]** whereupon the soloist enters with a cadenza,** his big opportunity to show off his technical agility in a longish section given over entirely to him. The cadenza is either apparently or actually improvised, but it must make prominent use of one or more melodies or fragments from the preceding exposition and development. When composers were likely to be their own soloists, cadenzas rarely were written out: it was taken for granted that they would be improvised on the spot. Mozart wrote out cadenzas for only a few of his concertos. Beethoven, however, composed cadenzas for all his concertos, even including one in the published edition of his Fifth Concerto for piano and orchestra, in E♭ major, Opus 79 ("Emperor"). Later composers, chary of the horrors that virtuoso pianists had composed for insertion at the drop of a six-four chord, almost invariably wrote out in full the cadenzas to which they had devoted all the care and imagination that they gave to any other element of composition.

The typical classical-concerto cadenza closed on the dominant key of the movement, thus allowing the harmonic motion back to the tonic to lend satisfying finality to the end of the movement.

[2] A six-four chord is the second inversion of a triad. In C major, for example, the tonic triad is C-E-G. The first inversion of this would be E-G-C, the second inversion G-C-E. If G-C-E were the six-four chord (so called because G and E are separated by the interval of a sixth, G and C by the interval of a fourth) upon which a concerto orchestra were to pause at the juncture under discussion, the deeper instruments very likely would insist upon the G in order to fortify in the listeners' minds the necessary position of the G as the bottom, root, or principal tone of this six-four chord.

A last movement in rondo-form became so usual in the classical solo concerto as to become an integral part of the concerto concept itself.

With these variants, then, and with composers feeling free to insert brief, cadenza-like passages elsewhere than in first movements, the concerto in general was simply an extended three-movement sonata for contending colleagues, the orchestra and one or more soloists. Piano concertos and violin concertos were composed in staggering numbers; soon there were also concertos for almost every conceivable instrument; double concertos for flute and harp, two pianos, violin and viola, and other combinations; and triple concertos like Beethoven's Opus 56, in C major, for violin, cello, and piano. When a concerto-like composition requires more than three solo instruments, it most often will turn out, upon being heard or examined more searchingly, to be closer in style to the baroque *concerto grosso* than to the classical solo concerto, even though its movement patterns follow those of the classical sonata.

CHAPTER XI

Emergence of the Pianoforte

While new ideas about harmony, temperament, instrumental ensemble, and musical patterns were evolving, events of future significance were taking place among the makers and players of the clavichord, harpsichord, and their younger relation, the *pianoforte*—sometimes then called the *fortepiano*, i.e., "loud-soft" instead of the now accepted name, which literally means "soft-loud." (One cannot help speculating that our abbreviation of this word to just *piano* may be unconscious compensation for the fact that we now almost always play it too *forte*.) These occurrences influenced both composers and the very nature of music.

The Psaltery

One of the most ancient of all stringed instruments is the psaltery, a name familiar to the men who translated the King James Bible, who used it to designate instruments that may or may not have been what we now call psalteries. All during the 1300s and 1400s, in fact, the psaltery was played throughout Europe, where it often was mentioned by poets and represented in both painting and sculpture. It then had a small flat surface with raised edges; in effect, it was a box with an open top. Between its raised edges extended strings that the player plucked either with his fingers or by means of a small pick called a plectrum. Whether the psaltery be classified as a variety of harp to which a resonating box has been added or as a rudimentary precursor

155

of that typically Tyrolean instrument the zither, it became an ancestor of the harpsichord, which differs from the psaltery mostly in that its strings are set vibrating by plectra activated from a keyboard rather than by the direct contact of fingers or hand-held plectra.

Dulcimer and Cimbalom

Related closely to the psaltery in basic design was an instrument whose strings were struck by small hammers, usually of wood and held in the player's hands. Of great antiquity also, the dulcimer (mentioned by Coleridge in *Kubla Khan* because of the evocative sound of its name) endured in Western Europe through the seventeenth century, after which it became less familiar there, though as the cimbalom (variously spelled) it survives today among the gypsies of Southeastern Europe. (The cimbalom was employed tellingly by Igor Stravinsky in the chamber orchestra for his "burlesque tale" *Renard,* 1916–17.) In basic principle, the dulcimer is to the pianoforte what the psaltery is to the harpsichord: the most important mechanical difference between a dulcimer and a piano is that the latter's hammers are activated from a keyboard instead of being held in the player's hands.

Clavichord and Harpsichord

The line of descent cannot be documented in equal generations, but what is all but certain is that the dulcimer led to the clavichord—with strings struck by "tangents" activated from a keyboard rather than by hammers held in the player's hands. In turn, the clavichord led to the idea of the pianoforte. Confusion entered the history of these interrelated instruments when early makers and players of the piano spoke and wrote about it as though it had been an "improvement" on the harpsichord—which it clearly was not —rather than as what it really was: an expanded, much more powerful, far more flexible child of the clavichord. The qualities at which these men were aiming as they experimented with the new instrument actually were derived from both clavichord and harpsichord. What they yearned toward was an instrument that could be heard at least as easily and as far as the harpsichord—a clavichord emits a faint sound that must be listened for attentively even in a small room. From the qualities of the clavichord they wished to retain the possibility of sustaining tone and of increasing and decreasing volume at will—the harpsichord could sustain tone scarcely at all, and its only shadings in volume depended upon the player's shifting hand-stops (later pedals) or, on larger examples of the instrument, moving his hands from one bank of keys to another and using coupling devices that permitted more than one string to be plucked by the depressing of one key.

The Earliest Pianofortes

During the seventeenth century, perhaps earlier, various instrument manufacturers had considered the project of applying the clavichord principle of hammer-struck strings to a larger, more powerful instrument. Not until early in the eighteenth century, however, did a harpsichord maker at Padua (later at Florence) make four *"gravicembali col piano e forte"* (harpsichords with loud and soft) that historians have come to accept as the first pianofortes. These four instruments made by Bartolommeo Cristofori (1655–1731) were modern pianos in all fundamental respects except that they had no pedals. They included an escapement mechanism because of which a hammer, having struck its corresponding string, returned to inactive position immediately, thus leaving the struck string to vibrate slowly into silence. They also included separate dampers that came into contact with the strings when the keys were released, thus allowing the player to cut off the sounding vibrations at will. By holding down a given key, that is, the player could keep a desired string vibrating briefly; by releasing the key, he could silence that string at once. At least two pianofortes made by Cristofori survived into the twentieth century. One is (or was) at Leipzig; the other, dated 1720, is in the Metropolitan Museum of Art, in New York.

About 1725, Gottfried Silbermann (1683–1753), a renowned builder of organs and clavichords then living in Dresden, having studied Cristofori's principles of pianoforte construction, imitated the Italian's instruments with superb craftsmanship. Sometime after 1726, Silbermann invited Johann Sebastian Bach, then well known as an authority on organ construction, to try critically two of his instruments. Bach played on them—and said bluntly that they had a heavy touch and that their higher tones were too weak. This seems to have discouraged Silbermann temporarily. But he lived to learn that Bach, visiting Frederick the Great at Potsdam in 1747, played on at least one of the king's three Silbermann pianofortes and found it good.

Developing Forms of Pianoforte

Neither Cristofori's nor Silbermann's pianofortes contained any of the three pedals to be seen on modern grand pianos. These early pianofortes were constructed in the harpsichord shape, roughly the one still used for the grand piano. In England about 1760, the first "square" piano—which is not a square, but an oblong, having its keyboard along one of its longer sides—was built. London became the greatest center of piano building during the heyday of John Broadwood (1732–1812). English pianos then were mostly of the "square" type. The only other basic piano shape, the upright, soon exceeded the square piano in popularity, but the fact that, because its strings run vertically, its dampers must be activated by springs—rather than, as in grand and square pianos, by gravity—has kept it a less satisfactory form. Today, as in the experiments of Cristofori and Silbermann, the best pianos retain the harpsichord shape.

Other important landmarks in the evolution of the modern grand piano and its repertoire were (1) the so-called Viennese action, (2) the American development of the all-metal frame, and (3) the addition of pedals. Other alterations have been numerous: changes in the nature of the strings, hammers, soundboards, and key mechanisms. (Additionally, attempts have been made to produce pianos with more than one keyboard—and therefore capable of producing quarter-tone intervals. To date, these efforts, though mechanically successful, have remained musically sterile.) The three landmarks mentioned above remain of sufficient significance to require brief explanation, particularly as they have influenced the music composed for the piano.

1. In Vienna, Johann Andreas Stein (1728–92) and his son-in-law Johann Andreas Streicher (1761–1833) developed a pianoforte notable for the ease with which its keys could be depressed (a "light touch") and for the elegance—some called it thinness—of its tone, especially as contrasted with the somewhat stiffer, more sonorous Broadwoods. So different were these Viennese pianos from their English contemporaries (which last were widely used as models in France and the Germanies) that they required different techniques of playing. This difference, in turn, had an appreciable influence upon the nature and style of the music composed for them. Both Haydn and Mozart were affected by the light Viennese action, whereas German and British composers almost invariably produced a somewhat "heavier" sort of piano music, influenced to some extent by the Broadwood action and the requisite technique for playing.

2. Whereas earlier pianoforte frames had been wood, upright pianos manufactured in Philadelphia early in the nineteenth century had an interior frame of iron. Not until 1856 did Steinway & Sons make the first grand piano with an all-iron frame. This stronger, more solid framework allowed the rapid development of the huge modern concert grand piano, able to produce auditorium-filling tones because its metal frame will withstand a pull (by the bass strings) of as much as thirty tons. As the size and volume of the piano grew, the thickness of the strings increased too; they too now were entirely of metal. Anyone who attempts to move or to lift a concert grand will retain a clear impression of its massiveness and enormous weight.

3. (a) In 1783, Broadwood patented the so-called "damper," or "sustaining," pedal. This applied to the piano a principle that earlier had been applied rather tentatively in the form of a board moved from side to side by the player's knee. That principle is the removal of all dampers from all strings simultaneously, the result being that no damper

cuts off the vibration of any single string when the player removes his finger from its corresponding key. This has the further result that all the strings are left "open" to vibrate sympathetically.**

(b) The second pedal, called "soft," formerly operated one way in grand pianos, another in uprights. The modern piano has one, two, or three separate strands of wire for each tone, depending upon pitch (the lowest tones requiring one long, thick string, now usually coiled about with thin wire, whereas the middle tones require two or three shorter, thinner strings, the highest tones three very short, very thin strings). In the grand piano, the soft pedal formerly moved all the hammers very slightly to one side, with the result that only one string would be struck for every tone, the unstruck strings thus being left free to vibrate sympathetically, the tonal result being a diminution of volume and an alteration of timbre. (This explains the directions in piano music: *"una corda"*—one string—for soft and *"tre corde"*—three strings—for loud.) But in almost all modern pianos, the pedal simply moves the heads of the hammers nearer to the strings, making it impossible for the player to strike the strings with the usual force. This method of reducing volume has lost the alteration in tone-quality inherent in use of the older mechanism.

(c) A third, middle pedal has been added to many American pianos since Steinway & Sons introduced it in 1874. This so-called "sostenuto" pedal—apparently invented in France in the 1850s—activates a mechanism that takes hold of any single damper at the instant it is raised by the depression of a key, holds it away from the corresponding string or strings, and releases it again only when the pedal (rather than the key) is released by the performer. This complex device makes it possible for the player to keep one tone or group of tones vibrating in isolation while he goes on to play other tones unaffected (except sympathetically) by the tones thus left vibrating. Some twentieth-century composers have evoked magical effects by the use of this pedal, but it never has achieved world-wide acceptance.

Growth of the Pianoforte

The earliest true pianofortes had a compass of four octaves or four and one-half octaves. This has increased gradually to the modern standard of eighty-eight notes, seven and one-quarter octaves. In Mozart's day, it was five octaves. The compositions of Chopin and Schumann were conceived for instruments not wider in compass than six and one-quarter octaves. Nothing in their music gives any evidence that they considered this compass cramping. The impatient Beethoven, however, was driven to altering the very contours of certain melodic passages repeated in various pitches by the fact that he wanted—but could not command—notes higher than any existing on the pianos of his day. Urgent demands by composers finally forced piano manufacturers to add more and more notes to their instruments.

The Kingdoms of the Pianoforte

Purcell and Handel in England; Johann Sebastian Bach in Germany; Couperin and Rameau in France; Domenico Scarlatti in Italy and Spain—these men and their coevals had composed for the harpsichord and, in some cases, for the clavichord. But beginning with C. P. E. Bach, Johann Christian Bach, Haydn, and Mozart, the composers who evolved the classical sonata and concerto forms conceived their keyboard music more and more for the pianoforte. By the era of Schubert and Beethoven, composers had begun to think in pianoforte terms inapplicable to performance on the earlier instruments. Mendelssohn, Chopin, Schumann, and Liszt at times drew the very texture and profile of their keyboard music from the piano's evolving capabilities. Debussy and Ravel intensified this tendency, until much of their keyboard music (Debussy's in particular) seems to have been produced almost as much by the character of the piano itself as by the composing imagination. Still another tendency, that of treating the modern concert grand piano as a percussion instrument—which in one sense, of course, it certainly is—became noticeable in the music of many later composers: Prokofiev, Bartók, and Aaron Copland are examples. These men have removed the style of keyboard music as far as it is now possible to imagine from the flowery traces and tripping graces of a Couperin.

Compositions for both clavichord and harpsichord were strewn with ornamental figurations of many sorts—so many sorts, indeed, that the mere accurate reading of much of this music sometimes parallels the solving of puzzles. The desired ornaments commonly were not written out as groups of visible notes, but either were left to the discretion of the performer or were indicated by conventional signs. Either of these latter procedures had the advantage, on the engraved page of music, of leaving the central harmonic and melodic outlines clear. The notes included in such ornaments as turns, appoggiaturas, mordents, and trills—dozens of others existed—thus were correctly indicated as extra or auxiliary tones, decorations or ornaments of the basic music. (For definitions of these and other ornaments, see the Glossary, pages 365–71.)

Music of the Harpsichord

The frequency of ornaments in harpsichord music was in part composers' response to the instrument's inability to sustain tone. Composers and harpsichordists had a feeling that they must somehow fill in the otherwise inescapable near-silences between tones, and without hurrying the tempo of the music. They accomplished this in part by filling the interstices with ornamental notes. This necessity was still felt with respect to the relatively weak early pianos, but it grew less imperative as later instruments expanded in sonority and became more and more capable of sustaining tone. The keyboard music of the sixteenth and seventeenth centuries (except that for organ, par excellence the sustaining instrument) remains dead when it is played without wisely chosen ornamentation. Early eighteenth-century piano music is scarcely different, though in it the performer usually is assisted by the increasing tendency to indicate ornaments by conventional signs. But late-eighteenth-century piano music has begun to shed ornaments, which by then have come to be used sparingly and largely for melodic reasons rather than in order to keep the instrument sounding.

Another reason for the profusion of ornaments in harpsichord music was that, when played before important melody tones, they made a kind of accentuation possible on an instrument on which otherwise what we now understand by accentuation—the playing of a note or a chord more forcefully than surrounding notes or chords—was all but impossible. The disappearance of this reason likewise diminished the frequent use of ornaments.

Several kinds of music were unsatisfactory, except in a relative sense, on the harpsichord. Undecorated slow or stately music, for example, came from the harpsichord as a series of widely separated tones or chords. Grand or thunderous effects of volume were beyond its strength, except—again—relatively. The style of keyboard playing known as *legato* (literally, bound), in which no perceptible silence occurs between one note or chord and the next, became fully possible only on the pianoforte, making available to composers and pianists effects of slow or stately music without ornamentation. In fact, the pianoforte opened up to composers a universe of keyboard-produced sound approximating that previously available only on the organ.

The Kingdom of the Harpsichord

Yet certain abilities of the harpsichord were lost to the piano. You cannot on a piano play more than one tone by striking a single key. Nor can you select one of several different timbres by shifting pedals or play interlacing melodies in two distinct but simultaneous timbres. These advantages disappeared with the older instrument. The twentieth century has had the great musical luck to hear the restoration of the harpsichord, after much too long a time away, to the company of living instruments. Largely, that restoration resulted from the determined labor of one woman, Wanda Landowska. What must be said, however, is that the metal harpsichord on which Mme Landowska commonly performed was a much more powerful instrument than the harpsichords in use when the pianoforte was invented. To hear her play, even if only by way of phonograph recordings, is a surpassing musical experience, but it would proliferate error to suppose that what is being heard is the exact equivalent of what composers for the harpsichord conceived for smaller rooms and far less sonorous instruments. Mme Landowska's performances always were far more exact historically when she played music composed for the harpsichord (and largely for her) by twentieth-century composers. But part of her passionate argument still defies contradiction: to hear the harpsichord music of Johann Sebastian Bach, Couperin, Rameau or Domenico Scarlatti played on a piano is to hear what amounts to a transcription of it. In order to realize what those composers intended, it must be heard on a harpsichord.

Triumphs of the Pianoforte

Haydn wrote a large amount of charming music for the piano, but his richest creations were in orchestral music, chamber music, and oratorio. With Mozart, however, the piano assisted at the birth of some of the greatest music ever composed, a series of concertos for piano and orchestra into which he decanted many of his richest musical ideas and structural inventions. Many critics have ranked Mozart's numerous piano concertos above all but the greatest of his symphonic and operatic music, as they certainly are superior to his violin concertos or his sonatas for solo piano. Only he up to the time of his death in 1791 had composed music for piano that no one would hesitate to consider alongside his best chamber music, *Le Nozze di Figaro, Don Giovanni,* and *Die Zauberflöte.*

Beethoven was not so prolific of piano concertos as Mozart had been, but three or four of those which he composed are music on the very highest level. More important than Beethoven's piano concertos to the historic evolution of music—equal in interest to his chamber music and symphonies—are his sonatas for solo piano. In them, at last, he may be said to have forced the piano to do more than it can do. Some of his famous "thirty-two" belong amid the most popular serious music ever created; scarcely one of them is less than a masterwork. In Beethoven's strong hands, as in Mozart's infinitely dexterous ones, the instrument invented so short a time before had become the expressive peer of the organ, the chamber ensemble, and the orchestra.

The most fruitful and enduring technical achievements of the period arching from the birth of Rameau in 1683 to the death of Beethoven in 1827 were equal temperament, the symphonic orchestra, the sonata concept in all its variations, and the invention and rapid development of the pianoforte. Other achievements were of equal importance artistically. But those four made possible most of the music we listen to most often today.

No other instrument since the era when the organ reigned supreme has attracted so many composers so strongly or has had so enduring an influence on the style, the very nature, of music itself, as the piano. The pipe organ once was properly known as the king of instruments. But whatever its powers and unique abilities, it has been no ruling monarch for more than a century now. No instrument, of course, genuinely "rules" music. But there is no doubt that the piano became—and to our day has remained—the single most important musical instrument of Western civilization.

CHAPTER XII

Instruments Played Together

Almost since the eras during which musical instruments other than the organ first came into being—and certainly from the hour at which they began to be played independently, apart from their roles in supporting or accompanying the human voice—they must have been played together. No documentary proof survives, but they probably were joined first in twos, then in threes, and then in increasingly larger numbers. Music for instrumental groups became a recognized form during the Middle Ages. It was composed by such musicians as Obrecht, Isaak, and Paulus von Hofhaimer (1459–1537?) in the fifteenth century; by Adrian Willaert and others in the sixteenth; by very numerous men in the seventeenth. The instrumental *canzona*, as some of these composers handled it, was an ancestral version of what we now call chamber music.

During the baroque era, the *sonata da chiesa* and *sonata da camera*, the two principal forms of trio sonata, likewise were ancestors of modern chamber music, though they led along diverging lines to two sorts of music between which musicians since the eighteenth century have tended to distinguish sharply: orchestral music and music for chamber ensembles. With the arrival on the musical scene of such composers as Boccherini, Haydn, and Mozart, it becomes essential to understand this distinction in terminology.

Chamber Music

Chamber music (*musica da camera*, literally music to be played in a room) is, in the modern understanding, for an

167

instrumental group of relatively small size, usually with only one player to each part. Its over-all emphasis is on ensemble activity; except in certain special cases, individual parts stand out from the general texture only temporarily and occasionally.

Chamber music for two players is comparatively rare. When it occurs, it usually is referred to as a sonata or duo. But music for two instruments (violin and harpsichord or piano, cello and piano, and so forth) often in reality is solo music with a keyboard-instrument accompaniment, and therefore cannot be called chamber music accurately. Music for three instruments is called a trio (string trio if all three instruments are stringed; piano trio if one instrument is a piano; horn trio if one is a horn, and so forth).

The String Quartet

Because four-part (four-voice) harmony has proved especially and enduringly satisfactory—it originated in the use of one high and one low male voice, one high and one low female voice—chamber music for four instruments has been composed in much greater quantities than any other sort. The quartet, and particularly the quartet for four stringed instruments (as distinct from the piano quartet, for example), became in the eighteenth century, and ever since has remained, the central type of chamber music. Luigi Boccherini (1743–1805) in Italy, France, and Spain, and Haydn in Austria set the form, if not entirely the classic texture, of the string quartet. The standard group of instruments came to be two violins (called first and second), viola, and cello. At the outset, the first violin tended to dominate this ensemble, so that violinists often spoke and wrote as if they played quartets by themselves. But the string quartet came more and more to be a genre in which the participating instruments played roles of approximately equal importance.

Purists point out that many early string quartets at first were performed by more than four players. Parts (voices), that is, were doubled and tripled, the result being quasi-orchestral, rather than chamber, music if our definitions of the two genres be applied with ironclad literalness. In the spirit of those definitions, however, we may doubt reasonably that any music for no more than four unchanging parts or voices is really orchestral, however many performers may be playing it.

Chamber-ensemble compositions for more than four players came to be known by numerical terms, beginning with quintet and going through sextet, septet, and octet to nonet. Chamber music for more than nine performers customarily goes under such other names as serenade, divertimento, chamber symphony, and rhapsody. Arnold Schoenberg, Paul Hindemith, and some other twentieth-century composers often have called it, in complete simplicity, *Kammermusik,* *i.e.,* chamber music.

The sonata form, as we have seen, soon invaded chamber music so completely as all but to banish other, older patterns from it. Trios, quartets, quintets all became sonatas for small ensemble. And though the conception of chamber music, and particularly of the string quartet, is difficult to date accurately, the genre certainly has maintained its position in the affections of composers and performers (though not always in those of audiences) without interruption from the time of that inception to the present day. Without as much alteration in its pervading patterns as has modified orchestral, solo instrumental, and vocal music, chamber music nonetheless has changed with the times.

Changes in Chamber Music

After the classical chamber compositions of Boccherini, Haydn, Mozart, and the early Beethoven, the man who began to expand, alter, and reinterpret the genre was Beethoven himself. Schubert led it toward romanticism; it was favored by such central romantics as Mendelssohn and Schumann. During the second half of the nineteenth century, it was employed by César Franck, Brahms, Dvořák, and others as an intimately personal vehicle. Such later composers as Debussy, Ravel, Schoenberg, Bartók, and Stravinsky have created notable chamber music; in much of it, the idiom differs greatly from that of Boccherini or

Haydn, but the structural patterns, the movement-by-movement layout or ground plan, have tended to change surprisingly little. Looked at structurally, the chamber piece has preserved its eighteenth-century patterns no matter what the musical ideas and dialects with which composers have chosen to erect and fill out those patterns.

Ideas of "Purity"

With knowing snobbishness, chamber music often is cited and looked upon as the "purest" variety of music. By this curious adjective apparently is meant that the string quartet, for example, is made of four melodic parts that can be apprehended distinctly and that it gets along stoically without the seductiveness of orchestral color, which the writer or speaker assumes to be used to cover up poverty of honest musical thought. But this sort of musical hierarchy, of distinctions in the void, is devoid of meaning. All forms of music are equally "pure" if they are used purely, employed with taste and understanding of what potentialities each of them possesses. A chamber piece by a sensitive creator often contains sovereign music of the noblest or the most delightful sort. But so, in the hands of a sensitive composer, does music for a solo instrument, for vocal soloist or ensemble, for full symphony orchestra, for all the varied forces of opera—and for various "impure" mixtures of them all. Any attempt to enthrone chamber (or any other variety of) music at the peak of musical society can be no more than a rationalization of personal preference. It should be accorded no more serious consideration than can be given to the opposite sort of judgment, which calls all chamber music dull, dry, "purely" intellectual scraping, striking, and blowing.

Listening to Chamber Music

By the same token, it is stultifying to listen to a Mozart string quartet, a Beethoven piano trio, a Schumann piano quintet, or a Ravel septet as though it were orchestral music in miniature. Its whole philosophy and psychology, so to speak, differ from the philosophies and psychologies of both orchestral and solo music. It is music whose fullest effect depends upon the audibility of several separate parts—not always, or even usually, in the polyphonic sense of independent melodies, but in a more purely instrumental sense. It is music in which, except to a narrow extent, the special tone colors or timbres of the instruments are not of first importance; and in which polyphony of one sort or another is likely to have a major constructive role. It cannot depend upon very wide-swinging changes of volume, for the range of volume change available to its performing instruments usually is limited. It is commonly softer than orchestral music, and it tends toward the intimate and the directly personal. Best listened to in a small auditorium (or, best of all, participated in by oneself as a performer), chamber music possibly requires more co-operation by the listener—particularly the uninitiate listener—than any other sort of music.

Orchestral Music

Orchestral music is composed for a large body of varied instruments in which many of the parts or voices customarily are played in unison by groups of the same instrument or of different instruments. (The band is a variant of the orchestra. A typical band, and especially a military band, contains no—or very few—stringed instruments, being composed chiefly of winds, among which the brasses are likely to dominate. The jazz band, however, very often is actually a chamber ensemble in which each player is assigned a part or voice.)

The Modern Orchestra

Except in special cases, the orchestra, from the day of the Mannheim ensemble to our own day, has contained more stringed instruments than any other kind. The modern orchestra usually has about half as many wind instruments as strings. The winds are about equally divided between woodwinds (especially members of the clarinet, flute, and oboe families) and brasses (especially horns, trumpets, trombones, and tubas). Somewhat fewer usually are the percussion instruments, which may include drums, xylophone, tambourine, cymbals, triangle, gongs, and various noise-makers. A modern symphony orchestra very often contains upward of sixty stringed instruments: violins in the two groups still known as "first" and "second" violins—the difference between them being in what they are assigned to play rather than in the instruments themselves; violas; violoncellos (cellos); doublebasses; and harp.

A modern orchestra may include from ten to fifteen woodwinds: flutes, oboes, English horns, bassoons, clarinets; the same number of brasses: horns, trumpets, trombones, and tubas; and ten or a dozen percussion instruments, including timpani (kettledrums), glockenspiel (a small metal xylophone of bell-like sound), cymbals, triangle, tambourine, celesta (in effect a glockenspiel with a keyboard), and piano. The piano also may be considered a nonorchestral instrument or an orchestral solitary. Every instrument—and the human voice—has at one time or another been included in a symphonic orchestra—from the organ to the saxophone, from the bugle to the policeman's whistle, and including such nonmusical instruments as the typewriter, the automobile horn, a paper bag full of sand, and shaken oyster shells. But the instruments fundamental to the constitution of most symphonic orchestras have remained about the same for nearly two centuries, though their number and relative importance have fluctuated. At full strength, and when playing Berlioz, Wagner, or post-Wagnerian music, a symphony orchestra well may consist of more than one hundred players all actively making their instruments sound.

The Earliest Orchestra

The orchestra did not begin as so gigantic a machine. Giovanni Gabrieli, who composed what many musicologists consider to have been the earliest truly orchestral music, was content with bassoons, cornetts, trombones, and violins as support for the human voices in his *Sacrae symphoniae*, composed near the end of the 1500s. Monteverdi used specifically orchestral group tone colorings for emotional-musical effect, but did not hit upon the string-dominated orchestra. His instrumental ensemble remained that of the Renaissance, in which wind instruments supply the foundation, the strings being brought in chiefly for pathetic or other specifically emotional effects.

The Baroque Orchestra

The baroque age, musically culminating in Bach and Handel, produced the string-dominated instrumental ensemble—almost, but not exactly, the classical symphonic orchestra. (It is as clear that the sonata-symphony produced the symphonic orchestra as it is that the emergence of the symphonic orchestra hastened the development of the classical symphony.) During the seventeenth century, no crucial importance was placed upon individual instrumental timbres, as is proved by the widespread practice of thorough bass, the writing out of parts only for melody and bass, the other parts being filled in more or less ad libitum. In such almost orchestral compositions as many of Bach's and Handel's, nevertheless, a transitional step is audible from the Renaissance ensemble (which in reality was a wind-dominated chamber group) to the modern orchestra and its division into "choirs" of instruments. Members of the violin family, gradually besting their viol cousins, made possible domination by the stringed instruments. The winds tended toward standardization: flutes, horns, and oboes (clarinets appeared later) were increasingly basic and normal.

Bach did not assign carefully to each instrument or choir of instruments—all meticulously indicated in a written score —a part that it could play better than another instrument or choir. When assigning a part to an instrument, Bach most often appears to have been considering only the instrument's relative audibility and its compass. As a result, no basic structural damage would be done to many of Bach's instrumental pieces if musical lines now assigned to flutes were transferred to violins. To make a similar change in music by Wagner or Rimsky-Korsakov, Berlioz or Ravel, would be to destroy a significant part of the composer's musical conception. In Bach's instrumentation, the parts very often actually are interchangeable. Nor did he often alter instrumental coloring midway in a piece or movement by changing instruments, a practice exceedingly common among later composers, a practice without which Gustav Mahler or Debussy or Stravinsky would have felt constrained if not frozen.

Handel, composing operas and highly dramatic oratorios, displayed more interest than Bach in the notable individualities of ensemble instruments, more awareness of the distinctive potentialities locked up in the timbres of instruments grouped within a larger group. He scored for special instruments briefly for special effects (the contrabassoon, for example, and the harp). He needed to be more constructively aware of the architectural possibilities of contrasted timbres than Bach had reason to be. But among the great composers, Jean-Philippe Rameau first showed some of that delicate care in selecting instruments for their color and special capabilities—as well as their volume and range—which became one of the fruitful constructive principles of symphonic music. Contrasts of timbre attracted Rameau, who not only established in French music a style that still was evident in both Debussy and Ravel, but also helped toward the formation of the classical symphony orchestra.

Importance of the
Mannheim Orchestra

The Mannheim orchestra was of enduring historic importance, as we have seen, chiefly for its development of effects and for its conclusive demonstrations of the values of rehearsal and precision. In the Mannheim ensemble, the importance of the stringed instruments was increased enormously, in part because the strings responded well to the desire of Stamitz and his associates for prolonged crescendos and decrescendos, trills, and sudden louds and softs. In the works composed with that ensemble in mind, instrumental ensemble music reached, from a technical point of view, an unprecedented complexity, though the compositions of the Stamitzes, Holzbauer, Richter, Cannabich, and the other Mannheimers have proved to be of smaller purely musical value than, on one side, the masterworks of Bach and Handel and, on the other, those of Haydn and Mozart.

The harpsichord was maintained in the ensemble in its *continuo* role even in symphonies that Carl Philipp Emanuel Bach composed nearly three decades after his father's death in 1750. These four interesting works, in which the sonata-symphony was all but born, require the later standard groups of stringed instruments and groups of eight (sometimes seven) winds: bassoons, flutes, horns, and oboes. Looking closely at most of the single instrumental lines in a C. P. E. Bach symphony, one can almost determine by their contours alone which instrument each of them was intended for. Similar examination of a part in one of his father's compositions often would produce only data for the vaguest guesswork. That is to say, the son, his father's inferior in most musical respects, belonged to a later, more nearly orchestral, era. He labored at the very portal to the age during which Haydn and Mozart would consolidate the orchestra and its primary position.

The Classical Orchestra
and the Modern

Experimenting with orchestral writing during a long lifetime, Haydn gradually dropped *continuo* and harpsichord from the ensemble. He slowly increased the proportion of strings to winds, brought instruments in or dropped them in the midst of symphonies or movements, often assigned leading melodies momentarily to a wind instrument chosen for its peculiar timbre, and at last formalized the make-up of the orchestral choirs. In Mozart's last orchestral works and the later among Haydn's more than one hundred symphonies, the orchestra commonly consists of first and second violins, violas, cellos, doublebasses, two bassoons, two clarinets, two flutes, two horns, two oboes, and two kettledrums. With this aggregation—perhaps the earliest that can be described accurately as a symphony orchestra—

these men created masterworks that really were something new. This orchestra sufficed (with constant changes, subtractions, and additions) for Beethoven and Schubert. Basically it sufficed until only yesterday, though it increased in size, though alterations in the manufacture of several instruments changed their powers and colors, and though new instruments occasionally (sometimes temporarily) have been added to it.

What has happened in less than two centuries to the size of the forces that a composer might demand can be seen vividly in a comparison of a "large" orchestra of Haydn's day[1] and a large orchestra of the twentieth century:

Orchestra of Haydn's "London" Symphony (No. 104, D minor-major), composed in 1795	Orchestra of Stravinsky's *Le Sacre du printemps,* composed in 1912–13
2 flutes	2 piccolos
	2 flutes
	1 flute in G
2 oboes	4 oboes (one interchangeable with a second English horn)
	1 English horn
	1 clarinet in E♭
2 clarinets	3 clarinets (one interchangeable with a second bass clarinet)
	1 bass clarinet
2 bassoons	4 bassoons (one interchangeable with a second contrabassoon)
	1 contrabassoon
2 horns	8 horns (two interchangeable with Bayreuth tubas)
	1 trumpet in D

[1] Great masses of instruments had been brought together on festal occasions during earlier periods. In London in 1749, for example, the overture to Handel's *Royal Fireworks Music* was performed in the open air by twenty-four oboes, twelve bassoons, nine trumpets, nine horns, one contrabassoon, three pairs of kettledrums, and a huge bass cornet known as a serpent. But that ensemble was a variety of ceremonial band rather than an orchestra, and in any case was notable chiefly for its rare monstrousness.

2 trumpets	3 trumpets
	1 bass trumpet in E♭
	3 trombones
	2 tubas
2 kettledrums	4 kettledrums; small kettledrum; bass drum; tambourine; cymbals; antique cymbals; triangle; tam-tam; rasp or scratcher
strings	strings

Leaving out of consideration the stringed instruments and the percussion, Haydn's orchestra in this case called for ten players, Stavinsky's for thirty-eight. Until Haydn went to London, he considered himself fortunate when, with strings and drums, he commanded any number of players in excess of twenty-four. *Le Sacre du printemps* cannot be played adequately by less than eighty. The point, of course, is not that Haydn did so much with so comparatively little, or that Stravinsky required huge forces. Supposing Haydn and Stravinsky to have been equally in command of the forces at their disposition, any contrast of importance between them cannot be made on the basis of size, but only on that of musical ideas conveyed or elicited by their music. Both were complete orchestral masters, though in wholly different ways.

The important point here is that the modern orchestra, starting out as an expansion of the chamber group,[2] has developed into the mightiest musical instrument ever devised. At each step of its development, men able to use it creatively have taken advantage of its tremendous flexibility and variety to convey many of their richest musical conceptions.

[2] Aggregations of instruments smaller in number than the great symphonic orchestras often operate under such designations as sinfonietta, symphonette, and chamber orchestra. "Chamber orchestra," though superficially self-contradictory, is the most useful term for this very useful ensemble of intermediate size: it truly is orchestral, but keeps somewhat to more intimacy of texture and aim than is possible to a group of eighty or ninety musicians performing in a very large auditorium. A considerable repertoire of music exists for which the chamber orchestra is far more appropriate than its larger relation: much of this was composed in the eighteenth century or is the work of twentieth-century composers.

CHAPTER XIII

The Evolution of Opera

Opera, which had been launched on its long, colorful history in the early morning of monody by Florentines yearning to revive Greek performances of drama, first had enlisted the services of a great musical creator when Monteverdi had turned his attention to it in *La Favola d'Orfeo* (1607). In it and in his other musico-dramatic works, Monteverdi exercised his genius on the combining of text, music, and theatrical presentation. Florence, Rome, and Venice thereafter had produced operas and almost-operas in huge supply. Many of these were composed by men of highly cherishable talent. They contained overtures, sinfonie, arias, concerted numbers, and choruses. Turning their backs on the dry recitative of the Florentine way-breakers, other composers had mixed polyphony with monody, coming to believe that almost any style or texture of music could be drawn upon in building operatic structures.

Opera in Rome and Venice

As the seventeenth century wore on, arias and concerted numbers (duets, trios, and quartets) became more than ever different in musical texture from the merely reportorial or plot-forwarding recitative. The chorus as employed by such Roman composers as Stefano Landi (1590?–1655?), Luigi Rossi (1598–1653), and Michelangelo Rossi (seventeenth century) played an increasingly dramatic role in the presentation of the libretto story. Comic episodes and interludes, both within serious operas and as performed between the acts, became common, being called for as contrast to and relief from the prevailing solemn classic-mythological or Graeco-Roman historical plots. The vocal agility of superbly trained singers—sopranos especially, both female and male (*castrati***)—won public enthusiasm and was catered to by composers. In the Venetian operas of Pietro Francesco Cavalli (1602–76) and Marc'Antonio Cesti (1618–69), the grandeurs and complexities of the still-young art form reached amazing intensity. Involving many singers in tortuous plots, filling well-equipped stages with eye-dazzling pictures, catering to the growing taste for comic interludes, and generally enlarging all the involved elements to a size that would have astonished and displeased Caccini and Peri, the Venetians set manners that have persisted ever since in the Italian conception of opera. With their works, in fact, opera as a theatrical spectacle in the Italian style had been born.

Opera in France: Lully

In France, meanwhile, that other Italian, Jean-Baptiste Lully, had begun to suggest the Franco-Italian manners of opera. In Italy itself, opera succeeded at once because it supplied attractive theater to a spectacle-hungry people. In seventeenth-century France, on the contrary, opera at first suffered strong competition from ballet and from the well-entrenched spoken drama of Corneille, Molière, and Racine. Lully simply imported ballet into the expansible precincts of opera and—from the French point of view—naturalized its presence there forever. He paid to the instrumental textures of his operas far more thoughtful attention than was lavished on that musical element by most of his Italian predecessors and contemporaries, Monteverdi being one notable exception. Too, with serious spoken drama alive and popular, Lully insisted more than most Italians on strength and theatrical credibility in the plots and situations of his librettos. Not for him the long *scene* (elaborate formal arias, often *da capo*) of an Alessandro Scarlatti, those magnificent musical outbursts that tended to congeal all dramatic action and attract attention to their own expressiveness. Rather, Lully favored brief, dancelike songs, called *airs,* often built over actual dance rhythms. (For Lully's treatment of the overture and of recitative, see pages 107–8.)

The Lullyan variety of opera was carried forward, not materially altered in structure, by Jean-Philippe Rameau, who arrived at opera when he was fifty years old and already a renowned composer and theorist. Immediately, he was attacked in Lully's name as a defiler of tradition; actually, he merely intensified tendencies clear in Lully's operas. He sacrificed interest in the voice itself to interest in the orchestra, and was not above suspending story and action for the time required by a good ballet. He wrote magnificent overtures in a manner somewhere between the so-called "French" overture and the sonata. He applied his advanced harmonic ideas and resources to opera just as he applied them to other musical genres. And he sought, in the opera orchestra as elsewhere, for characteristic instrumental effects, for the touches that each individual instrument could produce better than any other.

Opera in Germany:
Handel and Keiser

On the operatic scene in Germany appeared in 1705 a composer greater than even Monteverdi or Rameau: at Hamburg in that year *Almira* was sung, the first of nearly forty Italian operas by George Frideric Handel. This was seventy-eight years after the first known opera to a German text, Schütz's *Daphne,* had been sung in 1627. Probably the first opera of any sort sung in Germany, *Daphne* was, as already has been pointed out, an adaptation of a translation of Peri's *Dafne;* unfortunately that early victim of the insuperable difficulties of translating opera has not survived—the score of *Daphne* fell victim to a fire in 1760. Handel's *Almira,* though produced at Hamburg, was composed to an Italian text. In no important aspect was it a Germanic opera, though Handel had absorbed much of what he knew about operatic techniques from another German, the director of the Hamburg Opera, Reinhard Keiser (1674–1739), a composer now recklessly neglected. Keiser, using both German and Italian texts, and Handel, using only Italian, composed mostly the variety of opera which has come to be called "Neapolitan" whether composed in Naples, Vienna, or Hamburg.

"Neapolitan" Opera

"Neapolitan" opera was, first of all, serious, usually tragic (of Handel's many operas, only one—*Serse*, which contains the world-famous "Largo"—is comic), what the Italians called *opera seria*. It displayed small tolerance for comic interludes, being closer in purely narrative solemnity to the concepts of the Florentine pioneers of opera. It most often was divided into three longish acts, each of them divided roughly into two sections: first, one devoted to getting on with the story, in recitative, mostly *recitativo secco;* then a section given over to commenting upon the recently revealed plot events, this mostly in arias. Neapolitan operas were singing operas, largely for solo singers, and in them very little of importance was assigned to the instruments once the overture, if any, had been played—though notable exceptions to this generalization occurred. Each of the chief singers was assigned arias of a certain importance at predetermined locations in the acts, and battles were fought if these recognized traditions were flouted even momentarily. The singer and what she or he sang were all-important. Neapolitan operas seemed more likely than most to develop into an essentially undramatic chain of arias.

Bel Canto and Virtuoso Singing

Wherever composed and wherever sung, Neapolitan opera was the special habitat of the surpassing vocal technique that later became known as *bel canto* (beautiful song). This technique was accused of sacrificing "feeling" (by which the accuser far too often meant a tearful vocal quality) and of subordinating to displays the "characteristic" vocal shadings and colorings made mandatory by the changing emotions and situations of the characters in the libretto. Its prime emphasis was on beauty, accuracy, and brilliance of tone production. As practiced by the best female sopranos, male sopranos, and—more rarely—other voices of the eighteenth century, it provided vocal exhibitions that now can only be imagined. Later eras have developed other vocal techniques and emotional emphases with other values, but the most important of the many reasons why operas in the Neapolitan style now are sung seldom is that few modern singers can surmount their difficulties and, at the same time, sing expressively. An idea of what a singer could be expected to do in the course of a Neapolitan-style opera can be derived from the following measures from a solo vocal line in an aria from *Vespasiano,* an opera by Attilio Ariosti (1666–1740?):

Vor-rei che dar di fos-ser gli sguar-di

per la-cer-ar-ti in mil-le par - - - -

- - - - - - - - - - - ti in pet-to il cor

The Opera Libretto:
Zeno and Metastasio

To composers' demands for librettos that would (in their view) be dramatic and at the same time credible, and simultaneously would supply each first lady (*prima donna*), first man (*primo uomo*), second lady (*seconda donna*), and so forth with the essential arias at the required junctures, two literary men of talent responded. The earlier of them, Apostolo Zeno (1668–1750), served as court poet both in

Vienna and in Venice. The other, Pietro Trapassi, known as Metastasio (1698–1782), court poet at Vienna for the last fifty-two years of his long life, excelled Zeno and became librettist to a century. He was so adept at ringing acceptable changes on the narrowly delimited form of the Neapolitan libretto that more than one thousand eighteenth-century operas used one or another of his texts. The same Metastasian text was set by ten, twenty, even forty different composers. Johann Adolf Hasse (1699–1783) set one of Metastasio's most popular librettos—*Artaserse*—three different times; he boasted that he had composed operas to all but one of the Italian's numerous operatic texts. Handel, Haydn, Mozart—even so purely nineteenth-century a composer in a different manner as Giacomo Meyerbeer (1791–1864)—found Metastasio's texts useful. His popularity as a provider of opera librettos never has been approached by that of any other writer.

Mostly stories about personages from Greek or Roman mythology or pseudo-history, the finest operas of the Neapolitan style were grave, exquisitely constructed, and prodigal of melody. From a later point of view, they became as static as a hall of statues. Aside from the stage pictures, often of extravagant complexity and notable beauty, they offered the eighteenth-century operagoer supremely supple and accomplished singers performing difficult feats with apparent ease, clusters of the most luscious melodies ever imagined, and opportunities to enjoy and contrast the highly conventionalized dexterities of librettists and composers and stage designers. The audiences did not object (as why should they have objected, being given so much?) if what they saw and heard really was a concert in costume performed before handsome scenery. They did not expect—nor should we expect when we listen to eighteenth-century opera—the emotional "realism" or stormy musical dramatics that the operas of Richard Wagner, Giuseppe Verdi, and Richard Strauss have taught twentieth-century operagoers to consider the normal ingredients of "good" opera. On its own terms, an opera by Handel or by such greatly gifted Neapolitans as Tommaso Traetta (1727–79) and Niccolò Jommelli (1714–74) is in its way as reasonable, as secure an artistic structure, as *musically* expressive, as *Carmen, Aida, Tristan und Isolde, Elektra,* or *Tosca.* It is only more strictly musical in its appeal and—all appearances to the contrary notwithstanding—far more difficult to sing.

Opera and the Comic Spirit

But Neapolitan opera, for all its stores of beauty, did not provide a home for the comic spirit. As mentioned earlier, comic interludes or episodes had made their way into Roman opera very early. Even Monteverdi's *L'Incoronazione di Poppea* (1642) had room for comedy. The future Pope Clement IX, while still Giulio, Cardinal Rospigliosi, wrote comic librettos that were used in the middle 1600s for some of the earliest known entirely comic operas. One composer, Marco Marazzoli (?–1662) was involved in two settings of Rospigliosi librettos: in *Che soffre speri* (1639) with Virgilio Mazzocchi (1597–1646), who was primarily a religious; in *Dal male il bene* (1654) with Antonio Maria Abbatini (1595?–1677), who once was invited by Pope Urban VIII to revise the Hymnal. This Rospigliosi-Marazzoli-Abbatini collaboration is notable because it helped to establish the practice of ending comic operas with ensembles in which all of the principal characters sing together.

Intermezzo and Opera Buffa

Zeno and Metastasio genuinely disliked the comic spirit in opera. Their librettos "reformed" opera by removing from it not only integral comic episodes, but also the very possibility of breaking the grave, mostly tragic surface of an opera by playing a frivolous, often hilarious, brief comic musical play between its acts. The comic *intermezzo,* responding as it did to an enduring human desire, and having been pushed out of *opera seria,* gradually evolved separately into *opera buffa* (comic opera), generally a one-act or two-act form. The most renowned *opera buffa* of the first half of the eighteenth century was *La Serva padrona* (1733), composed by Giovanni Battista Pergolesi (1710–36), which still occasionally is staged. Having only three characters, one of them a mute, *La Serva padrona* is easy to stage, and it became internationally popular. It is marked by broad farce, music often of the warmest good humor, and great swiftness of action.

Operatic "War" in Paris

Pergolesi's masterly trifle was performed in Paris in 1752 by a company of players known as Les Bouffons (the comedians). And that performance led directly to a protracted controversy that became known as the *guerre des bouffons;* in that "war of the comedians," the ever-double nature of opera was clarified again, but not reconciled to itself. On one side of this peculiarly Parisian "war" stood Louis XV, Mme de Pompadour, a large section of the high nobility, and most of the wealthiest merchants. This party said (and believed) that it was defending French opera—the French brand of serious opera as practiced by Lully, Rameau, and their successors—though in actual fact it was involved in a foredoomed attempt to keep alive the pure baroque spirit that had given birth to *opera seria,* and which in France had begun to die out by 1752. Against that pro-baroque party stood the queen, Marie Leszczynska, the most learned and accomplished French musicians, such intellectuals as Jean Le Rond d'Alembert, Denis Diderot, Baron Melchior von Grimm, and—most important and vociferous of all—that apostle of the natural, Jean-Jacques Rousseau, himself a musician of learning and some talent. This party, whatever its stated motives and published tenets, was defending the newborn spirit of the rococo, which was destined to replace the baroque.

The actual, as against the literary, war of the comedians lasted one day. It was won by the "queen's party" for the rococo, but its supporters were very unclear as to what they had won. The manager of the theater at which *La Serva padrona* had set off the war announced an opera called *Les Troqueurs,* which, he said, was to be sung in French though it had been composed in Italian. The use of an Italian composer was intended to win over the "queen's party," which believed that it was fighting for Italian opera; that the opera was to be sung in French was intended to please the King-Pompadour party, which said that it was defending opera in the national tongue. *Les Troqueurs* succeeded in pleasing almost everyone, though it appears to have been indifferent stuff. Then the daring manager revealed that in reality it was the work of Antoine d'Auvergne (1713–97), a Frenchman. In short, it was *opera buffa* in French: *opéra-bouffe*. Other French composers, Rameau among them, earlier had tried in vain to interest Parisian audiences in other forms of comic opera. But it had taken a Paris "war" and a cleverly stage-managed deception to win that public to it. Operatically speaking, the *guerre des bouffons* ended the exclusive dominance of baroque *opera seria* in France. On the international scene, it made way for the so-called "operatic reform" of which the central figures were Christoph Willibald von Gluck (1714–87) and his librettist and private pamphleteer, Ranieri da Calzabigi (1714–95), neither of whom had more than a passing interest in comic opera.

Gluck and Operatic "Reform"

For the first two decades of his opera-composing career, Gluck had evidenced little difference from a dozen other non-Italian (or, for that matter, Italian) manufacturers of Neapolitan opera. He was forty-seven years old when he brought forth the ballet *Don Juan* (1761), from which a clever soothsayer might have predicted that Gluck was going to compose something different in kind from the twenty-five or so comic and tragic operas and *pasticci*[1] with which his past was starred. *Don Juan* demonstrated that Gluck was weary of reusing the same conventions over and over.

Gluck encountered in Calzabigi exactly the mildly revolutionary mental refreshment that he craved. In their *Orfeo ed Euridice* (1762), these collaborators served preliminary

[1] The *pasticcio* was a commonplace of the period. Literally "paste" in the sense of pastry, it was either an opera composed by two or more men in collaboration or a medley of operatic excerpts by various composers or a single composer which were strung together on a thread of frail plot. The most famous of all *pasticci* is *The Beggar's Opera*.

notice that their ideal of opera was severe, restrained, a partial return to the ideals of Peri and Caccini. Even though *Orfeo* is only a halfhearted revolt, it was strange enough so that the Viennese audience did not take it to their hearts. Five years passed, during which Gluck went back to composing Neapolitan operas to Metastasian librettos. Then he collaborated with Calzabigi again. And when their *Alceste* was sung in Vienna in 1767, it seemed that the two men conscientiously were mixing Metastasian-Neapolitan usages with their own ideals. In place of the *recitativo stromentato* used throughout *Orfeo ed Euridice*, dry recitative had returned in part; the libretto of *Alceste* reused some of the least fresh of Metastasio's conventions. But Gluck's music to it was very far from the bright and charming irrelevancies of many Neapolitan operas. Instead, it was dramatic, strictly related to the classic tragedy it supported (until a tacked-on happy ending) in a spare, powerful way. Gluck often has been called a poor harmonist, a charge that is perhaps correct but certainly meaningless. For the harmonic starkness of his music is precisely Gluck's revolution, his method of banishing baroque scrollwork, of leading both melody and rhythm forth in naked power.

The Preface to Alceste

But *Alceste* itself was not so revolutionary, so firmly set against the other employers of Metastasio, as was the preface to the published edition (1769) of the opera. In it, a single sentence crystallized the aim and creed of an operatic school that has waxed and waned throughout the entire history of the art: "I have tried to restrict music to its true office of serving poetry by means of expression and by following the situations of the story without interrupting the action or smothering it in a useless superfluity of ornaments . . ." Later in this brave document, Gluck (or Calzabigi in his name) wrote: "I did not think it my duty to pass quickly over an aria's second section, the text of which is perhaps most impassioned and important, so as to repeat regularly four times the text of the first section and to finish the aria where its meaning may perhaps not end, this for the convenience of the singer, who wishes to prove that he can vary a passage capriciously in a number of ways. . . . I have felt that the overture should inform the spectators of the nature of the action to be represented . . . that the concerted instruments should be introduced in proportion to the interest and intensity of the text. . . . I believed that my greatest effort should be devoted to seeking a beautiful simplicity, and I have avoided making displays of difficulty at the expense of clarity . . . and there is no rule that I have not thought to set aside willingly for the sake of the intended effect."

Except for one, those sentiments lie beyond criticism: some of the greatest musicians to create song and opera never could have been forced to agree that the true office of music is to serve poetry. More than once, a strong case has been made for exactly the opposite proposition: that in song and opera the true office of poetry is to serve music. But the Gluck-Calzabigi manifesto stated the tenets out of which they had brought *Alceste* and out of which, in 1770, they were to bring *Paride ed Elena*. Although both are superior operas, neither of them pleased Vienna. After the relative failure of *Paride ed Elena* (which contains *"O del mio dolce ardor,"* one of the most persuasively amorous of arias), Gluck left Vienna. Soon he was established in the Paris that had fought the *guerre des bouffons* two decades before.

The Masterpieces of Gluck

Gluck found himself famous in Paris, not so much because of his music as because of the preface to *Alceste* and the scarcely less challenging one to *Paride ed Elena*. Audiences were waiting to applaud him when he should apply the Calzabigi-Gluck principles fully to a libretto in French. The far-seeing composer already had composed most of such an opera, *Iphigénie en Aulide*. In 1774, that opera took Paris completely. It is removed a great distance from the ornate decorativeness of typical late Neapolitan opera or from a concert in costume. Grand, simple, dramatic—in short, the result of one method of mating text and music successfully

—Iphigénie en Aulide is an indivisible work of art. Gluck
may have believed that his music was serving the indifferent
poetry in which his French librettist had clothed the great
Greek story, but in fact he had absorbed that text into his
music, combining the two elements into something greater
than the sum obtained by adding together the virtues of
each. And Gluck was to surpass the first *Iphigénie* with a
second, *Iphigénie en Tauride* (1778), an opera entirely
worthy of the Euripides play of which its libretto is a French
adaptation.

Gluck's Mixed Victory

But the Parisians, while appreciating Gluck, loved "wars"
and realistically remained hospitable to more than one kind
of opera. An Italian appeared, or was imported in the hope
of starting a war, and was built up into a rival for the Austrian. Niccola Piccinni was a very talented composer of late
Neapolitan opera. Hoping for something as scintillating as
the *guerre des bouffons,* the Paris amateurs were seriously
disappointed when Gluck and Piccinni simply declined to
fight, each remaining content with the sort of opera he
could compose best. Modern taste wastefully has forgotten
Piccinni; it has remembered Gluck, though incompletely
and dimly. But this is far from indicating that Gluck's "revolution" triumphed decisively or that the tuneful, demonstra-
tive Neapolitan style, with its emphasis on *bel canto,* or the
Lully-Rameau heroic opera vanished forever. All varieties
of opera, including several later sorts, have been composed
since, in all purity and in every degree of compromise and
miscegenation. Gluck triumphed in another sense: he made
musico-dramatic masterpieces that can be restored to life two
centuries later. He reasserted the dramatic ideals of the
Florentine founders of opera, reasserted them in musical
terms more complex than theirs, and passed them on to the
future. Without his intervention or that of someone operating on beliefs much like his, opera might have degenerated
into a form that neglected drama entirely. What Gluck's
best operas achieved and preserved was to be of overarching

importance to composers as varied as Mozart, Hector Berlioz, Wagner, Verdi, Debussy, Puccini, and Richard Strauss.

Mozart and Opera

As Dante was the first universal genius in Italian literature, Cervantes the first in Spanish, and Shakespeare the first in English, so Mozart was the first anywhere in the history of music. He did everything musical with mastery, understood all existing forms with ease, and amalgamated contesting forces into satisfying artistic wholes. Before he was twenty-five, he had composed *opera seria* and *opera buffa* in Italian, as well as operetta[2] in German. In 1782, he wrote *Die Entführung aus dem Serail (The Abduction from the Seraglio)*, a comic opera in German. With its spoken dialogue between arias and concerted numbers, this type of German opera came to be known as *Singspiel*. *Die Entführung* nonetheless was full of Italianate, "Neapolitan" music. It required expert *bel canto* and included one of the most taxing arias ("*Martern aller Arten*") ever composed to show off the *colorature* of an agile soprano. When Mozart was thirty (1786), he composed an *opera buffa, Le Nozze di Figaro*, that comes as close as any human production to being wholly without flaw. The next year it was *Don Giovanni*, which he labeled *dramma giocoso* (jocose or mirthful drama) because it mixes tragedy and comedy, is neither all *buffa* nor all *seria*. One of the greatest of all operas, *Don Giovanni* mingles traits from Neapolitan *opera seria*—including its florid, elaborately decorated vocal line—with traits clearly Gluckian. Three years later, Mozart all but matched *Le Nozze di Figaro* with *Così fan tutte*, again *opera buffa*. And in 1791, the year of his death, he composed *Die Zauberflöte (The Magic Flute)* to a German libretto that stirs together Masonic symbolism, cheerful nonsense, and serious philosophy, putting into it some of the most exalted music ever composed (in Gluck's style) for the human

[2] The Italian word *operetta* was used in its literal meaning of little opera in the eighteenth century. Its later application to a text mated to light music intended wholly for popular entertainment then was only hinted at.

voice as well as a florid aria (the Queen of the Night's "*Der hölle Rache*") that asks for a fiendishly agile display of *colorature*. He was a dying man at thirty-five, but in that same year he ended his operatic career with a reversion to unadulterated Neapolitan *opera seria* in *La Clemenza di Tito*.

Mozart, Genius, and the Libretto

Mozart was gifted with unique virtues as a maker of opera; they were in addition to his stupendous, all but unbelievable, mastery of the techniques of composition, his surpassing fertility of melody, and his rarely faltering sense of proportion. He never has been equaled in the ability to depict in musico-dramatic terms a wide variety of human beings. In *Le Nozze di Figaro*, *Don Giovanni*, and *Così fan tutte* he was assisted ably by Lorenzo da Ponte, a more accomplished librettist even than Metastasio or Calzabigi. But though not even he could have created so nearly perfect an opera as *Le Nozze di Figaro* on a clumsy or inadequate libretto, his finest operas certainly multiply the best qualities of their texts. In *Die Zauberflöte*, in fact, he won out over an often witless, sometimes pompous, and never solidly constructed libretto. In the creation of stage personalities who take a place among real human beings, he is of the Shakespearean order, evoking men and women who, once they have become familiar, never can be remembered as less than living. With godlike swiftness and the assurance of genius, he gave to the important protagonists of *Le Nozze di Figaro*, *Don Giovanni*, and *Die Zauberflöte* music at once serenely or stormily beautiful and entirely appropriate to their own constant inward nature and shifting outward circumstance.

Opera as Unity

Mozart's music was not the servant of poetry. In that respect, he stood midway between Gluck's expressed ideals and those of the opposed extreme. His music was elaborated for its own sake, for those esthetic-psychological effects of communication which only music (or music best) can create. So delicate was this balance that Mozart not only absorbed libretto into opera as Gluck and other major operatic composers always had absorbed it, but also created drama—comic, tragic, or both together—from musically existing characters in the round both on the stage and in the mind, characters who live precisely in the music he assigned to them for expressing the text of their roles. Despite the universes of beauty in Mozart's symphonies, chamber pieces, and concertos, this special achievement—one never entirely equaled by another composer and perhaps most closely approached by Verdi—makes it seem to many that his greatest work was the composition of opera.

By the time when Mozart composed his theatrical masterpieces, the full eighteenth-century orchestra had been evolved. In his sonatas, concertos, chamber pieces, and symphonies, the varieties of classic sonata form had matured, as they had matured simultaneously in Haydn's symphonies and chamber music. With these two Austrians, the rococo-classical techniques reached summits above which it became impossible for music to continue without leaving the rococo behind altogether. A new force, some tendency to a different manner and style, was required if, after Haydn and Mozart, music was not to sink into repetitive imitation. At whatever then-existing technical element or device of construction we may look—whether at orchestration, the string-quartet style, modulation, the concerto style, opera, classical harmony, whatever—we find it used with perfect grace in Mozart's masterworks and the masterworks of Haydn's marvelous last years. Here was the finest musical result of the gallant rococo world built from Austrian, Italian, German, and French elements, the world whose eclipse was announced with terrible symbolic finality by the fall of the Bastille in 1789, when Mozart had but two years to live and Haydn already was a man of fifty-seven.

CHAPTER XIV

Beethoven:
Classicism and Romanticism

When dealing with Beethoven, a writer is especially wise to define his terms, particularly those words which refer to generalizations about style, manner, and content. What, for example, does he mean by "classical"? What by "romantic"?

One too common use of the word "classical" with reference to music can be discarded at once as useless to serious discussion. "Classical" music is not the opposite of "popular" music; for this necessary distinction between the supposedly weighty and enduring and the supposedly frivolous and temporary, no satisfactory terms have evolved. Many writers use such terms as "art music" and "serious music" when referring to whatever is not folk music or the music of light entertainment. But such terms will not serve: folk music is an art expression too, and the adjective "serious" is a heavy burden for many of Haydn's symphonies, *Il Barbiere di Siviglia*, Sir William Walton's *Façade*, or Stravinsky's Suite No. 2. Any attempt to label this distinction, as in the case of the waltzes of Johann Strauss, Jr., usually proves bothersome and meaningless rather than helpful.

Another traditional use of "classical" in discussion of music has more value. This is as a historical label for the period from about 1750 to about 1800—that is, from the end of the baroque era as bounded by the death of Johann Sebastian Bach, through Mozart's whole life and Haydn's creative life, to a year chosen because it is a round number and because it coincided roughly with the appearance of unmistakable new musical forces in the works of Beethoven and Schubert. In that sense, "classical" is a technical word: it remarks on the perfection of the sonata form in various guises, on the ripe maturity of euphonious, predominantly diatonic, consonant harmony, and on an overtopping concern with proportion and balance among the existing musical elements. The "classical period," that is, was in one sense introduced by the final evolution of rococo art, of which it became an extension and expansion. Despite the fact that Gluck was a Bohemian, Haydn and Mozart were Austrians, and Beethoven was a German, the most "classical" of their music is marked deeply by both Italian and French manners. When "classical" is used in this way, to label the period containing the finest achievements of Gluck, Haydn, and Mozart—and the early, somewhat Haydnesque and Mozartean works of Beethoven and Schubert—its opposite may be either of two other labels, depending upon the direction in which the writer is facing. If he means to contrast the 1750–1800 musical period with what had preceded it, the antonym of "classical" is "baroque"; if with what succeeded it, the antonym is "romantic."

A third critical use of the word "classical" is common to all the arts. It is difficult to define, and the indefinition of its limits constantly creates confusion. Not only does "classical" always necessarily suggest the meanings thus far mentioned; it also refers to the art of ancient Greek and Rome. More immediately, in our predominantly psychological age both "classical" and "romantic" have acquired psychological meanings that are vague in relation to their other, more clearly definable uses. In this psychological sense, "classical" suggests art produced by men whose ruling interest is in the creation of objective entities of certain size, shape, and content, impersonal (*relatively* impersonal) works in which their own private personalities and emotions are present only incidentally, as by-products. Similarly, the "romantic" artist is thought of as interested chiefly in "expressing" through his art his own character, personal emotions, and ideas, in making artistic creation an extension of his self.

The meaning of this psychological application of "classical" and "romantic" becomes unmistakable only at the extremes. Haydn, in his symphonies and chamber pieces, can seem to few listeners to be telling them symbolically how he saw the world, loved, felt about God and the universe, or thought of his fellow men. But a Chopin scherzo or a suite of piano pieces by Schumann scarcely can help seeming to be—in addition, of course, to being several other things— an attempt by the composer to communicate his own emotions and ideals or beliefs. It has been said that "classical" music creates and evokes ideas and emotions in the listener, whereas "romantic" music transmits them or conveys them from the composer to the listener. All possible shadings lie between such neat extremes, for which reason the terms themselves easily turn into battlegrounds distant from reality. Nonetheless, this use of "classical" and "romantic" will go on plaguing all discussions of art, and of music in particular, because it responds to a felt reality.

Musical Conservatives
and Liberals

Artistic traditionalists cling to the dubious belief that new forces and conditions could, if only they would, continue to make use of old, perfected forms. Revolutionaries claim, with little more certainty, that forms always are prisons from which the present must escape. The history of any art provides a graph of the oscillations between traditional "classical" periods marked by insistence on formal probity, emotional reticence, and the increasing perfection of existing formal elements and rebellious "romantic" periods shaped by the irruption of new or new-seeming ideas and forces and of those artistic personalities who tend to break up existing patterns, insert novel-appearing emotional tones, and dissolve the old, established mixtures. A "classical" era must be born out of a "romantic" one. It becomes more "classical" as it evolves its patterns and practices, and then starts to break apart in the demanding presence of new forces that it, in turn, cannot contain. The result of such a breaking-apart is a new period of "romanticism," always likely to appear disorderly as it opens, but to become more orderly as it extends itself in time and evolves toward another "classicism." In this view, classicism is consolidation, romanticism is experiment.

Within that usage of the terms, Orlando di Lasso, Palestrina, Johann Sebastian Bach, Handel, Gluck, Haydn, and Mozart were "classical." The era of Machaut, Dufay, and Okeghem, most of the musical seventeenth century, and all of the period from about 1800 almost to the end of the nineteenth century were romantic. An interesting brief could be drawn up for calling Carl Philipp Emanuel Bach the center of a truncated romantic period containing little but his own music. For in the view of those who depend upon this classical-romantic contrast, such a romantic intrusion was essential between the baroque classicism of Handel and Johann Sebastian Bach and the rococo classicism of Boccherini, Haydn, and Mozart. Obviously, these periods were not defined sharply at either limit: one extends into the other. A composer often is alternately classical and romantic and vice versa. What is important for us here is the general statement, derived from observation of what actually has occurred, that no classical period long outlasts the apogee of its particular perfections, that a romantic period tends from its outset to become more and more classical.

The End of Classicism: Beethoven

The Viennese classical era could not prolong itself beyond the culminating master efforts of Mozart and Haydn, not only because of the collapse of the world to which they responded, but also because the forms and patterns that its composers used were germane only for their purposes. Those forms and patterns would not, *therefore* would not, serve the different needs of a later day. The men appointed by genius and the nature of their eras to fail at attempts to continue them, but destined in the process of that failure to break up those eras and institute a new romanticism, were Ludwig van Beethoven (1770–1827) and Franz Schubert (1797–1828).

Four of the musical genres in which Beethoven excelled were the piano concerto, the piano sonata, the symphony, and the string quartet. The earliest of his five mature piano concertos was composed in 1794; the earliest three of his thirty-two piano sonatas were published in 1797; the earliest of his nine symphonies was composed by 1800 and published in 1801; and the first six of his sixteen string quartets also were published in 1801. All of this music, then, existed within ten years of Mozart's death and while Haydn was completing *The Seasons*. What characteristics can we determine as common to Beethoven's Piano Concerto No. 2, his Piano Sonata No. 2, his Symphony No. 1, and his earliest string quartet?

They all are Mozartean-Haydnesque. They all may be called classical under any of the meanings of that word advanced above. They all are very accomplished from a technical point of view. They all fully represent a composer already about thirty years old: they are not juvenilia. Not one of them, in spite of a wealth of beauties, would have guaranteed Beethoven an important position in the history of music.

Beethoven's Piano Concerto No. 2 is molded in the rapid-slow-rapid three-movement pattern favored by Mozart. It is altogether Mozartean, in fact, without approaching Mozart's sovereign mastery. It is conventional and a little tame in almost every element.

The Piano Sonata No. 2 uses the rapid-slow-minuet-rapid pattern favored by Haydn (with whom Beethoven studied briefly). It is altogether Haydnesque without approaching the originality or stature of the best of the older composer's sonatas. Only in its final, *prestissimo*** movement is something quite unclassical suggested by pell-mell power and insistence that threaten to overstep the borders of the polite.

The first of Beethoven's nine symphonies suffers from a truly nonclassical disproportion that has forced many of its apologists into tortuous explanation. It breathes a composer not satisfied with the eighteenth century but not yet at home in the nineteenth. It is a prevailingly comic work with traces of melancholy. Its orchestration, generally that of the string-dominated classical symphonic orchestra, nonetheless becomes overweighted in favor of the wind instruments. Beethoven's voice often is drowned out by echoes of Haydn and hints of Mozart. This otherwise persuasive work somehow gives the impression of being a little unsteady on its feet, as though uncertain, there in the half-light of a new day, where the next step may be taken safely.

The String Quartet No. 3 (generally believed to have been composed first of the six quartets in Opus 18) is too close to both Haydn and Mozart for it to have occasioned much surprise had it been found among the published works of either.

Beethoven Late

Now let us look at the final examples of Beethoven's creative intentions in the same four genres. The Piano Concerto No. 5 was completed in 1809; the Piano Sonata No. 32 was completed in 1822; the Ninth Symphony in 1824; and the last String Quartet, Opus 135, in 1826. In span of time elapsed between earliest and latest examples, Beethoven's piano concertos cover thirteen years, his piano sonatas twenty-five years, his symphonies twenty-four, and his quartets at least twenty-five. In measuring the span of their stylistic differences, however, no mathematical gauge will suffice. The last compositions do not sound so much like more mature works of the composer who had produced the earliest ones as like creations by another man, one somewhat influenced by the composer of those earliest works. Their very atmosphere, as contrasted with that of Beethoven's earliest compositions, represents a greater change than had occurred in any other composer's career up to that time. This shift is easy to hear; what is much more difficult to isolate is the most important of the technical means by which it had been brought about.

Hearing Beethoven's Piano Concerto No. 2 and his No. 5 (called the "Emperor"), we may be struck first by their disparity in size, both that of physical lengths and that of the size of development within those lengths. Then we notice that in No. 5 the second movement has no real ending, but closes on a whispered piano introduction of the chief melody of the final rondo, thus making a bow in the direction of unifying the concerto by more than key relationships among its separate movements. More—late in that final rondo, the violins briefly comment upon that closing whisper of the preceding movement. Everything about No. 5 is grand, assertive, imperial enough to justify its otherwise meaningless nickname. No one ever can have thought of No. 2 as imperial, for its every gesture is that of an elegant, bright, by no measure slavish courtier.

Now let us place the Sonata Opus 111, beside the Sonata Opus 2, No. 2. At once we can see that the earlier piece is made up of equivalents of the four customary classical movements: fast-slow-minuet-fast. (The third movement of Opus 2, No. 2, actually is a scherzo rather than a minuet. But any hard-and-fast distinction between the two was not maintained at the time. The difference between a Haydn sonata minuet and a Beethoven sonata scherzo is precisely the difference in personality, era, and technique which is here under discussion.) The final sonata, Opus 111, has only two movements, fast-slow. As Beethoven called it a sonata, we sensibly have enlarged our definition of sonata to include it, but it is not a *classical* sonata. In one standard edition, the four movements of Opus 2, No. 2, occupy twenty-eight pages, the two movements of Opus 111 thirty-one. An examination of Opus 2, No. 2, promises no insurmountable technical barriers to a pianist who can play the notes of an average Haydn or Mozart sonata. But one glance at the final pages of Opus 111 discloses such a passage as:

The principal technical problem here is that of keeping three trills going at the same time, two in the right hand, one in the left. But it is of first importance to understand that this new difficulty resulted, not from a desire by Beethoven to display virtuosity or to dazzle by agility, but from a profound, unceasing search for methods by which to set forth new musical ideas, new *compositional* emotions. This sonata inhabits both a pianistic and a musical world very far from the princely court of Opus 2, No. 2.

Placed beside Beethoven's First Symphony, his Ninth looks like a monster. The First requires two flutes, two oboes, two clarinets, two bassoons, two horns, two trumpets, two kettledrums, and the usual groups of violins, violas, cellos, and doublebasses. To this orchestra the Ninth adds two additional horns, three trombones, four vocal soloists, and a mixed chorus. The First Symphony is shaped in the four classical movements: fast (with a slow introduction, a useful idea that Beethoven borrowed from Haydn), slow, minuet, fast; in the Ninth we find fast, faster, slow, fastest, with the second movement being a minuet-scherzo in everything but label (it is headed *molto vivace: presto*). And the opening chord of the finale of the Ninth Symphony speaks a new musical world. It is an unvarnished discord:

Quickly, too, this movement abandons the purely instrumental character of the classical symphony, introducing a recitative for baritone voice, a quartet of vocal soloists accompanied by a chorus, two choral sections, and a final vocal quartet with chorus. If the First Symphony might be thought of as a small bright star, the Ninth might be likened to a galactic system of which large areas still remain in the process of creation.

Beethoven's final string quartet, Opus 135, is not so far

from his first as are some of the quartets that immediately preceded it. In Opus 130, for example, which was composed in 1825 and 1826, he originally wrote a six-movement quartet of which the finale was a vast fugue. Not only were six movements too many for a Boccherini-Haydn-Mozart period quartet; but also, several of these six were in musical patterns not previously employed in a string quartet. The Great Fugue in itself was so huge that Beethoven's friends persuaded him to replace it with a less fatiguing *allegro* finale (the Great Fugue was published separately as Opus 133).

In the Opus 131 quartet, completed in 1826, Beethoven composed what in reality is a seven-movement work. Because the movements are relatively brief, however, and are played without pause, being very closely interrelated in tone and character, the quartet may seem to be in one continuous movement. Neither seven short movements nor one extended movement would do for a *classical* string quartet. And over the slow third movement of Opus 132, a quartet completed in 1825, Beethoven wrote: *"Heiliger Dankgesang eines Genesenen an die Gottheit, in der Lydischen Tonart"* (Solemn Thanksgiving of a Convalescent to the Godhead, in the Lydian Mode). That is, the movement has autobiographical significance. Further, it is not composed in a major or minor key, but has reverted to the ecclesiastical Lydian mode, here placed so as to look much like F major. With a vengeance, this quartet, in comparison with any quartet of the period that preceded Beethoven, proclaims his untiring search for new realms of expressiveness.

In the last quartet, Opus 135, Beethoven returned amicably to the four-movement classical pattern. This is a relatively short quartet, and at first glance may seem to be a return to the truly rococo-classical manner of Beethoven's own earliest quartets. But above the last movement this curious legend appears in Beethoven's script:

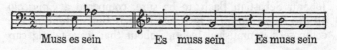

Muss es sein   Es muss sein   Es muss sein

"Must it be? It must be! It must be!" Here, again, is autobiography, this time allied to specific melodic fragments. What did this question and its answers signify? Probably, in view of what we know of Beethoven's life, "Must I accept life as it is, with illness, deafness, the stupidities of men, the infuriating minutiae of existence? Yes, I must! I must!" And the atmosphere engendered by that nonmusical question and its equally nonmusical answers haunts the music. Here is one full-fledged aspect of romanticism: music used by its composer in an attempt to communicate personal thoughts directly to the listener. (Whether anyone not seeing the words would suspect either their existence or that of a philosophical question and an answer in the music is another question.)

Music and Self-Expression

The point here is double, if not triple, and of first importance. Obviously, all music by all composers always has been influenced by their extramusical lives, as well as by the situations in which they found themselves while composing. When musical works still were composed mostly to order and their pervading character thus was defined for the composer in advance, his own mental condition nevertheless inevitably led him to select certain kinds of melody, certain rhythmic devices, certain modes or keys, a certain expansiveness or brevity. But when composers began to produce either what they thought would earn them money or what they were driven to by inner urgings—Handel and Beethoven were among the earliest to compose primarily for such reasons—then the very forms selected were dictated to them, whether they were aware of the dictation or not, at least in part by nonmusical factors in their inherent make-up and daily living. But there is a difference between that sort of extramusical effect on music and the direct, conscious intention to make music a vehicle for the transmission of nonmusical ideas or emotions. (About 1704, Johann Sebastian Bach, to be sure, composed a *Capriccio on the Departure of a Beloved Brother*. But nothing of the composer's nonmusical feelings about that leave-taking can be proved present in it, though it does contain an imitation of the sound of post horns.) Even Igor Stravinsky, who has been quoted as saying that music cannot really communicate anything, cannot escape the first, really inevitable sort of extramusical effect on music. But the conscious sort became a determining characteristic of romanticism. It could not help breaking up the harmonies, melodic styles, and formal patterns that had served as the containers and conveyors of classical music.

Music as Communication

By its nature, nonetheless, music cannot communicate with any degree of clarity specific emotions, logical thoughts and ideas, or pictorial figurative statements. Attempts to make it do so always must be bolstered up with titles, captions, superscriptions, onomatopoeic imitations. And inevitably it follows that such attempts and their results cannot be the central excellences of a good musical creation. Early eighteenth-century composers delighted in elaborating huge pieces purporting to describe or evoke one or another famous battle. With a considerable portion of willing cooperation by their listeners, they came as near to success in this attempt as possible. But most of them were less than first-rate composers, and their battle pieces, one and all—including one by Beethoven himself entitled *The Battle of Vittoria*—are dead. Richard Strauss a century later was to portray the creaking of windmills very convincingly in his *Don Quixote*—but a listener unaware of the title of the composition or of what that particular section of the composition had been intended to portray certainly could not deduce the presence of windmills from the sound of the music itself.

Yet if imitative, autobiographical, literary, or pictorial music is also good music in itself, no reasonable grounds exist for taking a severe attitude toward titles, superscriptions, onomatopoeia, or other nonmusical matter attached to music by its composer. The music always is what counts. Except as it joins sung or spoken words in opera or melodrama or is fused with dancing in ballet, it *alone* counts, but no tenable law exists against subtitling a symphony *"Eroica"* or calling three symphonic sketches *La Mer*. What we as listeners must guard against is listening to the *"Eroica"* for its heroism or *La Mer* for its wetness.

Music that does not convey cogent musical ideas in musical terms will not convey anything else either well or long. But a strong musical fabric can be, often has been and is, sufficiently durable to carry by suggestion and imitation a freight of nonmusical matter. Beethoven, bursting apart the purely musical reticence of the eighteenth-century classicism, introducing more and more "romantic," literary, and philosophical ideas into his inspiration, his titles and subtitles, rarely failed to weave his strictly musical strands into fabrics of the very highest tensile strength.

The Demonic Beethoven

Beethoven was a vividly energetic, mentally vigorous, and constantly dissatisfied and therefore experimental creator. He came, by force of necessity—necessity growing from his own character and his many-sided relationship to the unsettled, stormy era in which he lived—to view the artist's lonely existence as a contest with Fate, a singlehanded struggle with heartless Destiny, even a challenge to God. His musical talents were strong and multiple: his grasp of the musical techniques he needed was all but absolute. But the chief single characteristic of his music is its unresting determination to be expressive in the ways it bodies forth his fiery mental and spiritual attitudes. His resemblance to Michelangelo often has been remarked. His experiments with melody, harmony, formal patterns, and other elements of musical construction were his direct ways of searching for new, highly individual, very romantic sorts of expressiveness.

Classicism-Romanticism: Schubert

In sharpest contrast to Beethoven's vigorously male, dynamic artistic personality stood the lyrical, at times almost feminine, and always temperate musical nature of Franz

Schubert, exponent of an altogether different aspect of romanticism. Schubert never was volcanic or dogmatically assertive. His energy showed itself chiefly in the enormous number of his compositions rather than in any unusual muscularity within single works. He was not an intellectual, and whatever experimental steps he took were not the result of direct or conscious ethical or philosophical purpose; they came out of a different search for expressiveness. Schubert's was primarily an art of sentiment, of a tenderness and intimacy of feeling to which his endlessly fertile imagination responded with hundreds of the most beautiful melodies ever penned. In his case, that is, the emphasis in our use of the word "romantic" must be placed largely on a sort of idealized love for and responsiveness to the intimate and quiet facets of man and nature.

Schubert and the Lyric Impulse

Schubert tried most musical genres (though he never composed a concerto). He wrote operas, operettas, symphonies, overtures, chamber works in many forms, sonatas and other pieces for piano, songs, Masses, and many other varieties of music. Into almost every genre he put some of the most heart-touching and beautiful of musical materials. In the song for the solo voice with piano accompaniment, his mastery of expressiveness earned him the affection of a world. In nearly six hundred songs, Schubert presented lyric impulses, mercurial reactions to poetry, visions of happiness that he seldom experienced. Such Lieder as *"Ave Maria," "Der Erlkönig," "Die Forelle," "Gretchen am Spinnrade,"* "Hark, Hark, the Lark," *"Heidenröslein," "Ständchen,"* and "Who Is Sylvia?" are simple-seeming, instantly convincing, and expressively so winning that they have come to seem folksongs. In them no restless Beethoven seeks to force back the limits of the world or assert man's central position in the universe.

The Lied had a long history before Schubert: he, of course, did not "invent" it. But he did invent the Schubert Lied, something unique and enduring. In that genre he has not been surpassed, though other composers—Schumann,

Brahms, Hugo Wolf, Richard Strauss, Debussy, Fauré, Francis Poulenc—have written songs entirely outside his capabilities. But when, with the same equipment of melody and feeling, Schubert turned to more extended, more intellectually elaborated musical forms (such as the string quartet or quintet or the symphony), he often brought to them no such shaping grasp or drive to the carving out of new, appropriate forms as became essential to the melodically less facile Beethoven. Whatever the exquisite beauty of many of the component sections and elements, the less successful of Schubert's longer works, especially in varieties of sonata form, seem to many listeners to hesitate, even to maunder.

Schubert and Unerring Form

For a symphony or a piano sonata or a string octet cannot be made entirely out of a single lyrical impulse or even out of several lyrical impulses. Its completely satisfactory creation requires an intellectual domination of musical architecture for which no impulse, however fresh, original, and momentarily beautiful, can be substituted. Nearly all of Schubert's extended compositions, though they may succeed in other ways, fail to supply that intense, specifically musical satisfaction which Beethoven almost always provides: the satisfaction of recognizing a form unerringly created to house and present exactly the musical ideas that it contains. (In his tendency to attenuate music's ability to make points swiftly, Schubert foretold that nineteenth-century decrease of tempo which at last led to the slow-moving gigantic compositions of Wagner, Anton Bruckner, and Gustav Mahler.)

In so unpretentious and magical a lyrical composition as Schubert's *"Forellen"* Quintet, so surpassingly expressive and movingly melodic a piece as his C-Major String Quintet, so original and fascinating a piano sonata as his in B♭ major, or even so massive an achievement as his "Great" C-Major Symphony, Schubert conquers us by his lyricism, the marvelous unexpectedness of his modulations, and his sensitivity to the timbres and other individual characteristics of separate instruments. But much of the time he was pouring essentially lyric, songlike ideas and intimate melodies into patterns that existed to provoke and convey drama, patterns that he had misjudged or had failed to reshape in his own image.

Listening to Schubert

Instead of cracking open the classical forms and then refashioning them in his own lyrico-romantic image—as Beethoven remade them in his dramatic one—Schubert dilated them and filled them with song. He was not a hero: nature and his background had not equipped him to lead a revolution. But it is senseless not to enjoy a Schubert symphony or chamber piece—even so seemingly interminable a distention of pattern as his F-Major Octet—because it cannot give Beethovian satisfaction. Music supplies rich satisfactions in addition to the supreme sensation of realizing that worthy material has become its own form. It is equally self-frustrating to approach a Schubert composition in sonata form in the hope or expectation that it will provide the formal pleasure that Haydn and Mozart supply so bountifully in classical-rococo ways, Beethoven in his individualized romantic way.

Beethoven the re-creator was certain to show the path to many later composers; Schubert's historical effect is to be located in the remarkable efflorescence, after him, of the German Lied and in a certain near-sentimentality of tone. The symphony, the quartet, and the piano sonata might have evolved substantially as they did evolve if he had not lived at all. But then we should have been deprived of his works, and they, whatever their failure to attain formal perfection, are full, page after page, piece after piece, of music of an unparalleled, wholly cherishable sort.

Other Romantic Roads

These men—Beethoven, with his overarching urge to speak like a hero and a god, Schubert with his intense lyricism—crossed from the eighteenth century and its rococo perfections into the romantic unruliness of the nineteenth. Both began as classicists and ended as romantics. But they did not reach all the portals to the romantic movement, which in northern Germany was to have other emphases than those of the Viennese postclassical period in which both Beethoven and Schubert matured. They did not, for example, display that side of romanticism which related it to the word "romanesque" and made it seem in part a revival of the artistic spirit of the eleventh and twelfth centuries. Such poets and literary philosopher-critics as Baron Friedrich von Hardenberg, known as Novalis (1772–1801), and Ludwig Tieck (1773–1853) reacted against what they took to be the boring flatness of their era; they preached and exemplified a return to the more flavorful manners of the romanesque Middle Ages, to the sense of mystery and wonder, to the knightly and the supernatural. Ernst Theodor Amadeus Hoffmann (1776–1822), composer and man of letters—and in this romanesque sense a romantic among romantics—helped to recruit composers to the movement sponsored by Novalis, Tieck, and Tieck's friend Wilhelm Heinrich Wackenroder (1773–98). Defining music itself as par excellence the art of subjective emotion, of longing and wonder, saying that it always was romantic by nature, Hoffmann called it *the* romantic art.

Another Romantic: Weber

Concentrating on the subjective, the directly emotional, and the wildly picturesque, this variety of musical romanticism emphasized the nonformal aspects of the art at the expense of formal considerations. In sacrificing the persuasions of formal balance and elegance in favor of ingenious attempts at direct communication between the mind of the composer and that of the listener, the lesser early German romantics denied an important part of the special nature of music as an art. But they were unimportant extremists, and as the widely scattered impulses leading toward romanticism flowed together and were united in more masterly hands, the new sort of music began to develop its own patterns of discourse. Carl Maria von Weber (1786–1826) discovered the bases of his own romanticism in patriotism, a penchant for the grotesque and supernatural, and the setting of high-flown opera librettos and other texts that unfortunately but inevitably have come to seem to later (and particularly to non-Teutonic) generations too absurd to be tolerated.

Weber and Opera

The most enduringly remembered of Weber's larger compositions are three operas—*Der Freischütz* (1820), *Euryanthe* (1823), and *Oberon* (1826)—and a *Conzertstück* (1821) for piano and orchestra. *Der Freischütz*, which found enormous popularity in Germany, deals with magic bullets, romantic love, pacts with the Devil, and supernatural interventions in the lives of ordinary human beings. *Euryanthe*, the plot of which is difficult to understand and all but impossible to present convincingly on the stage, deals with a wager between two courtiers of Louis VI of France, the subject being the fidelity of the girl betrothed to one of them. A monstrous serpent appears, a girl goes insane and is murdered by her bridegroom, and the soul of an unhappy woman is given peace only when the tears of an innocent girl fall on the poisoned ring by which she had committed suicide. *Oberon*'s cast of characters includes mermaids, the King and Queen of the Fairies, Puck, Harun-al-Raschid, and a pirate. Even the *Conzertstück*, according to Weber's own program for it, deals with a knight in the Holy Land, a sorrowing medieval lady, and the way his last-minute return to the castle saves her from a swoon of death. That most of this literary material now appears meretricious does not mean that Weber was led astray: it means that we have been carried to a great distance from the heyday of German romanticism. Tastes have changed, but the qualities of Weber's music have been little affected.

Weber had a special talent for an unmistakable sort of richly curved melody, alternately nostalgic and declamatory, worked up on highly imaginative harmonic supports to climaxes of great intensity. Its texture is brilliantly colored and loosely knit, removed about as far as possible from the cooler-tinted, tightly woven fabrics of the Viennese classical period. Weber was not Austrian, but very consciously German. His was perhaps the first deliberately chauvinistic music ever composed, his nationalism having been one natural response by many young Germans to the waxing and waning of French Napoleonic imperialism. And in some manner that is psychologically unmistakable but impervious to analysis except in so far as its basis in folk practices can be isolated, his private melodic-harmonic nature coalesced with the prevalent nationalism to make his musical speech, for the Germans of his time, the very voice of Germany.

Weber, the Libretto, and Form

The mental universe in which Weber's music first was heard can only appear somewhat quaint and faded to most twentieth-century minds. To let that fact deafen us to the conquering fervor and horn-haunted mellowness of his best music, however, would be wasteful. His operas, except perhaps for *Der Freischütz*, probably now are beyond all possibility of successful stage revival: we could not absorb their stories and texts with any measure of seriousness, and either to face them without it or to attempt applying his music to new stories is to deface his qualities. But all of his mature operas contain overtures, arias, duets, and other separable sections that bring Weber's unique quality across the fences of literary taste. So magnificent an aria as Rezia's "Ocean, thou mighty monster" in *Oberon,* so glimmering a breath of pure aspiration as Agathe's prayer, *"Leise, leise, fromme Weise"* in *Der Freischütz,* the expertly fabricated overtures to those operas and *Euryanthe,* the *Conzertstück,* and a handful of other excerpts and pieces bring us his still-convincing voice (music being ever vaguer about nonmusical matter than literature is) speaking of the spells, dedicated loves, midnight enchantments, and woeful virgins that we almost certainly would find unbelievable and ludicrous in the operas themselves.

Weber's music almost always does without larger formal perfection, that seemingly inevitable progression of musical events in which every expectation aroused, every promise made by what happens first is fulfilled and kept by what comes next or at last—in which, to be sure, musical ideas are placed first, next, or last largely to make that arousing and satisfying of expectations possible. But not to listen appreciatively to the best music of lesser masters is to deny ourselves a whole world of secondary musical pleasure and fall victims to the cult of the masterpiece. Weber's dashing or sighing emotion-soaked melodies, his rich, highly flavored harmonies, his waywardly shifting rhythms—these make E. T. A. Hoffmann's dictum seem undeniable: music is *the* romantic art. In *The Harvard Dictionary of Music,* Willi Apel summed up the virtues and defects of this sort of high romanticism in a brilliant figure of speech. Having written that it tries to shorten the distance between composer and listener by eliminating so-called "unnecessary formalism," he says: "Not unlike a real short circuit, music has by this method immensely gained in 'high tension,' but as might well be expected, at the expense of sustaining power."

Toward the Later Nineteenth Century

In the musical practices evolved by Beethoven, Schubert, and Weber can be found the beginnings of the qualities by which much of the music of the later nineteenth century was to be defined and dominated. That music was generally to be emotionally expansive, often on the basis of underlying literary or philosophical ideas and ideals. It was to deal much with love and struggle and death and redemption, to have many supernatural and utopian visions. Restlessly seeking new forms and patterns—and in the process developing some of long-lasting value, it was to aim less, or less successfully, than its predecessors at concision and balance. Its melody was to become constantly more lush, its harmony ever richer and more highly seasoned. Seeking fresh musical means, it was to expand the size of the orchestra beyond anything Mozart, Haydn, and the young Beethoven had required; it was to experiment with many new instruments and to discover new aspects of old ones.

213

Fragmentation and Individualization
of Styles

Seeking personal communication, direct transference of
emotion and idea and belief from composer to listener, the
romantic musicians of the nineteenth century came inevitably to lean on nonmusical assistance, on programs, titles,
superscriptions, thus tacitly giving the game away by admitting that music unaided and unalloyed cannot directly
express anything but itself, whatever else it may symbolize
or accompany. As a response to increasing nationalism
among the states of Europe, romantic music also developed
national musical dialects, beginnings of which had been
present in the great international musical language of the
preceding centuries, but now each having its own increasingly prominent peculiarities and distinctive habits. Specifically German, French, Italian, Spanish, Russian—and even
Norwegian, Bohemian, and English—musical dialects would
result. And each national "school," pursuing the necessary
breakdown of the former international standards, also would
encourage the breakdown of its special dialect into an individual idiom for each composer, making the style of each
more and more personal, less and less like that of any other
composer. We easily may mistake some of Handel for some
of Vivaldi, some of Georg Philipp Telemann for some of
Bach, some of Haydn and early Beethoven for Mozart, so
much at each period in the eighteenth century were an
over-all texture and vocabulary of music common currency
universally recognized and sought after. But it is impossible
to mistake Beethoven for Schubert or Weber, Schumann
for Chopin, Berlioz for Wagner, Liszt for Mendelssohn, or
any of them for any other.

Romanticism and Idiosyncrasy

Nineteenth-century romanticism produced the great age
of musical idiosyncrasy. It discovered the composer as a
separate, unique individual and deemed individuality rather

than universality a crowning virtue. In a sense unknown to Haydn, a sense that Mozart was at the very edge of reaching when he died, each symphony, concerto, sonata, quartet, or trio by the mature Beethoven is a world unto itself. Each work by the composers of the classical period naturally contains its own special characteristics and differs from every other composition in its genre. But it clearly was thought of—and it remains—the best example of that genre which the composer could create at a given hour. It is a well-made, lovingly articulated, even (if we will) inspired setting-forth of the general over-all characteristics then considered native to its genre. With the later-than-youthful Beethoven, the emphasis was changed drastically. That change is precisely what makes Beethoven's musical atmosphere so different from that of his predecessors and early contemporaries. What he overtly was symbolizing in tones was his personal world, not the generally known and accepted world of music's universal material.

(The above remarks do not refer with equal cogency to music written to accompany, support, or collaborate with words or dancing. Mozart's operas or Haydn's songs differ from one another widely because of the composers' sensitivities to the meaning, color, and weight of the text words. In this respect, instrumental music after the middle of Beethoven's creative life tended to become more and more literary, more and more operatic. Almost every instrumental piece now came to be the wordless setting of a text either kept secret or published separately. This becomes a certainty easily visible, of course, in the numerous cases in which the composer published or told fragments or all of the nonmusical ideas and emotions that had been in his mind while he was composing.)

Classical and Romantic Forms

In easily recognizable ways, almost every late Beethoven composition in an instrumental genre is unique, as though while composing it he had evolved a new genre. Each piece was to him not so much the best music-making to which he could adapt the inherent capacities of a universally accepted pattern or form as it was the use of such an existing form as one of several means toward the presentation of a novel, a unique, world of musical matter related by various ties to a personal grouping of nonmusical ideas. From earliest to latest, Haydn's symphonies, sonatas, and quartets, Mozart's concertos, sonatas, symphonies, and chamber pieces evolved and altered in inclusiveness and mastery, in expressivity and polish. But they remained instances of the same forms and patterns, used in all consciousness for the same or very similar purposes, though used with firmer command as the composer experienced and matured. Between Beethoven's Second Symphony and his Third ("Eroica"), between his Third Piano Concerto and his Fourth, and at related points in the lists of his other compositions, vastly wider changes took place.

Beethoven's Second Symphony may be viewed as a straining at the leash of classical reticence; his Third ("Eroica") is wholly nonclassical, a massive epic of the composer's interior world. The "Eroica" is unlike any other composition. Never before had it occurred to a composer of genius to use the symphonic pattern for so literary-philosophic, so poetically personal, a purpose. That difference in fundamental conception of what a symphony is was the major reason why classical composers wrote symphonies in large numbers—Haydn more than one hundred, Mozart forty-one—while Beethoven composed but nine, Schumann and Brahms only four each. When the twentieth-century Russian composer Nikolai Miaskovsky, reapproaching the classical conception of a symphony as exemplary music-making in a given form rather than intense personal expression, composed more than two dozen symphonies, that number became the most discussed aspect of his music.

Classicism of the eighteenth-century variety operated on the principle of variety in uniformity. The composers of the nineteenth century transferred romantic literary and philosophic ideas to music by breaking away from uniformity to shape their creations to the principle that each piece must discover or create its own universe and formal patterns, sometimes by altered uses of past patterns, but increasingly by performing the extremely difficult double task of conceiving and presenting musical materials and *at the same time* evolving a pattern for them, a wholly new pattern that probably could be used only that once, being wholly fitted to the specific materials in hand. All argument as to which method is better or more true to the nature of music as an art is pointless unless based on judgment of the success or failure of individual compositions. But the importance of acknowledging and remembering the difference is great.

Listening to Classical and Romantic Music

A modern listener often finds it necessary to pay the closest possible attention to a classical composition if he is to be able to appreciate its individual characteristics, its particular expressivity, the ways by which it differs from other works by the same composer and by his near contemporaries. He must lavish the same careful, co-operative attention upon romantic compositions if he is to discern in such of them as are labeled only symphony, sonata, concerto, and quartet the uses that they make of classical principles, their resemblances to other compositions similarly labeled. For the uniqueness and personal urgency of a piece of "pure" (as opposed to programmatic) romantic music often is so intense and attention-capturing that its forms and patterns, the machinery of what may be called its uniquely musical attributes, are hidden from the unwary or inattentive ear. To appreciate the architecture of Beethoven's Fourth Piano Concerto, the string quartets of his Opus 130, 131, 132, and 135, his Piano Sonata Opus 111, his Ninth Symphony, is far harder, but no less rewarding than to make the same essential conquest of the most complex instrumental pieces of Haydn and Mozart. Not that musical architecture is solely a matter of patterns visible upon the page or audible to the attentive ear: it involves also the appropriateness and interrelationships of the instrument or instruments employed, subtle effects of modulation and key relationship, and very numerous other factors.

Less assistance toward this understanding, toward this really basic "appreciation" of music, can be obtained from knowledge of general principles or general awareness of formal usages if a piece was composed late in the nineteenth century than if it was composed late in the eighteenth. Although the success of any musical work of any complexity finally depends upon its use, adaptation, or creation of a structure substantially inseparable from its purely musical contents, in each romantic composition we no longer are dealing so much with a differing example of a known quantity as with something entirely new and therefore comprehensible in formal terms only by greater effort. This, and no general failure of talent or technical ability in the composers of the full nineteenth century, allows us to view the Viennese classical era as orderly and serene, which very often it was not, and to see the romantic period as tempestuous and disorderly. Conversely, it long has underlain the maiming error of viewing the music of Haydn and Mozart as, by comparison, cool, superficial, and almost wholly unemotional.

CHAPTER XV

The Last Operas of Mozart

Mozart had composed two astonishingly different operas during 1791, the last year of his life. One of them, *Die Zauberflöte* (*The Magic Flute*), is a fairy-tale pantomime with religious and philosophical overtones. In it, music of mostly classical texture is joined to a typically romantic libretto. But into its musical procedures intrude now and again (not unwelcomely or so as to destroy the opera's over-all integrity of style) hints of those romantic turns of melody, harmony, and instrumentation which also had been present in the last act of *Don Giovanni* (1787). All to the contrary, Mozart's other 1791 opera, *La Clemenza di Tito*, a setting of a remodeled libretto by Metastasio, often suggests a throwback to the decorous, severe *opera seria* of an earlier time. Although *La Clemenza di Tito* contains beautiful and persuasive music, as a stage work it already was an anachronism when Mozart composed it. So passionate a Mozartean as the late Edward J. Dent wrote: "For the stage of today it can only be considered as a museum piece." To listen to it in the hope of encountering vividly living characters such as people *Le Nozze di Figaro* and *Don Giovanni* is to listen for the wrong thing.

Fidelio, *or Opera as Ethos*

The most indicative musical stage work of the twenty-nine years between *Die Zauberflöte* and Carl Maria von Weber's *Der Freischütz* (1820) was Beethoven's only opera,

Fidelio (1805, later revised). Its theatrical values are intermittent and indecisive. It towers above the other operas of the first two decades of the nineteenth century only because of its strictly musical values. In its four overtures,[1] in separate scenes, every so often (but not all the time), *Fidelio* provides music of full Beethovian power. But it always has failed to sustain itself as a stageworthy opera. To Beethoven, who was engaged in elaborating the techniques he had inherited from Mozart and Haydn, and in molding them into means for communicating struggle and revolutionary significance, music itself was becoming drama. But he had no more than a wavering sense of theatrical activity in terms of those clashes of well-defined character by which it largely exists. The "Leonore" Overture No. 3, not a part of *Fidelio* as Beethoven last revised it, contains more consistent and cumulative drama than the whole of the opera itself. When exceptional passages in *Fidelio* have been noted and admired, it nonetheless remains a patchwork of abstract music resembling Beethoven's instrumental works, of living but quite unremovable connective tissue, and of intermittently theatrical outcroppings. By far all the best of what Beethoven put into it is contained in the "Leonore" No. 3, the baritone aria *"Ha! welch ein Augenblick,"* the tremendous soprano aria *"Abscheulicher! Wo eilst du hin?"* the prisoners' chorus *"O welcher Lust!"* and the tenor aria *"Gott, welche' Dunkel hier!"*

Weber, theatrically adept almost from birth, knew more about opera as stage music than Beethoven, for his purposes, ever needed to understand. In *Euryanthe* (1823) and *Oberon* (1826), however, Weber was defeated by librettos at times frivolous and always cumbersome. Yet his sense of what is theatrically possible in musical terms, of what can be sung and what cannot, and of how to hold the attention of audiences was all but flawless. The faults we sense in his operas are not the faults of *Fidelio*. Weber's last stage

[1] That is, in the so-called *Fidelio* Overture and in the three other overtures—known by the name of the opera's heroine as "Leonore" No. 1, No. 2, and No. 3—which Beethoven composed for the opera at different times. Of these last, the No. 3 foretells the symphonic poem or tone poem of later composers.

works were to beget a numerous line of recognizable descendants; *Fidelio* has remained childless, whatever Richard Wagner and some others have said to the contrary. Wagner was consciously, at times overwhelmingly, influenced by Beethoven, but by Beethoven the symphonist (and particularly as the composer of the Ninth Symphony) rather than by the composer of *Fidelio*.

Weber's Descendants: Marschner and Wagner

Appearing first in the long line of German composers bearing close family resemblance to Weber was the now unjustly neglected Heinrich Marschner (1795–1861). In such essentially romantic, moodily macabre operas as *Der Vampyr* (1828), *Der Templer und die Jüdin* (1829), and *Hans Heiling* (1833), Marschner built parts of the bridge from Weber to Wagner. As early as 1841, attempting, in *Der fliegende Holländer*, a carefully unified setting of folklore touched with the grisly and the supernatural, Wagner showed that he had been listening to both Weber and Marschner. Constantly discarding other, extraneous influences, Wagner was becoming more and more German, more and more Weberian—though with a difference. The early influences he had to cast off, teachings and methods inimical both to his own development and to his success, had come from Italian opera, French opera, and the international works of a Frenchified German. These displayed aspects of romanticism which were not specifically German or folkloric enough to contribute successfully to Wagner's intensely Teutonic conception of the art of music.

Romantic Opera Buffa: Rossini

Beginning in those early years of the seventeenth century when Peri and Caccini had initiated the long course of opera, Italians had composed a profusion of musical stage works. *Opera seria, opera buffa,* variants and combinations thereof—all had flowed from Italian and Italianate pens unceasingly. The last great fabricator of *opera buffa*, touching it with romantic and sensuous overtones, was Gioacchino Rossini (1792–1868). His comic masterpiece *Il Barbiere di Siviglia* (1816) remains in the active repertoire of opera houses everywhere because of its abounding vigor and melodic inventiveness, because of the effervescence of its musical wit and humor. Its chief characters (incidents in whose later life are recounted in the libretto of Mozart's *Le Nozze di Figaro*) are not living people in the Mozartean way, but they are enormously lively and funny types, perhaps all that legitimately can be asked of them in *opera buffa*.

The enduring qualities of *Il Barbiere di Siviglia* are present in varying quantities and strengths in others of Rossini's *opere buffe*: *L'Italiana in Algeri, La Cenerentola, Le Comte Ory* are examples. But Rossini's position in the evolution of musical manners derives rather from his effect upon recitative, upon the inviolability of the text as composed, and on grand opera. He gradually abandoned *recitativo secco* for recitative with orchestral accompaniment, thus pushing it toward incorporation into the over-all texture of the music. And he temporarily forestalled virtuoso singers, formerly tempted (and able) to decorate their vocal lines with flashy, difficult ornaments of their own devising—forestalled them by meticulously writing out all the ornaments he desired and then insisting that his operas be sung exactly as he composed them. Rossini's own vocal melodies were difficult and showy enough for singers in one of singing's golden ages, for which reason star sopranos and tenors could find little reason for fighting the losing battle against his insistence that the music sung in one of his operas be his alone. The justice of Rossini's position in this matter can be estimated by trying to imagine a singer interpolating passages of extraneous music into *Die Meistersinger, Pelléas et Mélisande, Der Rosenkavalier,* or *Wozzeck*.

(Sopranos, a persistent race, have triumphed over Rossini in one renowned instance. When *Il Barbiere di Siviglia* was weakened by transposition of the leading role of Rosina from the contralto range for which Rossini composed it to that of high soprano, the music that he had supplied for her to sing in the "Lesson Scene" was abandoned. Since then, Rosinas have taken their singing lessons by warbling everything from "Home, Sweet Home" to samples of showy brainlessness especially composed or arranged for them. We have the right to judge *Il Barbiere di Siviglia* only when Rosina is sung by a contralto or mezzo-soprano and the "Lesson Scene" consists solely of the music that Rossini composed for it. Similarly, we have every right to demand that in Act II Bartolo sing Rossini's aria beginning *"A un dottor'"* rather than interpolate—an action sanctioned by "tradition"—an aria beginning *"Manca un foglio,"* the work of a composer named Pietro Romani, who at Florence dashed it off for a bass who found Rossini's *"A un dottor'"* beyond his powers.)

Bellini, Donizetti, and Melody

Somewhat younger than Rossini was Vincenzo Bellini (1801-35), a very original composer who exerted influence out of proportion to the brevity of his life. An artist of Keatsian temperament, Bellini evolved a sort of melody which was to echo down through the rest of his century into our own, a long-breathed, highly decorated *cantilena*** of hushed, intense ecstasy, of all but perfumed melancholy. In his finest operas—*La Sonnambula* (1831), *Norma* (1831), and *I Puritani* (1835)—he supplied the stages of Italy and Paris, and then of the world, with romantic serious operas almost as exquisitely fashioned, though naturally not so lively, as Rossini's *opere buffe*. Their widespread popularity, along with that of Rossini's operas and those of Gaetano Donizetti (1797-1848) made certain the prolonged cultivation of the techniques of beautiful singing and added to the vocabulary of musical romanticism that unmistakable melodic intensity which often is thought of as the invention of Chopin. That Bellini's operas now are heard relatively seldom, that we can be acquainted with only a scattering of Donizetti's nearly seventy operas, that Rossini's reputation now depends largely upon *Il Barbiere di Siviglia* while his serious operas are neglected—all this can be explained in large part by the refusal of modern singers to undergo

the years of training and persistent practice required to sing
them properly and effectively.

Perhaps the most remarkable of all the remarkable Bel-
linian melodies, equally astonishing for its length and for
its poetic evocativeness, is that of the soprano aria *"Casta
diva"* in Act I of his Druid opera *Norma:*

This truly was something new. As an expansion of music's
resources, it proved as important in the final evolution of
romanticism as Weber's coloristic orchestration and Cho-

pin's chromatic harmony. Without these condiments, indeed, nineteenth-century music would have meant something other than the music we know, that music which fortunately or unfortunately still supplies most of what is called the standard repertoire.

Interim Men: Cherubini and Spontini

An anomalous position both in musical history and in the library of living music is occupied by Luigi Cherubini (1760–1842), an Italian long resident in Paris. Cherubini's music was admired by Beethoven, Weber, Brahms, and many other composers. Born when Mozart was four years old and dying fifteen years after Beethoven, Cherubini spanned the interregnum between the climax of Viennese classicism and the full tide of romanticism. He was a magnificent artificer of lofty-toned Masses; he composed a Requiem that many critics have called the splendid final representative of the old Italo-German religious music. Cherubini's operas (out of which we now hear only occasional performances of his *Médée*—and that in Italian translation and with accompanied recitatives replacing his spoken dialogue—and the Beethovian overture to *Anacréon*) were superbly made and so noble in ethical atmosphere that they fascinated Beethoven. *Fidelio* scarcely could have been composed without their example. Cherubini was a musician of compendious learning, a strong teacher and administrator, and a composer of all but the highest quality. But his music, semiclassical in a romantic age, now seems to lack the personal profile and warmth that might have kept for it the place among the living which it otherwise demands.

Historically even more important than Cherubini was another interim and largely expatriate Italian, Gaspare Spontini (1774–1851). Responding cannily to the pseudo-classic romantic pomp of Napoleon as conqueror and emperor, Spontini evolved from a second-rate confectioner of outmoded *opera seria* into an inventor of grand opera. "Grand opera" is a much-abused term: the reality that it covers is easier to sense than to define. But for purposes of identification it can be said to have the following characteristics: it has orchestral accompaniment throughout, and therefore minimizes the distinction between full song and recitative; it is preponderantly tragic in text; and it involves very large amounts of panoply, pageantry, and elaborate stage action. It characteristically makes use of chorus, ballet, procession, and set scenes of splendor and brilliance. Napoleon's glory brought it forth. Its first unmistakable exemplar was Spontini's *La Vestale,* produced at Paris in 1807 under the patronage of the Empress Josephine. Romantic in its physical appurtenances, the score was almost Gluckian in its dignity, or seemed so to those for whom it was composed. Its classicism now looks and sounds like romantic pseudo-classicism, much resembling the pseudo-classicism of the empire's painting, architecture, and interior decoration. Like those visible expressions of the First Empire, *La Vestale* has very considerable beauties. Basically sincere and moving, it is a little static and very self-consciously grand.

Spontini grew grander with time. His *Fernand Cortez* (1809) required crowds of supernumeraries, a troop of horse, and complex stage machines evoking the conquest of Mexico. With *Olimpie* (Paris, 1819), he finally set the manners of grand opera in a groove from which they could be turned aside only with difficulty. When *Olimpie* was sung in Berlin for the first time (May 14, 1821), Spontini's Italo-Napoleonic magnificence seemed on the way to conquering the Germanies too. To the struggling Weber that opera was anathema: *Der Freischütz,* essentially Teutonic and in no sense "grand," intensely romantic both inwardly and outwardly, was to be sung in the Prussian capital five weeks later. Weber understood that it altogether lacked the numbing magnificence of *Olimpie.* But because it spoke directly to the inmost childhood memories and hot nationalism of its first audiences, it triumphed. Spontini's German reign was cut short; it seemed that the future of German opera was Weber's future. Paris might keep its grand opera. Berlin and the other German cities and towns would take the Weberian *Singspiel,* with its weird atmospheres, the folk-like warm simplicities of its human relationships, its almost cozy musical colorings.

Yet the kind of opera that Spontini had evolved was to dominate the opera houses not only of Paris, but also of other world metropolises for much of the rest of the century and the first decade of the twentieth. Grand opera indeed were *La Muette de Portici* (also known as *Masaniello*), which was composed in 1828 by Daniel-François Auber (1782–1871), and *Guillaume Tell*, by Rossini, both operas composed by men now remembered chiefly for lighter, less ponderous works. And in 1831 Paris heard *Robert le diable*, a blazingly romantic opera of the grandest proportions by Giacomo Meyerbeer (1791–1864). In Meyerbeer's talented, synthesizing hands, grand opera was to achieve positively Babylonian gorgeousness. In *Les Huguenots* (1836), *Le Prophète* (1849), and the posthumously staged *L'Africaine* (1864), Meyerbeer purveyed operas of unfailing theatrical impact to the singer-enthralled audiences of Paris, London, and New York. His purely musical gifts were considerable, but his energies were expended chiefly upon supplying instant stage effectiveness of the most reliable sort. At the business of showing off beautifully trained singers, of keeping costumers and stage designers occupied lavishly, and of supplying opportunities for dramatic, vividly pictorial stage groupings, Giacomo Meyerbeer never has been surpassed. He joined the sensuous melodic idioms of Rossini, Donizetti, and Bellini to an expansion of the Weberian orchestra; he took well-digested hints from everywhere. The popularity of his operas became so great that for many decades other composers—Berlioz and Wagner among them—found them blocking all roads to advancement, particularly toward the greatest summit of all, the Paris Opéra.

The influence shed by the grand operas of Cherubini, Spontini, Rossini, and Meyerbeer was enduring and incalculable. It can be found without difficulty in Wagner's *Rienzi* (1838–40) and *Tannhäuser* (1834–35)—between which, to be sure, Wagner composed *Der fliegende Holländer,* a child of Weber more indicative of his own future style; in Verdi's *Nabucco, Don Carlos, Aïda,* and *Otello;* in Berlioz's *Les Troyens* (1858-59), and in hundreds of other operas by Frenchmen, Italians, Germans, and others. Much of what has been called Wagnerian in operas by other composers (notably the late Verdi) turns out, on more careful inspection, to reflect Meyerbeer's concentration of grand opera's taste for expansiveness, pseudo-historic grandeur, and sure-fire theatricality.

Weber's Orchestra

In Weber's operas, the orchestra's multiple voice had been romanticized by coloristic use of instruments, particularly of wind instruments, and of them particularly the wood-winds. He had made special dramatic use of those sections of instruments' ranges which other composers had left alone because they were not those instruments' "normal" voices. He had made effective use of the mute, that device by which the tone colors of the violin and viola in particular can be rendered muffled and mysterious if somewhat nasal. But he had been content to individualize his orchestra without greatly adding to its complement.

The Orchestra as Giant

Meyerbeer, Berlioz, and Wagner expanded the orchestra to giant size, building it into a pliable instrument capable of ear-shattering volumes and varieties of sound that would have surprised and perhaps repelled Bach, Haydn, and Mozart. Like grand opera, this vastness of means was in itself an aspect of high romanticism. Sometimes it illustrated the pathetic belief that size insures greatness. But music for eighty, ninety, or one hundred players is not necessarily mere furious noise. Here, as everywhere, the problem of evaluation is that of deciding, in each case on its own terms and merits, whether or not the result justifies the means employed. When, for example, Weber divided his strings, giving each of several subdivisions of the orchestral violins its own melodic line and similarly multiplying the voice of the violas and cellos, he was not merely showing off. He required the resulting harmonic richness for the expression of his musical or musico-dramatic ideas, for the creation of the texture that he had heard in his imagination. Haydn, it is true, had composed great music without dividing his strings. But Haydn was not composing Weber's music.

What must seem megalomaniac excess in the scores of a third-rate composer can be abundantly justified in the outbursts of a Berlioz, a Wagner, a Gustav Mahler. Justified or unjustified, that enormousness of orchestral means became a central characteristic of the romantics' prolonged attempt to conquer new musical worlds.

Orchestration and Exoticism

Weber contributed importantly to the use of local color in nineteenth-century music. In various works he included actual folk or composed melodies, harmonies, and rhythms from Turkey, Poland, China, and Spain. Haydn, Mozart, and other earlier composers had introduced Turkish, Hungarian, and other non-Western usages into their classical-textured music. But the prevailing idiom of music in their noonday of Viennese classicism had been so absorbent that it diminished rather than increased the exoticism of foreign elements introduced into it. So to say, the classical composers of the eighteenth century had twined a few brilliant foreign threads into the otherwise homogeneous stuff of their music. With Weber, however, the exoticism of the Chinese melodies that he introduced into his incidental music for Schiller's *Turandot* and the Spanish ones in that for P. A. Wolff's *Preciosa* was a deliberate attempt to produce noticeable foreignness: it insisted upon its own divergence from the manners of the prevailing idiom. Because of the harmonic implications of both real and imitation exotic melodies, often widely divergent from those of Western European folk music and from those of classical music, they became ways of insinuating new harmonic practices into the vocabulary of romanticism.

Chopin and Harmony

Of even more far-reaching influence than Weber in this respect was Chopin, who brought over into Western European music both Slavic practices from Poland (notably in his mazurkas and polonaises, both Polish dance forms) and those of his own highly original invention. It was said above that during the classical era harmonic evolution was marked by "rapidly enlarged importance of the tonic, dominant, and subdominant as harmonic centers; rapid modulation to remote keys, achieved both enharmonically and by passing rapidly through intervening keys." The influences of Weber's carefully cultivated exoticism, of Chopin's native Slavic coloring, and of the naturalization of the liberties that they and others had begun to legitimatize was to initiate a gradual disintegration of all the harmonic suppositions, reticences, and "laws" of classicism. This psychological development cannot be dated exactly, but it was perhaps the greatest single factor in the development of twentieth-century music, and it is useful here to note that it began roughly in the 1820s and was complete by the 1920s.

The Deliquescence of Classical "Laws"

It will be recalled that four different triads may be based on any tone. Taking C as our fundamental tone, we may build (1) a major triad, C-E-G; (2) a minor triad, C-E♭-G; (3) a diminished triad, C-E♭-G♭; or (4) an augmented triad, C-E-G♯. And any one of the four can be inverted once or twice. Taking our major triad as our example, C-E-G may be inverted first to E-G-C and second to G-C-E. The first inversion (E-G-C) is called a sixth chord because the interval between its outside tones, E and C, is a sixth; the second inversion (G-C-E) is called a six-four chord because the interval between its outside tones is a sixth whereas that between its lowest tone and next higher tone is a fourth. These chords are not, of course, separate musical events by themselves, but functions of harmonic forward motion; they necessarily or usually lead to other chords, which also are functions. In romantic nineteenth-century harmony, the triad and its inversions maintained their central roles. As more and more of their hints and suggestions were explored and accepted, classical notions of consonance or concord gradually fell away. The romantic composers began to use as pleasant in themselves many combinations of tones which the classical composers would have thought unwarranted unless used very warily and with very special purpose.

Romantic Chromaticism

Relatedly, though the nineteenth-century romantics still thought of diatonicism as the central fact in manipulation of keys and scales, they employed chromaticism with increased freedom and frequency. Chromatic alteration—that is, the use, at junctures in melodic motion and harmonic progression at which tones in the prevailing diatonic scale formerly would have appeared, of tones alien to that scale —became normal. Neither Chopin nor any other one composer, not even the nineteenth century collectively, "invented" chromaticism. It had appeared early in the sixteenth century, when such a lonely experimenter as Carlo Gesualdo had used it for compact emotional effects. Both the principal melodies and the secondary themes of fugues by Bach and others often were chromatic in the eighteenth and seventeenth centuries. Examples of chromaticism in patches, inserted by composers for special, momentary effects, can be found in all varieties of music from *canzona* to concerto, from cantata to oratorio. But the composers of the Viennese classical period largely had dispensed with chromaticism, or at least had not exploited its possibilities.

A composer of any period who wrote a scale passage reading (upward) G-G♯-A-A♯-B-C or (downward) G-G♭-F-E-E♭-D-D♭-C obviously was writing chromatically. But in cadenzas or passages of rapid *colorature* such scales most often were nothing more than passing effects devoid of harmonic weight or meaning. Romantic composers later than Weber and Chopin began, however, to hear almost constant chromatic alteration of tones as entirely commonplace. This naturally complicated the interrelationships of chords, making harmony denser and richer. What those composers at first failed to realize fully was that constant chromatic alteration, by its very nature, could not continue long to be considered an "alteration," but soon enough would establish chromaticism as a parallel to diatonicism in importance and validity, would in itself become a prevalent harmonic-melodic scheme. That culmination of the chromatic revolt finally was to amount to a total (if perhaps temporary) breaking down of all harmonic interrelationships in the former sense. It did not reach that extreme until the end of the nineteenth century or the beginning of the twentieth: throughout most of the romantic post-Beethovian period, the development continued to be considered chromatic invasion of diatonic territory.

Romantic Dissonance

Romantic composers increasingly asserted their right to employ "unprepared" and "unresolved" dissonances. A tone causing a dissonance is said to be unprepared if it is not a repetition of a tone used just previously as part of a consonance. Obviously, then, a tone causing a dissonance cannot be thought of as prepared if it either does not appear in the preceding chord or in that preceding chord also is used dissonantly. A tone causing a dissonance is said to be resolved if it is succeeded immediately by a tone that would have been consonant in its place. A dissonant tone, then, is unresolved (at least, immediately unresolved) if it is not succeeded at once by a tone that would have been consonant in its place. Classical harmonic procedure placed great importance on both preparation and resolution. Haydn, Mozart, and their contemporaries introduced unprepared dissonances rarely, left dissonances unresolved rarely—and then only for specially determined reasons. But Chopin and the later romantics not only disregarded the preparation and resolution of dissonant tones in chords; they also extended that nonclassical attitude to unprepared and unresolved dissonant chords. Of these perhaps the most important structurally is the so-called "appoggiatura" chord.

Let us say that in a passage in D♭ major, a classically trained ear is expecting a chord consisting of C-E♭-G♭-A♭, with harmonic support in the bass of a chord including A♭ and E♭. Instead, the composer writes a chord consisting of B-D♭, G♭-B♭—with A♭ and E♭ in the bass. In this position, the B and the D♭ certainly are appoggiaturas—that is, nonharmonic, dissonant, and sounded instead of harmonic consonant tones from which they usually are removed by the interval of a second. (In the views of some, the B♭ is also an appoggiatura, but it may also be interpreted in other ways; any decision about that is beyond the scope of this brief illustration.) The B strikes the prepared ear as having taken the place of an expected and certainly consonant C; the D♭ as taking the place of an E♭. If neither the B nor the D♭ was used consonantly in the immediately preceding chord, both of them—in addition to being dissonant and to being appoggiaturas—are unprepared.

If, in the same harmonic passage, the chord succeeding our B-D♭-G♭-B♭ does not read C-E♭-A—or, at least, if the G♭ in our first chord does not disappear, the B move to C, and the D♭ move to E♭—the dissonant appoggiatura chord remains unresolved, at least for the time being. The lack of preparation and the failure to resolve would have been arresting in Mozart, but would cause little surprise in Chopin and none in Richard Strauss. This sort of unprepared and unresolved dissonance employing nonharmonic, often chromatic, procedure tended still further to expand harmonic complexity and to debilitate the basic assumptions of classical harmony.

The Blurring of Boundaries

Modulation too achieved new, extreme freedom. The necessity to prepare the way for a change from one key to another, or to move from an established key to a distant key only by prescribed passage through intervening keys, was more and more disregarded. Schubert had begun to treat modulation with great freedom; later composers came to

233

deal with keys as units that might be placed side by side and intermixed almost as notes may. They began to assume that the listening ear will take in without assistance of intervening signposts the harmonic relationships involved, implied, and set up. So little did late romantic composers scruple to employ major chords in predominantly minor passages and vice versa that the formerly clear distinction between major and minor began to become exceedingly and often excitingly blurred.

Classical and Romantic Harmony

Using "thin" and "thick" without implying any preference for one condition or the other, classical harmony can be described as thin, full romantic harmony as thick. And the leading result of all this divergence from classical harmonic manners was the consequent, constant weakening of those types of musical structure which developed their very logic and strength from the firm ever-present sense of a central tonality or key. In a much-used variety of exposition in the first-movement form of classical sonata, for example, the pattern depended in part on its "first system" being in the tonic key of the movement and its "second system" being in the dominant if the tonic was major, in the relative major if the tonic was minor. Nearly everything in a typical classical composition or movement existed in clearly felt relation to the basic key and to the greater and smaller importance of the tones of its diatonic scale. But in an advanced romantic composition or movement this no longer could be the case in the same sense or to the same degree. Some of that sort of structural logic still stood, but not enough of it to give romantic composers the sensation of formal probity which they inevitably sought. Even while they still thought of themselves as evolving their patterns and forms out of the harmonic interrelationships of the preceding era, romantic composers felt uneasy, sensing (even before they understood intellectually) that they were engaged in the impossible task of refilling old forms with new materials quite unsuited to that purpose. Increasingly, therefore, they sought out and invented new principles of organization.

These developments of useful romantic forms and patterns must be understood in their true relation to the constantly more fluid condition of romantic harmony, as well as in formative relation to the kinds of melody which summoned up romantic harmony and then appeared as its by-products.

The Tyranny of the Sonata

One of the commonplaces of unfriendly criticism often leveled against romantic music by writers with classical prejudices has been that such men as Chopin, Liszt, Schumann, Tchaikovsky, and Brahms could not compose formally satisfying works in sonata forms. This charge has been made equally against piano sonatas, symphonies, concertos, and chamber pieces. And if romantic music is approached and judged by classical standards, the accusation is unanswerable. The reverse attitude, judgment of classical music by romantic standards, produces the same measure of truth, finding Haydn and Mozart superficial, unemotional, all but inhuman.

The truths thus discovered are, of course, only justifications of predilections or preconceptions. They damage our ability to listen to music in the only honest and useful state of mind: that of approaching an individual composition as an individual case to be understood and enjoyed, as far as is possible, on its own terms, to be judged by its own successes and failures with its own solutions of its own self-created problem. The extension of preconceived classical and romantic standards to the postromantic music of the twentieth century has blocked enjoyment and stultified understanding of much of the most important creation by our own musical contemporaries.

Just possibly, the careful elaboration of certain critical tools could produce standards that would be applicable to any individual musical work. But those standards would have to be free of any lingering belief that the fully developed patterns and working methods of one musical period were in themselves superior to those of another. The varieties of sonata form, for example—and the prejudice in favor of that form has been perhaps the strongest in exis-

235

tence, and therefore the most damaging to judgment—were evolved and employed by Haydn, Mozart, and Beethoven for the apt and absolutely convincing setting-forth of their musical ideas and matter. The musical structures that they built by those means have proved enduring. But to assume that only they had the mental power to handle the sonata forms is to convict oneself of arrested sympathy and to misunderstand the meaning of form. The sonata forms provided a foundation of miraculous rightness for exactly the kinds of melody, harmony, and rhythm which the evolution of resources up to their time had placed within the classicists' reach. The exact degree of freedom in harmonic movement, the precise varieties of melody, and the shades of rhythmical relationship conceived and developed by the classical masters themselves were what made the sonata forms and then proved them to be the miracles they were.

Romanticism and the Evolution of New Patterns

So great was the admiration of later musicians for the sonata-based music of the eighteenth century that they naturally, and all but unthinkingly, continued to work their own sorts of musical material into replicas of those forms. If the immediate postclassicists can be convicted of any intellectual absent-mindedness, that conviction must be based on their natural failure to realize quickly that their own melodies, harmonies, and rhythms could not supply the tensions, the measured interrelations, the levels of structural variety, that gave the classical sonata forms their own special solidity. One result of that cultural lag was the romanticists' slowness in developing the new patterns and procedures which, alone, could bear to romantic musical substance a structural relationship resembling that which the sonata had borne to classical thought. Another result has continued to be the preposterous charge already mentioned: that composers such as Chopin, Berlioz, Liszt, Schumann, Tchaikovsky, and Brahms were deficient in mental power and simply could not learn their sonata lessons.

Form in Romantic Music

Let us consider a few significant romantic compositions: Chopin's B-Minor and B♭-Minor Piano Sonatas and G-Minor Cello Sonata; Berlioz's *Symphonie fantastique* and *Roméo et Juliette,* Schumann's symphonies, piano sonatas, and chamber music; Liszt's *Faust Symphony* and B-Minor Piano Sonata; Tchaikovsky's symphonies, string quartets, and piano trio; and Brahms's symphonies, piano sonatas, and chamber pieces. To approach this astonishing variety of musical experience, much of it in pieces endowed with original, vivid, and beautiful musical ideas, in the hope of finding those ideas handled classically, with Haydnesque or Mozartean clarity of formal interrelationships, is to guarantee self-defeat. Doing so, further, we are almost certain to miss the real significance of the music. For the romantic intensity crowded into short phrases by harmonic and rhythmic abundance, the enfeeblement of differences in key, the extreme freedom of modulation—all this had rendered the sonata patterns of the eighteenth century useless as molds to be reused and at the same time had cried out unmistakably, in the long run, for the casting of new molds.

Like many arguments about esthetic form, this one is partly a war of terminology. If Chopin's B-Minor Piano Sonata is a successfully contained piece of musical architecture, but not a true classical sonata, then we must either enlarge our definition of "sonata" to include it or insist that Chopin should have given it another label. Neither mental process, however, will tell us anything about this music itself. That is not to deny the general point: Chopin clearly placed obstacles in his own way and ours by trying to force into sonata patterns musical matter ill suited to them; then, by using the still rigidly interpreted form title "sonata," he appeared to invite listeners to employ classical standards in judging what he had composed.

Most romantic musical substance responded best to extended treatment only in relation to literary texts, particularly operatic; in the form of suites of linked short movements; and in new or adapted patterns evolved in response to its texture and weight. (It may be noted similarly that postromantic music, opera having declined for both musical and extramusical reasons, found continuing valid use for the suite of short movements and the semiliterary, but text-free, ballet. An appreciable portion of the finest early twentieth-century music was composed to accompany dancing.) To say this is not the same as saying that longer romantic compositions labeled sonata, concerto, symphony, or quartet inevitably were weak in structure and deficient in unity. It is to point out that to listen to them primarily in the hope of hearing them make *classical* sense is to act against them: they do not and in most cases could not make it. The typically romantic achievements lie elsewhere or are brief passages imbedded in these often moving and beautiful but nearly always quite unclassical forms.

Chopin and Musical Form

Had Frédéric Chopin composed nothing but his two early piano concertos, three piano sonatas, cello sonata, and cello trio, he would not bulk very large in the living repertoire of performance or in musical history. But he was gifted with almost unfailing formal insight, which he displayed in the elaboration of numerous short, perfectly proportioned pieces in forms at least as relevant to his musical personality as the sonata forms had been to Mozart's. In *étude*, ballade, impromptu, mazurka, nocturne, polonaise, *prélude*, waltz, and a few other categories, Chopin instinctively discovered the perfect homes for his musical children. The finest of the resulting masterpieces-in-small lack only scope, the inclusiveness that can accompany only forms of greater extension, to belong with the greatest music ever composed.

Their very lack of scope proves Chopin's genius: for him to have distended his ideas would have been for him to misjudge their nature and therefore to produce jerry-built structures. Small though they are, and compacted of the most intensely personal, romantic inspirations, they have at their best the solidity of rock.

On a few occasions, indeed, Chopin conceived groups of closely related ideas which demanded more expansion than any one of his exquisitely understood short patterns permitted, but which he did not therefore unthinkingly and foolishly try to house in sonata patterns. For them he evolved, through a process of intense intellectual concentration, new formal patterns, new romantic patterns of total rightness. These patterns, by the very necessity that had brought them into being, were suited only to the materials out of which he had constructed them. They are not suitable for reuse by other composers; Chopin himself did not reuse them. Examples are to be found in his four scherzos, his only barcarolle, and—most notably—in his F-Minor Fantaisie. Either the barcarolle or the fantaisie will prove, on analysis, to be so indissoluble a fusion of matter and manner that its mere existence should have prevented the ridiculous accusation that Chopin could not think consecutively or handle an extended composition. In thematic development, in subtlety and probity of key relationships, in rhythmic variety and justice, in harmonic tension and resolution —indeed, in every department of musical architecture—the fantaisie is masterly.

Schumann and Musical Form

Similarly Robert Schumann. Nobody ever has been completely at ease with the formal setting of any of his four symphonies. His chamber pieces, rich though they be in melodic beauty, harmonic charm, and his unique epigrammatic concentration, are far from notable for formal propriety. But his songs and many of his short piano compositions are beyond the reach of any negative criticisms of their forms. In such chains of linked brevities as the piano suites called *Carnaval, Papillons, Fantasiestücke, Kreisleriana,* and *Études symphoniques,* in the song cycles *Dichterliebe* and *Frauenliebe und Leben,* Schumann discovered for himself entirely apposite ways of making the presentation of his essentially undevelopable materials formally satisfying through the equivalents of long compositions. Even in the hands of Schubert, the Lied and the song cycle had begun to be romantic; in Schumann's they glow at the heart of romanticism. In view of them, what importance can be attached to the fact that Schumann could not obey the classical rules when playing the symphonic game or the sonata gambit? How should he have so played them when he lived altogether in an unclassical world?

Largely because of Chopin and Schumann, the short piano piece and the Lied, the suite of piano pieces and the song cycle, as well as the extended piano piece in one unique movement, became available to other romantic composers, supplying them with methods of summoning forth and properly displaying their new kinds of musical ideas.

Liszt and Musical Form

Franz Liszt, much more worldly and theatrical than either Schumann or Chopin, but native to the same area of musical evolution as they, attempted again and again to build huge musical structures. As long as he clung to the skeletonic outlines of classical pattern, these proved inhospitable to his intensely romantic cast of mind. Brilliant as are many of the individual musical phrases in the *Faust Symphony,* *Dante Symphony,* piano concertos, and B-Minor Piano Sonata, none of these convinces us that its form was inevitably derived from its content. But in the volumes of brief piano pieces that Liszt called *Années de pèlerinage,* in separate piano compositions, and in songs, he drew closer to that special musical success. He went farther, taking hints from many other composers: in the process of evolving the "symphonic poem," he discovered a way to present romanticism with one of its most useful procedures.

The Symphonic Poem

The symphonic poem descended from mixed ancestors. One of them was the operatic overture; others were the overture to spoken plays and the concert overture. From the brief *sinfonie* that early composers of opera had placed before their first acts, the operatic prelude had expanded, drawing to itself greater importance and autonomy. By the beginning of the nineteenth century, it was being separated into two general types by diametrically opposed purposes. One type was a potpourri, the loose stringing-together of the opera's chief or most alluring melodies. The other type, at first retaining elements of first-movement sonata form, often had a more integrated purpose: that of prescribing the emotional weather in which the opera would be played. Examples of the potpourri type are several of Rossini's overtures, including the extended one to *Semiramide*; outstanding examples of the other type are Beethoven's three "Leonore" overtures. This second type largely suggested (or perhaps evolved into) the concert overture.

Standing somewhere between the opera overture and the concert overture in purpose are the musical pieces intended for performance before spoken plays, during which other pieces of incidental music often were heard. When the plays themselves drop from sight as stage works or are performed rarely, the overtures perforce become events in isolation. Thus Weber's *Turandot*, Beethoven's *Egmont* and *Coriolan*, Mendelssohn's *A Midsummer Night's Dream*, and Schumann's *Manfred*. The true concert overture, however, was in reality not an overture to anything, but a composition intended from the first for performance by itself. Thus Beethoven's *The Consecration of the House*, Mendelssohn's *Hebrides*, Berlioz's *Le Corsaire*, Brahms's *Tragic Overture*, Tchaikovsky's *1812*, and innumerable others. Not one of these but was meant by its composer to carry philosophic, pictorial, narrative, or other nonmusical suggestions and conceptions.

241

Berlioz and Program Music

When Franz Liszt began to wrestle with the idea of the symphonic poem, he had before him, in addition to such of these overtures as already existed, the example of Berlioz's astonishing five-movement *Symphonie fantastique*. That blazing orchestral work was proclaimed by Berlioz to be the telling of a story. He said that movement by movement it recounted the adventures of a man delirious with passion and opium. The lesson of its apparent marriage to the actual machinery of storytelling was not lost upon Liszt. Also, he understood the great importance of Berlioz's so-called *idée fixe*, a short musical phrase occurring in each of the five movements of the *Symphonie fantastique* as representing the hero's beloved. To symbolize a person or idea or situation by an easily recognizable musical tag was not an idea original with Berlioz: Monteverdi, Mozart, and others had made use of it, mostly in opera. But Liszt fastened upon Berlioz's special employment of the *idée fixe* as lending unity to the movements of a long composition and used the device in his symphonic poems in such a way that Wagner later was able to evolve his complex, subtle system of leading motives in part from it.

Understanding well the overture in its then most recent manifestations, absorbing the lessons taught by Berlioz's program symphony, Liszt began to work out an extended one-movement orchestral form based on literary or philosophical materials and/or pictorial suggestions. The earliest of his compositions in the class that he later called symphonic poems was *Ce qu'on entend sur la montagne*, written for piano in 1840, orchestrated in 1849. The most lastingly known of them are *Orpheus* (1854–56), *Les Préludes* (1856), and *Mazeppa* (1858). Liszt used the symphonic poem more for reflecting the pervasive character of its program than for rendering specific narrative or pictorial details. *Les Préludes*, the most often played of his works in this genre, is said to be a musical transformation of poetic lines by Alphonse de Lamartine, though it certainly was not composed with them in mind and originally may have been conceived as illustrating an altogether different program—or simply as music devoid of extramusical notions.

Liszt and "Transformation of Themes"

Simultaneously, Liszt worked out that highly original method of melodic-harmonic unfolding through a composition which has come to be called "transformation of themes," and by means of which he succeeded in lending each of his later symphonic poems a considerable appearance of unity. Making as much use as he wished or needed of strict key relationships, imitation, traditional modulatory practices, and other fragments borrowed from classical patterns, he concentrated on evoking emotional intensity. Most of this he extracted from his flamboyant melodies by stating them and then altering them constantly, either one by one or in combinations. The fabric of such a consciously conceived symphonic poem as *Hamlet* or *Die Ideale* (both 1859) is continuous and continuously more complex, though all of one piece, or nearly so. Here, in short, Liszt had developed a romantic form capable of scope and extension. It had emerged directly from the nature of his musical ideas and extramusical philosophy, both of which naturally were related to those of his contemporaries. Liszt's symphonic poems have not, for the most part, remained in the active repertoire, perhaps owing to what strikes many later listeners as his posturing and insincerity; their silence is not a result of any formal inferiority.

Later Symphonic Poems

Quickly the symphonic poem became a standard romantic orchestral form. Popular examples of it were composed from Russia to Spain, from France to the United States. Nineteenth-century and twentieth-century symphonic concerts would have been incomparably less varied without—to name but a few very popular symphonic poems—Debussy's *Pré-*

lude à *L'Après-midi d'un faune,* Smetana's *My Country* (six thematically linked symphonic poems, one of which is familiar as *The Moldau*), Tchaikovsky's *Francesca da Rimini,* Respighi's *The Fountains of Rome,* and Sibelius's *The Swan of Tuonela.*

Richard Strauss
and the Tone Poem

Almost the entire reputation of Richard Strauss until he composed *Salome* in 1905 resulted from a series of tone poems (a label that he preferred to "symphonic poem") which began in 1886 with *Don Juan,* included *Death and Transfiguration* (1889), *Till Eulenspiegel's Merry Pranks* (1895), and *Also sprach Zarathustra* (1896), and concluded in 1898 with *Ein Heldenleben.* With the last of these, a climax in musical autobiography was reached: *Ein Heldenleben* portrays Strauss himself as the hero of the title and quotes extensively from his own earlier tone poems. Particularly as it does not otherwise offer Strauss's finest musical ideas, many modern listeners have difficulty in not finding it absurd. Strauss's two largest orchestral compositions later than *Ein Heldenleben*—the *Symphonia domestica* of 1903 and *Eine Alpensinfonie* (1915)—curiously attempt to introduce into symphonies the essentially nonsymphonic procedures of the tone poem.

The Nineteenth Century and Variety

The music and composers usually classified as belonging to nineteenth-century romanticism present the listening ear with a far wider variety than is obvious in the music and composers generally considered as eighteenth-century classical. From the later music of Beethoven and Schubert to that of Wagner, Brahms, Tchaikovsky, Gustav Mahler, Anton Bruckner, and Jean Sibelius, the nineteenth century (extending a little back into the eighteenth and a little forward into the twentieth) included such shadings of character as the classical romanticism of Mendelssohn, the romantic classicism of Brahms, the theatrical romanticism of Verdi, and the nationalistic romanticism of the Russians and Bohemians. Almost everywhere, composers went on producing pieces that they called symphonies, concertos, sonatas, and (intending the appellations to serve as formal labels almost as much as they intended them as purely instrumental descriptions) trios, quartets, and quintets. By the very nature of the common store of musical thought available to them in the atmospheres in which they lived, they were not writing classical music. Prevailingly, their melodies were freighted with more intensity and deliberate meaning than classical melodies had held. Their harmonies were much more complex and much less sharply defined. Their rhythms were much less decisive. Their prevailing tempo tended to be slower. In the brief piano piece and the Lied, the suite of piano pieces and the song cycle, the symphonic poem and the tone poem, they were successfully demanding of themselves the creation of new (or newly used) ways of relating their substance to self-justifying forms.

Misreading the Nature of Form

To enter upon highly debatable ground, one might say that the notable failures of some of the most gifted composers of the romantic era to create extended compositions in which form and idea had become indivisible resulted from a misreading of the nature of form itself. Those who feel that some of the symphonies of Schubert, Schumann, Brahms, Bruckner, and Mahler, whatever their other great qualities, are formal failures—huge, finally un-unified structures to which the remnants of classical patterns add little or nothing of value—argue that those men, in these instances, were mistaken in their worship of the classical symphony, that they would have done better to perform the labor of working out for their rich and attractive musical materials forms and patterns growing out of them rather than out of a merely formal tradition.[2] Writers holding this

[2] The opposite procedure sometimes has been followed with success. Serge Prokofiev composed in 1916-17 a symphony making use of the movement patterns of Haydn's and Mozart's symphonies, de-

view define musical form as a constantly unique interaction between musical materials—melody, harmony, rhythm, and the others—and the best patterns and other means of setting forth those particular materials.

Romantic Culmination and Synthesis:
Wagner

Certainly the most tremendous, and in many ways the most interesting and influential, attempt on the part of a single composer at any time to remake the art of music in his own image, to create very extended compositions, and to relate all the elements of his own mind to the results of his composing was Richard Wagner's. Except for a few youthful works of little importance, he wrote nothing in classical patterns. He composed one symphonic poem (*The Siegfried Idyll*) and one other piece that might be classified as one (*A Faust Overture*). But nearly all of his colossal store of energy and genius went into operas and the new sort of opera which he preferred to call music drama. The most challenging formal effort of nineteenth-century romanticism culminated in Wagner's stage works, and particularly in *Tristan und Isolde* and *Der Ring des Nibelungen*.

Gathering together into his powerful synthesizing and transforming grasp ideas exemplified by the late Beethoven, the chromatic harmony of Chopin, the symphonic-poem concept of Liszt, the orchestral expansiveness of Berlioz, the folk romanticism of Weber and Marschner, and the operatic magnificence summed up in Meyerbeer, Wagner created musical units of unprecedented size. They would have represented the merest megalomania had he not been a great natural musical genius. But he was—and until very recently it could be said that no man composing music later than *Tristan* and the *Ring* has been free of Wagner's influence. Until only yesterday, that is, every post-Wagnerian com-

liberately creating the kind of musical material which best would fit into them. The resulting *Classical Symphony* is a charming pastiche rather than a deeply expressive work, in large part because it is an imitation rather than a native product of Prokofiev's present.

poser was either a Wagnerian or an anti-Wagnerian. In either case, Wagner and his music dramas stood colossus-like in the near background, athwart history and esthetics as the overtowering summations of nineteenth-century romanticism.

CHAPTER XVI

Musical Media and
Characteristic Style

Increasing distinction between vocal music and instrumental music has provided one of the constantly decisive forces in shaping new manners of composition since the Renaissance. Music for instruments differed from music for voices almost from its inception because instruments and voices possess widely varying capabilities. As the number of instruments in ensembles grew, the variety of instrumental styles also increased: any given instrument has different capabilities from all other instruments. Within an orchestra, for example, a violin can play well a musical line all but impossible for a trumpet, and vice versa. A symphony orchestra obviously can perform music beyond the reach of a string quartet.

Such critical beliefs as that certain combinations of melody, harmony, and rhythm are properly "orchestral," "violinistic," "pianistic," or closely related to the capacities of a string quartet or an orchestra became enormously more decisive in the nineteenth century than they had been earlier. This is not to say that Haydn's materials or his manipulations of them did not differ when he was composing a piano sonata from those he used and manipulated when composing a symphony; it is rather to say that in Haydn's time this difference commonly was little wider than the separate mechanical natures of the instruments employed made inevitable. Comparing Mozart and Bach, we may sense that Mozart's textures, melodic profiles, rhythmic ways, and har-

monic motion grew far more ascertainably and directly than
Bach's from the special characteristics of the forces for
which, at the moment, he was composing. This tendency to
specialization increased swiftly during the eighteenth century. But if we extend the comparison from Mozart forward
in time—to that of a piece for piano by him and one by
Chopin (born only fifty-four years later than Mozart), we
can hear for ourselves that early in the nineteenth century
this specialization increased suddenly. The contours and
manners of a Mozart piano composition do not differ in materials and handling from those of a Mozart work for orchestra in the same degree as a Chopin piano piece differs from
any piece of orchestral music whatever.

Materials and Choice of Means

We have come to feel that Bach possessed (or was able
to imagine and embody) an endless supply of musical ideas
complete in themselves as to melody, harmony, and rhythm,
but very loosely related to the technical capacities of a given
instrument or ensemble. (This is an exaggeration, but one
that suggests a useful idea.) Setting these ideas down on
paper so as to make their performance possible, Bach assigned them to such instruments or groups of instruments
and/or voices as he could command at the moment, as he
had been ordered to supply music for, or as were equipped
to project them—equipped, that is, to supply the number
of contrastingly colored melodic lines he desired, as well as
to sustain tones and make them clearly audible. By Mozart's time the creative process had changed. Mozart responded to the problems of composing for a string quartet
with musical ideas that would not have occurred to his
imagination when he was writing for piano, for voices, or
for orchestra. No longer were the questions, much of the
time, what instruments were available, what class of musical employers or patrons was involved, or which producing
means could project a certain number of melodic voices or
produce sustained or brief, perhaps percussive, tones. Far
more than with Bach and his contemporaries, the process
now consisted of conceiving *simultaneously* the musical ma-

terials and their means of projection. One aspect of musical creation reacted upon the other so constantly that they began to become inseparable steps of one process. When a Mozart composition is transcribed for another medium, far more of its complete original nature is sacrificed than when a Bach piece is similarly transcribed: far more of the individual aspect of Mozart's music resides in an organic relationship between its materials and its instrumentation.

Influence of Media on Composition

With Chopin and the other composers of the high romantic period, moreover, this process began to pass beyond the line of relatively equal interaction. To some extent—often to a very large extent—a Chopin composition for piano is an emanation of the piano itself, grows as it does partly because Chopin was exploring the piano's unique abilities and accepting musical materials suggested to him by them. A Beethoven piano sonata, particularly a late one, often sounds like orchestral music transcribed; no one of Chopin's piano works could have been conceived for any other medium. Nor could Berlioz's orchestral pieces have been composed for anything but the orchestra, which in itself is an important component of their very size, shape, and physiognomy. This quality of characteristic relationship, in which the performing medium plays a definitive part in the shaping of the music, is pre-eminently a nineteenth-century procedure. It was to reach its most intense application early in the twentieth century. Guesses from close quarters always are dangerous, but it appears to have been losing force as our century has unrolled.

Recomposition and Transcription

Maurice Ravel, a master of instrumentation, composed *Ma Mère l'Oye* (*Mother Goose*) in 1908 in two forms: for two pianos and for orchestra. He composed the six-section *Le Tombeau de Couperin* for piano solo in 1917 and recomposed four of its sections for orchestra, thus repeating what he had done earlier (1911) with his *Valses nobles et sentimentales.* He apparently felt that two other sections of *Le Tombeau de Couperin—Fugue* and *Toccata—*would be served badly by the orchestra. In Ravel's hands, the orchestral versions of his own works for piano are not "orchestrations" in the usual sense, but entirely new compositions in which he made use of the same (or very nearly the same) melodic, harmonic, and rhythmic materials.

Bach had composed *The Art of the Fugue* abstractly. He did not, that is, even indicate the instrument or instruments by which it was to be realized as sound. It has been arranged by later musicians for two pianos, for string quartet, and for orchestra. Much of it can be performed successfully on the piano and could be sung wordlessly by several accurate human voices. Mozart composed a serenade for eight wind instruments (K. 388) and himself recomposed it for string quintet (K. 406); although he appears to have written the wind version because he wanted to, the quintet version because he needed money, enthusiasts still dispute the relative qualities of the two. But such orchestral transcriptions as have been made of high romantic music—of Schumann's *Carnaval* and of a group of Chopin pieces as *Les Sylphides* —simply denature the music: they remove from it one of the central causes and reasons for its having existed at all, its integral relationship to the piano. Similarly, a four-hand piano transcription of a Haydn symphony loses much; a transcription of a Berlioz orchestral composition loses much more; any transcription of any mature piece by Debussy loses almost everything.

Musical Media and Musical Ideas

By the time of Debussy, the partnership between material and medium had become equal—if, indeed, to say that the medium had become a pervasive element of the material would not be both more illuminating and more exact. In extreme cases, in fact, the piano or the orchestra or other medium may seem to have played more part in selecting and shaping the musical ideas than the composer himself. The human voice can produce only one musical tone at a time. But two human voices can produce two simultaneous tones, one hundred voices one hundred tones. These irreducible facts rule all vocal music. The human voice can, within the physical limitation of breath supply and breath control, sustain tones well for a relatively long time, but it cannot produce well *staccato*** tones or sharply percussive tones. And these facts, too, shape all vocal music.

The violin sustains tone easily, can be made to produce *staccato* tones, but can produce not more than two tones at a time and is limited in volume, whereas the piano excels at *staccato* (it often is classed as a percussion instrument), can produce only a relative *legato*,** and (under the hands of a single player) can produce ten (at moments more) tones at a time. It has a much greater potential volume than a violin. These facts explain much of the difference between truly "violinistic" and truly "pianistic" music. And the fact that a large symphony orchestra—to which piano, organ, and other not strictly orchestral instruments may be added—can produce all at once *staccato, legato,* loud tones, and soft tones, and has a tremendous potential volume—all these physical facts dictate the kinds of music composed for orchestra.

Criticism of Means

Critics often say of a composition that it is or is not well conceived for its performing medium. A composition for piano may evoke in well-trained listeners the uncomfortable sensation that its composer was trying to make a solo piano do what only an orchestra really could do or could do easily and without strain. Or a very percussive piece, largely of *staccato* tones, composed for a stringed instrument, may seem to them wrongly scored in that it would have projected its percussive nature better through the piano keyboard. When this aspect of criticism is just, the composer has failed as badly as he would have failed if his melodies were poor, his harmony was awkward, or his rhythms were monotonous. The important fact to notice is that these are nineteenth-century and twentieth-century critical conceptions, end results of the romantic concentration on coloristic, characteristic instrumentation.

Wagner's Evolution of Himself

Richard Wagner did not, early in his career, hit upon the all-inclusive medium most germane to his esthetic and psychological nature or his ideas. The vastness of the musico-theatrico-moralistic notions that he was to evolve in his maturity would turn out to require not only a combination of orchestra and human voices, but also a monster orchestra and voices specially used. He composed one symphony when he was nineteen; piano sonatas when he was sixteen and eighteen; other early piano pieces; seven settings of lines from Goethe's *Faust* when he was nineteen. Not only were these pieces little more than juvenilia; they also were false starts. But Wagner made the right start, also at nineteen, when he began to compose an opera to a libretto written by himself (*Die Hochzeit*, never completed). Only in his own highly personal version of opera could he find his own way.

Wagner composed six operas from *Die Feen* (1833–34) through *Lohengrin* (1846–48) by following Spontini and Marschner and Weber and Meyerbeer, by using a full orchestra, setting semihistorical and legendary texts of his own writing. These six operas are typically early romantic in both detail and whole effect. Through them increasingly runs the underlying belief that opera could and should exemplify and inculcate ethical and moral ideas. The texts of all six are in dead earnest. They are serious works of art with messages to convey. In short, they are romantic not least in being hopefully employed as a means of communicating nonmusical ideas directly to listeners.

Wagner and Operatic Means

In all matters of musical syntax and grammar, Wagner's operas became constantly more complex. Through *Tannhäuser* and *Lohengrin* his form still was preponderantly that of eighteenth-century opera as adapted to the purposes of grand opera. It consisted, that is, of an overture or prelude[1] followed by a series of separable solos, duets, trios, and so forth, connected (or separated) by orchestra-accompanied recitative, arioso, and purely instrumental fabric. But Wagner already was making novel use of the *leitmotiv* ("leading motive") and showing clear signs of something like Liszt's "transformation of themes." That is, he was interested increasingly by methods of breaking down the separate-number scheme of operatic architecture; he was moving toward new methods aimed at over-all operatic unification.

The Leitmotiv and Continuous Texture

Wagner had a rare talent for inventing short musical phrases that would prove highly useful for identifying, expressing, or characterizing an idea, a protagonist, or an object. He had begun to weave these leitmotivs into a continuous musical fabric, subjecting them to transformation, contrapuntal combination, and rhythmic alteration. By the time when he came to compose *Tristan und Isolde* (1857–59), the four operas of *Der Ring des Nibelungen* (*Das Rheingold*, 1853–54; *Die Walküre*, 1854–56; *Siegfried*, 1856–71; and *Götterdämmerung*, 1869–74), and *Parsifal* (1877–82), he had succeeded in reforging opera in his own image.

In Wagner's later "music dramas," formal arias and other separable numbers has been dispensed with except where Wagner's own text called for a special effect. (*Die Meistersinger von Nürnberg*, the other opera of Wagner's maturity, stands apart from the rest: it is a comedy; it lacks magical or supernatural content; its text, revolving about a singing contest, required some extended use of set-number construction. Still, most—but not all—of the remarks above concerning his other late music dramas apply to it equally well.) Except for changes of scene, the texture was continuous. Full-blown melody in the classic or early romantic man-

[1] In Wagnerian terminology, an overture comes to a full stop before the stage action begins, whereas a prelude leads without break into the opening of the act following it.

ners had given way to continuous semimelody in which numerous leitmotivs appear and disappear in response to hints in the text. Because Wagner desired uninterrupted texture, he made his harmonic movement more and more chromatic and thus avoided those formal cadences which give listeners the sense of finality or break. He used a very large orchestra and then demanded that singers be heard clearly above and against it—and therefore finally required not only a new sort of singing, but also the erection of his own theater (the Festspielhaus at Bayreuth) for acoustic reasons including the proper placing of orchestra and singers. Because of the kind of singing that Wagnerian roles require, the singers must be of very ample physique and must nearly always belie in appearance the romantic youthfulness that many of them are supposed to express.

Wagner's Beliefs and Triumph

Richard Wagner believed himself a hero destined to revolutionize the art of music and, while doing that, to educate the German people for its predestined leading role in world affairs. For combined genius, egotism, and force of will he has no equal in the history of art. What is more important than the fascinating story of his prolonged struggles is that he finally won a gigantic, a Wagnerian triumph, enlisting across the civilized world such hordes of intense admirers as usually are enlisted only by religious or political leaders. His belief in the desirability of a synthesis of all the arts—and he finally intended his music dramas to be nothing less —his beliefs about every aspect of music, his practice of the leitmotiv, his development of the constantly unfolding musical fabric, the effect of his mammoth orchestration and voluminous singers—all of his proclamations and polemics and achievements—seemed to be at the edge of drowning out the music of the past and obliterating that of his contemporaries.

That Wagnerian sovereignty only recently began to fail. In order to understand Wagner, in order to comprehend the contemporary and later reactions to him, we must examine some of the techniques by which he created his most origi-

nal masterworks: *Tristan und Isolde, Der Ring des Ni-*
belungen, and *Parsifal* (*Die Meistersinger,* again, being less
germane to our purposes here).

Wagnerian Techniques:
Tristan und Isolde

Tristan und Isolde is divided into three acts because its
story requires three stage settings and three times: on shipboard, later at a castle in Cornwall, still later near a castle
in Brittany. The Prelude to the first act merges into the
opening of the shipboard stage picture without a break,[2]
but each of the acts necessarily comes to a concluding cadence giving a temporary sense of repose. Ernest Newman,
analyzing *Tristan* in his masterly study *The Wagner Operas,* quoted from it sixty themes, fragments of themes, and
versions of themes, nearly every one of which has more than
one symbolic meaning in relation to the text, or several shifting symbolic meanings. These motives appear, disappear,
and reappear, winding sinuously in and out of the chromatic
harmonic fabric woven of frequently chromatic melodies.
The opening of the Prelude:

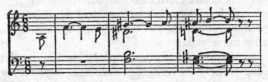

accurately indicates that by the date of its composition Wagner had agreed to the full decay of the classic harmonic
system and had made it inevitable that the harmonic developments to follow his own works could be nothing short of
deliberate rejection of even so much of that system as survived in them. What key is this? Lacking a key signature,
is it C major? No. A minor? Probably. Both C major and

[2] Wagner supplied the *Tristan* Prelude with a formal ending to be
used when it was played separately in concert. Making this arrangement, he also altered some earlier passages, his aim being to make the
form of the Prelude satisfactory as detached from the opera's action.

A minor? Possibly. Neither? That depends on the eyes, ears, and brain examining it.

If, with Ernest Newman, we regard these measures as containing two motives—one from the opening A to the D♯ at the beginning of the second full measure, the other beginning with the G♯ at the opening of that second full measure and running to the final B—we can discover that one of the two motives is predominantly chromatic (A-F-E-D♯ being chromatic except for its first step), the other (G♯-A-A♯-B) altogether so. Wagner himself suggested the presence of two distinct motives here by assigning the first to the cellos, the second to oboes above a support of bassoons, English horns, and clarinets.

Slowly, with all the deliberateness of much late-nineteenth-century romantic music, *Tristan und Isolde* lengthens out by the addition of new melodic ideas and treatments that are not simply stated and then abandoned, as in most older operas, but are referrred to, hinted at, and used outright again and again throughout the acts. At moments of tension in the story, the melodic-harmonic intensity and complexity become very great, but rhythmic intensity remains much less noticeable. This music induces a sensation of continuous, dreamlike unfolding which is formed out of the sinuous chromaticism of melody, the slowly revolving richness of the chromatic harmony, and the pervasive (anti-Wagnerians would say the enervating) absence of well-defined rhythmic pulse.

A few sections of *Tristan und Isolde* can be detached from the entirety for concert performance or recording. The Prelude (in Wagner's concert arrangement); the Narrative and Curse, sung by Isolde in Act I; the second-act Love Duet; Isolde's Love-Death (*Liebestod*) in Act III—these and a few other passages often are performed apart from the whole. But this questionable practice does not contradict the fact that *Tristan* is an uninterrupted continuity in three sections. If the listener's purpose be to absorb the meanings of the music (not to mention the libretto) or to judge Wagner by it, it can be listened to adequately only as he composed it (or nearly as he composed it—few performances of Wagner's operas today are complete; they nearly always are staged with extensive cuts). The over-all form of this music drama is as relevant to its contents and intentions as the form of a Mozart concerto or a Beethoven sonata is to its contents and intentions. By the time when Wagner had reached maturity, he had evolved a grasp and a command of his endlessly complex materials which were nearly absolute. Serious disagreements with him necessarily must be conducted on the level of disagreement with his purposes and aims, never (or seldom) on that of his consciousness of what he was intending to do or with his success in doing exactly that.

Wagner and the Human Voice

One indicative peculiarity of the late Wagner music dramas is well exemplified by Isolde's Love-Death. A concert performance of this excerpt without a singer to perform the tones sung by Isolde or an instrument to play them loses the narrative continuity; but it sacrifices almost nothing of the strictly musical structure or fabric. The notes assigned to the heroine easily are managed by a good singer; this is not awkward vocal writing. When properly sung, they can be heard above the orchestra. But they add almost nothing *musically*. As Sir Donald Francis Tovey points out (*Essays in Musical Analysis,* vi, 104), Isolde here sings for sixty-eight measures, in twenty-five of which "she is able to deliver the main theme, constantly broken, sometimes quite awkwardly, by pauses and other necessities of declamation." During the other forty-three measures, the notes assigned to her are mostly nonmelodic counterpoints, the omission of which in a concert performance by purely instrumental forces robs the music of nothing essential to it.

"Surely her [Isolde's] last notes should be memorable?" Tovey asks: she is the pivotal figure of the entire music drama, and here she is dying of love. "They are the right notes in the right declamation; they easily penetrate the orchestra, and they will do justice to the most golden of voices. How many music-lovers can quote them? They have never been heard in the concert-room, except when a singer was engaged; but I should not be surprised if many of the music-lovers who go to every stage performance of *Tristan* found themselves unable to quote them." What Tovey describes here is a climactic example of one Wagnerian procedure: that of assigning a majority of the musically important materials to the orchestra and of using the human voice largely for the prime purpose of pronouncing the text words so that they may be audible.

Any peformance of the waltzes from Richard Strauss's *Der Rosenkavalier* represents only the accompaniments to singing in various scenes. In arranging these waltzes for concert performance, no effort whatever has been made to introduce instrumental equivalents of the notes given to the singers. Contrarily, concert and recorded performances of Violetta's *"Sempre libera"* from Act I of Verdi's *La Traviata* usually assign to the orchestra (or to the piano if the aria is so accompanied) the notes supposed to be sung offstage by the tenor: the musical structure is incomplete without them. Thus opera in which the vocal line is of essential musical importance differs in texture and construction from opera (Wagner and Richard Strauss are examples) in which that assigned to the orchestra is more important.

Der Ring des Nibelungen

Tristan und Isolde is very long. But it shrinks beside *Der Ring des Nibelungen,* four complete operas constituting together perhaps the longest interrelated series of musical compositions in existence. The *Ring,* though not necessarily Wagner's greatest accomplishment, remains the fullest demonstration of his unique manner of creation. In that huge concourse of musical means he summed up (and in many senses impaired the future usefulness of) romanticism's chief syntactical and grammatical contributions to music: the furthest development of chromaticism conceivable within the classical-romantic harmonic assumptions; the effort to make music a language for expressing the nonmusical, the didactic, the autobiographical, and the philosophic; the doing-away, in opera construction, with both the aria and the Lied and their derivatives; and the substitution for them of continually unfolding melody pieced together out of themes and thematic fragments. (Analyzing the *Ring*, Ernest Newman found it essential to quote one hundred and ninety-eight themes, fragments, and transformations.)

The clarity, crispness, and clearly outlined rhythms of classical music, as well as most of its transparency, are almost totally absent from the *Ring*. In their stead, we find something like the flow of a great continental river, a stream sometimes clear, but more often translucent; a stanchless flood moving slowly forward except for occasional falls and rapids, a prehistoric current in which monsters lurk and the denizens of nonhuman kingdoms carry on a strange sublife. Those who first fell under the intensely potent bewitchments of the late Wagner were often as though literally under a spell; the increasing numbers of later listeners who can enjoy *Tristan*, the *Ring*, and *Parsifal* only in excerpts or as cut drastically most often are found yearning for the crisp sunlight or decorous candlelight of Viennese or French classicism, the sweet emotions of the Renaissance, or the anti-Wagnerian impressionism and relatively impersonal neoclassicism and neoromanticism of a later day.

The Uniqueness of Wagner

The case of Wagner (and it is significant that Friedrich Nietzsche, once an ardent admirer of Wagner's art, wrote a book under that title only five years after the composer's death) remains unique. In order to be an informed and confirmed admirer of Monteverdi or Handel or Mozart or Beethoven, it is not necessary to know what they as individuals thought or believed. On the contrary, in order to be a confirmed Wagnerian it is inescapably necessary to admire even the messages embedded in his texts. To an unprecedented extent, Wagner really succeeded in making his music, his texts, and his stage business indivisible. Nothing would have displeased him more than to have learned that less than a century after his death hundreds of thousands of music-lovers would be familiar with all or fragments of his operas from *Rienzi* to *Parsifal* while only a few among them would know his artistic, philosophical, and religious beliefs and preachments. He would be positively shocked to know that a significant number of today's continuing admirers of some of his music never have witnessed a stage performance of a single one of his operas.

At this hour the truth appears to be that Wagner survives as a composer and as nothing else. Wagner the teacher, the arguer about ethics, religion, race, and politics, the conceiver of artistic syntheses—Wagner the dabbler in so many nonmusical fields of which he wished music to be no more than an equal partner (if not a servant)—has ceased to matter except to historians, biographers, and a scattering of orthodox Wagnerians. But some of his music, torn in fragments and patches from its mammoth contexts, appears relatively immortal.

Giuseppe Verdi, Romantic and Nonromantic

In persistent, dramatic contrast to Wagner's evolution—and significant both for producing music of enduring popularity and for tending to mitigate Wagner's overweening influence—was the comparatively calm development of Giuseppe Verdi. Born, like Wagner, in 1813, the Italian by 1840 had produced two operas (*Oberto, Conte di San Bonifacio* and *Un Giorno di regno*) not far removed from the *opera seria* and *opera buffa*, respectively, of his era. If the name of Rossini or Donizetti were signed to both of them, students probably would note that these operas were early, undeveloped works by those masters. They differ from, say, *La Gazza ladra* and *Lucia di Lammermoor* only in a certain robustness and sinewiness—and by being inferior to them.

But Verdi lived more than sixty years after 1840, composing twenty-four more operas and a large Requiem Mass. Like Wagner, he was always a full-blown romantic who felt somewhat the puissance of the grand-opera manners of Spontini and Meyerbeer. But his texts nearly always were devoid of legend, free of supernatural interventions, human in their action. If Verdi held well-formulated ethical, moral, religious, or political (as distinct from patriotic) beliefs, they did not appear in the texts he set, none of which was of his own writing. Except for the early *Un Giorno di regno* and the final *Falstaff*—completed when he was nearly seventy-nine—all of Verdi's operas are tragic. But none of them conveys any urgent nondramatic or nonmusical message. They do not attempt to communicate extraoperatic ideas directly to listeners except in so far as they represent and support theatrical stories built around characters who have and who express such ideas.

The contrast in mental atmosphere between Verdi's *Otello* and Wagner's *Tristan und Isolde,* between *Aïda* and *Der Ring des Nibelungen,* between *Don Carlos* and *Parsifal,* is in part national. But it is much more importantly individual, the difference between a man who aimed at the noblest and most movingly human sort of musical entertainment and a man who believed that he was shaping a synthesis of all the arts in the direction of a ritualistic philosophy or religion.

The Evolution of the Verdian Opera

Musically, in most matters of grammar and syntax, Verdi was nearly as complex in his early operas as he ever was to become. But he tended, in a manner distinctively his own, toward a continuous musical web freed in part from the separate-number layout of classical opera. Through his long life, his orchestration became more and more expressive and effective. He made no extensive use of the leitmotiv or the Lisztian transformation of themes, but he occasionally employed methods related to them, uses noticeable and startlingly effective because of their rarity and because he placed them dramatically. In *Otello,* for example, the Moor, just having murdered Desdemona and stabbed himself, recalls the rapturous melodic phrase allied, in their first-act love duet, with the words *"un baccio"* (a kiss). The poignancy of this musical quotation is intense and wholly un-Wagnerian.

Song and the dramatic interactions of human passions interested Verdi. He was a prodigiously bountiful melodist, and many of his melodies have achieved almost the status of folk song. He learned how to characterize complicated individuals musically in an almost Mozartean manner: from his middle-period and late operas have stepped such rounded human beings as Rigoletto, Violetta, the elder Germont, Aïda, Amneris, Otello, Iago, and Falstaff. All of the characters mentioned, Aïda and Amneris excepted, had existed previously, though sometimes under other names, as personages in renowned plays, but the individuals created by Verdi from the outlines handed him by his librettists are musical characters, not merely singing versions of personages originally created by Victor Hugo, Dumas *fils,* and Shakespeare.

Except for his constant diminution of the distinction between aria and recitative, Verdi's plan of operatic construction differed but little from that of Spontini, Meyerbeer, or the Wagner of *Tannhäuser.* Yet *Rigoletto, La Traviata, Aïda, Otello,* and *Falstaff* at least are as stylistically unified as any operas ever composed. To the end of his career, Verdi maintained a seldom-flawed balance in the partnership of singers and orchestra. It is impossible to think of a transcription or performance of one of his arias or concerted numbers with the singers' notes omitted. Equally integral is his orchestration; piano transcription does small justice to his music.

Verdi and Modern Taste

Verdi expressed and incarnated very few theories except purely musical ones and practical dramatic and theatrical ones. His harmony, increasingly subtle as he grew more experienced, seldom was daring or experimental. His finest operas grew organically from opera's past as interpreted by a dramatic composer of genius. They differ from the operas of Gluck and Mozart in myriad details and in atmosphere, but they recognizably are blood descendants of the operas that had preceded them. Even *Aïda, Otello,* and *Falstaff* nonetheless once sounded old-fashioned alongside *Tristan,* the *Ring,* and *Parsifal,* at least to non-Italians. More recently, their fierce sincerity, the masterliness of their vocal writing, the vital endurance of their characters, and their unbreakable mating of music and text once again have made them new. No more indicative revolution in the musical taste of the large music-listening public has occurred in the twentieth century than that which has elevated Giuseppe Verdi to the universally recognized company of the very great. He was not Wagner's intellectual peer. He had not Wagner's all-conquering egoistic energy and drive. But no justification survives for the former tacit belief that Verdi's operas are, for these or any other reasons, inferior to Wagner's as works of musical art.

Wagner's influence on instrumental music, his harmonic ripeness, his structural expansiveness, and his dedicated seriousness of intention have been fixed in several lines of descent. But his influence on the structure of opera has not proved fertile or lasting: the "music drama," that synthetic omnibus of the arts as he envisioned it, has not evolved beyond his own operas, the last of which was completed and first staged in 1882.

Richard Strauss
as Heir of Liszt and Wagner

The most obvious heir of Wagner was Richard Strauss, such of whose operas as *Salome* (1905) and *Elektra* (1909) made use of the Wagnerian continuum, the assertiveness of Wagner's orchestra, and Wagner's usual separation of the vocal lines from the meaning of the orchestra's music. But these are brief operas, for which reason they resemble a Lisztian symphonic poem or Straussian tone poem with vocal lines added. They are intensely serious, tragic works. In *Der Rosenkavalier* (1911), however, tragedy and earnestness gave way to a waltz-beguiled semiserious frivolity; here the discordant texture of the psychological tragedies made way for something sweeter and more overtly old-fashioned. And then, by one of the most curious twists in musical history, Strauss persisted in the musical idiom of *Der Rosenkavalier* for the rest of his creative life, using it alike for comedy and tragedy until it came to seem neuter and wholly undramatic. Not one of his numerous operas later than *Der Rosen-*

kavalier but contains music of charm and great expertness; not one of those operas as a whole approaches the force or beauty of its three most notable predecessors in the list. Except for an upthrust here and there, the music of the aging Strauss came to seem all but automatic.

Engelbert Humperdinck's *Hänsel und Gretel* (1893) also was somewhat Wagnerian in that its somewhat continuous music was evolved from melodic leitmotivs. A number of less talented, less successful, now largely forgotten German, French, Belgian, and English composers tried vainly to follow in Wagner's large footsteps. But formally speaking, Wagner has proved to be a massive door closing the operatic period of high romanticism rather than a gateway through which other composers could move forward into new territories.

The Influence of Verdi
and Verismo

On the contrary, the influence of Verdi—a simple re-affirmation of long-standing Italian traditions that Rossini, Bellini, and Donizetti had followed—has been continuous and certain. Giacomo Puccini, combining with some Verdian vigor the sort of realism that Georges Bizet had manipulated so brilliantly in *Carmen* (1875)—but modifying both by his own less forthright, more feminine, personality —brought that phase of Italian opera to what now seems to have been its terminus. When Puccini's *Manon Lescaut* (1893) and *La Bohème* (1896) followed soon after Pietro Mascagni's *Cavalleria rusticana* (1890) and Ruggiero Leoncavallo's *I Pagliacci* (1892), their contemporaries thought that a new school of opera—called *verismo* (literally "truthism")—had been founded on realism. But just as no German opera since *Der Rosenkavalier* stays regularly in the active repertoire of major opera houses in world metropolises, so no Italian opera since Puccini's *Turandot* (1924, left incomplete) has established itself with seeming permanence.

The Decline of Opera

Almost every important composer of the twentieth century has composed at least one opera. (Alban Berg's *Wozzeck*, 1914–21, regarded by many critics and enthusiasts as a towering musico-dramatic peak, is discussed in Chapter XXI.) But because the production of opera has become enormously costly, an opera must win the support of a very large audience to pass the test of the box office; at the same time, the taste of the widest music-listening public and the style of the foremost contemporary composers have continued to diverge extremely. The result has been that the most accomplished modern operas have been heard relatively few times before being relegated either to silence or to intermittent revival, often in less costly concert performance. Also, the primacy of opera among musico-theatrical forms now seems to have ended in the close of the romantic nineteenth century and its dying afterglow. The repertoire of large opera houses more and more has tended toward the condition of a museum collection: opera houses today have become mostly a means for displaying the art of the past rather than a means for producing the art of the present or that of the future. Opera has not regained the formerly unquestioned primacy among the musico-theatrical forms which it lost to ballet early in our century.

CHAPTER XVII

Belated Romanticism and
Neoclassicism

Later than the intensely individualistic romanticism of the first half of the nineteenth century, contemporary with or following Wagner's gigantic effort to sum up romanticism and synthesize the arts, large-scale attempts to pour new wines into the old classical bottles developed a classicizing movement. It formed largely around the massive orchestral compositions of two men active in Vienna: Johannes Brahms (1833–97) and Anton Bruckner (1824–96), important counterparts and extensions of whose formal procedures were to become evident in the somewhat isolated later compositions of Gustav Mahler (1860–1911) and Jean Sibelius (1865–1957).

These four greatly dissimilar composers shared an implicit belief in the enduring self-disciplinary value of sonata patterns, of the symphony, and of other extended forms shaped in large part by the example of the classical eighteenth century. They did not question the wisdom of adapting those examples to musical matter and conceptions native to the nineteenth century and—with Mahler and Sibelius—to some extent the twentieth. None of them ever composed an opera. Mostly they used the originally dramatic sonata procedures for meditative, epic, philosophical, autobiographical, or other nondramatic purposes.

Brahms and the Problems of Form

In Brahms's earliest surviving music, the romantic contours of his melodies and the warm ripeness of their related harmonies seem to be direct reflections of Schumann, whom Brahms knew personally and admired intensely. But the patterns over which the young Brahms stretched his Schumannesque matter were brought forward, little changed, from Beethoven's middle and late periods. This unsuitable and unstable relation of manner and matter becomes particularly noticeable in the three piano sonatas and the piano scherzo composed between 1851 and 1853 and in the Concerto for Piano and Orchestra in D minor (1854). The musical mind and personality that this music discloses are quintessentially romantic, whereas the employment of the extended formal patterns too often reins in prematurely the material's intense, clearly discursive nature or prolongs beyond necessity the development of some of its sections. Brahms, that is, had not yet found an appropriate vehicle for transporting his musical messages. During the last forty-four years of his life he notably composed no more piano sonatas, though he produced much piano music and several sonatas for other instruments with piano.

Brahms as a Later Beethoven

Brahms openly considered the symphony the loftiest of instrumental forms. He edged up to the composition of his own First Symphony (1855–76) with timidity and extreme caution, experimenting meanwhile with two orchestral serenades (1857–60). In the four symphonies that he wrote between 1855 and 1885, classical patterns persist—but whereas the models in the serenades largely had been Beethoven's chamber music, those for the symphonies were Beethoven's symphonies. Brahms's melodies swell, conveying romantic, sometimes fruity, emotion; the harmonies become more and more intricate. The formal conservatism, combined with the steady discipleship to Beethoven, at times battles with the innate, self-sufficient nature of the musical thought. In the eyes of others, this music won Brahms the undesired leadership of the anti-Wagnerian forces; he came to be looked upon as the last white hope of classical romanticism in the "war" against the formal as well as material romanticism of Liszt and, particularly, Wagner.

But the mature Brahms did not compose only symphonies, the gigantic Concerto for Piano and Orchestra in B♭ Major (1872–81), and that huge partial parallel to Beethoven's *Missa solemnis, A German Requiem* (1857–68)—works which, however otherwise admirable, do not fairly represent successful attempts to house Brahms's idiosyncratic musical personality. He composed many Lieder. In them, too, he was at first slavishly Schumannesque, but he matured into a song-writing method of his own by means of which he produced some of the most satisfying poetic settings of the post-Schumann era. Curiously, Brahms never made significant use of either the song cycle or the suite of brief piano pieces—both forms that Schumann had made his own —or of that native romantic orchestral idea, the symphonic poem. But, perhaps influenced by Chopin's nomenclature (though not often by Chopin's comparatively unclassical melodic habits or persistently daring harmonic motions), Brahms composed many short piano pieces—ballads, capriccios, intermezzos, rhapsodies, romances, waltzes, and *études*. In them, as in his finest Lieder, the musical materials and the forms by means of which they are deployed are coextensive. In harmonic and melodic ideas, these later piano pieces are as unabashedly romantic as Schumann or Chopin, and by their individual success of form belong to the canon of romanticism's characteristic achievements. Of classicizing they are wholly free: they are, in fact, free superb forms produced simultaneously with and by the materials that they contain.

Listening to Brahms

For many decades, all attitudes toward Brahms were based on the assumption that he was a belated classical composer. This assumption started to lose its immediacy in the 1920s, when, for almost the first time since Brahms's youth, voices were heard saying that his claim to be considered an original master of music must be based chiefly on his Lieder, his pieces for solo piano, and (in a formal, technical sense) on his command of a new extension of the variation principle. These were voices speaking against the background of a critical axiom that it is difficult to controvert. Any great artist necessarily is one of his own era's representatives in the stream of artistic evolution: he either perfects already existing forms or evolves new ones. No claim ever has been put forth that Brahms's use of sonata forms bettered that of Haydn, Mozart, and Beethoven. He was no more a revolutionary than Bach or Handel had been, and the new criticism asserted that he—coming as late in the romantic period as they had come in the baroque—had to be a romanticist to be a great composer. They were asserting that he was not a classical master at all, but a romantic one, no rebel of the Liszt sort, the Wagner variety, or any other kind, but a composer nonetheless able and ready to forge his own forms.

Brahms and the Variation

In a remarkable series of extended sectional compositions in variation form, Brahms hit upon and then with great intellectual command perfected a compositional method peculiarly fertile for him. In the sense of liberating and concentrating Brahms's own significance, his discipleship to Beethoven became most fruitful here, formally speaking. He found preliminary hints toward his variation technique in such Beethoven compositions as the piano variations on a theme from the *"Eroica"* Symphony, those in the *"Appassionata"* Sonata, Opus 57 (*andante con moto*); those on a waltz by Diabelli; those on an original theme in C minor; and—for orchestra—the *adagio* movement of the Ninth Symphony. Brahms's own sets of variations include those on a theme by Schumann (1854) and culminate in the Variations on a Theme by Haydn (both for orchestra and for two pianos, 1873); the Variations and Fugue on a Theme by Handel (1861); the *études* known as Variations on a Theme by Paganini (two volumes, 1862–63); and—for orchestra—the passacaglia finale of his Fourth Symphony (1884–85).

Later Manners of Variation

Variation remains possible in many ways: on a more or less set progression of harmonies, on a melody, on a rhythm or group of rhythms. In the baroque and rococo periods, most continuous variation patterns and sectional variations maintained either a complete melody or a ground throughout. They were likely to maintain harmonic continuity between the varied theme and the variations. Up to Mozart, one notable aspect of all sorts of variation was the relatively small difference (harmonic, melodic, or rhythmic) between a theme and its variations. The differences, that is, had been largely occasioned by slight shifts and decorations. With Mozart, however, and more with Beethoven and Schubert, variation began to be envisioned in a more far-ranging sense. The interrelations between the chosen melody or melodic fragment and the variations farthest removed from it still usually were easy to determine—but in the remote variations the melody in particular often was so altered that, if isolated, it might be unrecognizable as a variant. Certain elements of the harmonic structure tended to be kept throughout, but the outline of the melody at times was lost almost completely.

With Brahms, an element that might be called controlled waywardness entered in. This was a manner of evolving some variations in a series from sparse hints in the melody or from materials newly developed during earlier variations. In his "Handel" and "Paganini" sets, whole groups of variations advance progressively, each variation being more closely derived from the variations preceding it than from the original theme. The most distant variations are related to the original melody by only tenuous threads, but sound inevitable as placed in this new sequence of musical events. In all probability it was from the *alla fuga* that ends Beethoven's *"Eroica"* Variations and the fugue just before the last of the "Diabelli" set that Brahms adapted the plan of using a passacaglia and a fugue in the highly satisfying finales of his "Haydn" and "Handel" variations respectively.

In the finest of his sets of variations, Brahms welded impressive musical ideas and impressively handled patterns into true musical form, evolving patterns none the less valuable because he never used them twice in the same way. The Variations and Fugue on a Theme by Handel, formally speaking, is as great a triumph of romantic musical design as Chopin's Fantaisie or Schumann's *Carnaval*. Among the many movements of Brahms's symphonies, concertos, and chamber pieces, few, if any, others display the composer so relaxed in the certainty of power as does the stupendous finale of the Fourth Symphony. Whatever else a passacaglia may be, it is not a dramatic form. Sir Donald Francis Tovey brilliantly suggested (*Essays in Musical Analysis*, i, 116) that Brahms, having satisfied himself dramatically during the first three movements of the Fourth Symphony, desired this finale to be "free to express tragic emotion without being encumbered by the logical and chronological necessities of the more dramatic sonata forms."

This passacaglia is made up of a theme, thirty variations, and something more. The theme, eight measures in length, first appears thus:

The extraordinary number of ways in which Brahms varies his treatment of this somber theme, altering it only by moving it from one pitch to another, is a measure of the distance that one sort of variation had traveled between the seventeenth century and the nineteenth. The seventeenth-century *arie* had often consisted of a chief melody sung above an accompanying brief semimelody sounded over and over (*basso ostinato*). Transferred from vocal-and-instrumental music to purely instrumental use, this pattern often was called either passacaglia or chaconne. And the final movement of Brahms's Fourth Symphony is fundamentally nothing else: what differentiates it from a seventeenth- or eighteenth-century chaconne or passacaglia is the wealth of instrumental, harmonic, rhythmic, and contrapuntal methods that Brahms has applied to its unfolding. He often has so manipulated the unchanging theme as all but to obliterate it completely, making it for a time just one element in what amounts to wholly new music.

Although Brahms's passacaglia is one continuous musical unit, it actually is plotted this way: the theme itself, fourteen variations, sixteen more variations, a coda. The second group (sixteen) of variations may be seen, in a typically Brahmsian sense, as variations on the first group of fourteen—though we must note again that the theme itself appears, substantially unaltered, in one instrumental range or another, as the base above which each section of this whole complex structure is erected. Of particular interest as an excellent example of the musical suggestibility that made Brahms a more original master of the variation than of the sonata forms is his derivation of several highly satisfactory sub-melodies and countermelodies from two small elements in the theme itself: the chromatic progression G, A, A♯, B in measures 3, 4, 5, 6 of the example (and especially the A, A♯) and the descent of one octave from B to B (measures 6, 7 of the example).

Brahms contrasts E major with the previously pervading E minor in the twelfth variation. When he begins the second group of variations with No. 15, he indicates what might be called a rebeginning by returning to E minor. He uses numerous sorts of contrapuntal devices: Variation 29, for example, is a canon. What is musically noteworthy about the entire passacaglia, however—as distinct from what technically causes this quality—is the sensation given to the listener that he is being carried toward a climax with no intervening feeling of repetition. And when the rather agitated thirtieth (final) variation has entered upon a ritardando, the coda is able at last to present overwhelmingly convincing proof that the climax has been attained, that all complexities have been gathered together and been unraveled.

Through the thirtieth variation, Brahms has for the most

part stayed rigorously in a single key in each division. The coda, again repeating (or so it seems at first) the original theme in the same key, gets through only its first four measures. Then Brahms uses the chromatic step and octave descent mentioned above, employing them as the convincing reason for a series of releasing modulations; employs an artful variety of imitation (the same theme two measures later and only a semitone higher); reiterates the theme in compacted quarter-notes; and finds one last sad, solemn comment to make about it. The totality is a formal masterwork just as right for its communicative purposes as are, for other, more dramatic, less emotionally packed purposes, the most superb uses of sonata forms.

Brahms and Ultimate Victory

Early in Brahms's creative life, he had mostly detractors, and the number of them was increased by the mistaken fanatic Lisztians and Wagnerians. Somewhat later, he became one of the most honored and popular of serious composers—justly for the loftiness of his musical aims, the creative grasp of his techniques, and the melodic and emotion-evoking richness of his finest works. But he became as mistakenly estimated in praise as he had been mistakenly depreciated by adverse Wagnerian criticism. He became, that is, the epicenter of the mistaken attitude that (he being taken for a classical composer) the sonata was the only road to the loftiest achievement in purely instrumental music. In more recent years, Brahms again has been criticized adversely, but much of that criticism actually has been directed at the mistaken picture of him. A fair statement of the most modern critical position regarding Brahms might be that unquestionably he was a great composer; that he was not a true classicist (having been born in 1833); that in general he employed classical forms only to triumph over them rather than with them—to triumph through sectional beauties, noble melodies, and engaging harmonic variety rather than by formal rectitude; that he took the variation principle to the most complex and widely expressive stage of development that it yet has reached; and that in Lieder and piano pieces he was a romanticist pure and simple, the forms of his songs having been determined by his sensitive responses to their texts, those of his piano pieces by their own idiosyncratic musical matter.

The Bruckner Problem

Since the middle years of Brahms's creative career he never has lacked very numerous admirers. Anton Bruckner, on the contrary, never (outside of Vienna and some German cities) has won more than a handful of admirers. He was an intensely religious man of somewhat naïve mind, propelled by lofty ideals, but quite devoid of Brahms's genial warmth, rather pretty sentiment, and earthy humor. Bruckner became an ardent Wagnerian (Wagner called him the only true symphonist after Beethoven), and unwary critics began saying that his music was as Wagnerian as he. If his eleven symphonies[1] be examined solely as music, they are discovered to be far more nearly Beethovian than Brahms: Bruckner derived much of his formal philosophy and the patterns for carrying it into action from the Beethoven of the Fifth Symphony. Gabriel Engel, an ardent Brucknerite, went as far as to state that each of Bruckner's symphonies was based on this formula: "I. The Drama of Inner Conflict (with the soul as hero). II. Adagio. The Song of Faith (Prayerful Communion with God). III. Scherzo. The Dance of Life (the Joys of Life in Nature). IV. Finale. The soul's decisive struggle and the triumph over all opposition." With the slightest shifts, this could be a crude diagram of Beethoven's largest symphonies.

Bruckner was fertile in melodies that he used for sonata-like treatment though most often they were romantic rather than classical in contour and not in themselves of arresting beauty. Often they were simply too long to be happy subjects for any sort of sonata development. He strove under-

[1] Bruckner's "First" Symphony (two others had preceded it) was composed in 1894. Of the nine numbered symphonies, only one pretends to be anything but absolute, nonprogrammatic music. The Fourth ("Romantic" or "Wagner," 1874) Symphony has a vague program that Bruckner himself warned his disciples not to apply literally.

standingly and often with success for rhythmic variety. His use of the orchestra was original, deviating from the symphonic usages of earlier composers chiefly in the way he used instruments in families. Again and again in Bruckner's symphonies, an entire orchestral family (the brasses, the woodwinds, or the strings) is made to sound together; variety and a peculiar, grudging sort of forward motion then are achieved by silencing that family to bring in another. Bruckner's craftsmanship was of the most scrupulous and he was constantly revising. He showed, in fact, most of the determinable qualities of a great composer. But except in the ears and eyes of a few fanatical admirers, he lacked all sense of punctuality, largely because he construed the sonata forms as epic rather than dramatic. He used them for ceremonial and prolonged meditative and expositional effects rather than for the aspects of drama native to them by ancestry and innate structure. Many times he distended the component sections of sonata form until their dramatic contrast—their very reason for existence—was lost to the ear, however clearly they may be visible to the examining eye on paper.

Musical Stasis

The musical result of Bruckner's unique combination of virtues and faults is that a Bruckner symphonic movement sometimes threatens to last forever as—sluggishly, with enormous pomp, and with persistent squareness—it moves concentrically toward no imaginable goal. Bruckner's String Quintet (1879), his only important chamber work, sounds like one of his symphonies on a smaller scale; it has their flaws without their orchestral virtues. Only in religious music, and perhaps especially in the concert Mass in F minor (1866) was Bruckner unable to impose upon himself the damaging need to fill out at incredible length the sections of a pattern prescribed and strictly interpreted. There, reined in by a text, he could not easily challenge the logics of musical time and a listener's patience. His religious music forcibly suggests, as passages scattered throughout his symphonies suggest, that he mistook the very nature of formal truth, that he might have become the romantic master he was in many ways equipped to be if he had not held in blind adoration the letter rather than the informing spirit of Beethoven.

The Problem of Gustav Mahler

Gustav Mahler and Jean Sibelius often are regarded as modern composers (of Mahler's major compositions, only the first four symphonies and the song cycle *Lieder eines fahrenden Gesellen* were composed during the nineteenth century; the later six symphonies—the Tenth remaining incomplete—and the song cycles *Kindertotenlieder* and *Das Lied von der Erde* belong to the twentieth century. All of Sibelius's larger works except the symphonic poem *En Saga* were completed after 1900). They are more easily and justifyingly understood as prolonged afterglows of the sunset of romanticism, a twilight attempt to re-establish classical forms by adjusting them to late romantic conditions.

Mahler was intensely self-centered and wholly romantic. Every measure of his music is colored unmistakably by and expressive of his peculiar nature: he is as instantly recognizable as wholly unique as Chopin or Berlioz. Yet even one of his most vocal admirers (Gabriel Engel, quoted above in reference to Bruckner) states that Mahler's music "is in no respect, save in its unprecedentedly abundant employment of solo-passages for all instruments, of a radical or revolutionary nature." (This statement, to be sure, would have astonished the audiences who heard Mahler's music when it was new, and who found it terrifyingly "revolutionary." But they were being distracted from its fundamental characteristics by its most noticeable surface features.) Mahler, that is, attempted to confine his unique musical ideas, his juxtaposition of the grandiose-tragic and the popular-vulgar, in a cage of hallowed usages and old formal patterns. As Mr. Engel pointed out, he gave an almost concerto-like importance to one solo instrument after the other within the texture and discourse of his symphonic orchestra. He did introduce both solo human voices and choruses into several of his symphonies, perhaps reflecting

Bruckner's special use of trumpet and horn statements as much as the choral finale of Beethoven's Ninth Symphony. But Mahler's musical material itself was exuberant, idiosyncratic, nervous, and wholly unclassical—if not anticlassical. Not interpreting the symphony's established patterns with Bruckner's literalness, and being willing to alter both the order and the number of a symphony's movements, Mahler nevertheless hewed to its broad outlines in nine completed symphonies, one incomplete symphony, and the huge song cycle *Das Lied von der Erde,* really a symphony with voices.

Later Attitudes Toward Mahler

The results of Mahler's twenty years of productivity are a body of music that has won a relatively small group of faithful admirers, a large body of indifferent listeners, and another small body of violent detractors. The admirers accurately point out the originality of his music, its often charming "Viennese" melodies, its intermittently intense expressivity, and the guiding effect on the composers who have followed him of his "lineo-coloristic" orchestration. The crux of the continuing argument over Mahler resides in their added claim that he evolved new forms in a "struggle to conform as closely to the tenets of absolute music as a new content would permit" (Gabriel Engel). The indifferent listeners to Mahler's music most often are merely bored by its length and seeming diffuseness. The detractors assert that his large works simply fail to hold together, falling into shards out of sheer overtension, from the over-development of highly personal musical materials that in fact either are undevelopable by the traditional symphonic procedures as Mahler altered them or simply appear as self-sufficient units. For many listeners, Mahler must seem to present the final *reductio ad absurdum* of the nineteenth century's ever-increasing tendency toward sheer size, toward slow tempos, toward the pouring of increasingly inappropriate musical raw material into distended, finally almost gaseously diffuse, versions of classical patterns. (This argument fails, of course, to deal with Mahler's individual

Lieder, many of which listeners of all stripes recognize and cherish as masterpieces in small.)

Pursuit of the Impossible

To look upon Johannes Brahms's musical life as a tragedy is impossible: he composed much music that was and that is greatly loved. But both Bruckner and Mahler may be seen as tragic in more than one light. Their music always has been more discussed than listened to, and the suggestion is inescapable that tragedy—apart from other, purely biographical, elements—lay in their pursuit of the impossible. They were anachronisms in that they failed to create for deeply romantic musical materials the related romantic forms. In the freedom of the symphonic poem or in forms that—had they been men of different training and mental equipment—they might have evolved spontaneously out of their own musical habits of speech, they might have evaded the aura of unsuccess that clings about their figures. They are found guilty, much of the time, of a mortal artistic sin: they did not discover the integral forms by which their ideas could have satisfied the expectations that they aroused. From the noblest motives—and despite heroic wrestlings with formal problems—their shared worship of Beethoven and their position in artistic time led them to find in variants of existing patterns a supposedly eternal virtue that for them those patterns could not have. This might not have mattered in a more superficial sense (they might have become as popular as Tchaikovsky) if they had been willing and able to succeed on any more superficial level and to curb their remarkably similar tendency to self-prolonging discursiveness. But neither Bruckner nor Mahler was content to be anything less than a very great composer, a Beethovian and/or Wagnerian Master of Music. Neither of them was willing, as Tchaikovsky was, to be in relative brevity whatever he might become if he was entirely, unadventurously himself. The result now appears to have been that, whereas Tchaikovsky became a greatly successful composer of the second rank, Bruckner and Mahler were damagingly flawed composers of the first.

Sibelius and the Symphony

Jean Sibelius seemed at first to have sprung, as a symphonist, straight from Tchaikovsky. His First Symphony was called "Tchaikovsky's Seventh," with reference to an earlier designation of Brahms's First Symphony as "Beethoven's Tenth." And in truth it is conventionally romantic. But Sibelius no more developed as a full-blown Tchaikovskyan romantic than he developed as a true descendant of Beethoven. He began to experiment with—and within—the symphonic patterns. Disregarding more and more the basic classical symphonic way of creating drama out of the contrast of strong and weak (or male and female) themes, he elaborated a highly individual method of movement construction. In several later Sibelius symphonies, a movement is built by gradual addition and grudging revelation. A fragment of melody is set forth; a second fragment is added to it; only at a climax or conclusion does the complete theme appear. By this method, Sibelius wrought movements of great strength and solidity. By themselves they can only be regarded as true examples of formal success. But this type of construction alters the inner relationships between a single movement and the other movements of a symphony. It tends to make the four-movement symphonic pattern itself unnecessary and even undesirable, for it greatly weakens the particular contrasts on which that pattern subsisted. Sibelius himself recognized this: his Seventh Symphony is in one movement.

Sibelius's Seventh Symphony contains the rudiments of slightly altered classical symphonic form written in a sort of musical shorthand and both condensed and run together. From one point of view, it may be thought of as a symphonic poem or tone poem without known program; in that view, its being called a symphony at all appears to have been mistaken piety. But Sibelius still was near enough to the dramatic bases of sonata structure so that his assertion that this is indeed a symphony must be considered seriously. It suggests what no symphony by Brahms, Bruckner, or Mahler suggests at all: that it might be the dependable herald of a new, sonata-derived, formal classicism. Its musical ideas—whatever influence they trail of the romantic effusiveness of the nineteenth century and of the harmonic restlessness of the twentieth, and whatever their attractiveness and power—are possible subjects for compact and condensed sonata-like treatment. The difference between Sibelius's Seventh Symphony (1924) and, say, his symphonic poem *En Saga*, composed thirty-two years earlier, is the result of a long march toward classical concision.

Sibelius as Anachronism

Sibelius's career, however, is tinged too by the tragedy more notably associated with the careers of Bruckner and Mahler: though at times—especially in England and the United States—he has won a far larger public than they, he has not spoken convincingly to his younger contemporaries or the musicians who followed after him. The tendencies ruling twentieth-century musical creation have led music farther and farther away from him. His finest works still are performed. But in the light of musical history he had, long before his death, become a noble, isolated anachronism. Much of the sometimes unjust bitterness in appraisals of Sibelius is the anger of younger men that a composer of such obviously major endowments should have clung, if only halfheartedly, to the outward symbols of the academic past instead of passing over with them into a new day.

Music of the Recent Past and
of the Future

The foregoing paragraphs have not been intended primarily as critical judgments of Brahms, Bruckner, Mahler, and Sibelius—each of whom could be discussed and criticized with wholly different emphasis from several other points of vantage. These pages are intended to portray four men coming just before, at, or past the end of the high romantic period of the nineteenth century, men who were not content to be adventurously romantic in formal behavior, as Chopin, Schumann, Berlioz, and Wagner had been, but who placed their consistent lofty labor at the service of probably foredoomed attempts to revivify the symphony and other sonata-based forms. Each was a composer of ample talent, and Brahms at least was a major creator. But all of them demonstrated a conscious or unconscious belief that enduring value existed in sonata-like forms themselves, almost without regard to the nature of the musical matter used to fill out those perhaps altered, but certainly pre-existing patterns.

The future of music, we now can see, was not with them. For while Brahms was composing his last symphony, while Mahler and Bruckner were at work on their unfinished final symphonies, and Sibelius—with thirty-three years more of life ahead of him—was finishing his last symphonies, the itinerary and destination of the art of music were abandoning romanticism and romantic adaptations of classicism to set out on a genuinely new road. They were the formidable last expressions of the nineteenth century. Alongside their remarkable efforts to preserve or prolong the immediate past, other men with other ideas and ideals were (slowly at first, then swiftly) creating a present farther removed from them and from their basic conceptions than any earlier musical period ever had been from the period immediately preceding it. This is to say that the artistic distance from Brahms or (even) Mahler to Stravinsky or Schoenberg would have to be measured in light years if we were to measure that from Haydn or Mozart to the late Beethoven in thousands of miles.

CHAPTER XVIII

Acceptance and Rebellion

During every period since the Middle Ages, a predominant style usually has been entrenched in each of the arts—a manner or group of manners already recognized and accepted as normal by listeners, readers, and spectators. Parallel with such "normal" styles and manners, and usually to some extent at war with them, have been "modern" or "new" manners and styles not yet recognized as entirely acceptable by the widest existing public. In many cases, though not always, these temporarily so-called "revolutionary" styles have endured and matured to become the predominant, entrenched styles of the succeeding period. Such "revolutions," which frequently are denounced as anarchic and destructive both by the largest public and by the artists still practicing the styles already acceptable to that public, often have been the representative constructive efforts of younger men. Whether musicians, writers, painters, architects, or sculptors, such newcomers traditionally have been asserting their unquestionable right to respond to their own world, as distinct from that of their elders, in ways attractive and useful to them. Sometimes, and notably in music, this rebellion has been that of classicists against romanticism; in the late Beethoven, in Schubert, Chopin, and the early Berlioz, romanticism produced and was produced by men struggling to pry open doors locked against them by a classicism that had begun to lose the freshness and relevance in which it had arisen some decades earlier.

Nationalism in Music

Loosely speaking, the nineteenth century was largely an expansive and emotion-cultivating period in all the arts. But at the hours when the representative romanticists were working out their own formal and expressive problems, forces were gathering for the task of disintegrating that very sort of highly personal creation, which was felt to be less and less relevant to general currents of life and thought as the nineteenth century sloped down to its close. As producing the musical art of the first half of the twentieth century, those forces were localized chiefly in three countries, in each of which they operated differently, by ways determined in the past and by what was being rebelled against. The regions in which postromantic music—"modern music" in the first-half-of-the-twentieth-century sense—burst from the enveloping embrace of romanticism were Russia, France, and Austria.

Music in Russia

In Russia the chasm between folk music and serious composed music had been all but unbridged for centuries during which vitality had been greatly present in the former and largely absent from the latter. For the folk music of the Romanov empire was, naturally, Slavic, more or less Oriental in rhythm, harmony, melody, and coloration, whereas its composed music was slavishly Italianate, with late, occasional infusions of the Teutonic and the Gallic. In that slowly stirring giant of a country, the first cause leading toward modernism turned out to be nationalism. It was mostly expressed at first by the determination of a small group of only partly professional musicians to relate their own work to the folk music and other truly indigenous expressions of Russian life.

The principal Russian composers involved, both before and after the self-consciously nationalistic efforts, were Mikhail Glinka (1803–57), Alexander Dargomizhsky (1813–69), Alexander Borodin (1833–87), Mili Balakirev (1837–

1910), Modest Mussorgsky (1839–81), Nikolai Rimsky-Korsakov (1844–1908), Igor Stravinsky (1882–   ), and Serge Prokofiev (1891–1953). Also from Russia during the period spanned by those men came two others: Piotr Ilyich Tchaikovsky (1840–93), one of the most widely performed of all composers since his death, and Alexander Scriabin (1872–1915), an interesting musical eccentric. For the most part, Tchaikovsky and Scriabin stood outside the line of technical and stylistic inheritance which stretched from Glinka to Stravinsky and Prokofiev.

Music in France

In France, music had been nurtured since the earliest times on a close relation to folk music. French musical nationalism therefore was not possible in anything like the Russian sense: an art cannot turn for renewal to what it already has in abundance. The Paris rebellion that opened one road to modernism was a rising against a conservative group of learned, imitative composers and academicians (respect for "the academy" long has been a French trait) who controlled the schools and theaters under state supervision. That fight had been begun by Berlioz, whose single-handed war had produced his own music and nothing else. In men who arrived later than Berlioz, the closest thing to signs of rebellion against the academicians had been the chromaticism and so-called "cyclical form" of César Franck[1] (1822–90) and the feeble transplanted French Wagnerism of Ernest Reyer (1823–1909). In the sense of either leading

[1] "Cyclical form" refers to the building of a composition of several movements, in all (or at least in several) of which the same melodies or other recognizable musical ideas occur. This idea was not original with César Franck, as often has been pointed out: Schubert had used it, for example, in his *Wanderer Fantaisie*. But Franck applied the idea in a manner closely related to that of the Lisztian "transformation of themes," and made the repetition of some material from movement to movement as important an agent of over-all unity as key relationships. His pupils and followers—notably Vincent d'Indy (1851–1931), Camille Saint-Saëns (1835–1921), and Gabriel Fauré (1845–1924)—were deeply marked by Franck's personal interpretation of cyclical thematic repetition.

to modernism or of actually evolving it, the composers of first importance in France after Berlioz were Claude Debussy (1862–1918), Erik Satie (1866–1925), and Maurice Ravel (1875–1937).

Music in Austria and Hungary

In Austria, following upon the widespread acceptance there of Wagner, Brahms, and Richard Strauss (to whom, in 1920, Paul Rosenfeld referred accurately as "the false dawn of modern music"), rebellion took still another form, being directed against the idiom and size of romantic composition rather than against its emotional attitudes. Largely intellectual in inception, it challenged at its foundation whatever remained of the classical harmonic system in romantic harmony, finally denying flatly the continuing validity of tonality itself. The important composers in this most drastic of all rebellions were Arnold Schoenberg (1874–1951), Anton von Webern (1883–1945), and Alban Berg (1885–1935).

Some important aspects of twentieth-century music arose in other places than Russia, France, and Austria. But its salient characteristics could have existed almost exactly as they became if no composer not mentioned in the preceding paragraphs had lived and worked. One possible exception to this statement may be called for by the music of the Hungarian composer Béla Bartók (1881–1945). Bartók compressed into his own creative life an evolution very like the course of Russian music from the folk nationalism of Mussorgsky and Borodin to the highly individual, only remotely nationalistic, idiom of Stravinsky.

The Position of Tchaikovsky

In order to understand the evolution of twentieth-century music, it is particularly necessary to take note of Tchaikovsky both in a positive sense and in a negative one. Tchaikovsky made possible the international efflorescence of Russian ballet, without which large areas of twentieth-century music never would have come to be what they have been.

Tchaikovsky composed three of the most enduring popular symphonies, one each of the most popular piano concertos and violin concertos, and several other orchestral compositions that can be grouped as symphonic poems which have been familiar since the 1890s to anyone at all aware of music. In those feverishly romantic, instantly convincing, and self-revealing pieces, Tchaikovsky remained, for the most part, formally quite unadventurous.[2] He was not a self-conscious nationalist, being far more cosmopolitan in taste and experience than most of his Russian colleagues. But enough Russian and other Slavic turns of musical thought found their way unself-consciously into his music so that his vast world-wide popularity has played a leading role in naturalizing them elsewhere.

In so far as Tchaikovsky's larger nontheatrical music won the widest possible audience for serious music throughout the world, it served as belated reinforcement of nineteenth-century romanticism. Standing almost as much as Wagner's music (and later that of Brahms and Richard Strauss) athwart the paths of young men desiring to find the future, the music of Tchaikovsky was for a time cordially and vocally detested, most particularly by propagandists of "modernism." Possibly no more instantly convincing and engaging music ever has been created, and modern criticism now takes the attitude that a liking for Tchaikovsky may indicate either a lack of musical sophistication or possession of a musical sophistication so complete as to be impregnable.

The Tchaikovskyan Ballet

Similarly, modern criticism—largely reflecting the attitude of Igor Stravinsky—often holds that Tchaikovsky's most gal-

[2] One of Tchaikovsky's signal deviations from usual procedures occurs in his *"Pathétique"* Symphony. Its finale violates the classical habits by being an *adagio lamentoso, i.e.,* a slow movement: classical finales customarily had been triumphant and joyous in tone and effect. Tchaikovsky unquestionably was led to this experiment by the emotions of a troubled man in a troubling world. Because the experiment provided an entirely satisfying capstone for his Sixth Symphony, this finale in its way is as self-justifying as the passacaglia finale of Brahms's Fourth Symphony.

vanic contribution to musical evolution was made by his ballet scores. This highly formalized dance, originally imported into Russia from Italy, had been popular in St. Petersburg and Moscow for at least a full century before Tchaikovsky turned to it. The music of pre-Tchaikovskyan ballets, however, either had been the thin, relatively characterless stuff composed for dancing by Frenchmen like Adolphe Adam (1803–56), Germans like Peter Ludwig Hertel (1817–99), or Italians like Cesare Pugni (1805–70), or had been Polish and Russian apings of their feeble compositions. The first great Russian ballet score was that of Tchaikovsky's *Swan Lake* (1876). To the elaboration of that music, carefully tailored to fit the ballet's scenario and choreographic needs, he brought his abundant melodic gift, his rich romantic harmonic idiom, his apparently endless supply of rhythmic variety, and his genius for instrumental color. The result is a series of short pieces full of fairy-tale sorcery and devoid of Tchaikovsky's sometimes wearisome autobiographical neuroticism. We do not, of course, look for large formal patterns in what is, by its very provenance, a suite of small, often unrelated pieces; but most of those pieces not only are flawless for balletic purposes, but also were shaped by an unfailing sense of small form.[3]

Tchaikovsky composed two other ballets after *Swan Lake*: *The Sleeping Beauty* (1889) and *The Nutcracker* (1891–92), both also to fairy-tale scenarios. After his death, his three ballets became (along with the compositions of later men) the basic repertoire of the Russian ballet companies that burst upon the cities of Western Europe and America, bringing with them the folk-dramatic literature of Russia, its Oriental colors, and its tradition of ballet's high seriousness. Tchaikovsky's ballet music and such of its descendants as were continually more responsive to Russian nationalism provided the receptive atmosphere needed for the creation of that later series of ballet scores by Stravinsky: in *The Firebird* (1910), *Petroushka* (1911), and *Le*

[3] Great ballet scores had been composed long before Tchaikovsky and the great era of Russian ballet. Lully, Rameau, Gluck, and many other pre-nineteenth-century composers (none of them Russian) had produced magnificent ballet music.

Sacre du printemps (1913), Stravinsky carried one sort of modernism right out of the fairy-tale atmosphere of *Swan Lake* and *The Sleeping Beauty* and of the picture-book realms of Rimsky-Korsakov's operas to perhaps the highest point it attained.[4]

The Heritage of Tchaikovsky

The romantic harmonic idiom of Tchaikovsky's ballet scores differed little from that of his other music. Those who have complained that Tchaikovsky's symphonies sound like ballet music really are saying only that they sound like Tchaikovsky. The historic importance of his three ballets resides in the history of ballet: musically it consists of the fact that he composed them at all, that a serious composer should have lavished all the compositional care he could on what had for some time been the proper work of second- and third-rate musicians.

With one hand, then, Tchaikovsky helped to increase the specific gravity and blocking power of that curious and incomprehensibly constituted body of music known to impresarios as "the standard repertoire"—as Verdi, Wagner, Brahms, and Richard Strauss similarly helped unwittingly to impose its supposedly stationary standards on the great musical audience. With the other hand, however, Tchaikovsky liberated ballet as a serious vehicle for modern music, signaling to many younger composers—Russian and foreign —a side door by which they could slip their novel idioms into the musical sanctum. Among those who eventually took most telling advantage of that portal were not only Stravinsky, but also Ravel, Paul Hindemith, Manuel de Falla, Serge Prokofiev, and Aaron Copland. The list could be lengthened considerably by adding to it composers of music not originally written to accompany dancing, but which has won acceptance, even widespread popularity, as adapted to balletic use.

[4] Another composer of carefully, elaborately constructed ballet scores was Léo Delibes (1836–91). For the Paris stage, Delibes wrote *Coppélia* (1870) and *Sylvia* (1876), both of which Tchaikovsky admired intensely, and both of which have kept their slim but definite musical vitality.

Glinka and Nationalism

Mikhail Glinka was a semiprofessional, semidilettante composer trained in Western European musical techniques both at home and in Italy and Germany. Much of his production is conventional nineteenth-century romantic tone-painting or Italianate opera different from other music composed during his lifetime only in its occasional employment of actual and synthetic folk melodies, folk rhythms, and—to a smaller extent—harmonies derived from or shaped by folk usage, largely Russian and Spanish. The widespread performance of such of his scores as the nationalistic tone picture *Kamarinskaya*, the *Jota Aragonesa*, and of at least excerpts from his two operas, *A Life for the Tsar* (1836) and *Ruslan and Lyudmila* (1842) served, as Chopin's polonaises and mazurkas served more importantly, to introduce to Western ears the previously unregarded colors and textures of Slavic-Oriental and Spanish-Gypsy-African music. The "Orientalism" of Viennese eighteenth-century "Turkish" music pales beside the splashed raw colors of *Kamarinskaya*.

Most of the salient characteristics of the Russian music of the second half of the nineteenth century and the first half of the twentieth are promised in Glinka's compositions. His use of orchestral instruments with great sensitivity to their individual and mixed colors, producing an over-all ensemble of notable transparency and brilliance;[5] his knowing use of choruses, particularly as an operatic method of expressing the natures and tempers of crowds; his tendency to build long compositions out of linked, brief musical fragments repeated with or without slight variations; his Orientalism, with its consequent (but perhaps mostly unconscious) harmonic daring—all of these set the norms for much in the art of his successors.

[5] Glinka was a pioneer in enlarging the orchestra to include the harp and the piano as naturalized members. Also, he was one of the earliest composers to write important characteristic parts for the so-called English horn.

Whole-Tone Scales and ⅝ Time

In *A Life for the Tsar*, one passage of notably Russian-Oriental texture is the wedding chorus. This is in ⅝ time, a rhythm frequently encountered in Russian folk music, but largely foreign to Western Europe (so foreign that many professional Western musicians cannot to this day feel it as anything but an artificial combination of two beats and three beats, or of three and two). After Glinka, it occurs often in Russian composed music, one of the most familiar examples of it being the second movement of Tchaikovsky's Sixth ("*Pathétique*") Symphony. Another Glinka passage notable for its progeny is an example of melodic-harmonic daring derived from folk practice. It is the leitmotiv that accompanies the baleful wizard Chernomor whenever he appears in *Ruslan and Lyudmila*:[6]

That passage frequently is cited by historians as the earliest appearance in composed music of the whole-tone scale, later to become an important auxiliary tool, particularly in the hands of French composers, for the destruction of the unique position of the classical harmonic system. On instruments of fixed pitch, only two whole-tone scales can be played: C, D, E, F♯, G♯, A♯, B♯(C) and C♯, D♯, F, G, A, B, C♯, either of which may begin and end on any tone it contains—and either of which can be notated with flats and in other ways. Nowhere in either of these scales are to be found two of the intervals central to the classical system of

[6] Chernomor's theme is quoted here as it appears in the finale of Act I of *Ruslan and Lyudmila*. The first notes of each of the bass tremolos (G, F, E♭, D♭, B, A, G, F, E♭) constitute an uninterrupted succession of whole-tone intervals.

major and minor tonalities: the perfect fifth and perfect fourth. Nor does any whole-tone scale supply the half-tone (minor second) step up to the tonic (as in C, D, E, F, G, A, B-C or in A, B, C, D, E, F, G♯-A—which is of fundamental importance, particularly to closing cadences, in both the major and the minor modes. Theoretically, of course, it is possible to build whole-tone melodies into a system of whole-tone harmony. But such a system must always lack the sensation of a "home" or tonic fundamental tone to which all other tones used bear affinities and kinetic relationships. The importance of the whole-tone scale from a compositional or creative point of view has proved transitory, but it was useful in lessening the hold of the classical harmonic system on composers' mental ears, and it supplied Debussy and a few others with added means for exploiting exotic and impressionistic effects.

Glinka, Russian Music, and Form

Glinka's *A Life for the Tsar* and *Ruslan and Lyudmila* are as fragmentary and unintegrated (both as to libretto and as to music) as any operas ever composed. This episodic lack of development, this failure of (or lack of interest in) integration also were to characterize much Russian music after Glinka. This sort of fragmentariness, as often has been pointed out by students of Russian culture, also is to be found in much Russian literature, including that of its greatest writers except Turgenev. This is perhaps to say that all Russian music, and perhaps all Russian art, of the nineteenth century is romantic art, in which the "what" is of much greater importance than the "how."

Dargomizhsky, the Libretto, and Realism

The libretto of *Ruslan and Lyudmila* was based on a fairy tale by Alexander Pushkin, who became as important to the development of Russian opera as Ariosto and Tasso and Metastasio had been to that of seventeenth- and eighteenth-century Italian opera. Alexander Dargomizhsky likewise based his first important work, *Rusalka* (1856), on a Pushkin play. But Dargomizhsky disliked the intervention of a librettist, whether himself or someone else, between the poet and his new audience. In his second, incomplete opera, *The Stone Guest*, he therefore attempted the extremely difficult and perhaps impossible task of setting to operatically viable music Pushkin's version of the Don Juan legend exactly as the poet had written it.

In *Rusalka*, Dargomizhsky took long strides toward the naturalizing of harmonic implications and rhythms native to true Russian and Eastern folk song and folk dance in composed music of harmonic texture. But he was a creative composer of intermittent and uncertain power, and his attempts to identify his music psychologically and pictorially with Pushkin's characters and situations too often sacrificed musical interest to prosy, unmusical declamation not unlike the least communicative recitative of older operas. He believed that music could be made to express "precisely what the words express," a delusion particularly damaging to his opera in those parts of the libretto which a dramatically wiser composer simply would have refused to set, knowing them unsuitable for musical treatment.

Dargomizhsky and "Melodic Recitative"

In *The Stone Guest*, an entire opera is built out of what Dargomizhsky called "melodic recitative," an uninterrupted almost-melody rising and falling mechanically in response to the meanings and accents of Pushkin's words. Except in those passages in which Dargomizhsky the composer rose to his very best, the opera remains theatrically ineffective because the text is much more alive than the music. (Dargomizhsky also subjugated his orchestra to the singers' unending recitative, thus unquestionably suggesting to Debussy something of the vocal-instrumental balance of *Pelléas et Mélisande*, a suggestion that the much more musically gifted Debussy transformed into a richer synthesis.)

This dogged application of a crippling theory of operatic construction, however, led Dargomizhsky to harmonic combinations never before written down seriously.

Because *The Stone Guest* so often is couched in harmonic combinations alien to the true constitution of major and minor tonalities, Dargomizhsky noted it without a key signature, thus again foreshadowing the practice of some later composers. His opera contains several melodic passages in whole-tone progressions, and at times seems to be on the verge of attempting a harmonic system depending from them. Thus, though the opera's juiceless, stiff texture and its paucity of arresting and expressive materials leave *The Stone Guest* thankless on the stage, its influence endured because of the hints it supplied to composers much more talented than Dargomizhsky.

The Five

Dargomizhsky's harmonic unconventionality had almost as deep an influence on the future as the politico-literary tenets of nationalism upon Borodin, Balakirev, and Mussorgsky, the three central figures of the "mighty handful" known to non-Russians as the Five. (The two other members of the group were César Cui, 1835–1918, more memorable for his sponsorship and championing of nationalism than for his generally mediocre practice of composition, and Rimsky-Korsakov, an erudite musician on whom Dargomizhsky's theories about operatic "truth"—as apart from his coloristic use of Russian, Caucasian, and other Eastern folk idioms—had almost no effect.)

Balakirev, Nationalism, and Decorative Variation

With the ably argued assistance of the critic Vladimir Stasov (1824–1906), Balakirev became the very heart of Russian musical nationalism, being both the intense preacher of a "war" against musical Westernism and himself an accomplished practitioner, in nearly pure form, of folk-based musical creation. In his symphonic poems *Tamar* (1881) and *Russia* (a revision, 1882, of an earlier work) and his piano fantasy *Islamey* (1869), Balakirev composed music that at once sums up intense Russo-Orientalism (much of which he had absorbed in the Caucasus) and displays the best integral method of setting them forth. Borrowing—or creating by sympathetic imitation—musical ideas essentially self-sufficient and therefore impervious to classical development, he made strength out of what might have been debility. Realizing the sectional nature that his extended pieces inevitably must have, he employed many sorts of decorative variation.

Nothing truly *develops* in *Tamar, Russia,* or *Islamey.* But their component melodies, harmonies, rhythms, and decorations are strong and attractive, and their interest is raised to climaxes and then abated with almost unfailing sense of the material's staying power. If "form" be used to indicate the fusion of material, pattern, and other elements, these pieces possess satisfactory form. Their structural devices have been employed to present and display completely the musical ideas that they contain.

Islamey *and Appliquéd Decoration*

Islamey in particular belongs with Glinka's *Kamarinskaya* among the legitimate ancestors of many Russo-Oriental compositions, both real and simulated. It consists almost wholly of two melodies, both of which are varied by decoration. A Western composer earlier than Balakirev probably would have considered the first melody unfit for any sort of musical extension—by variation or by any other method —the second too weak to play an important role anywhere. But out of these highly unpromising basic materials, Balakirev evolved a brilliant piano composition of satisfying proportions. Despite its fragmentary look to the eye, he managed in it, by apt variation and by insight into the piano's special possibilities, to produce a fairly long composition. In the deepest sense, *Islamey* perhaps lacks real variety, as it certainly lacks all sense of struggle or drama. It nevertheless holds the listener's attention without wearying it.

It may be said that *Islamey* is "virtuoso" music and therefore will not hold the listener's attention through numerous hearings. If this is true—and general experience strongly suggests that it is—the flaw lies in the folklike themes, which are recalcitrant to treatment other than decoration, a form of appliquéd variety which has strict limitations, in music as elsewhere. Certainly *Islamey* soon begins to sound monotonous and shallow if contrasted with a fine movement from a classical sonata, with Schumann's *Carnaval,* or with Mussorgsky's *Pictures at an Exhibition.*

If all but the greatest successes of the Five be looked at for their similarities, we can see that both their virtues and their flaws are those of *Islamey.* Except for the masterpieces of Borodin and Mussorgsky, these brightly colored, melodically pungent, rhythmically various, and harmonically seductive Slavic-Oriental compositions substitute surface variation for the real development that is foreign to the possibilities of their very subject matter. They remain fragmentary; and their sections generally are short-winded and gain length only through bare repetition or repetition-with-decoration.

Borodin and Problems of Form

Only Borodin among the nationalists and Tchaikovsky among their Russian contemporaries succeeded occasionally in creating extended organic compositions in which musical ideas really develop, in which at least some of the drama that gave birth to the sonata and the symphony is worked out without patchiness, or at least without the sort of patchiness that shows too obviously. Borodin composed three symphonies (the third left incomplete) and two string quartets that are marvels in view of the excessive difficulties he set himself by using melodies of Slavic-Oriental cast which can be manipulated by sonata techniques only with great, concentrated effort, both because of their very definiteness and because of the harmonic meshes that they generate. Borodin's symphonies and quartets are suavely euphonious. And yet, for all their superb facture, they become a little boring. In the first movement of his Second (B minor)

Symphony, for example, the opening theme, which is repeated again and again, at last becomes almost maddening, however justified its reappearances may look on the printed page.

No such reservations are possible about Borodin's tone picture *In the Steppes of Central Asia* (1880) or his incomplete opera *Prince Igor*. In these, the fragmentariness persists. But in the symphonic poem the form is thrown off by the material, nowhere required to do more than it can do; and in the opera—actually a series of pseudohistorical tableaux, a very conventional old-fashioned set-number opera completely lacking any musical development in any Wagnerian or Verdian sense—the charmingly relevant Oriental tone-coloring, the handsome use of choral effects, and the sensitivity with which most of the music is related to the fragmentary libretto combine to make the musical fragmentariness unobjectionable. Borodin often has been criticized adversely for banalities in *Prince Igor*, many of which have proved, on scholarly examination, to be additions by Rimsky-Korsakov or Alexander Glazunov, who "completed" it. The extremely undistinguished overture, for example, is more Glazunov than Borodin.

Listening to Russian Nationalist Music

To criticize the Russian nationalist composers adversely for their obvious failures to find or evolve the requisite formal means for housing or sustaining their musical materials is fair and useful when their attempts to adapt forms extrinsic to those materials make failure both obvious and certain. But such criticism is bootless when it leads to belaboring Balakirev's *Islamey* for not being a sonata movement, Mussorgsky's *Boris Godunov* for its lack of Wagnerian symphonic development, his *Pictures at an Exhibition* for not being a classical suite, or Rimsky-Korsakov's dazzling *Le Coq d'or* (*The Golden Cockerel*) for not being profoundly serious. One rule for critical behavior covers all these cases: if a work of art succeeds in being precisely what its creator intended it to be, criticism of it for not being something else is gratuitous nonsense—though criticism of the creator's intentions may not be.

Folk Music and Composed Music

True folk music is of fundamental service in refreshing by suggestion the idiom of composed music, but is almost impossibly hard to manipulate in strict pre-existing forms—as difficult, in fact (and for much the same reasons) as the German and other high romanticisms had found their own individual, intense musical epigrams. Its basic self-completeness, shortness of musical breath, and sharp, quickly revealed harmonic color make it peculiarly useful in songs, in regional and historical effects in opera and ballet, and in the building of extramusically inspired symphonic poems or piano pieces of brief, self-determining patterns. The later Russian composers who have written symphonies, concertos, string quartets, and sonatas to popular approval or critical acclaim or both have drawn away more or less absolutely from the employment of true folk tunes and rhythms as well as from overt imitation of them. Serge Rachmaninoff (1872–1943) and Serge Prokofiev were intensely Russian, as is Dmitri Shostakovich—but none of these men can be classified as a nationalist artistically in the sense that Balakirev was one. Even in the Soviet Union, the nineteenth-century sort of folkloric nationalism, though approved of by the state, appears to be left to second-raters like Aram Khachaturian.

Glinka and Later Russian Opera

In opera, contrarily, Glinka's suggestive use of folk materials mated to stories from the national treasury of legend, history, and fiction signaled the dawn of a brilliant, prolonged outburst of highly colored masterpieces. If the Five had produced nothing more than Borodin's *Prince Igor,* Mussorgsky's *Boris Godunov* and *Khovanshchina,* and Rimsky-Korsakov's *The Golden Cockerel,* its major tenets would have been justified fully. The creation of scenic atmospheres; the reflection, underlining, and creation of lively human types; the lifelike evocation of historical eras; and the musical pictorialization of the fantastic supernatural—none of these has been achieved more happily elsewhere.

The sadness of unfulfillment that pervades much of the musical story of the Russian nationalist composers is borne out by the facts. Dargomizhsky's *The Stone Guest,* left unfinished, was "completed" by Cui and orchestrated by Rimsky-Korsakov. Borodin's *Prince Igor,* in turn, was filled out by Rimsky-Korsakov and Glazunov; his Third Symphony was "set in order and scored" by Glazunov. *Boris Godunov,* though existing complete as Mussorgsky arranged it for performance in 1871–72, is known chiefly in a revision by Rimsky-Korsakov which prettifies it, and in "versions" tampered with by other composers. Mussorgsky completed a vocal score of four acts of *Khovanshchina,* but did not orchestrate them, and left Act V in rough sketch; the opera was "arranged" by Rimsky-Korsakov. *The Fair at Sorochinsk,* another opera left incomplete by Mussorgsky, has been "completed," "arranged," and "orchestrated" by others at least three times—and all without becoming what he himself might have made of it.

Genius Not Wholly Fulfilled: *Borodin and Mussorgsky*

Elements in the lives of both Mussorgsky and Borodin can be blamed in part for their failure to complete so many very promising works. But maybe it also would be just to lay some blame for the incompleteness of their works on technical incompetence—if that phrase is nicely interpreted. Borodin and Mussorgsky were musical geniuses of a high order; the music of both men deserves the enthusiasm that any critic may wish to display toward it. But neither of them was either highly trained or successfully self-trained in overcoming small difficulties that a thousand of their inferiors could have solved easily without either talent or thought.

No such technical and formal uncertainties beset the earlier nationalists when they composed songs. The cosmopolitan Tchaikovsky wrote beautiful and moving songs touched by Slavic gaiety and Slavic melancholy. But Mussorgsky's songs, such as the six called *Sunless* and the four *Songs and Dances of Death,* are often great dramas in small, evidencing the genius for musical character revelation which makes *Boris Godunov* a masterwork of musico-literary art whether or not it suffers from over-all formal flaws. Mussorgsky's emotional power and great talent for the most convincing sort of pictorial evocation also are evident in his renowned suite of piano pieces, *Pictures at an Exhibition.*

Rimsky-Korsakov as Chameleon

Rimsky-Korsakov is a peculiar figure among the nationalists. He was prodigiously learned, a very accomplished professional composer. His techniques, most notably as an orchestrator, were certain and unbounded. He believed that music was a bright-colored deception, and he devoted his chief energies to a series of pictorial folk-tale and fairy-tale operas with the shallow attractiveness of splashily painted illustrations. His ability to adapt the outsides of other men's styles and manners was astounding. He paid obvious tribute to Glinka in the operas *May Night* and *Snyegurochka (The Snow Maiden)*; to Dargomizhsky in *Mozart and Salieri*; to Borodin in *Sadko* and *The Tale of the Invisible City of Kitezh*; and to Mussorgsky in *Pskovityanka (The Maid of Pskov)*.

Rimsky-Korsakov's operas attempt no musical character-creation as Mussorgsky and Borodin understood it. In his best fairy-tale opera, *Le Coq d'or* (1906–07), this fact is unimportant, at least through the first few hearings. This opera is crammed with superficially very attractive melodies, gay rhythms, and harmonic effects that pall only through familiarity. His symphonic poem *Scheherazade* and the scarcely less renowned *Capriccio Espagnol* and *Russian Easter Overture* are mines of instrumental effects from which other composers have been extracting ore ever since. On the surface much of Rimsky-Korsakov's music is as instantly winning as Tchaikovsky's. But Tchaikovsky was investing his entire being in what he composed, whereas

Rimsky-Korsakov often seems to have been busy creating a collection of dazzling effects. Suffering from the same inabilities of formal development as the other nationalists, he did not—as at least Borodin and Mussorgsky did—compensate for that lack by intense expressiveness. He was perhaps the last man in Russia who should have tampered with the musical works of his betters.

In addition to completing fifteen operas in thirty-nine years, Rimsky-Korsakov also composed three symphonies, numerous fantasias, symphonic poems, overtures, a piano concerto, and chamber music. Although he believed that he was composing in various different styles, he really had only one style, and that dictated by his taste (and all but unparalleled gift) for a Glinka-like transparent instrumentation in primary colors. In his operas, Rimsky-Korsakov simply added human voices to that individual palette. His great stores of technical knowledge and his pervasive conviction that music is a decorative deceit combined to lend a childlike thinness to almost everything that he composed. He evoked a storybook Russia distant from the bitter realities summoned forth by *Prince Igor, Boris Godunov,* and *Khovanshchina.* Harmonically he was a conservative and a pedant. But he was also a nationalist, and therefore admitted into his rule-governed harmonic universe harmonies related to folk and folklike melodies that he borrowed and invented. Historically speaking, the result was that he, too, played a part in the final overthrow of the classical-romantic interrelations among form, scruple, manner, and euphony.

Mussorgsky, Opera, and Academic "Laws"

The styles, methods, and even mannerisms of Mussorgsky and Rimsky-Korsakov, so polar to one another, indeed jointly affected the evolution of both Prokofiev and Stravinsky, though in different ways than those later men were influenced by Tchaikovsky. Mussorgsky disdained the accepted norms of musical procedure, partly because he never understood them fully, but more importantly because he was not traveling toward the musical terminals to which they led. His music is frequently modal—in passages that emerged spontaneously from modal usages in Russian and Oriental folk music. Unknowingly, in opera he was a descendant of Peri and Caccini, of the manifestoes of Gluck, and of some of Dargomizhsky's and Wagner's theoretical pronouncements. He wanted operatic music not to be an end in itself, but to be one more means of projecting the text and realizing the characters.

Mussorgsky did not care at all whether one chord "correctly" succeeded another in the convention derived from Western practices during the eighteenth century and later. If the sound of two chords in succession appeared to him to assist in projecting the significance of the libretto or in drawing the lineaments of an individual or a crowd, he used them. He disregarded the theoretical proprieties of modulation, moving from one tonality to another without preparation as, and exactly when, he was impelled to do so by the meaning he was trying to convey or evoke. He was much more interested in what he believed to be dramatic truth than in smoothness or euphony. His orchestration was rough, powerful, and not always capable of producing exactly the results at which he directed it. He was not a polite or a well-bred composer, but the vividness and force of his best music *as he wrote it* are unique. (Maurice Ravel's orchestration of *Pictures at an Exhibition* is not a prettification of the original in the sense that Rimsky-Korsakov's version of *Boris Godunov* is. Ravel's instrumentation is an attempt to re-create Mussorgsky's suite in another medium, and it leaves the highly original harmonies intact. Even so sympathetic and comprehending a transcript, however, never should be mistaken for genuine Mussorgsky.)

Mussorgsky's vividness and force were native qualities of his creative imagination, but they survive for us because of the methods he evolved for representing and conveying them. To regard Mussorgsky as a fumbling illiterate is to misconceive the meaning of musical originality. That he was not more secure technically is sad only because that insecurity prevented him from achieving and completing more than he was able to compose during his forty-six years of life. His contribution to the stream of musical evolution —a different reality from his value as a composer—was in operatic realism, in the song as a faithful intensification of text, in harmonic freedom, and in still further disintegration of what remained of the classic-romantic harmonic system.

The Five and Dancing

Notably, no member of the Five composed a ballet, though Borodin, Mussorgsky, Balakirev, and Rimsky-Korsakov all composed large amounts of danceable music. The Dances of the Persian Slaves from *Khovanshchina*, the Polovtsian Dances from *Prince Igor*, the Hopak from *The Fair at Sorochinsk*, and twenty excerpts from Rimsky-Korsakov's opera—including the familiar Dance of the Buffoons from *Snyegurochka*—entirely demonstrate their ability to write music for dancing and the special applicability of their styles to the expressive, pantomimic, and evocative powers of ballet. But whatever of their music (most notably *Scheherazade*) has had any part in the history of ballet has been adapted to that purpose rather than being composed for it.

Now, long after the fact, we see that an important chapter in the history of ballet and an equally important one in the evolution of early-twentieth-century music lay in the combining of Tchaikovsky's serious handling of ballet music and the harmonic freedom and rhythmic variety of the Five. What was needed to usher that combination into existence was an impresario of daring and fresh vision. Opportunely, he appeared. He was Serge Diaghilev (1872–1929), whose brilliant sense of theater, knowledge of advanced pictorial art, and hospitality to the latest manifestations in music were to affect deeply the history of twentieth-century art. Diaghilev found precisely the composer able to combine Tchaikovsky's attitudes toward ballet with the musical idiom of the Five—and particularly of Rimsky-Korsakov and Mussorgsky—and to go on from that confluence to become the single most influential composer after Wagner and Debussy. That composer was Igor Stravinsky.

CHAPTER XIX

Music in France after Berlioz

Despite the music of Berlioz, Debussy, and Ravel—to name only three French composers out of many—the notion that France has been a comparatively unmusical nation since the days of Jean-Philippe Rameau persists stubbornly. Whatever part of this misjudgment does not merely represent a holdover from the musically pro-German second half of the nineteenth century has been derived from the smooth conventionality of much French music before and after Berlioz. Additionally, the nineteenth century having far too long been foremost in the minds of music-lovers, the fact that many of the brightest musical luminaries of Paris during that century were foreigners—Chopin, Liszt, Rossini, Donizetti, Meyerbeer, and Offenbach are examples—has added to the apparent plausibility of the belief in France's musical decadence. The talented, agile, and musically erudite Camille Saint-Saëns, the soberly classic-romantic Gabriel Fauré, and the stately, somewhat pedantic Vincent d'Indy, producing pleasant, sometimes delightful, often enduringly persuasive music part of the time, failed to make the native French scene musically very lively. The first intensely, disturbingly original French composer after Berlioz (Franck was a Belgian) was Claude Debussy.

Debussy, Literature, and Painting

Chopin, Liszt, Berlioz, and Franck had imported some of the techniques of musical romanticism into conservatory-dominated Paris; others, too, had evolved new elements of romanticism on the spot. But the first large and significant French attempt to relate music to literature and the other arts in the way so characteristic of German romanticism occurred when the central technical procedures of nineteenth-century musical romanticism already had begun to wear thin elsewhere. And so it happened that the oblique mentality and peculiar imagination of Debussy evolved music related to symbolism in literature and impressionism in painting. Except in technique, Debussy long remained a romantic; for most of his creative life, that is, he was a technical postromantic composing the last bright pages of romanticism. Only very early and very late in his life did he compose notable music that made no use of verbal text or poetic-plastic title: his String Quartet of 1893 and the three chamber sonatas of the final three years of his life. Between these poles in time lay many compositions of exquisite facture, unquestionable technical rightness, and revolutionary originality, compositions entirely able to engage the mind without reference to their flowery and suggestive titles. Nonetheless, that music is related with complete appositeness to the names by which Debussy identified it.

The Evolution of Debussy's Style

Debussy's art, beginning in feeble echoes of Saint-Saëns and of the ardent operatic lyricism of Charles Gounod and Jules Massenet, drove constantly toward concision, self-sufficiency of form, and an emotional reticence in direct contrast to the expansiveness and assertiveness of high—and particularly of high German-Austrian—romanticism. He made comparatively little use of classical patterns (the sonata included), but instead attacked the central romantic task of unifying form and material freshly in each given instance. (That was, of course, the central romantic task even when the pattern used was a pre-existing one: romantic materials made the task inescapable under any condition.) Falling under the spell of Wagner after visiting Bayreuth in 1888, Debussy encountered his own very different future the very next year, when he became well acquainted with Mussorgsky's *Boris Godunov* and heard Southeast Asian music at the Paris Exposition Universelle.

Within a few years, Debussy had composed the *Prélude a L'Après-midi d'un faune,* his String Quartet, and the three unexampled *Nocturnes (Nuages, Fêtes, Sirènes)* for orchestra. As early as 1880, he had begun setting Paul Verlaine to music, and shortly he was using texts by Paul Bourget, Théodore de Bainville, Alfred de Musset, Stéphane Mallarmé, and his friend Pierre Louÿs. His music for the solo piano, beginning with innocuous salon pieces, by 1904 included the three *Estampes (Pagodes, Soirée dans Grenade; Jardins sous la pluie)*, in which his mature manner is unmistakable. Between 1892 and 1905, he completed, besides much else, his largest masterworks: the opera *Pelléas et Mélisande* and the "three symphonic sketches" (really a tripartite symphonic poem), *La Mer.* He later added to the list of his compositions in almost every genre, but with these large central works he already had influenced the entire course of Western music.

The Liquidation of Harmony and Rhythm

Debussy was fascinated by shadowy, fine-spun emotions, by the "iridescence of decay," by powerful, subdued eroticism—the very aspects of human life most dealt with by the symbolist poets. He also was moved by the shifting, momentarily fixed, evanescing play of light and tint which the impressionists were painting. Whatever was compelling, likely to depart, and (at least on the surface) charming, all that seemed aristocratic and rare, impelled him to composition. Reflecting the sources of his inspiration in literature and painting, he evolved and perfected in the structure and coloring of his music a stylish technique that has remained unique (for the easily understood belief that Ravel imitated it is false). He dissolved rhythm and then remade it in smooth complexity. He weakened harmonic logic without making use of astringent dissonance. He mixed instrumental colors much as Claude Monet and Georges Seurat mixed pigments and as Mallarmé and Arthur Rimbaud mixed words. Debussy seldom was awkward and never was excessive. He used the whole-tone scale, but followed its implications only as far as they could be retained in solid structures preserving a sense of tonal "home"—and then dropped them, or mixed whole-tone passages with his own very individual versions of diatonic and chromatic harmony.

Pelléas et Mélisande

In Count Maurice Maeterlinck's symbolist drama *Pelléas et Mélisande*,[1] the lovely heroine, first encountered lost in a forest, does not know whence she came, why she lives, or why she must die. The members of the royal family of Golaud (whom she marries) and Pelléas (whom she loves) inhabit a gloomy castle above caves at the edge of the sea. As closely as such an impossibility can be approximated, Debussy's score for this misty text retells it in musical terms. Nothing in this music is definite or clear, but everything in it is relevant. It contains no arias, no real set pieces of any sort. It presents no crowds, no triumphal scenes, no dances —none of the things that made grand opera grand. Significantly, the only true supernumeraries in the opera—three blind beggars—are seen only once, briefly, and that once asleep.

Pelléas et Mélisande emerges, flows, mounts, continues, subsides. Debussy believed that he was composing an anti-Wagnerian opera. But in disposing of the sectional construction of the older opera; in reducing what is sung to a variety of unbroken heightened recitative; and in performing on a continuous web of interrelated drama and music, *Pelléas* may be the most Wagnerian opera composed since *Parsifal*. Yet Debussy was right: *Pelléas* is anti-Wagnerian: its entire ethos and atmosphere are subdued, nonimperial, un-Teutonic, Gallic. It triumphs by restraint, by half-statement and less. When Wagner would have repeated and

[1] Maeterlinck's drama *Pelléas et Mélisande* fascinated composers. Arnold Schoenberg, in 1902, composed a symphonic poem entitled *Pelleas und Melisande*—his Opus 5—and in 1905 Jean Sibelius composed incidental music for the play.

expanded, Debussy blurred and hinted; where Wagner would have gathered many strands together toward a towering climax, Debussy shifted a tint from one end of the gamut to the other.

Rebellion Against the Nineteenth Century

Even at Debussy's most massive and voluminous, as in *La Mer,* his music denies the nineteenth century and its tendency toward personal and direct communication, its prolonged attempts to storm Parnassus with shattering masses of sound. When his brasses cry out, they cry out briefly and just before sinking back into his heaving, murmurous orchestra. In this seascape there are no people (just as, in reality, there is no water), not even Debussy himself. No attempt whatever is made at communicating any kind of nonmusical, ethical, moral, religious, or other ideas from composer through performer to listener. *La Mer* is music for its own musical sake, titles and subtitles not withstanding.

Debussy's Late Sonatas

Even more impersonal—indeed, so reticent that romantically minded listeners often mistakenly find them meaningless—are the Sonata for cello and piano (1915), the Sonata for flute, viola, and harp (1915), and the final Sonata for piano and violin (1916-17). These pieces are as French as Couperin *le grand,* and of an almost dandyish refinement. The subtly sensuous composer of the *Prélude a L'Après-midi d'un faune,* the piano *Préludes* and six *Images* for piano, and many of the exquisite songs here has shed the last tatter of his own romanticism. These sonatas are pure abstract constructions of patterned sound. They show as little trace of either nonmusical intention or extramusical support as a Handel fugue or a Haydn symphony. In the second decade of the twentieth century they indicated, though perhaps not for the first time, the change of musical weather to what later was to be called neoclassicism. They are, as Edward Lockspeiser wrote, "creations of a hedonist who had become a stoic." Journeying from his own image of romanticism to a new classicism, Debussy paralleled the artistic career of Berlioz. But Berlioz had lived too early to stem the swelling tides to which he himself earlier had given great impulse, whereas Debussy matured at a moment ripe for the emergence of a new sort of classicism.

Debussy and the Piano

Debussy's influence on rhythm, which he helped to resubtilize and make nervously responsive after the nineteenth-century sluggishness, and on harmony, which he conducted even farther from classical-romantic norms, was decisive. Even more original was his conception of the piano. He found means to make that percussive giant glide and murmur, left it speaking mistily and with clangor. He exploited chords and successions of tones in which struck sounds emphasized the overtones of others sounded previously. He made the piano evoke and whisper, suggest and dance. On that instrument, as on the orchestra and the human voice, he imposed his enigmas, his ambiguous personality and shadowy esthetic meaning, investing it with impressionist-symbolist magics. In this the immediate future was not with him: the last decade of his life and the years since his death most often have heard the piano employed as percussively as possible at the bidding of later composers.

Debussy almost never made the foredoomed attempt to transfer visible, tactile, audible realities into musical terms. He used his isolated art to evoke a visionary universe, sometimes very like a hallucination, a universe that existed nowhere before he imagined it. By unexpected, instantly self-justifying modulations, by swift, quiet, sudden irruptions of tones, he composed a new world.

Elements of Debussy's Style:
A New Harmony

How did Debussy mold an art so striking in its idiosyncrasy once it had emerged complete? By rhythmic, harmonic, and melodic originalities that he seems to have developed because he knew that music could not sound as he wanted it to sound if he continued to employ the dynamic, dramatic, classical romanticism of Beethoven or the chromatically rich, rhythmically indecisive romanticism of the nineteenth century, especially the Teutonic nineteenth century.

Debussy treated both consonant and dissonant chords almost as though they were single tones. Constantly present in his music are the dissonances that result when seconds, fourths, sixths, and sevenths are added to triads—and these most often are left unresolved. But they are not so characteristic an element of the Debussyan technique as is his manner of placing them. For he ignored, when he chose, the germinal tenet of harmony as it had been practiced for two centuries: that chords have normal functions, are mostly the result of what has preceded them and mostly move on by logical resolution to other normal chords. He placed both consonant and dissonant chords in series without regard to their "normal" functions, quite baldly because he liked the way the series sounded.

Parallel motion—successions of chords differing from one another only in pitch, and therefore preserving the same intervals in the same relative positions—was considered improper by classical harmonists. In the case of parallel fifths, indeed, it was flatly forbidden by all academic teachers. But Debussy used parallel motion freely, not only for thirds, fourths, and ninths (which, under urgent circumstances, classical purists might have approved in moderation), but also for fifths and octaves. As early as 1888, setting a poem by Verlaine, he began "C'est l'extase" with "sideslipping" or "gliding" parallel ninths.

In one of the most popular of Debussy's piano pieces, "La Cathédrale engloutie," he suggested the undersea tolling of cathedral bells by an unclassical (in one sense, a totally unharmonic) series of parallel octaves. Handling chords so, as though they were complex single tones, Debussy mixed his characteristic colors. Most of them reside in a whole-tone scale. In such a prélude as "Voiles," an extreme example, the misty, unsettled nature of the sail-evoking music derives almost wholly from totally unclassical whole-tone progressions.

Nor was Debussy frightened by that *"diabolus in musica,"* the tritone (augmented fourth), which earlier composers had labored earnestly to avoid. His music is starred with tritones: such combinations as F-B, A-D♯, and G♭-C. Where classical harmony had sanctioned use of this interval only as one component of a more complex chord, Debussy delighted in its unfamiliar effect for and by itself, feeling no compunction over leaving it unresolved, denying by implication that logic which requires resolution. Similarly, he often disregarded the "leading-tone" principle—the upward approach to the tonic of a scale by a half-tone step. In strict usage of whole-tone scales, of course, no half-tone was present, but even when Debussy was not moving entirely by whole-tone steps, he saw nothing wrong, when closing a phrase, section, or even composition, in having his melodic lines approach their tonics by other than half-tone intervals.

Another color-giving chemical applied to Debussy's strongly individual palette was the employment of modal passages not native to any diatonic major or minor scale or any chromatic scale (and not derived from the nonexistent "whole-tone system")—and thereby still further disrupting and rendering void of meaning the logical implications of both classical and romantic harmony. He came to place chordal and tonal tints very much as Monet and Seurat placed primary colors side by side, using unprepared and apparently inexplicable irruptions for contrast and integral decoration. His harmony, if such it may be called, was that of a sensualist more interested in—and more certain of—effect than in physico-acoustical logic. His methods are dangerous because they depend upon an extremely sensitive composing ear, on "logics" of a highly personal sort. No one but Debussy ever has used them with complete success; the seemingly similar art of Maurice Ravel differs from Debussy's both spiritually and technically.

Debussy and Musical Pattern

In developing the layout of a composition, Debussy very often avoided long phrases and any appearance of dramatic conflict. He found more germane to his conceptions a type of mosaic formed from fragments of divergent sizes and shapes. Again his inner ear was triumphant, but he did not develop means that would serve other composers well. He eschewed clear, sharply profiled melodies, creating instead a new sort of melody which moves up and down in zigzags with apparent willfulness and its own finally convincing and unmistakable rightness. In most of the compositions of Debussy's maturity, in fact, melody no longer is a separable element, any more than is rhythm or harmony or counterpoint. Melody has been assumed into fabric until, in any classical sense, it no longer truly is melody at all. Better it might be said that everything in this music has been merged into melody, melody subtilized, refined, broadened, and softened. Seldom has a composer amalgamated the chief musical elements to this extent, mixing them until they scarcely can be isolated even for discussion.

Debussy's musical cosmos was doomed except as it has endured in the music in which he evoked and created it, for it depended wholly upon him. It was intensely romantic in every meaning but that of technique, a belated summation in musical atmosphere of the romantic world of Baudelaire, Verlaine, Rimbaud, and Maeterlinck. And by 1900 romanticism was moribund, even in Paris. Neither Erik Satie nor Maurice Ravel was, in that sense, romantic at all except on the rarest occasions.

Erik Satie and Musical Wit

A highly accomplished jester, Satie helped both to orient the very late Debussy toward a sparseness related to new views of classicism and successfully to ridicule to younger French composers the more sensuous and idealistic aspects of musico-pictorial-literary romanticism. He kept his harmonies and textures unclothed to the point of nakedness. He deliberately exploited vulgarities of music-hall brashness. He used composition titles and musical directions that most often were nonsensical or utterly cryptic. Not a composer of the greatest strength, Satie nonetheless came justly to be regarded as a *petit maître* because his music helped to clear the air by reducing somewhat the too indoor temperature in which Debussy had chosen to exist. If, as Gerald Abraham has said, Debussy's music was concerned "with sensation instead of emotion (and hence often with the sensation of pure sound for its own sake)," Satie's is devoid of emotion altogether and is concerned solely with the wittiest juxtapositions of pure sound.

Satie was a full antiromantic, being opposed by the scope of his musical equipment to the subjective expansiveness of late German-Austrian romanticism and by temperament to the technically advanced but characteristically impressionist-symbolist romanticism of Debussy's middle, longest period. By such of his titles (having nothing whatever to do with the music they head) as *Embryons desséchés, Heures séculaires et instantanées,* and *Trois pièces en forme de poire*—and whatever the inherent value of the music—Satie laughed publicly and damagingly at Debussy's poetic nomenclature. More important for the future of music, he also laughed at all shoring up of music on poetry and painting and on its relationship to symbolism and impressionism. In his ballets *Socrate* (which may be an opera) and *Relâche* and in the wistfully antique *Gnossiennes* and *Gymnopédies,* with the merest wash of ambiguous and silvery nostalgia, he adumbrated the aristocratic, dandified classicism and the sheer delight in craftsmanship that were to propel much of the music of Ravel and younger Frenchmen. This was dandyism mixed with music-hall echoes and snatches of folk song. It was much else as well, but even in its lack of attempted personal communication it foretold no return to the eighteenth century or earlier. What was clearest about it was that it had bade willing farewell to the nineteenth century and to all of Debussy except his unfaltering taste and some of his newly wrought technical devices.

Ravel and His Critics

Ravel began much like Debussy, in the sentimental train of Gounod and Massenet. But those earlier men had known nothing of his sardonic heartlessness, his sheer pleasure in highly varied sonority as an aim of composition divorced as much as humanly is possible from the composer's extra-musical beliefs and emotions. Although the music of the mature Ravel has been called *pointilliste* because of its use of tiny areas of color, its structural outlines suggest a draftsman more than a colorist. He was a sovereign master of the large modern orchestra, a composer of songs of persuasive charm and peculiar expressiveness, a creator for the piano able to proceed on from the point at which Debussy had desisted, a man capable of following the implications of a purely musical logic to a cold, orgiastic frenzy. Scarcely one of Ravel's admirers has failed to sense that even his best-made music lacks something with which it might have become great. They surely are correct, however, in protesting that to condemn him to mediocrity is to speak foolishly in the sense of confusing nonmusical with musical weight. Ravel had not the adult Debussy's implacable sense of proportion, but the composer of *L'Heure espagnole, L'Enfant et les sortilèges, Miroirs, Le Tombeau de Couperin,* and *Gaspard de la nuit,* of the finest songs, and of the chamber pieces and piano concertos was not an imitator or an empty vessel.

Like Debussy, Ravel made effective uses of parallel chords in series, notably sevenths, with which Debussy had concerned his texture but little. He mostly avoided the whole-tone scale and its chords, which were too indefinite for the sharper outlines he desired. In his *Sonatine* for piano, Piano Trio, String Quartet, piano concertos, and some other pieces, he adapted classical forms to his own very unclassical purposes, not hesitating to season them with borrowings from American jazz. He composed, in such a piece as *"Scarbo"* in *Gaspard de la nuit,* virtuoso piano music that recognized procedures in Fauré and Debussy as ways of proceeding with some of Liszt's intentions. He composed much music about the world of children, but not for them—in *Ma Mère l'Oye* of a sophisticated adult's vision of fairyland, in *L'Enfant et les sortilèges* (to a libretto by Colette) playfully, but sometimes brutally, sardonic.

Ravel as a Man of the Twentieth Century

In his music, Ravel became what Debussy—thirteen years his senior—had not quite been: a twentieth-century man abraded by twentieth-century frictions, the framer of entirely postromantic structures and sensations. Greatly admiring the *clavecinistes,* notably Couperin and Rameau, Ravel brought something of their refinement into his own fully modern terminology, writing (as in *Le Tombeau de Couperin*) music of which past musical manners and meanings might be said to be the subject rather than the significance. And in *Daphnis et Chloé,* a ballet composed for Serge Diaghilev, though he did not match the tonal violence of Stravinsky's *Le Sacre du printemps,* Ravel proved that his techniques could be enlarged with complete success for the typical purposes of the actor, those which make emotions and meanings foreign to his own nature the very stuff of an overwhelmingly convincing performance.

Debussy, Ravel, and Harmony's Absorption of Melody

With both Debussy and Ravel, something peculiarly modern had occurred to the relations between melody and harmony. Harmony, freeing music and itself of rules and becoming an element of texture which required more and more of the listener's attention if he was to understand the composer's intentions and discourse, had begun to lose its separable importance. Having evolved gradually as a logic of the relationships among simultaneous and successive sounds—having, that is to say, emerged from counterpoint as a servant of melody, it had asserted a sort of autonomy gradually. But romantic chromaticism was, in this connection, self-defeating: as composers started to deal with chords and their web of interconnections with complete freedom, chromaticism lost its original significance. It could no longer be looked at or heard as a "coloring" in predominantly diatonic music for the reason that diatonicism itself no longer prevailed.

This may seem a paradox: that harmonic liberty again reduced harmony to the status of a servant to melody. But it is no paradox. For when composers began to treat the most complex chords as though they were single tones—and went on to write what might be called chord-melodies, melodies of which the constituent integers are groups of simultaneously sounded tones, harmony could be nothing more than a method of widening or "thickening" melody. When chords (both those academically labeled "consonant" and those scowled at as "dissonant") are being moved *en bloc* from pitch to pitch, they are being treated melodically. Debussy and Ravel were not the initiators of this special twentieth-century manner of creating texture, but they first brought it to fruition. In their mature compositions, melody had taken harmony and what remained of counterpoint back into itself. At the very hour when an understandably bewildered (and sometimes angry) wide public began to feel and say that melody was wasting away, it was in reality reasserting its primacy among musical means. This is easier to hear in Debussy and Ravel, who had not discarded repetition of melodic sections or the use of melodic series, than it is in the music of the polytonalists, atonalists, and twelve-tone composers—who in their search for great brevity generally have avoided the least repetition. What still is true is that there can be no music without melody; it is the special trait of contemporary music that melody again rules all, even the characteristic employment of instrumental and vocal colors, the intense complications of rhythm, and the other devices that also denote modernity.

The Six and Parisian Modernism

Following (when it did not accompany) the music of Debussy, Satie, and Ravel went the nose-thumbing, often deliberately vulgar music of the "Six," among whom the most notable composers were Francis Poulenc and Darius Milhaud. Under the pyrotechnic cover of Jean Cocteau's wit, Paris heard, during the 1920s and later, the small ex-

319

plosions of a sort of music which delighted in transmuting banalities into destructive humor, sentimentalities into oblique exegesis. The Parisian modernists adapted from the more emotional and intellectually violent modernisms of Central Europe, Germany, and Russia only those attitudes and technical ways which best could serve their own antiromantic quests. Polyrhythm, polytonality, the exploitation of jagged rhythms, even atonality in measured portion tickled rather than seared the ears of the French and their outland audiences.

Seldom attempting (except in some rather overblown compositions by Arthur Honegger) to erect large structures or convey their own religious, emotional, or sexual feelings, the composers of the "Six" sounded trivial to ears still bewitched by Wagner or even by Debussy. But it is useless to proclaim that the composers were out of joint or that music must be overtly romantic to be music at all. Milhaud, Poulenc, Georges Auric—these men were not at all frightened by the seeming truth of the charge that they were not great poets or likely to become culture heroes in any Beethovian sense. They were interested in music as music and were sensibly willing to leave poetry to poets and heroism to heroes. It scarcely would be absurd to say that the "meaning" of French music from the 1880s to this hour (aside from the welcome reassertion of entertainment as a good and aside from some special composers not discussed here—Olivier Messiaen being one) is the divesting of nonmusical accretions from music, the reiteration of the incontrovertible statement that what music can do best is what music alone can do at all.

CHAPTER XX

Stravinsky and One Way out of
Classical-Romantic Harmony

Igor Stravinsky, the most influential inheritor of musical legacies from late-nineteenth-century Russian music, began as a close disciple and imitator of Rimsky-Korsakov. Even the earliest of his music still played is extremely clever and well made. But nothing about it suggests either a revolutionary experimenter or a great composer. Only when Stravinsky began to compose scores for Serge Diaghilev's seasons of Russian ballet in Western Europe did he embark upon his own discoveries. The first Diaghilev-Stravinsky ballet was *The Firebird* (1910). In atmosphere and technique, most of it strikingly resembles pages from Rimsky-Korsakov's operas. In it, however, we hear the "Dance of Kashchey." Kashchey is a demon out of Russian mythology. His dance is accompanied by jagged rhythms, explosive bursts of dissonant sound, a brutality new to music. This section of *The Firebird* is much closer to the witches' sabbath at the close of Mussorgsky's symphonic poem *A Night on Bald Mountain*, nearer altogether to the harmonic novelties of Dargomizhsky and Mussorgsky than it is to the idiom of Rimsky-Korsakov's fairy tales.

Petroushka *as Announcing*
the Later Twentieth Century

The Firebird was followed by *Petroushka*, a landmark in the music of the first half of the twentieth century. As in

The Firebird, the scenario deals with purely Russian matter, but with an important difference: the three central characters of *Petroushka* are not mortals and supernatural presences, but marionettes that come to temporary life to act out an abrupt tale of faithlessness and tragic jealousy. Stravinsky's musical raiment for this melodrama (1910–11) is remarkable for the success with which it reflects the semihuman nature of these animated toys, for its ways of diminishing the world to their spiritual, mental, and emotional dimensions without lessening its own suggestiveness and power to engage listeners. The score naturally is fragmentary if listened to or looked at apart from scenario and choreography, but even under such conditions what becomes certain is that it has peculiar psychological verity and that its rhythms and its metrical constitution both are something new. *Petroushka* is a final farewell to the harmonic, melodic, and rhythmic manners of the nineteenth century, even the Russian nineteenth century. Into it, what is more, Stravinsky introduced rhythmic and harmonic usages without which the later music of the twentieth century must have become something other than what it has been becoming.

In *Petroushka,* Stravinsky gave to shifting meter and rhythm—to definite, noticeable, but constantly altering beat —an importance that it never before had been allotted in the composition of either Russian or Western music. He elevated rhythm as a compositional element to a position as central to the achievement of his conscious purposes, as significant to his listeners and his disciples, as the places that long had been held by melody, counterpoint, and harmony. To some extent, of course, characters in ballet always had been revealed to rhythms that were meant to be characteristic of them. But in *Petroushka* the three central characters are not so much accompanied as created by the rhythmic profiles of the music associated with them. In themselves the rhythms of *Petroushka* presuppose and prefigure this special choreography.

The Firebird had been Russian nationalist music marked by only enough new elements to suggest that its year was

1910, not 1890. With a difference, *Petroushka* may be thought of as a further refinement of that nationalism. Stravinsky was reducing to skeletonic essentials the folk-derived melodic contours and consequent harmonies and rhythms that had distinguished the music of Balakirev, Borodin, Mussorgsky, and Rimsky-Korsakov. So reducing them, Stravinksy propelled himself along a one-way road toward a new musical idiom in which forceful, constantly shifting rhythmic beats, often in the form of *ostinati*,** would become a major tool of musical composition.

Petroushka *and Bitonality*

One of the passages in *Petroushka* which evoked most comment from its early commentators was this:

The historically significant fact about this passage from *Petroushka* is that it is composed in two simultaneous tonalities or keys: C major and F♯ major. The four introductory notes in the right-hand part are C-E-G-C (C-E-G, the tonic triad of C major, with the root [C] doubled at the top); the four simultaneous notes in the left-hand part are A♯-C♯-F♯-A♯ (F♯-A♯-C♯, the tonic triad of F♯ major inverted to A♯-C♯-F♯, again with the root tone of the chord [A♯] doubled at the top). In the eleventh measure of the example, observe that, while the left-hand notes remain unaltered, those played by the right hand, still in C major, make up the triad built up from its dominant, G (G-B-D, once again with the root tone doubled at the top). By some views of analysis, these notes may be looked at as appoggiaturas, especially when, in the measures immediately following the example, Stravinsky spreads all the notes out like this:

Polytonality

Nevertheless, as introduced and worked from, this is an example of bitonality, of music couched in two tonalities at

the same time. This postharmonic device was to become of some utility to Stravinsky himself later on, as well as to many other twentieth-century composers, notably Alfredo Casella and Darius Milhaud. When, at times, more than two tonalities came to be used simultaneously, the practice became known as polytonality, which, by extension, has also been used to include bitonal usages as well. Whatever its enduring value per se—as distinct from its occasional use for special effects—polytonality became one possible component of all specifically dissonant modern harmonic texture. It appears not to have been the most important texture of any compositions of first quality, but it always is too early to know what use a great composer may make of any musical method or device.

The human ear and brain are capable of apprehending several tones simultaneously—else we should be unable to hear chords. The listening mind can follow two or more melodies simultaneously: if it could not, polyphony would be a meaningless jumble. So the first supporters of polytonality asked: why not two, three, four—more—tonalities at once? The usual answer was a string of epithets: "Anarchy! Impossibility! Ugliness!" But *Petroushka* and music far more extensively polytonal became popular stage and concert fare nonetheless. The ears and brains of more hospitable and better-trained generations have found Stravinsky's score at first exciting and then acceptable. To sophisticated listeners, indeed, *Petroushka* now contains no measure that for any harmonic reason sounds incorrect, ugly, or anything but justified in its place. This music has come to seem little more "advanced" than *Boris Godunov.*

Musical Explosion:
Le Sacre du printemps

In 1913, two years after *Petroushka,* the Diaghilev-Stravinsky collaboration culminated in a ballet that stirred up such tempests of commentary as remain unparalleled in musical anecdotage, a score that many of those who first accepted it as a surpassing masterpiece still tend to view as the central fact of Stravinsky's long career—and therefore of an entire hemisphere of twentieth-century music. This was *Le Sacre du printemps* (*The Rite of Spring*). Unlike the music of *Petroushka*, which remained sufficiently respectful of romantic-classical concepts of tonality so that its printed score includes several temporary key-signatures, that of *Le Sacre du printemps* has dispensed with signatures altogether. For in it tonality as an element of composition is taken some advantage of here and dispensed with or suspended there. The ballet employs a huge orchestra (see pages 176–77), and goes forward from the jagged rhythms of the "Dance of Kashchey" in *The Firebird* to a rhythmic insistence that perhaps never has been matched in nervous, kinetic force. The final seven measures of the full orchestral score of *Le Sacre du printemps* are given on pages 328–29.

Here thirty-one staves are needed. The constant changes in time-signature (5/16, 3/16, 5/16, 3/16, 4/16, 3/16) are typical of many areas of this score (Mussorgsky similarly had alternated 5/4–that peculiarly Russian meter–and 6/4 in the "Promenade" that occurs several times in his *Pictures at an Exhibition*). Here, as elsewhere, the music is full of searing, unprepared and unresolved dissonances. Try–with all your force (and the assisting fingers of two friends)–putting down on a piano the following chord, which contains all the tones of the first beat of measure 5 in the page of full score on pages 328–29):

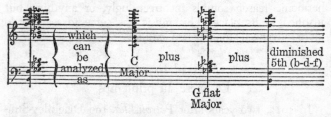

Played thus close together and all in one timbre on the piano, these tones produce an effect vastly different from that which they produce as performed by numerous different instruments and with the tones spread out. But no number of differing timbres, no amount of "spreading-out," could make this chord consonant in any traditional sense. It is only one of hundreds of chords as dissonant in *Le Sacre du printemps*, music that temporarily marked the complete rejection of the harmonic assumptions evolved during the preceding two hundred years.

Although many of those who first heard *Le Sacre du printemps* assailed it as the death of melody and therefore of music, it is music—and by definition therefore inevitably compacted in part of melody. A dozen or twenty entirely distinct melodies can be isolated from it; part of its shocking effectiveness, in fact, derives from the contrast between simple, mostly diatonic tunes and their intricate harmonic, rhythmic, and instrumental investiture. The startling simultaneities of tones are somehow intensely appropriate to the pagan prehistory that is the ballet's scenario—which certainly does not mean that music of this sort existed in prehistoric times, which it emphatically did not. What animates this music, what produces its savage, hypnotic power is rhythm, rhythm set free from sequence and from any repetition of the same groupings of fundamental beats. At its most powerful, this music seems to act, through rhythm, directly on the auditor's nervous system (while, at the same time, others of its constituent elements—melody, postharmonic texture, tone color, variations in tempo and volume—continue to affect those reacting centers to which all composed music later than Gregorian chant had directed itself).

Stravinsky and Musical Anarchy

Whether *Le Sacre du printemps* really lifted the lid of a musical Pandora's box or not, as its enemies asserted, it appeared to have done so to all musical conservatives who lived through the two decades that followed its first performance in 1913. Experiment in disregard of all "rules"—indeed, at times, the searching-out of "rules" so that they could be broken in the most startling way—became habitual and self-conscious, especially during the 1920s. It sometimes led to vitality, but it also led to considerable vacuous nonsense from the studios of the untalented, just as the "rules" themselves had led to vacuous nonsense in the hands of untal-

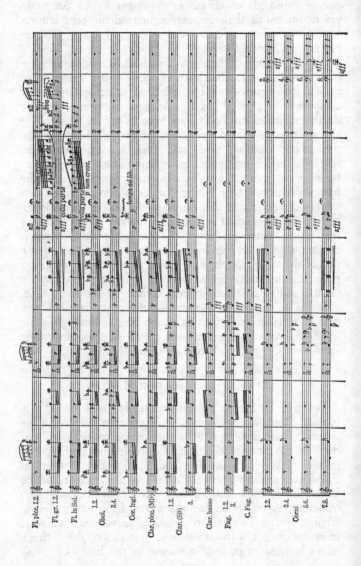

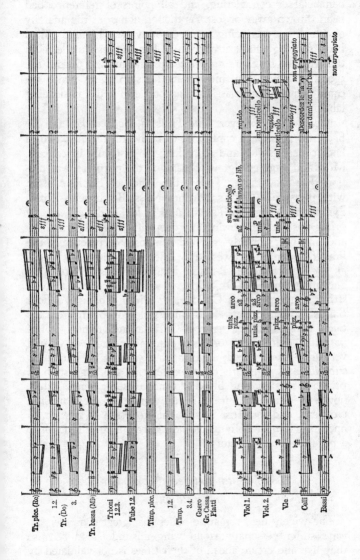

ented composers earlier. For a time, it seemed that all rules, beneficial or constricting, and all points of reference had been thrown away or lost. As though aghast at the anarchy of which he was being accused, Stravinsky himself pulled back, starting almost at once to be less and less "modern" in the terms of *Le Sacre du printemps* and moving toward the special revaluation of musical methods and aims which became known as neoclassicism, a poor term and a misleading label.

Meanwhile, however, *The Firebird, Petroushka,* and *Le Sacre du printemps* continued to be heard, the first two as both concert suites and as ballets, the last only in concert. More and more ears grew adjusted to the purposeful revolution that they made. Today, thousands of listeners listen with pleasure to Bach's B-Minor Mass, Beethoven's Ninth Symphony, Wagner's *Tristan und Isolde,* and *Le Sacre du printemps* without sensing any deep rift between Stravinsky and any other greatly talented composer of practically unlimited technical prowess. No listener in his sense would choose to listen to the B-Minor Mass when his state of mind and attention called for a Mozart piano concerto, a Haydn string quartet, Bizet's *Carmen,* or Virgil Thomson's *Four Saints in Three Acts.* It is impossible to obtain from *Le Sacre du printemps* a sense of Christian resignation (it is a pagan program-piece) or quiet entertainment (it is in part very loud), or, indeed, anything but what it pre-eminently supplies and calls up: deep excitement, the suggestion of primeval mystery and blood violence close at hand. It has, however, established itself in the canon of great musical creations, and to refuse at this date to listen to it with an open mind and wholly unprejudiced ears is to fall victim to a peculiar trick of history.

The Gap Between Composer and Audience

The widely held romantic belief that great composers always suffer personally from being misunderstood because they live and create ahead of their times is not validated by a study of musical history. Nevertheless, it contains a measure of truth: any important new artistic creation, and particularly in one's own times, must differ in several of many possible aspects from everything that was created earlier. This difference was blatantly noticeable during the second half of the nineteenth century, when—in music as in painting and the other arts—the breakdown of academic "legislation" had become unprecedentedly swift. Listeners could scarcely begin to catch up with one new aspect of musical texture before two or three much newer ones had begun to assault their ears and their minds. The gap between the harmonic textures used by the most advanced composers, for example, and those textures familiar to (and therefore accepted by) the great body of people attending concerts, recitals, and performances of staged music began to widen rapidly. By 1913, the year of Stravinsky's *Le Sacre du printemps*, that gap had become dangerously wide. To many implicated individuals the danger seemed real that it already was too wide to be bridged—or to be bridged quickly enough.

The ensuing situation, comical when its tragic possibilities were not too patent, was perilous to the continuing vitality of the ancient art of music. Composing scores that stirred immediate, enthusiastic responses from highly trained small groups of listeners, men like Igor Stravinsky learned that their most recent music struck the great public (only recently converted to Richard Strauss's tone poems) as meaningless, ugly, and infuriating. This could have signaled the end of the constant changes that provide the vitality of any organism. What actually happened? *Le Sacre du printemps* (1913) and *Les Noces villageoises* (*The Village Wedding*, 1914–17) proved to lie in a forward territory beyond which Stravinsky's own personal sort of rhythmically dominated, dissonant, harmonically detached music was not to advance (perhaps was incapable of advancing). Stravinsky himself began to face toward other regions: his disciples and imitators began to search for diverging paths. And gradually the chasm between the Straussians of 1913 and the small advance guard of Stravinskyans began to be filled in by the detritus of time itself. Very slowly, and with some painful puffing, the giant strides that Stravinsky had taken from 1910 to 1913—from *The Firebird* to *Petroushka* to *Le Sacre du printemps*—were made in small steps by the Western world's audiences for serious music.

Stravinsky: Change of Direction
after Le Sacre

But the comical-tragical results of Stravinsky's career as the foremost composer of his era did not end when the music of his three big ballets had become firmly imbedded in the "standard repertoire." By that time, he himself had left the evolving methods of those scores far behind. He had begun to react against their elements of romantic emotion, their increasing expansiveness, and their exploitation of extramusical materials. *Les Noces villageoises,* which achieved its definitive form as late as 1923, when Diaghilev staged it, displayed one of the first large steps away from *Le Sacre du printemps*. Although Stravinsky described it as "Russian choreographic scenes in four tableaux, with song and music," it was mechanistic in its abstractness, another evidence of twentieth-century music's determination to be unliterary, nonphilosophic, unpictorial—if necessary, inhuman. In this score, unquestionably, the modern dependence upon machines was reflected.

Stravinsky and "Neoclassicism"

Increasingly involved in the elaboration of pure music built from essential elements of melody, chordal relations or lack of them, and metric-rhythmic patterns, Stravinsky passed through a period during which he used the characteristic styles and manners of earlier composers as subject matter for his own composing. In the "ballet with songs" *Pulcinella* (1919) what the music was "about" was really certain compositions of Giovanni Battista Pergolesi (1710–36), from which some of it was directly borrowed. In *Oedipus Rex* (1926–27), an opera-oratorio seemed to anatomize the musical style of Handel. *Le Baiser de la fée* (1928) dealt with parts of the sound-world of Tchaikovsky. Adverse critics suggested that Stravinsky borrowed the styles—and even the melodies—of other composers because he now had no style and little melody of his own. The truth, however, was that he was merely asserting sharply that the most important value of the art of composition lies in what is done with its basic materials rather than in their provenance and exact nature. This stoic impersonality alienated larger audiences as certainly as had the kinetic, discordant violence of *Le Sacre du printemps* and *Les Noces villageoises*. To listeners still under the persisting influence of nineteenth-century romantic communication, this "neoclassical" abstractness sounded devoid of the very warmths and pleasures they always had sought in music.

Continuing to Listen to Stravinsky

But Stravinsky continued to delight the *avant-garde,* that often-derided but nevertheless extremely powerful group of highly attentive and trained intellectuals which often seems either to be closely allied to the evolving spirit of the age or to be producing that spirit. He remained "the style" in world capitals, not with the mass audiences of symphony orchestras and opera houses, but with the intellectual critics and performers who are looked up to covertly even by many of the "average" music-lovers who deride them. His music, which he continued to send forth from his worktable with something like abundance, would not be downed. It was—and remains—par excellence, music that must be listened to with intense attention again and again. Doing little, most of the time, to be gracious or winning, it nevertheless wins and has grace. Increasingly, man after man, music-lovers who at first had found Stravinsky's "neoclassic" music unappetizing if not altogether desiccated and dead have begun, much later, to "hear" it. It has become clear to them that its business is the business of, say, Bach's *Well-Tempered Clavier* or Beethoven's last string quartets: that of building solid musical edifices out of inner tensions and interrelationships. Of Stravinsky's mastery over the means and manners of his ever-changing art no doubt ever has been raised; his eventual vindication was, again, a question of time.

Stravinsky and Music as Expression

Stravinsky and his enthusiasts often confused those who paid more careful attention to composers' pronouncements than to their music. His often-expressed admiration of Carl Maria von Weber and Tchaikovsky, for example, appeared paradoxical from the lips of so implacable a postromantic. And then, in his autobiography (1935), he wrote: "For I consider music, by its essential nature, powerless to express anything at all, whether a feeling, an attitude of mind, a psychological mood, a natural phenomenon, *etc*. . . . Expression never has been the immanent property of music. That is by no means the purpose of its existence. If, as nearly always is the case, music seems to express something, that is only an illusion and not a reality. It is simply an additional attribute that, by tacit and inveterate agreement, we have lent it, thrust upon it, as a label, a convention—in brief, an aspect that we have come, unconsciously or through force of habit, to confuse with its essential being." Affronted commentators seized upon one section of this statement—that music is "powerless to express anything at all"—and said that it proved Stravinsky to be an anti-Music. What they neglected to notice was that what he had written was correct: that the extramusical "anythings" that we believe music to be "expressing" are not in the music, but in ourselves, however much we have agreed to let the patterned sounds symbolize them. Here, as everywhere, Stravinsky was merely asserting in simple, shocking terms the autonomy of music as an art, its right to be musical rather than literary or philosophical or pictorial.

The Later Stravinsky

And so, despite the obvious disappointment of those who waited for Stravinsky to go on from the romantic *Schrecklichkeit* of *Le Sacre du printemps*, and despite the wrongheadedness of those who have hoped to find, in each of his new compositions, a return to the textures of romanticism, Stravinsky has gone on being a master. To say that is not to suggest that every item in the long list of his compositions (which now includes symphonies, concertos, ballets, operas —one of them to a libretto in English—and numerous small works) is a lofty masterpiece. But if the passing decades have taught us anything about Stravinsky and his creations, that lesson is that with a little effort we most often can catch up with him and then find the catching-up worth all effort. His craftsmanship is his most sincere tribute to the art he has practiced so long. Whoever cannot enjoy craftsmanship in any art cannot really appreciate that art at all *as an art*, for if he enjoys it nonetheless, he certainly enjoys it for nonartistic reasons.

Stravinsky and the Limits of Tonality

Except in a very few, very late compositions, none of Stravinsky's music entirely abandoned some sense of "home" tones and "home" chords to which others of the composition's tones and chords bear distinguishable relationships. The most important tones in any passage from a work by Stravinsky (and, again, except for a few late flirtings with dodecaphony**) are heard with a sensation that they have been located in relation to an at least temporarily established fundamental or "home" tone. In fact, the remoteness and complexity of his most remote and complex measures are remote *from* something present or understandably implied —and are complicated in relation to some basic simplicity likewise present or implied. While inviting the music-lovers of his time to share his enormous gifts for design, structure, and continuous internal relevance, Stravinsky has journeyed as far as seems possible within the boundaries of tonality— and even, toward his eightieth year, has crossed over them.

But it was in the third leading branch of twentieth-century music—the Viennese—that tonality itself first was deliberately flouted. If judged by the procedures permissible under the Viennese harmonic government of Haydn's and

Mozart's time, the state of rule in much of Stravinsky's music looks like anarchy, though it is not. In reality, Stravinsky's harmonic administration is a very liberal democracy preserving significant elements from the procedures that had been evolved during a millennium of musical creation and codified to some extent during the eighteenth and nineteenth centuries. From the same point of comparison, the harmonic rule of Arnold Schoenberg and his followers at its strictest would have to be called an autocracy from which tonality had been exiled by ukase, an arbitrary replacement of the past's constantly evolving ways by a series of complex formulas imposed from above by fiat.

CHAPTER XXI

A Harmonic Side Road: Scriabin

Driven to verbal explanation and the compounding of abstract formulas by some need to justify the promptings of forces within their artistic selves, composers from time to time have experimented with abstruse harmonic "systems" lacking any divinable connections to the audible physical make-up of sound. Alexander Scriabin (1872–1915), for instance, was natively fascinated by chords built up out of fourths (the conventional diatonic chords, it should be remembered, are basically superimpositions of thirds). One of these chords of fourths, a central fact in Scriabin's orchestral "poem of fire" entitled *Prometheus* (1909–10) he called the "mystic chord." It consisted of a superimposed series of fourths: C-F♯-B♭-E-A-D (or A-D♯-G-C♯-[F]-B-E) and variants thereof. As Scriabin—a composer whose value perhaps has been unduly depreciated by lack of sympathy with all the nonmusical freight that he asked his music to carry—employed these synthetic chords and built a harmonic pseudo-system on them, they unquestionably lent his musical textures a peculiar sound that momentarily seemed very original. But the flaw in his pseudo-system was double: only those who learned it outside his music really could "understand" the music in which it was set forth, and they proved to be few; the resulting harmonic textures defied constructive evolution, and the final result of that defiance was music of necessity centripetal, rhapsodic, and finally static.

Revolution as Romanticism:
Hauer and Schoenberg

Experimentation itself, it already has been suggested, is a romantic activity, classicism being defined as creation out of materials already accepted as being in a satisfactory state of development—and originality within classicism being demonstrated in ways of manipulating those materials. To this pattern Scriabin fitted: everything about his personality and the extramusical machinery attached to his largest compositions places him full in the nineteenth-century romantic tradition, however harmonically "modern" his harmonic idiom may at first have appeared to be. Equally romantic, by this definition, was a much more stern and rigorous defiance of ordinary concepts of key and tonality which emerged from Vienna, specifically in the theories of Josef Matthias Hauer (1883–1959) and both the theories and the compositions of Arnold Schoenberg (1874–1951) and his disciples. Today, many decades after its first appearance, both that overt defiance of tonality and the system that it demanded—a remarkable mental achievement—remain subjects of acrimonious debate. On the side of Schoenberg speaks a group of ardent, convinced adherents, many of them with key positions in academic life; against him speaks the flat indifference of most audiences, some facts about the mathematical constitution of musical tones, and the circumstance that even today his music still is performed only very occasionally.

Adapted, mixed with other elements, and thereby in a sense contradicted, the Schoenbergian techniques have produced one towering masterpiece, Alban Berg's opera *Wozzeck*, and several other compositions that have won a modicum of general acceptance. In undiluted form, those theories and techniques have produced nothing that has succeeded in crossing the bristling fence between cultists and large audiences.

The Evolution
of Schoenberg's Teachings

Schoenberg was born in Vienna in 1874. At the age of twenty-five he composed a string sextet entitled *Verklärte Nacht* (*Transfigured Night*). Passionately, yearningly romantic, this conventional piece (in both its original instrumentation and as Schoenberg expanded it for string orchestra) won and has maintained some world-wide popularity. Unless the most advanced harmonic speech of Brahms, Wagner, and Richard Strauss be considered modern, *Verklärte Nacht* is not modern. The only other composition by Schoenberg which ever has won a fraction of music's larger audience is his *Gurre-Lieder*, a vast cantata or oratorio for soloists, chorus, and orchestra of text by Jens Peter Jacobsen. It is as lushly romantic as *Verklärte Nacht*—and has no more to do with "modernism." By turns, it is Brahmsian, Wagnerian, Mahlerian, Debussyan, Brucknerian, and Straussian; it was completed in 1911. In its full romantic expansiveness it is a product of the romantic strain kept blooming in Vienna from Schubert to Brahms and beyond: it is only very mildly experimental, being entirely friendly to tonality and to chromatic and other aspects of late-romantic harmony.

The Denial of Tonality

Before Schoenberg completed the *Gurre-Lieder*, however, he also had composed three short piano pieces whose implications were to rock the more intellectual sectors of the musical world—and to keep them rocking to this day. These, the *Drei Klavierstücke*, Opus 11, composed in 1908–09, occupy but eleven pages; they were followed by, among other compositions, the *Sechs kleine Klavierstücke*, Opus 19 (1911), which occupy only seven pages (only the first of them is more than one page in length, and three of the six contain only nine measures each). Their explosive content, out of all proportion to their lengths, resulted from their

339

overt, complete denial of the principle of tonality. Thus briefly and assuredly did Schoenberg contradict the basic assumption by which, for the centuries since the earliest counterpoint, the music of Western civilization had been held together.

"Atonality" and the
Twelve Chromatic Tones

Critics and other writers on musical subjects at once began to call this music "a-tonal" or "atonal." Schoenberg objected to the word, saying that this music has "tonality," but adding that the pieces thus miscalled were composed "by means of twelve tones among which there is no relationship except the relationship of one of them to another." (The twelve tones to which Schoenberg refers are all the component parts of a one-octave chromatic scale, such as A-A♯-B-C-C♯-D-D♯-E-F-F♯-G-G♯.) As the very meaning of tonality is that, in a given instance, the temporary functions of certain tones lend them a significance of which other tones then are devoid, the last part of Schoenberg's phrase must seem to non-Schoenbergians the definition of a musical texture to which the word "a-tonal" perfectly applies.

In the piano pieces of Schoenberg's Opus 11 and Opus 19, no tone is a home tone; no point of rest or finality appears (for which reason the ending of each piece seems as arbitrary as its beginning); and no dominant or leading tone emerges anywhere. Chords, mostly dissonant, are built arbitrarily, having been dictated solely by the composer's psychic-aural-intellectual being. The organizing principles of these compositions—that which differentiates them from accidental collections of tones—defy both deduction and imitation—as Schoenberg himself admitted when he pronounced, somewhat later, the need for imposing principles from outside and by rule on what he still insisted was not "atonality."

Listening to Schoenberg

For the ordinary listener no "way" to listen to the Schoenberg *Klavierstücke* can be formulated or suggested except that of letting the unobstructed sound of their arranged tones act upon him. Nothing that he can bring to such listening, no memory or preceding concept of musical significance or pleasure or comprehension, can prove anything but a barrier to accepting this music at all. In most cases, the experiment of such pristine listening proves comparable to that of facing an entirely abstract painting or sculpture that suggests nothing pre-existent or of reading one of Gertrude Stein's most willful and abstract arrangements of words. The listener may be baffled, irritated, pleased, moved, or amused. What he cannot obtain from these piano pieces is any of the responses that he has been accustomed to experiencing when listening to earlier seriously intended Western music, from Gregorian chant to the most extreme experiments of Stravinsky (except Stravinsky's late flirtations with atonality).

Schoenberg did not move directly from the deliquescent, overripe romanticism of *Verklärte Nacht* and the *Gurre-Lieder* to the several *Klavierstücke*. Some of his earlier pieces had been richly seasoned by a taste for romantic harmony lush with chromaticism and complex counterpoint. And in his D-Minor String Quartet, Opus 7 (1905), and elsewhere, he had composed architecturally baroque music in which the extreme complexities of chromatic and other counterpoint had borne him to the farthest edge of tonality. In that music a definable tonality always is to be discovered by looking, but cannot always be heard by listening.

The Absence of Tonality

A Viennese, pervasively romantic by nature, Schoenberg was driven by an interior demon. A man of formidable intelligence, he was—once he had become convinced—utterly logical and fearless of the results of his own logic. Not every composer could have faced the consequences of the steps that Schoenberg took. In his F♯-Minor String Quartet, Opus 10 (1907–08); in the cycle of fifteen songs with piano accompaniment on texts from Stefan George's *Das Buch der Hängenden Gärten*, Opus 15 (1907); and in the *Klavierstücke*, already discussed, he did several things that in sum resulted in what clearly was atonality though he said that it was not. He combined all previously existing harmonic practices—including whole-tone scales and chords, as well as chords not unlike Scriabin's towers of fourths—and added new devices of his own. He moved indecipherable chords sidewise in *en bloc* progressions. And the result was a complete and final absence of tonality.

The Absence of Development

Now, development in the classical sense or the romantic sense is, by definition, an activity within tonality. So Schoenberg implacably let development follow tonality to oblivion. This stoicism tended to curtail the native expansiveness that he had demonstrated in the *Gurre-Lieder*. Another force tending in that direction was the sharply defined limitation of the amount of continuous nontonal texture which even well-disposed listeners can attend to with concentration. And so Schoenberg's first consciously atonal pieces were gnomic, cryptic, silent before the ear and mind could absorb from them any impression but that of much present discord and that of the absence of all known landmarks. The number of performances which these epoch-shattering compositions have won in the decades since their creation remains smaller than that which has been awarded any other pieces of like fame. They have no wiles with which to seduce those who come to them without preconceptions, with only a full musical background and willing attention. Again excepting converts to Schoenberg's theories, no matter what the nationality of the listeners, these pieces always are likely to seem to him to be in a language other than his own.

Schoenberg and Expressionism:
Pierrot lunaire

In 1912, however, Schoenberg composed, to a German adaptation of moodily romantic French poems by Albert Guiraud, his Opus 21, *Pierrot lunaire*, described as "three cycles of seven poems" and as a "melodrama for recitation and chamber orchestra." In this expressionist[1] masterpiece, the female vocal soloist is instructed to speak the heated, overwrought words on definite pitches, which are indicated meticulously throughout the score. Schoenberg had used a "reciter" among the soloists in the *Gurre-Lieder*. His employment of song-speech, known as *Sprechstimme*, is terrifyingly effective in setting forth the neurasthenic, intermittently almost demented, meanings of the *Pierrot lunaire* poems. Equally effective for that purpose are the intense, seemingly dislocated, arbitrary lines of the melodies that Schoenberg here sets forth by means of a chamber orchestra delicately fragmented. The result can be a literary-aural experience of crushing power. With the best will in the listener's heart and mind, and despite the decades that have passed since 1912, it is extremely difficult to think of this power as a strictly musical function. But to escape its impact is even more difficult.

Pierrot lunaire at once suggested to wary listeners two ideas about Schoenberg which passing time has done nothing to contradict: he would always find the best employment of atonality in relation to a verbal text; his whole conception of music was pre-eminently suited to the support and projection of exacerbated nervous conditions and deranged mental states.

[1] Expressionism—a word borrowed, as "impressionism" had been, from the vocabulary of painting—was a term often applied to Schoenberg and his disciples. It covered their attempts to express or transmit by music the contents of their real, or subconscious, selves. In a technical sense, expressionist music almost always is exactly coextensive with atonal and twelve-tone music. Its psychoanalytic pretensions, of course, are added—and extramusical—qualities. But it is interesting and thought-provoking that all three of the leading atonalists were born in Vienna.

Despite the relatively few performances of Schoenberg's music, he continued to be a very active composer. Following *Pierrot lunaire* came *Vier Lieder* with orchestra, Opus 22 (1913–15); *Fünf Stücken* for piano, Opus 23; a serenade, Opus 24 (first performed in 1923); and a suite for piano, Opus 25 (1924). In this uncompromisingly atonal music (Schoenberg in later years occasionally wrote tonally) what gradually became apparent was that Schoenberg was in the process of forging for his atonality a system logical and workable enough to satisfy a mathematician.

Imposing Order on Atonality

Schoenberg had fabulous contrapuntal learning, a titanic grasp of harmonic and contrapuntal devices from every musical era, which made him the century's greatest preceptor and theoretician. Using old contrapuntal methods, he inverted his often widely skipping melodic lines; he reversed them and combined the original form with the reversion; he built them into canons and crab canons. From about 1915 onward, both his music and his remarks made clear that he was working on a way to impose order on atonality. Any such system, of course, could only be abrupt, complex, and difficult.

The Twelve-Tone "System"

Hints for important constituent elements of this system were borrowed from the music and writings of another remarkable man (whom most of the musical world has forgotten), Josef Matthias Hauer. A prolific composer, Hauer (like Schoenberg a native of the Vienna that also produced Sigmund Freud) also published a series of pamphlets and monographs in which he advocated grouping the twelve tones of a one-octave chromatic scale into patterns that he called *Tropen*. Hauer's theories partook a little of mathematical legerdemain, of the sheer fun of discovering the number of different patterns in which the twelve tones could be arranged. Schoenberg's ideas were different. What was important to Schoenberg in Hauer's conceptions was the notion of making a particular "row" of twelve tones—a melody of twelve tones in which none of the twelve is repeated—the basis of composing in somewhat the way that a tonality had been the basis of tonal composing.

Coming fully formulated at last from Schoenberg's formidable brain, this second of his history-altering steps soon came to be called "the twelve-tone system." This frankly arbitrary imposition of laws from without, however hard to understand by hearing the resulting music, is easy to explain in words:

1. Each twelve-tone composition is built out of a tone row containing all twelve tones of a chromatic one-octave scale. Arranged at will, these twelve tones (none of which is repeated within the row) are presented over and over in the same unchanging sequence or one of three variants thereof;

2. Besides the original pattern of the twelve tones in the row designated, they may at any juncture be presented upside down (inversion), backward (retrograde progression), or both upside down and backward (retrograde inversion);

3. Both in its original form and in any of the three variants thereof, the tone row (usually called a *Grundgestalt*) may at any time be transposed whole so that its first tone is any tone at all—but then the row's internal pitch relationships from tone to tone must be renewed intact in the new pitch;

4. Any of the twelve tones of the designated row may at any time appear in any octave; the tones may be presented vertically (in chords) as well as horizontally (in melody);

5. Both melodies and chords may be derived from the tone row, but all twelve of its tones, in whichever of its forms, must be employed before the series is rebegun. (In later manifestations of the dodecaphonic, or twelve-tone-row, system, Schoenberg somewhat relaxed this rule. He himself sometimes used segments of a row without completing the row each time.)

If an arrangement of the twelve tones within an octave is not to sound like a simple chromatic scale, few of the tones must appear in continguous sequence: the typical Schoenbergian tone row therefore contains many wide skips. Here is the "basic tone row" or "basic set" from his Wind Quintet, Opus 26 (first performed in 1924):

As used upside down (inverted) at a descent of one octave, this row reads:

And here is a comparatively simple passage from the Wind Quintet which demonstrates one actual treatment of this row to create musical texture:

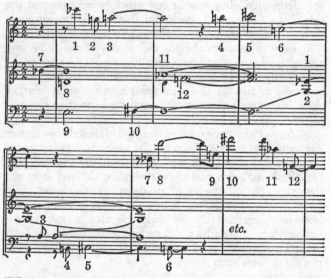

"This example," Schoenberg said in a lecture delivered at the University of California at Los Angeles in 1941, "shows how an accompaniment can be built. As octave doubling should be avoided, the accompanying of tones 1–6 with tones 7–12, and vice versa, is one way to fulfill this requirement." That statement explains not only something of the method itself, but also the ineradicably dissonant and mechanistic "counterpoint" always characteristic of twelve-tone music in pristine purity.

Listening to "Serial" Twelve-Tone Music

These examples from Schoenberg's Wind Quintet show one application of a twelve-tone procedure in relative simplicity and absence of complication. The invitations to tremendous complexity within it are numerous, and Schoenberg and his disciples accepted most of them. In some of their scores, even the examining eye is all but prevented from following the gyrations of the tone rows. And it is difficult, often to the edge of impossibility, for the listener to hear what really is happening in such cross-textured music, though that fact would be of no importance if the music itself were available to him without such awareness. Of most of the tone rows or basic sets, non-Schoenbergians say that, though certainly these are nonaccidental successions of tones and may very well be true melodies, it is possible to hear them again and again without being able to hear them as performing a truly melodious function. In fact, it is possible to hold a naturally hospitable attitude toward any music presented (or even to cultivate a conscious preference for *le dernier cri*) without therefore being able to obtain from much of Schoenberg's music any specifically musical rewards or values—or to obtain from it, at last, any sortable impressions whatever.

The Possible Position of Schoenberg

Certainly this is not true of all listeners, for there are many convinced Schoenbergians who rank his most arcane compositions—and perhaps even more those of Anton von

Webern—as the most important musical events of our century. Nor should any intelligent listener who finds himself utterly baffled or even angered by this music write down the dodecaphonists as charlatans or signs of a musical tragedy. First, such a listener must face the lively possibility that the familiar time lag is operating here: that one day he will be able to catch up with Schoenberg as he can catch up with Stravinsky and as the whole musical world eventually caught up with Wagner and Debussy. Second, he must recognize in Schoenberg's twelve-tone procedures this century's most single-minded attempt to give solidity to musical form of postharmonic nature. In effect, that purpose—of constructing whole compositions from one germinal idea, the tone row—goes back beyond the sonata forms (which by nature are built from several contrasting ideas) to the baroque way of unity through singleness. Or, if looked at another way, it makes variation of a single thematic integer the central principle of musical pattern. And, last, it easily may turn out (though many are much inclined to doubt it) that the quality in Schoenberg's music which so sets on edge the teeth of many well-disposed listeners is not its techniques at all, but its dogged and decayed romanticism.

Mosco Carner, rightly calling Schoenberg "a typical exponent of later German romanticism," spoke bluntly of his "monomaniac urge for unrestricted self-expression." Schoenberg's compositions in tonal textures—both the early ones and those which he interspersed among the atonalities of his later period—confirm this judgment. For both personal and historical reasons, Schoenberg was an unhappy and often a neurotically disaffected man. Being a clear end-product of the Teutonic romanticism that led from the late Beethoven and Schubert through Weber, Mendelssohn, Schumann, Liszt, Wagner, Brahms, Bruckner, and Mahler to himself, but living in a technically advanced age, he became an expressionist. And his music, whether tonal or atonal, expressed *him*, both as all creation somehow and to some extent must express its creator and self-consciously, by fierce determination. When Schoenberg used his atonal, expressionist, twelve-tone techniques in support of a literary text, they perhaps were best used. But he chose texts that conveyed in literary terms the exacerbations, neuroses, angers, frustrations, and violences of his own uprooted nature—and in that way the very integrity of his self-expressive purpose denied us the benefits we might have won if he had been capable of objectivity either in selecting texts for cantata, opera, and song or in the creative employment of his great talent and magnificent knowledge.

Prospects for Atonal and Serial Music

Because atonality and the twelve-tone procedures were felt to be the only logical outcomes of one historic line of musical development, they undoubtedly have great value. It is, in a sense, our duty to give their foremost exponent the benefit of every doubt, to take as many steps as we can toward meeting him halfway. Still, not ruling out the hopeful possibility already mentioned—that one day we shall come to accept his products as integral parts of the canon of meaningful music—we need not altogether discard the possibility that we shall not. Some reasons certainly exist for supposing that even in the hands of a more balanced and sanguine human being (supposing that such a composer would find Schoenberg's techniques relevant to his own personality and purposes), unmitigated atonality and the twelve-tone techniques still would prove to be a musical side road leading to a dead end. All of that titanic mental effort may turn out to have produced, in the light of subsequent musical evolution, a few technical devices to be absorbed into the general textures of music, there to have no more enduringly important a position and place per se than the whole-tone scale or Scriabin's chords of superimposed fourths.

Webern and Musical Cryptograms

Of the two foremost Schoenbergians, Anton von Webern was an atonalist and twelve-tone composer of uncompromising conviction. His extraordinarily brief compositions might be the music of another planet or another form of life, so little resemblance do they bear to anything that the peoples of Western civilization considered to be music before they were composed or have come to accept widely as music since then. Webern even added new rules, new limiting clauses to the legislation of the twelve-tone system: in his ensemble pieces, for example, he did not allow any single instrument to sound any two tones from a tone row in succession, thus presenting the components of such a row in a predetermined variety of timbres. About the most that these cryptograms suggest to all but a small handful of dedicated listeners is a floating and unmotivated intensity and a curiously selfless dedication.

Alban Berg, Impure Schoenbergian

The other leading Schoenbergian was Alban Berg. A composer of genius, he was not so orthodox as Webern. His finest compositions suggest, more forcefully than any verbal argument, that atonality and the twelve-tone techniques eventually will find their proper places when employed for special purposes among the numerous other musical techniques evolved over the last ten centuries.

Berg, like Schoenberg (but apparently unlike Webern) was a belated romantic seeking roads to self-expression. But his self was less insistent on iron introversion; his sympathies were broader; humor never for long deserted him —and he finally was more interested in expressive music than in any theory or system of procedures. Schoenberg doubtless was the most important single influence upon his practice, but he seems even more clearly to have been a descendant of Brahms, Bruckner, Mahler—and Debussy. He was only fifty when he died in 1935, and he had not been prolific. The subsequent curve of his reputation and the insistence with which his opera *Wozzeck* was kept alive by discussion until it was returned to the stage suggest what little that has happened with Schoenberg's or Webern's music can suggest at all: that Berg's finest works will take their place in the active repertoire as the fascinating final postscript to Viennese nineteenth-century romanticism.

Berg's Evolving Style

Berg approached atonality spontaneously and by easy stages. But he already had composed his *Vier Stücke*, for clarinet and piano, Opus 5 (1913), dedicated to Schoenberg, and the more important *Drei Stücke*, for orchestra, Opus 6 (1914) before he began to work on *Wozzeck*. The three orchestral pieces, entitled Prelude, Round, and March, strained the then-existing means almost to the snapping point. Elaborate directions to each player indicate Berg's intense occupation with dynamic values; the counterpoint is extraordinarily luxuriant; no melodic voice is doubled anywhere; in any conventional sense, no development occurs; the insistence upon the individual timbre of each instrument is final; and great care is taken to make each chord not only a combination of tones, but also a combination of instrumental timbres, for each note of each chord is assigned to an instrument of its own. This music—and notably the March—is as complex and as hard to follow as anything in Schoenberg. But a *sensation* that understanding may follow, that this multiplicity of learned means was at the service of a meaning that finally we shall be able to extricate from it, precedes even a rewarding study of the score itself. Everything about the facture and presentation of this highly romantic musical stuff indicates, even to an unfriendly ear, that the intelligence at work behind it is primarily at the disposition of a truly musical urge to expression rather than a primarily intellectual one or a complex of self-revelation.

Wozzeck

In May 1914, Berg was deeply moved by a staging of *Woyzeck,* an incomplete, somewhat disorderly, but powerful drama of poverty and hallucination by Georg Büchner (1813–37). This loosely interrelated series of twenty-five scenes, some of them of extreme brevity, was peculiarly germane to Berg's twentieth-century moods and perceptions. He

worked at making a usable libretto from it, completing
that part of his task in 1917 after having reduced the essentials of the narrative to fifteen scenes. By the autumn of
1920, he had the complete opera in orchestral sketch; he
finished the orchestration in April 1921. Although excerpts
from it were performed in 1924, the first complete performance had to wait until December 14, 1925, when the Berlin State Opera staged it. By the time when the Nazis got
round to banning *Wozzeck* as decadent art or *Kulturbol-
schewismus,* Berlin had heard it twenty-one times; it now
has been performed entire many times in the cultural capitals of the Western world, and its popularity is growing.

This story of an army captain's regimental soldier-servant
who is driven by mistreatment and the blurring of his sanity
to murder the mistress by whom he has had a child and
then to commit suicide was a full predecessor of expressionism in the drama. It often wavers hysterically near in-
coherence; it is savagely and cruelly disturbed and feverishly
intense. Berg cast it in three acts of five scenes each, organizing the patterns of the mostly atonal music (not yet
dominated by the twelve-tone usages) through the use of
rigid formal patterns and informal usages adapted from the
baroque, preclassic, and classic past, as well as from both
folk and popular music. Formally analyzed, the three acts
of *Wozzeck* are made up of the following movements and
patterns:

I. 1. suite, 2. rhapsody and hunting song, 3. military
   march and cradle song, 4. passacaglia (twenty-one
   variations on a melody), 5. *quasi rondo;*
II. 1. sonata form, 2. fantaisie and fugue on three melo-
    dies. 3. largo for chamber orchestra, 4. scherzo, 5.
    martial rondo (the entire movement being "a sym-
    phony in five movements");
III. 1. invention (variations) on a theme, 2. invention on
     a tone (pedal point), 3. invention on a rhythm,
     4. invention on the chord A♯-C♯-E♯-G♯-E♭-F♭, 5. in-
     vention on the tonality of D minor, and a toccata-like
     section in persistent eighth-note pattern.

No listener, clearly, is expected to hear these movements

and forms as such: they were of importance to Berg as tools of composition. Their meaning to any but the most studious listener best is absorbed without concentration on that process.

Listening to Wozzeck

As Ernest Newman once pointed out, the idiom of *Wozzeck* is not uniform throughout. Berg cast it in wide variants of several idioms, not only in response to the demands of the shifting dramatic substance, but also because he himself was changing during the years of its creation. The way to enjoy *Wozzeck* (and thus to approach understanding of it through the best-located entrance) is to pay attention to the text and follow the characters. Despite all of its technical legerdemain, despite its long sections of atonality (which are interspersed here and there with elaborate but semi-"tonal" treatments of recognizable tunes), the music will not obstruct that attention. A good performance of Berg's *Wozzeck* is an overwhelming human experience—from which most members of the audience hearing it for the first or the second time probably will emerge bearing no more specific memory of the music itself than they would bring from a first or second hearing of *Pelléas et Mélisande*. They will, that is to suggest, likely recall the music as an atmosphere, the environment in which the drama and the characters had their being.

Only gradually do we begin to realize that Berg's emulsion of late-German chromatic harmony, atonality, pre-existing patterns, and peculiar song-speech is one perfect clothing for characters so manic-depressive or actually schizophrenic, situations so compulsive, explosive, and irrational, subjects so morbid, mortal, and real. What Berg accomplished in composing *Wozzeck* is music magnificent for exactly the purpose of being absorbed into hectic drama, for tightening the shuddersome horrors and slashingly macabre humors of Büchner's drama. To say that most of this music has small significance when parted from the libretto is to tell a meaningless truth. For Berg performed his selected task successfully: he has convinced us that the tonal utterances of instruments and singers provide the inevitable speech of precisely these characters, spontaneous emanations of the tragedy in which they are so hopelessly involved. In this respect, though in few others, *Wozzeck* lies very close indeed to *Pelléas et Mélisande*.

The Later Berg and Lulu

In the few compositions that Berg completed after *Wozzeck*, he increasingly used twelve-tone methods, though very seldom with the rigidity of Schoenberg or Webern. His Chamber Concerto (1924), for example, is erected out of a tone row derived from those letters in the names Schoenberg, Webern, and Berg which also are (in German) the names of musical tones. The Lyric Suite of 1926 is dodecaphonic music with a difference. And in 1928, Berg began to compose his second opera, this one to a telescoped version of two related "tragedies of sex" by Frank Wedekind. When he died in 1935, *Lulu* was complete in sketch, but he had not fully completed or orchestrated its third act. The whole melodic-harmonic fabric of this dizzying musico-dramatic story of "the eternal feminine manifestation of evil," the sex-crazed woman who sinks through layer after layer of degradation, is derived by astonishing manipulation from this single tone row:

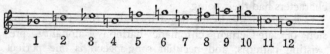

Adolfo Salazar pointed out one example of the ingenuity of Berg's compositional methods. By dividing the tone row quoted above into four groups of three successive tones each and then making chords of them, we can get:

354

If we next evolve a new tone row by reading the notes of these four chords from left to right, top notes first, middle notes second, bottom notes last, we get:

And precisely this new tone row, derived from that of the first example above by these methods, and then couched in waltz time, is what Berg actually used to symbolize Lulu, the heroine-villianess of his opera.

Although incomplete, *Lulu* has been winning increasingly frequent stage performances. Berg himself never accurately set forth his intentions in this bewildering but emotionally powerful score. But careful listening to the suite of Five Symphonic Pieces which he extracted and arranged from it shows that he was in the process of developing a non-atonal twelve-tone texture. Some of this music *sounds* tonal when in fact it is not; some of it, in intermittent passages, discovers a definable tonality even in the printed score. No inescapable reason exists, of course, why a twelve-tone theme must be treated atonally. That Berg indeed was on the verge of producing a new mixture of tonality and atonality seems proved by the texture of his last and finest purely instrumental work, the Concerto for Violin and Orchestra.

Berg's Violin Concerto

Berg's Violin Concerto is predominantly atonal; it mostly follows the twelve-tone schemes. After an introduction apparently intended to announce the sorrowing mood (the piece was in memory of a young friend who had died), it begins with a tone row cleverly drawn from implications of the mood-opening, which is made up of a series of perfect fifths; these appear as alternates in the row. In this row, three successive tones form a major triad, three other successive tones a minor triad—and the presence of these triads casts at least a glimmer of tonality over the row itself. Also, the final four tones of the row are elements of a whole-tone

355

scale, and not accidentally. For in the final movement—derived, of course, from the same row—Berg emphasizes those four tones as a way of introducing smoothly, with its original harmonies very little altered, the chorale "*Es ist genug*," from Bach's cantata *O Ewigkeit, du Donnerwort*. He had no hesitation, then, about mixing tonality and atonality.

Berg could equal any man in the concocting of musical ingenuities, and often did so. But he was first of all pervasively musical, and he seldom sacrificed expressiveness (which he did not conceive inevitably as self-expression) to the tenets of any system. Instead, he triumphed over the methods that he used, having been powerful, individual, talented, and liberal enough to start breaking them apart and then—with the help of other elements, both borrowed and created—remaking them in the image of his own needs and desires and objective artistic intentions. He digested what was useful to him, using it to grow a style and idiom entirely his own. What rigidly doctrinaire atonalities and twelve-tone-method proponents seem not to have noticed is that Berg, who surely was a heretic, won nothing but praise from Schoenberg. If it is too much to propose that Schoenberg was a voice crying in the wilderness, was he not perhaps an old man not destined to enter the promised land?

Roads into the Musical Future

Certainly a talented composer, rich in inherent musical feeling and intellectual acuity, can evolve living music from textures mixing tonal procedures and those of twelve-tone atonality. The twelve-tone usages may be the most salient ingredients of such music; they even may occupy ninety-five per cent of its length—but the essential catalyst, if they are not to remain bristlingly rebus-like, is some small ingredient of tonality, something to suggest the home from which we have been exiled—and even though we may never sight it clearly again. This mixture, in fact, appears to be the useful present and future of the lessons taught by Schoenberg, Webern, Berg, and the eminent musicologist-composer Egon Wellesz: the methodology of the twentieth-century Viennese school is an additional means of value, an enriching adjunct, to the supply of compositional tools. But no more reason exists today than existed a century ago for believing anyone, however persuasive, who proclaims that the future of music is the exclusive possession of one region or one group or "school" of composers. No one can predict by which (or by how many) of the possible routes open to the art of music it will proceed onward into its future.

POSTLUDE

Repeating what was said earlier, this book tries to be help-ful "by sticking very close to the notes out of which music is made. The book tries to show how they are arrranged by composers and performed by instrumentalists, singers, and conductors, how they can be apprehended, understood, and enjoyed most easily by listeners without technical musical training." Its business, then, certainly is not that of predic-tion and only to a small extent is it that of critical judg-ment. And because large parts of the most advanced experimental—*"avant-garde"*—music of today and yesterday dispense with what we have thought of as notes and get along without instrumentalists, singers, and conductors, the task of sorting out or even of merely describing—not to men-tion estimating or evaluating—much of the production of the musical vanguard since World War II remains beyond this book's scope and purpose as well as beyond its author's sym-pathetic understanding.

Therefore, it being impossible here to help the reader to apprehend, understand, and enjoy this presently "far-out" music, let us merely mention some of its most noticeable characteristics and then wait for time (both physical time and mental time) to perform the explaining and winnowing and appreciating.

Among the chief elements in much of the current experi-mental musical production are: 1. the total discarding, con-sciously, of as much as possible of what has come out of the musical past, not only in relation to melody, harmony, rhythm, meter, and the forms that have housed and evoked them, but also in relation to the aims, expressivity, and sig-

359

nificance of music itself as a human activity; 2. the use of sound-producing means other than the human voice and the traditional musical instruments; 3. the most finicking attention to tone color, this at its most extreme in *Klang-farbenmelodie,* in which every constituent of a melody differs from every other constituent in tone color, perhaps even being played on a different instrument, noisemaking machine, or substitute therefor; 4. the negation of conscious planning and the substitution for it of chance or happenstance as a chief determinant of musical events, which thus become "aleatory"—that is, accidental and unique (in the sense of being improvised and unforeseen and not being subject to repetition unless mechanically preserved).

"Musique concrète"—concrete music—began in Paris in 1948, when Pierre Schaeffer started to create sound-structures out of already existing sounds. At first he used sounds on existing gramophone records, which he could play at reduced or increased speeds, run backwards or forwards, and otherwise alter, arrange, distort, and combine, at the same time allowing the resulting sounds to be listened to or themselves recorded. When the use of magnetic tape became easy, this concrete music could in itself be altered or distorted or combined during the recording process, or even after it. In one variety or another, *musique concrète* has been used as accompaniment to films, as a ballet score, and in some extended works to be listened to for their own sake alone. Besides Schaeffer, musicians who have done some notable work with *musique concrète* have included Pierre Henry, Olivier Messiaen, and Pierre Boulez.

Related to *musique concrète* is electrophonic music, a German development that chiefly has remained anchored to the Cologne experimental laboratories and broadcasting station of the North-West German Radio. Sprouting late in the 1940s, it consisted of "pieces" in which the constituent musical sounds or noises were themselves produced by and on electrophonic instruments. This music dispenses with performers, does not make use of pre-existing recordings or external sounds, and has been in the process of evolving several types of notation. The sounds generally are recorded onto magnetic tape, after which they may be arranged, distorted, combined, and altered much as in *musique concrète*. They are preponderantly noises rather than imitations of the musical sounds produced by traditional instruments or the singing human voice. The aim of the most prominent electrophonic composers has been the creation of wholly novel edifices of sound. Among its best-known champions have been the German Karlheinz Stockhausen (1928–   ) and the Italian Luciano Berio (1925–   ).

Abstruse mathematical relationships among complex rhythmical and metrical elements, as well as other constructive principles inaudible as such, but probably valuable as organizing means, mark the music of Elliott Carter (1908–   ), a leader of one wing of the American avant-garde, of which another wing is led by John Cage (1912–   ), in whom a large component of witty shock is joined to complete disregard of everything that the past and most of the present musical world has taken to be the meaning, purpose, or proper employment of music. Other American composers not so "far out" as Cage have been trying (as in the music of Gunter Schuller, 1925–   ) to marry elements of jazz to formal patterns uprooted from sonata, concerto, and symphony; still others, such as Lukas Foss (1922–   ), have been trying the probably impossible task of combining pre-composed music in classico-romantic patterns with improvisation and the evocation of apparently or actually "aleatoric," accidental mixtures.

Not much of this most advanced or experimental music is to be heard in the average concert or recital hall or opera house; only a smattering of it has become available on gramophone records. It is written about, analyzed, and criticized in very advanced publications and discussed in classes in the universities and music schools as well as by its creators and (where they exist) its performers. A glance, however cursory or summary, at the past history of music will convince us that, whereas some of this music almost certainly will turn out to have enduring significance, much of it—like the music of any historic period whatever—will prove to have been ephemeral.

I hope that I may be forgiven for intruding an autobiographical confession here. The first time I heard Stravinsky's *Le Sacre du printemps* (it was a concert of the Chicago Symphony Orchestra conducted by Frederick Stock), I was excited and engaged as I have been excited and engaged by few other compositions. I felt that, in some ill-defined way, *Le Sacre* was for me, was *my* music. I was about twenty-one years old, and I made the mistake of discussing that music during an intermission with several people of about the age I have now reached. They loathed it, describing it as "pure noise . . . the death of music . . . destructive barbarism." On the basis of that and a few related experiences, I made myself a solemn vow. When I am the age of those elders, I said, I will not have shut my mind as they have shut theirs. I always will keep abreast of the latest developments in music. When I am nearly sixty, no young man is going to approach me full of enthusiasm about some new composition and hear from me that it represents "pure noise . . . the death of music . . . destructive barbarism."

Alas, I am nearing sixty. And I have been unable to keep my vow to myself. I have been unable, despite rather constant effort, to keep sympathetically abreast of the post-Stravinskyan, post-Schoenbergian music. For now what we are faced with is not so much radical developments of what came earlier as it is a complete break with the conscious and unconscious aims and purposes of the arts, perhaps most notably painting and music. I feel strongly that music as the art largely dealt with in this book has, for the time being, stopped being created anew. I take refuge from my inability to be eagerly in touch with the musical avant-garde by appealing to an Aristotelian notion. At a certain age, that notion holds, we all have the right to feel that our education has reached a point at which we may properly enjoy what we have learned, enjoy it without feeling any moral compulsion to learn more. I intend, that is, to enjoy the music I like most (from Gregorian chant to the second decade of this century) to the full wherever and whenever I can. I shall, of course, go on listening too to the music of my youngest contemporaries as long as I live. But I shall do so from now on without the prickly sensation that I am under an ethical or moral obligation to like it. I suggest that a similar attitude on the part of many other listeners would free them from a needless discomfort. I do hope, however, that no one will believe that I am inviting him to develop a closed mind.

Some present-day signs, moreover, point in directions different from those taken by the several vanguards. They indicate a new consolidation, the sort of expanded handling of musical means which always has succeeded a romantic (and portended a classic) period. Never has a young composer had at his command, if he but wishes to exercise it, half the wealth of musical tools which a novice today can acquire from his immediate predecessors and more mature contemporaries. The nurture he may need for achieving greatness, it is said with numbing repetitiveness, remains scarce in our alarum-ridden world. But need greatness be the only aim? Perhaps it will prove to be true that the musical tendency toward a new classic balance has been arriving at a historic juncture unfavorable to its flowering. But one cannot help wondering whether or not the era preceding, during, and just after the French Revolution really was favorable in that sense to the classicism that soared to its apogee during those violent decades.

Prediction always is dangerous; it is perhaps almost as silly as the drawing of exact historic parallels. Let us leave it to the soothsayers. The world of music remains incalculably rich. We can turn again to listening. For listening— with an open mind, a trained ear, and a growing awareness of methods and means—is itself the only key to one of the enduring pleasures of living: an understanding and enjoyment of the marvelous music of the Western world.

GLOSSARY OF MUSICAL TERMS

The following glossary includes, not only all terms double-starred in the preceding text, but also some other basic musical terms that can present difficulties to readers not previously trained in their use. For finer distinctions and for the historical evolution of many musical terms, readers are urged to turn to a musical dictionary (such as the *Harvard Dictionary of Music*) or a musical encyclopedia (such as *Grove's Dictionary of Music and Musicians*), as the definitions below pretend to supply nothing more than skeletonic and indicative information.

adagio, see tempo indications.

allegretto, see tempo indications.

allegro, see tempo indications.

andante, see tempo indications.

andantino, see tempo indications.

appoggiatura, in general modern usage, a very briefly sounded nonharmonic (grace) note performed on the beat or, particularly in nineteenth- and twentieth-century music, just before it.

broken chord, a chord of which the constituent tones are sounded in rapid succession rather than simultaneously.

cadenza, a musical passage originally intended for improvisation by the performer, but in later periods written out by the composer, editor, or performer in improvisatory style. The cadenza is particularly native to the concerto.

cantilena, in postmedieval music, a melody—either vocal or instrumental—of which the dominant character is lyrical rather than dramatic or virtuosic.

castrato, a male soprano or contralto whose preadolescent vocal range has been preserved artificially by castration.

chord, in harmonic music and some of its immediate predecessors, the simultaneous sounding of three (rarely two) or more tones.

chromatic (the noun is chromaticism) describes music in which important use is made of intervening tones not native to the diatonic scale, whether major or minor. The period of composition extending from Beethoven's late years to the 1930s made extensive (some would say excessive) use of chromaticism.

clef, a sign placed at the beginning of a staff to indicate pitch. In piano music, the G, or treble clef (resembling a reversed capital script S), indicates that the second line up represents the G above middle C; the F, or bass clef (resembling a reversed capital C), indicates that the fourth line up represents the F below middle C.

coloratura, see ornamentation.

concord, see consonance and dissonance.

consonance and dissonance, extremely moot terms referring to the supposedly pleasant (consonant) effect of some intervals, such as the octave and the third, and the supposedly unpleasant (dissonant) effect of other intervals, such as the second and seventh. Originally employed (like the related terms concord and discord) in a technical sense, consonance or concord and dissonance or discord more recently have come to be regarded as matters of historic evolution and personal or subjective reaction.

cornett, as distinct from cornet, an obsolete instrument consisting of a bent octagonal tube with fingerholes and a cup mouthpiece. Forms of cornett were called *Zink* and serpent.

diatonic refers to music couched largely in the natural scale made up of five whole-tones and two half-tones (as C-D-E-F-G-A-B-C or A-B-C-D-E-F-G♯-A). Music is called diatonic when it is predominantly confined to the tones of such a major or minor scale. When many tones not native to such a diatonic scale are employed, music is said to be chromatic (*which see*). The music of Western composers during, just before, and just after the heyday of the Viennese classicists, and most notably that of Haydn and Mozart, is very largely diatonic.

discord, see consonance and dissonance.

dissonance, see consonance and dissonance.

dodecaphony, a word artificially compounded from the Greek terms for "twelve" and "sound" and now employed to refer to the twelve-tone or serial music of Arnold Schoenberg and his followers.

fioritura, see ornamentation.

imitation, the musical procedure of restating a melody, motive,

366

or other melodic element in rapid succession at different pitches within a polyphonic or contrapuntal texture. The most familiar forms of imitation are *ricercar(e)*, canon, fugue, and round.

interval, the distance in pitch difference between two musical tones. Two tones of the same pitch are said to be "in unison." An interval represented, for example, by A-B is called a second, A-C a third, A-D a fourth, A-E a fifth, A-F a sixth, A-G a seventh, A to the next A above or below it an octave. Intervals wider than an octave are said to be compound; for example, that from A to the second B above it is a compound interval referred to as either a ninth or a compound second (that is, an octave plus a second). Any interval is called major, minor, augmented, diminished, or perfect according to the number of semitones it encloses. Thus, for example, a major third (as A-C) contains four semitones, a minor third (as A-C♭) three semitones, an augmented third (as A-C♯) five semitones, a diminished third (as A♯-C) two semitones. Seconds, thirds, sixths, and sevenths have the four forms exemplified. Fourths, fifths, and octaves, however, have no major or minor form, but only a "perfect" form—the fourth with five semitones (as A-D), the fifth with seven (as A-E), the octave with twelve (as A to the A next above it), plus forms augmented by one half-tone (as the fourth A-D♯, the fifth A-E♯, and the octave A-A♯), and diminished by one half-tone (as the fourth A♯-D, the fifth A♯-E, and the octave A♯-A).

largo, see tempo indications.

legato and staccato, Italian words meaning "linked" and "separated," used to indicate, respectively, a manner of performance in which tones succeed other tones without noticeable intervening breaks and a style in which tones are made to sound less (commonly about half) of their indicated mathematical value, so that noticeable spaces occur between them. *Legato* commonly is indicated by a slur, a curved line placed above or below the series of notes to be linked. *Staccato* commonly is indicated by a small dot or wedge-shaped sign placed above each note to be sharply abbreviated in performance.

lento, see tempo indications.

libretto, literally "little book," the literary text of an opera, oratorio, or related composition with sung words.

melisma (plural *melismata*), in Gregorian chant (and, by extension, in other music) the performance of several tones to one syllable of text (and, by extension, that of several tones on a single beat or portion of a beat).

metronome markings, see tempo indications.

moderato, see tempo indications.

mordent, indicated by a short, thick, wavy horizontal line with a thin slanting stroke through it, an ornament in which the written note is alternated rapidly once or twice with the adjacent note below it. Mordents usually begin on the beat of the written note.

movement, an extended, at least partially self-contained division of a sonata, symphony, concerto, or other composition constructed in more than one section.

octave, the amount of pitch difference enclosed between a note and the note seven diatonic steps above or below it (as from C to the C next above or below it).

opus (literally "work"), sometimes written as Op. or op. and commonly followed by a numeral (as Opus 64), from Beethoven's time on, an approximate indication of the chronological position of a work in the composer's complete output. Useful as designations, opus numbers are not always dependable as chronological signposts.

ornamentation, the addition of a tone or tones to those essential to the melody or harmony. Ornaments are called for by composers by such signs as grace-notes, trills, turns, and mordents; in some music the performer adds them *ad libitum*. Such Italian words as *coloratura* and *fioritura* (literally coloring and flowering) refer to varieties of ornamentation, most commonly in singing.

ostinato (literally "obstinate"), a recognizable melodic or submelodic unit repeated throughout a composition or one section of a composition, commonly at the same pitch.

passacaglia, a composition or movement in slow triple meter, consisting of continuously developing variation of melody and harmony.

prestissimo, see tempo indications.

presto, see tempo indications.

ritornello, an Italian word used with a variety of musical meanings, but now most usually employed to indicate either (a) a purely instrumental section among vocal sections in the operas of Claudio Monteverdi and his immediate successors and (b) the recurring sections of a *concerto grosso* in which the larger body of instruments takes part.

rondo-form, as found in final movements of concertos, sonatas, symphonies, and chamber music in related patterns, a form consisting of five or more sections, of which the odd-numbered sections are a repeated refrain, the even-numbered ones distinct episodes. Rondo-form thus is represented as ABACADA, etc.

scherzo (literally "joke"), a rapid movement, ordinarily in triple time like the minuet (which, in this sense, it succeeded in Beethoven's time), often employed as the third movement of a sonata, symphony, or chamber piece. Like the minuet, it usually is in ABA form: the scherzo proper, then a trio, then a repetition of the scherzo proper. Scherzos not necessarily in the ABA form have been composed as separate pieces, notably for the piano by Chopin.

staccato, see legato and staccato.

staff (sometimes stave), the horizontal lines—grouped in fives in most postmedieval music—upon which notes are written or printed.

sympathetic vibration, vibration of a sound-producing medium set up by vibrations external to it, as when, for example, a silently depressed piano note will be heard vibrating after the same note in another octave is struck and released.

tempo, the speed at which music is performed.

tempo indications, the words or conventional symbols by means of which composers indicate the speed at which they wish music to be performed. The commonest of the Italian words thus employed are, in descending order of speed, *prestissimo* (extremely fast); *presto* (very fast); *allegro* (fast); *allegretto* (reasonably fast); *moderato* (moderate); *andante* (slowish); *andantino* (confusingly, either slightly slower or slightly faster than *andante*); *adagio* (slow); *lento* (noticeably slow); *largo* (broad and very slow). Other qualifying or descriptive Italian words often are added to these basic superscriptions. Thus *ma non troppo* (but not too much so), *con brio* (with dash or vigor), *con moto* (with movement—that is, rather quickly), and *maestoso* (majestic). Such conventional symbols as M.M. 80♩ and M. 90♩ are markings with reference to the metronome, a machine that can be set to ticking or clicking at a regular desired speed. The examples given mean that the machine should be set to giving off its sound, respectively, eighty and ninety times per minute and, again respectively, that each click or tick is to indicate the duration of a half-note and a quarter-note.

third, the interval between one note in a diatonic scale and a note removed from it by two whole tones (major third) or by one whole tone and a half-tone (minor third).

thorough bass, with particular reference to the baroque period, a composer's way of indicating accompanying chords by writing out only their bass notes, thus requiring the performer to improvise the chords actually sounded. When such notes are accompanied by numerals, the procedure often is called "figured bass."

timbre, the color or distinctive quality of a tone. It defines the difference between two soundings of the same tone, one on a violin and one on a flute, for example, or soundings of the same tone by two singers.

tremolo (literally "trembling"), a term with several meanings, the most commonly met with of them being (a) the rapid repetition of a tone on a stringed instrument as produced by swift alternations of upward and downward strokes by the performer's bow and (b) in singing, either such rapid repetition of a single tone or rapid alternation of a tone and tones differing from it very slightly in pitch. The last-mentioned alternation is more usefully called *vibrato* (literally "vibrated").

triad, a chord made up of a root tone, the tone a third above it, and the tone an added third higher. Reading upward, a triad may consist of major third-minor third—as C-E-G (major triad); minor third-major third—as C-E♭-G (minor triad); minor third-minor third—as C♯-E-G (diminished triad); or major third-major third—as C-E-G♯ (augmented triad).

trill, an ornament consisting of rapid alternation of a principal note and the adjacent note above it. A trill may begin on either of its constituent notes as required or taken for granted by the composer.

trio, a term with several distinct musical meanings, of which the most commonly encountered are (a) a composition for three voices, three instruments, or (especially in baroque music) three melodic lines or parts and (b) the B or middle contrasting section of ABA forms such as minuet and scherzo; it is so called because early composers commonly scored such sections for only three instruments.

turn, an ornament consisting of the rapid sounding of a principal note and the adjacent notes above or below it—as (with C as the principal note) in Chopin's Nocturne in G minor, Opus 37, number 1, CCdCbD. In modern performance, a turn uses up duration value borrowed from the principal note preceding it. Turns are printed in smaller size than principal notes.

variation, the procedure of composing by presenting one or more subsequent modifications—melodic, rhythmic, harmonic, or some combinations of the three—of an already stated melody, theme, rhythm, or other recognizable musical constituent.

A BRIEF BIBLIOGRAPHY

For readers wanting to probe farther into the techniques, history, and lore of music the list below points a way to a few of the best standard reference books and some other books of general interest to which they can turn for the usefulness of information and the fascination of interpretation. Any reader desiring to probe deeply into any of the aspects of music discussed herein is directed to one of the scholarly bibliographies to be found in the standard textbooks on musical history (a notably useful one is included on pages 668–94 of Professor Donald Jay Grout's *A History of Western Music*, New York, 1960). Only books available in English are included below.

Reference books

Baker's Biographical Dictionary of Musicians, fifth edition, revised by Nicolas Slonimsky, New York, 1965

Grove's Dictionary of Music and Musicians, 9 volumes, fifth edition, edited by Eric Blom, New York, 1954; supplementary volume, New York, 1961

Harvard Dictionary of Music, by Willi Apel, Cambridge, Massachusetts, 1947

A New Dictionary of Music, by Arthur Jacobs, Baltimore, 1958 (paperbound)

Aids to listening

What to Listen for in Music, by Aaron Copland, New York, 1939

The Structure of Music, A Listener's Guide, by Robert Erickson, New York, 1955

Hearing Music, A Guide to Music Appreciation, by Theodore M. Finney, New York, 1941

The Craft of Musical Composition, by Paul Hindemith, New York, 1945

The Enjoyment of Music, An Introduction to Perceptive Listening, by Joseph Machlis, revised edition, New York, 1963

The Musical Experience of Composer, Performer, Listener, by Roger Sessions, Princeton, 1950

Listening to Music Creatively, by Edwin J. Stringham, New York, 1943

Essays in Musical Analysis, by Sir Donald Francis Tovey, 6 volumes, New York, various dates

Comprehensive historical and philosophical books

A History of Musical Thought, by Donald N. Ferguson, second edition, New York, 1948

A History of Western Music, by Donald Jay Grout, New York, 1960

Music in Western Civilization, by Paul Henry Lang, New York, 1941

Music in History, The Evolution of an Art, by Howard D. McKinney and W. R. Anderson, New York, 1940

The Rise of Music in the Ancient World, East and West, by Curt Sachs, New York, 1943

Biographical and general books

(The following titles are listed in roughly chronological order with reference to the periods and composers dealt with.)

MEDIEVAL TO BAROQUE

Music in the Middle Ages, by Gustave Reese, New York, 1940

The Italian Madrigal, by Alfred Einstein, 3 volumes, Princeton, 1949

The English Madrigal Composers, by E. H. Fellowes, Oxford, 1921

Contrapuntal Technique in the Sixteenth Century, by R. O. Morris, Oxford, 1922

Palestrina, by Henry Coates, London, 1938

Sixteenth-Century Polyphony, by A. T. Merritt, Cambridge, 1939

William Byrd, by E. H. Fellowes, London, 1948

Purcell, by J. A. Westrup, New York, 1937

374

The Technique of Chordal Composition, by Archibald T. Davison, Cambridge, Massachusetts, 1945

A Short History of Opera, by Donald Jay Grout, 2 volumes, New York

The World of Opera, by Wallace Brockway and Herbert Weinstock, New York, 1962

Monteverdi, by Leo Schrade, New York, 1937

Venetian Opera in the Seventeenth Century, by S. T. Worsthorne, Oxford, 1954

Men of Music, Their Lives, Times, and Achievements, by Wallace Brockway and Herbert Weinstock, second edition, New York, 1958 (paperbound)

THE BAROQUE

Corelli, His Life, His Music, by Marc Pincherle, New York, 1956

Music in the Baroque Era, by Manfred Bukofzer, New York, 1947

The Sonata in the Baroque Era, by William S. Newman, Chapel Hill, 1959

Jean-Philippe Rameau, His Life and Work, by Cuthbert Girdlestone, London, 1957

Bach, A Biography, by Charles Sanford Terry, second edition, Oxford, 1933

Johann Sebastian Bach, His Work and Influence on the Music of Germany, by Philipp Spitta, 3 volumes, New York, 1951

The Bach Reader, by Hans David and Arthur Mendel, New York, 1945

Handel, by R. A. Streatfeild, London, 1909

Handel, by Herbert Weinstock, second edition, New York, 1959

Handel's Messiah, A Touchstone of Taste, by Robert Manson Myers, New York, 1948

Handel's Dramatic Oratorios and Masques, by Winton Dean, London, 1959

Concerning Handel, His Life and Works, by William C. Smith, London, 1948

Domenico Scarlatti, by Ralph Kirkpatrick, Princeton, 1953

The Bach Family, by Karl Geiringer, New York, 1954

THE LATER EIGHTEENTH CENTURY

Gluck, by Martin Cooper, New York, 1935

Gluck, by Alfred Einstein, New York, 1936

Haydn, A Creative Life in Music, by Karl Geiringer, second edition, Garden City, 1963 (paperbound)

The Symphonies of Joseph Haydn, by H. C. Robbins Landon, London, 1955

Mozart, by Eric Blom, New York, 1949

Mozart, His Character, His Work, by Alfred Einstein, New York, 1945

Mozart and His Times, by Erich Schenk, New York, 1959

Mozart's Operas, A Critical Study, by Edward J. Dent, New York, 1947

Mozart and His Piano Concertos, by C. M. Girdlestone, Norman, 1952

The Letters of Mozart and His Family, edited by Emily Anderson, 3 volumes, London, 1938

Mozart, The Man and His Works, by W. J. Turner, New York, 1938

The Life of Ludwig van Beethoven, by Alexander Wheelock Thayer, Carbondale, 1960

The Life and Works of Beethoven, by John N. Burk, New York, 1943

The Letters of Beethoven, edited by Emily Anderson, 3 volumes, New York, 1961

Schubert, A Critical Biography, by Maurice J. E. Brown, New York, 1958

The Schubert Reader, edited by Otto Erich Deutsch, New York, 1947

The Music of Schubert, edited by Gerald Abraham, New York, 1947

THE NINETEENTH CENTURY

Music in the Romantic Era, by Alfred Einstein, New York, 1947

Rossini, A Study in Tragi-Comedy, by Francis Toye, New York, 1934

Donizetti and the World of Opera in Italy, Paris, and Vienna in the First Half of the Nineteenth Century, by Herbert Weinstock, New York, 1963

Donizetti, by William Ashbrook, London, 1965

Mendelssohn, by Philip Radcliffe, London, 1954

Schumann, by Joan Chissell, New York, 1949

Schumann, A Symposium, edited by Gerald Abraham, New York, 1952

Chopin, by Arthur Hedley, London, 1947

Chopin's Musical Style, by Gerald Abraham, London, 1939

Chopin, The Man and His Music, by Herbert Weinstock, New York, 1949

Berlioz and His Century, by Jacques Barzun, New York, 1956 (paperbound)

Johannes Brahms, His Work and Personality, by Hans Gal, New York, 1963

Brahms, by Peter Latham, New York, 1955

Brahms, His Life and Work, by Karl Geiringer, New York, 1961 (paperbound)

The Music of Franz Liszt, by Humphrey Searle, London, 1954

Liszt, by Walter Beckett, New York, 1955

The Life of Richard Wagner, by Ernest Newman, 4 volumes, New York, 1933, 1937, 1941, 1946

The Wagner Operas, by Ernest Newman, New York, 1949

A Hundred Years of Music, by Gerald Abraham, New York, 1938

Opera as Drama, by Joseph Kerman, New York, 1956 (paperbound)

Hugo Wolf, by Frank Walker, New York, 1951

Dvořák, by Alec Robertson, New York, 1955

Tchaikovsky, by Herbert Weinstock, New York, 1943

Tchaikovsky, A Symposium, edited by Gerald Abraham, London, 1945

César Franck, by Norman Demuth, New York, 1949

Giuseppe Verdi, His Life and Works, by Francis Toye, New York, 1959 (paperbound)

The Man Verdi, by Frank Walker, New York, 1962

Masters of Russian Music, by M. D. Calvocoressi and Gerald Abraham, New York, 1939

The Musorgsky Reader, edited by Jay Leyda and Sergei Bertensson, New York, 1947

Modest Mussorgsky, by M. D. Calvocoressi, London, 1956

My Musical Life, by Nikolay Andreyevich Rimsky-Korsakov, third edition, New York, 1942

The Music of Spain, by Gilbert Chase, New York, 1941

French Music from the Death of Berlioz to the Death of Fauré, by Martin Cooper, New York, 1951

Bizet and His World, by Mina Curtiss, New York, 1958

Bizet, by Winton Dean, London, 1948

Bruckner and Mahler, by Hans F. Redlich, New York, 1955

THE TWENTIETH CENTURY

Jan Sibelius, by Harold E. Johnson, New York, 1959

Puccini, A Critical Biography, by Mosco Carner, New York, 1959

Richard Strauss, A Critical Commentary on His Life and Works, Volume I, by Norman Del Mar, New York, 1962

Recollections and Reflections, by Richard Strauss, edited by Willi Schuh, New York, 1953

Debussy, by Léon Vallas, London, 1933

Debussy, His Life and Mind, 2 volumes, by Edward Lockspeiser, New York, 1962, 1965

Maurice Ravel, by Roland-Manuel, London, 1947

Ravel, by Norman Demuth, New York, 1947

Erik Satie, by Rollo H. Myers, London, 1947

Music since 1900, by Nicolas Slonimsky, third edition, New York, 1959

Studies in Contemporary Music, by Wilfred Mellers, London, 1947

Autobiography, Articles, Reminiscences, by Sergei Prokofiev, Moscow, n.d.

Eight Soviet Composers, by Gerald Abraham, New York, 1943

The Life and Music of Béla Bartók, by Halsey Stevens, revised edition, New York, 1964

America's Music, by Gilbert Chase, New York, 1955

Music in a New Found Land, by Wilfred Mellers, New York, 1965

Aaron Copland, by Arthur Berger, New York, 1953

Our New Music, by Aaron Copland, New York, 1941

Notes Without Music, by Darius Milhaud, New York, 1953

Poetics of Music, by Igor Stravinsky, Cambridge, Massachusetts, 1947

Conversations with Igor Stravinsky, 1959; *Memories and Commentaries,* 1960; *Expositions and Developments,* 1962; *Dialogues and a Diary,* 1963—all by Igor Stravinsky and Robert Craft, Garden City

Composition with Twelve Notes, by Josef Rufer, London, 1954

Style and Idea, by Arnold Schoenberg, New York, 1950

The Works of Arnold Schoenberg, by Josef Rufer, New York, 1963

Arnold Schoenberg Letters, sel. and ed. by Erwin Stein, New York, 1965

Alban Berg, The Man and His Music, by Hans F. Redlich, New York, 1957

Schoenberg and His School, by René Leibowitz, New York, 1949

INDEX

Abbatini, Antonio Maria, 185
  Dal male il bene (with Marazzoli), 185
Abraham, Gerald: quoted, 316
A cappella, 86
Accompaniment, 17–18
Adam, Adolphe, 290
Adam de la Halle, 13
Aleatory (aleatoric) music, 360, 361
Alembert, Jean Le Rond d', 186
Angelico, Fra, 23
Apel, Willi, 89; quoted: 213
  Harvard Dictionary of Music, 89; quoted: 116, 213
Appoggiatura chord, 233
Arcadelt, Jacob, 44
Aria, 83, 89–91, 127, 260, 274
Aria da capo, 90–91, 113, 129, 149, 180–81
Arioso, 83, 90, 95
Ariosti, Attilio, 183
  Vespasiano: quoted, 183
Ariosto Lodovico, 40, 294
Aristotle, 118
Aristoxenus, 118
Ars antiqua, 9 ff, 16, 29
Ars nova, 10, 15 ff, 22, 23, 29, 31, 37
Atonality, 340, 341–42, 343, 344 ff, 349 ff, 353, 354–55. *See also* Dodecaphony
Auber, Daniel-François, 227–28
  Muette de Portici, La (*Masaniello*), 228
Audiences, 330–32
Augmentation, 146
Auric, Georges, 320

Auvergne, Antoine d', 187
  Troqueurs, Les, 187
Avant-garde, 333, 359, 361

Bach, Carl Philipp Emanuel, 92, 133, 141, 142–43, 161, 175, 198
  Auferstehung und Himmelfahrt Jesu, Die, 133
Bach, Heinrich, 68
Bach, Johann Christian, 161
Bach, Johann Sebastian, 32, 41, 43, 54, 55, 60, 65, 66, 67, 68, 71, 86, 88, 91, 97, 100, 104, 105, 108, 109, 113, 117, 118, 119 and n, 120, 128, 129, 130, 132, 134, 136, 137, 138–40, 141, 143, 158, 161, 164, 173, 174, 175, 195, 198, 204–5, 214, 228, 249–51, 252, 272, 330, 333, 356
  Art of the Fugue, The, 252
  "Brandenburg" Concertos, 88, 137, 143
  cantatas, 100, 131, 356
    O Ewigkeit, du Donnerwort, 356; "Es ist genug," 356
  Capriccio on the Departure of a Beloved Brother, 204–5
  Italian Concerto, 143;
  Magnificat, 104;
  Mass, B minor, 131–32, 330
  Passacaglia, C minor, 94
  Passions, 41, 100, 131, 132
    John, 41, 100, 131; "Es ist vollbracht," 131

379

381

389

390

ANCHOR BOOKS

ART AND ARCHITECTURE

ANCHOR BOOKS

MUSIC

DOLPHIN HOME REFERENCE BOOKS

DOLPHIN RECREATION AND TRAVEL BOOKS